TREASURES IN TRUSTED HANDS

Sidestone Press

TREASURES IN TRUSTED HANDS

NEGOTIATING THE FUTURE OF COLONIAL
CULTURAL OBJECTS

Jos van Beurden

© 2017 Jos van Beurden

Published by Sidestone Press, Leiden
www.sidestone.com

Imprint: Sidestone Press Dissertations

Printed and bound in Great Britain by
Marston Book Services Ltd, Oxfordshire

Lay-out & cover design: Sidestone Press
Photographs cover and parts: © Jos van Beurden

ISBN 978-90-8890-439-4 (softcover)
ISBN 978-90-8890-440-0 (hardcover)
ISBN 978-90-8890-441-7 (PDF e-book)

Contents

Preface

Thirty years ago, I met a poet. Me'aza made poems about her dream – self-determination for her country and the whole of Africa. She knew them by heart, had never written down a single line and made new verses on the spot. People loved Me'aza. I met her in the eroded mountains of Northeast Africa. Her hamlet was under control of rebels. We had walked all night, as it had been too cold to lie down and sleep. The double local whiskey that she offered us at six in the morning was, in more than one sense heart-warming. I estimated her age between 60 and 70. When I asked how old she was, Me'aza answered that she was four! Four? Yes, four! How come? *'Four years ago, I really started my life. I became aware of what was going on in the world. I began to make poetry. So it was then, that I was born.'* At the age of four, one watches the world as something that is still unknown, and that is yet to be conquered, while being both threatening and thrilling. One is explorer, open-minded, self-confident and naive.

I am now of the same age as the poet then was and I have a dream too. On top of a round table stands a cultural object, acquired in the European colonial era and far removed from its place of origin. Its major stakeholders sit around the table. They talk about their involvement with the object and help to compose its biography. The exchange can be tough, but in the end they jointly decide about the object's future and choose where the object will be in trusted hands.

Four years ago, I began an academic project, picking up the subject of what to do with treasures that had left their country of origin for far-flung destinations during the European colonial era. Until then I had studied the illicit trade in art and antiques from vulnerable countries to art market regions and had begun to understand the mechanisms of the trade and its local variations. A lot of sad news came out of it. To focus on return would enable me to keep studying the same subject from a more constructive angle.

At the start, I did not realise how much the new research would turn my insights into how one can deal with contested cultural heritage upside down. I felt four years old, making a new world my own. Unlike the poetess, I have written down my lines. Nor have I been under control of rebels or anyone else. I am solely responsible for the contents of this book, but like Me'aza, I welcome you to take my lines to you. Hopefully they are heart-warming.

About this book

This study is the result of a fascination with the fate of the material cultural heritage of mostly vulnerable countries. The large-scale presence of cultural and historical objects in public and private collections in the countries of the former European colonisers raises serious questions. I discovered that my own country, the Netherlands, returned a few colonial cultural objects to Indonesia in the 1970s, but that after this return nothing had happened, even though Indonesia and other former colonies had been outspoken about their desire for such objects.

Whether anything can and should be done to change the maldistribution of these cultural and historical objects is the subject of this study. It charts and analyses the disappearance of cultural objects from their places of origin during the European colonial era and the returns that have taken place in order to develop a model for negotiating the future of such objects.

The study consists of six parts.

Part I, Introduction, explains why the future of colonial cultural objects is a pertinent subject and introduces the three main questions of this book. The 'how' of the answers – research methodology, use of sources, etc. – is presented. Frequently-used concepts are described. A typology of colonial cultural objects is offered.

Part II, Colonialism and cultural objects, aims at an overview of the disappearance of cultural objects during different periods of European colonialism. It defines decolonisation as an unresolved conflict and colonial cultural objects as a major, be it underexposed, element in this conflict.

Part III, Colonial cultural objects and the law, considers legal and protective measures taken in the colonial era and thereafter. It lists the first return claims by former colonies. A comparison is made with colonial human remains and Nazi-looted art. The question is raised whether the 1998 Washington Conference Principles for Dealing with Nazi-Confiscated Art can be translated into Principles for Dealing with Colonial Cultural and Historical Objects.

Part IV is a case study of the Netherlands and Indonesia. It analyses in two steps the ambiguities in the negotiations in the 1970s between the two countries for new cultural relations and the return of objects. The first step is based on contemporary archives and documents. The second is a complement to the first, with insights of recent research. Based on this, elements are sought that can become part of a model for negotiating the future of colonial cultural objects.

To better map the one-way traffic of objects and find more elements for the model, Part V offers case-studies of other negotiations for bilateral agreements in the 1970s and 1980s – those between Belgium and Congo, between Denmark and Iceland and Denmark and Greenland, and between Australia and Papua New Guinea. The on-going dialogue between Nigeria and some Western museums about the Benin objects in their possession is also included.

Part VI, New insights, a new approach, answers the three main questions and presents principles for dealing with colonial objects and a model with seven phases for negotiating their future.

This book is an adjusted version of the doctoral thesis, defended by the author at VU University Amsterdam on November 30, 2016.

Keywords: *Australia, Belgium, booty, collecting, colonialism, objects, colonial human remains, conflict studies, cultural heritage, decolonisation, Denmark, DR Congo, Europe, gift, Greenland, history, Iceland, iconoclasm, Indonesia, legal studies, Nazi-looted art, the Netherlands, Papua New Guinea, restitution, return.*

Acknowledgements

I am greatly indebted to many people in the academic world and heritage sector. I mention specifically Rogier Bedaux, Evelien Campfens, Peter Carey, Katja Lubina, Silvie Memel Kassi, Zuozhen Liu, Staffan Lundén, Wim Manuhutu, Adriana Munoz, Wayne Modest, Francis Musonda, Lyndel Prott, Barbara Plankensteiner, Bambang Purwanto, Hildegard Schneider, Samuel Sidibé, Jim Specht, Harm Stevens, Hasti Tarekat, Sarah Van Beurden (no relation), and Boris Wastiau. Others occur in various chapters or unfortunately remain unmentioned. Your readiness and time over the years have inspired me and have helped to develop my thoughts. I have built on many of your suggestions, documentation and questions. A major thanks to all of you.

Jill Bradley and Mark Hannay have improved my English. Thank you for your help and generosity.

I am also grateful to my children, my family and in-laws, my friends, neighbours and other people close by who gave moral support or showed interest into the topic. It has strengthened our bonds.

A special word of thanks is due to my supervisors. First of all, chief supervisor, Prof. Dr. Susan Legêne. From the start you were enthusiastic about my topic. You helped me in the transition from research journalist to academic researcher and taught me what discipline means in academic terms and how I was to enjoy this new acquirement. You were generous with advice and shared part of your own archives. You never forced your own opinions on me but helped me discover my own path and focus. Prof. Dr. Wouter Veraart, my second supervisor, with patience, precision and suggestions you helped me to better master principles of law and justice and their relevance for colonial cultural objects. You challenged me to keep focussing on the main argument in this book.

Finally, Louise Boelens, my partner who supported my undertaking from the beginning and lovingly accepted all the time-consuming disquiet surrounding it: thank you for this and even more for being a valuable and critical sparring partner for developing so many ideas in this book.

I dedicate this book to Louise and our sons, Olmo and Benji.

Utrecht, February 2017

PART I

INTRODUCTION

Part I - Introduction

Chapter 1 explains how a growing awareness about the pillage and smuggling of cultural heritage from vulnerable countries, visits to sites and museums in former colonies, investigations in the port of Rotterdam and other experiences inspired me to take up this research. For a description of the global context, a few far-reaching changes are mentioned, including some that impact on colonial cultural objects. The three main questions of this book are formulated, followed by a description of how they will be answered.

Since return and colonial cultural object are key terms, Chapter 2 gives their definitions. Other concepts – provenance, violence, hard and soft law and others – are also described. The biggest challenge comes at the end – a typology of colonial cultural objects, consisting of five categories. They are based mostly on the way in which they were acquired. This typology will be used throughout the research.

Photograph previous page: Borobudur temple complex, Indonesia.

Chapter 1

A neglected issue in an evolving world

During negotiations about cultural relations in the 1970s, the Netherlands and Indonesia did not solve the question of the whereabouts of a *kris* (dagger) of national hero Pangeran Diponegoro.[1] This kris, which the Javanese rebel leader had to surrender to the Dutch in 1830, is crucial to Indonesia, but nobody knows where it is. Inquiries of museums in the Netherlands, Austria and Indonesia have only helped to discover where it most probably is not.[2]

In March 2013, the National Commission for Museums and Monuments of Nigeria, a representative of the Oba (traditional King) of Benin and curators of some European ethnological museums met in Benin City, Nigeria to discuss treasures in European and Nigerian museums, which had been seized during a violent British action in 1897. On the occasion of an exhibition in Vienna's World Museum in 2007, the Oba had put forth the possibility of a return of some objects,[3] but the museum's answer had been a decided negative, as they were state property and thus inalienable. The uneasiness that this created led to the meeting in Benin City.

Why is it difficult to search for the kris and to conduct a dialogue about the future of the Benin treasures? Why has a Dutch-Indonesian commission not ended the uncertainty? Why did the Viennese World Museum respond so brusquely to the Oba's modest request? What had happened before, when these and many other objects changed hands in the European colonial era? Were the European possessors allowed to take them then? What makes these objects crucial for the countries of origin? What happens when these countries claim objects that went missing during the European colonial era? Do they have a basis for their claims?

1.1. Decisive experiences

From the early 1990s, I have studied the current looting, smuggling and preservation of cultural heritage in Asia, Africa and Eastern Europe. Africa curator Rogier Bedaux of the National Museum of Ethnology – henceforward called Museum Volkenkunde – in Leiden made me face the facts of the one-way illicit

---

1 Susan Legêne and Els Postel-Coster, "Isn't all culture? Culture and Dutch Development Policy in the Post-Colonial Period", in *Fifty Years of Dutch Development Cooperation 1949 – 1999*, eds. J.A. Nekkers and P.A.M. Malcontent (The Hague: Sdu Publishers, 2000), 359.

2 Jos Van Beurden, *The Return of Cultural and Historical Treasures: The Case of the Netherlands* (Amsterdam: KIT Publishers, 2012), 58 – 62.

3 Barbara Plankensteiner, *Benin Kings and Rituals – Court Arts from Nigeria* (Vienna: Museum für Völkerkunde, 2007), 13.

traffic in cultural heritage from vulnerable countries. During a visit to Djenné in Mali, I noticed how looters had damaged almost half of the archaeological sites around the city.[4] Samuel Sidibé, director of Mali's National Museum, impressed me by not exclusively blaming colonial powers for the destruction and the loot. Both vulnerable countries, such as his own, and art market countries are part of the problem. The exhibition of ancient *Tellem Textiles* from the Bandiagara burial caves, held in the Netherlands and Mali in 1991, was an example of cooperation on an equal footing. Mali owned the textiles, Dutch scientists helped to clean and preserve them and, in exchange, Museum Volkenkunde was allowed to keep half of them on a long-term loan.[5] The exhibition *Treasures from the Niger Valley*, travelling through Europe, the USA and West Africa from 1993 onwards, indicated the necessity for improved protection. When I visited Mali again in 1998, the looting of sites around Djenné had increased to two-thirds of all archaeological sites. To call a halt to the looting and smuggling, the country had by then entered into a bilateral *Cultural Property Agreement* with the United States. It covered the illicit trade in objects from the Niger River Valley, the Tellem burial caves and Palaeolithic era sites.[6]

In 1996, I witnessed how a Dutch art dealer was caught at the port of Rotterdam, smuggling two celestial nymphs from the Angkor region in Cambodia and thirteen bronze Buddha heads from Ayutthaya in Thailand. Both were World Heritage sites. Due to media coverage, public outcries and outrage in the Dutch parliament, the objects were returned. In the Netherlands it created sympathy for the 1995 *UNIDROIT Convention on Stolen or Illegally Exported Cultural Objects*. For Cambodia it was the first time that a Western country helped to return stolen treasures. During a visit in 2004 the Cambodian authorities failed to show the two nymphs, which their ambassador had received from the Dutch in 1997. At the time of their return, they explained, conditions in the country were chaotic, but with more cultural police and temple guards the Angkor Wat complex was now better protected. It was somewhat reassuring that the National Museum in Phnom Penh made special exhibitions of other returned objects.[7]

These experiences made me advocate a dialogue between the different stakeholders, aiming for more cultural self-determination for source countries.[8] In 2002, a network with like-minded professionals from cultural and enforcement agencies in Europe for the preservation of cultural heritage was set up, and returns of illicitly acquired objects began to attract my attention.

---

4   M. Dembélé, Annette Schmidt and Diederik van der Waals, "Prospections de sites archéologiques dans le delta intérieur du Niger", in *Vallées de Niger*, ed. Collectif (Paris : Editions de la Réunion des Musées Nationaux, 1993), 218 – 232.

5   Rogier Bedaux, *Rendez-nous notre bélier – Het Behoud van Cultureel Erfgoed in Mali* (Leiden: CNSW, 1998), 18.

6   http://eca.state.gov/cultural-heritage-center/cultural-property-protection/bilateral-agreements/mali (April 20, 2016).

7   Jos Van Beurden, "The Dutch Treatment of Tainted Objects", in *Sense and Sensitivities: The Dutch and Delicate Heritage Issues*, ed. Steph Scholten (Rotterdam: ICOM Netherlands, 2010), 23.

8   Jos Van Beurden, *Goden, Graven en Grenzen: Over Kunstroof uit Afrika, Azië en Latijns Amerika* (Amsterdam: KIT Publishers, 2001), 102, 104.

Also in 2002, some major Western museums asked in the *Declaration on the Importance and Value of Universal Museums*[9] for the recognition of the consideration that objects acquired in earlier times had to be viewed in the light of different sensitivities and values, and promised to act more ethically with future acquisitions. In the same period the People's Republic of China, South Korea, Turkey, Greece, Egypt, Ethiopia and Peru listed objects and collections outside their territories to which they made claims to be returned. Italy challenged museums in the United States for illicit acquisitions and retrieved important treasures. Italy also summoned a Dutch museum, the National Museum of Antiquities in Leiden, to court because of the purchase of an Etruscan cuirass at the annual TEFAF art fair in Maastricht. Its hoped-for return would be the first contribution from Europe to an exhibition in Rome of illicit acquisitions, which otherwise had been retrieved from museums in the USA. When a Dutch judge rejected the claim due to lack of evidence, the Italians lost interest. Later on, the Leiden museum let the Italian authorities know informally that it was willing to discuss the case. Italy never responded.[10]

I discovered more returns of tainted acquisitions that had been acquired in recent and colonial times, by the Dutch state and public institutions. Of the thirty-four instances that I found, eleven concerned colonial cultural objects. Most returns had taken place in the 1970s and 1980s. The former Dutch colonies of Indonesia, Australia, Suriname and Aruba were among the recipients.[11] Since then, there have been scarcely any returns of colonial cultural objects.

Recent decades have witnessed increasing consensus on how to deal with human remains outside their place of origin and with artworks that disappeared during the Second World War. For both categories soft law instruments have been developed. The 1970 UNESCO *Convention on the Means of Prohibiting and Preventing the Illicit Import, Export and Transfer of Ownership of Cultural Property* has opened avenues for tackling the current theft and smuggling of cultural heritage.

However, there is no consensus on what to do with objects and collections that were acquired in a contestable manner during the European colonial era. This challenged me. What sort of objects is meant? How were they acquired and how did they come to the Western world? Who were involved then, who are involved now? What was and is justice in this case? The focus on colonial cultural objects is prompted by developments that have influenced the world since, say, the end of the Second World War.

1.2. Changes that matter

The risk of oversimplification makes it hard to describe changes in the world after the Second World War. The following section focusses, therefore, on those changes that are relevant for this study. An obvious one is the independence of colonies in Asia and Africa, as most South American colonies had already gained

9   Lyndel Prott, ed. *Witnesses to History: Documents and Writings on the Return of Cultural Objects* (Paris: UNESCO, 2009), 116 – 118.
10   Jos Van Beurden, "An Etruscan Cuirass", in *Culture Without Context*, newsletter of the Illicit Antiquities Research Centre (Cambridge: IAR, Spring 2006), 10.
11   Jos van Beurden, *Return of Cultural and Historical Treasures*, 53.

independence at the start of the 19th century. Another change is globalisation. The increasing interconnectedness of humans and places is hardly a new phenomenon. Early in the 17th century the silver-for-silk trade connected global players: The silver came from Spanish controlled South America, the silk from China, while the two precious goods were exchanged in the Spanish trading post of Manila.[12] The spread of agricultural products and diseases and the trade in enslaved Africans during the European colonial era were as much expressions of globalisation as the present dispersion of Asian IT instruments over the globe.

The present wave of globalisation began in the 1960s. Thanks to computer networks, connections became faster, intellectual resources more available and mass media were boosted.[13] Globalisation influences people differently – captains of industry more than female heads of remote households, port cities more than their hinterland, *near* things and events more than *distant* ones.[14] Terrorist attacks, the economic crisis and the refugee crisis are no longer isolated events, but rather expressions of global imbalances with direct consequences for more and more people. Globalisation has given rise to often-populist nationalism and protectionism; national borders '*still matter a great deal* [...] *so do flows across them*'.[15]

There is an unmistakable global power shift. In the mid-19th century, European countries were '*challenging the Chinese, pushing Persia out of its sphere of influence in the Caucasus, invading north Africa, forcing the Ottomans to open up their markets, promoting Christianity in Indo-China and eying a long-secluded Japan*'. They could do so thanks to their '*new technologies, superior information gathering and attractive trade terms*' and their '*capacity to kill*'.[16] Europe's domination became Western supremacy when the USA made territorial gains after the Mexican-American War (1846 – 1848), and when it captured three Spanish colonies, Cuba, Puerto Rico and the Philippines, in 1898.[17] In the 1870s, Japan joined the Western colonial powers when opening up Korea, Taiwan and China for free trade.[18] In 1895, it defeated China and gained control over Taiwan and parts of Manchuria. In 1905, Japan won the Battle of Tsushima against Russia. After the Second World War, West European and East Asian countries passed their power to the USA and the Soviet Union. Nowadays, the USA, China, Russia and some others dominate the world. Some scholars argue that the European colonial domination was an interruption of Asian, and particularly Chinese, domination and that Europe deserves a smaller place in the global order.

---

12   Charles Mann, *1493 – How Europe's Discovery of the Americas Revolutionised Trade, Ecology and Life on Earth* (London: Granta Books, 2001), 161.

13   Arjun Appadurai, *Modernity at Large – Cultural Dimensions of Globalisation* (London/Minneapolis: Minneapolis University Press, 1996), 3.

14   Pankaj Ghemawat, *World 3.0 – Global Prosperity and How to Achieve it* (Boston: Harvard Business Review Press, 2011), 55, 57.

15   Ibid., 17.

16   Pankaj Mishra, *From the Ruins of Empire – The Revolt Against the West and the Remaking of Asia* (London: Allan lane, 2012), 39 – 40.

17   Jane Burbank and Frederick Cooper, *Empires in World History – Power and the Politics of Difference* (Princeton/Oxford: Princeton University Press, 2010), 265, 321, 322.

18   Ibid., 302.

At the moment, three global changes can be mentioned as having direct consequences for colonial cultural objects: (1) cultural globalisation and cultural localisation, (2) more supranational legal measures and (3) a renewed discussion about restitution.

Globalisation has two seemingly opposite dimensions. Globally, a transnational business elite is emerging. Popular cultures and an intellectual culture are being created. Transnational social movements are arising. There is ample evidence of business elites in former colonies that collect and repatriate (colonial) cultural heritage and start new museums.[19] This is seen in the People's Republic of China with its growing art market and expanding cultural heritage activities abroad. Russia and the United Arab Emirates boast serious numbers of wealthy collectors. Governments of Gulf countries support new museums and other cultural infrastructure.[20] In Africa, there is an increase of wealthy art collectors, but this has remained largely unnoticed because of a focus on European and American collectors of African art.[21] In source countries, civil society organisations have become active. They either operate because of the absence of government efforts, or act as a complement to them.

The other dimension is an *'increasing emphasis on cultural difference'*, a cultural localisation. People use their cultural heritage *'creatively in finding their own path through the modern world'*.[22] It can result in both positive and negative developments. The positive leads to a stronger self, without antagonising the external world or deprecating other cultures. The rise of regional and local museums and cultural festivals in numerous places expresses this tendency.[23] A negative expression is increased antagonism towards the external world. In the material cultural heritage field this can lead to iconoclasm, as will be shown next.

Iconoclasm is the wilful, intentional and humiliating destruction of other people's religious and cultural images. The concept has long been applied in a European-Christian centred way and covers three waves: in the Byzantine church in the 8th and 9th century, in Christian North-western Europe in the 16th and 17th century and in the aftermath of the 1789 French Revolution. In some instances the iconoclasm was aimed

---

19   Kiran Nadar Museum of Art, India, http://www.knma.in/ (October 6, 2014); Nasser D. Khalili: Iran, Islamic, Japanese, Swedish, Spanish and enamels collections http://www.khalili.org/ (July 29, 2012); Carlos Slim Helú, Mexico: pre-Columbian and colonial art, http://www.artnews.com/2013/07/09/the-2013-artnews-200-top-collectors/6/ (February 20, 2015); Femi Akinsanya, Nigeria: bronze, brass, copper alloys and iron, http://akinsanyaartcollection.com/ (September 18, 2012); Sindika Dokolo, DR Congo: African art, www.fondation-sindikadokolo.com/ (December 23, 2015); Frank Huang, China: porcelain, http://www.artnews.com/2013/07/09/the-2013-artnews-200-top-collectors/3/ (February 20, 2015); Patricia Phelps de Cisneros and Gustavo A. Cisneros, Venezuela: colonial art and Orinoco ethnographic objects, http://www.coleccioncisneros.org/collections/colonial-art (February 20, 2015).

20   Robert Kluijver, *Contemporary Art in the Gulf – Context and Perspectives* (Self-published, http://www.sciencespo.fr/psia/sites/sciencespo.fr.psia/files/Contemporary%20Art%20in%20the%20Gulf%20for%20print.pdf, 2013), 138.

21   Sylvester Okwunodo Ogbechie, *Making History: African Collectors and the Canon of African Art*, see http://olaleredot.blogspot.nl/2012/02/making-history-femi-akinsanya-art.html (September 18, 2012).

22   Peter Geschiere, *The perils of belonging – Autochthony, citizenship and exclusion in Africa & Europe* (Chicago: University of Chicago Press, 2009), 156, 157.

23   Regional and local museums were visible at the conference *'Museum of our own: In search of local museology in Asia'*, November 18 – 20, 2014, Yogyakarta, Indonesia.

at one's own religion or denomination, in which case it is not only humiliating but also purifying.[24] James Noyes links iconoclasm with the construction of the modern state and expands the spotlight to include iconoclastic eruptions in the Arab world.[25] Recent evidence supports this.[26] UNESCO has named these eruptions '*cultural cleansing*', which is a war crime.[27] Gamboni, Noyes and most others[28] do not mention one of the most extensive waves of iconoclasm – the wilful destruction and confiscation by foreign missionaries of ritual objects from other religions and cultures in the colonial period. This is dealt with in the next chapter (2.3.4.).

The second change affecting colonial cultural objects is an increase in the number of global and regional institutions and legal instruments that promote global justice and human rights. This increase was a reaction to the horrors of the Second World War[29] and was furthered by the on-going discussion about the impact of the slave trade and violence in the colonial era.[30] Recent expressions of the latter are the 2014 *Declaration of Latin American and Caribbean countries for reparations for slavery and the genocide of native peoples*[31] and the reparation payments for alleged atrocities, which are claimed by countries as Indonesia, Kenya, Namibia and Tanzania from the Netherlands, Great Britain and Germany.[32] UNESCO Conventions and other hard law instruments for the protection of cultural heritage and the adoption of principles for dealing with Nazi-looted treasures are more specific expressions. This change made it possible for the International Criminal Court in The Hague to impose a nine-year sentence on an alleged fundamentalist for the destruction of mausoleums and a mosque in Timbuktu in 2012, on 27 September 2016.[33]

The argument often heard in former colonies that these instruments for global justice are white Western inventions is debatable. Such ideas were found everywhere. Indian Emperor Ashoka (3rd century BCE) argued against intolerance and in favour of understanding. Moghul Emperor Akbar (16th century CE) studied social and political values and legal and cultural practices.[34] Representatives of

---

24   Dario Gamboni, *The destruction of art – Iconoclasm and vandalism since the French Revolution* (London: Reaktion Books, 1997), 246.

25   James Noyes, *The politics of Iconoclasm – Religion, violence and the culture of image-breaking in Christianity and Islam* (London/New York: Tauris, 2016), 92; 166 ff.

26   Examples are the destruction of, or damage inflicted upon the Buddhas of Bamiyan, Afghanistan (2001), the Sufi shrines, northern Mali (2012), Christian churches, Egypt (2014), and archaeological sites and museums in Syria and Iraq (2014, 2015) https://www.youtube.com/watch?v=Kgvakdb-gBM (February 27, 2015).

27   http://en.unesco.org/news/director-general-irina-bokova-firmly-condemns-destruction-palmyra-s-ancient-temple-baalshamin (June 14, 2016).

28   Raymond Corbey and Frans-Karel Weener offer an exception in "Collecting while Converting: Missionaries and Ethnigraphics", in *Journal of Art Historiography* (Birmingham: University of Birmingham, 2015), https://arthistoriography.files.wordpress.com/2015/06/corbey-weener.pdf (December 6, 2016).

29   Siep Stuurman, *De Uitvinding van de Mensheid: Korte Wereldgeschiedenis van het Denken over Gelijkheid en Cultuurverschil* (Amsterdam: Bert Bakker, 2010), 472, 436.

30   Achille Mbembe, *Kritiek van de zwarte rede* (Amsterdam: Boom, 2015), 254.

31   http://www.lacult.unesco.org/docc/reparaciones_esclavitud_final_En.pdf (May 27, 2016).

32   http://bigstory.ap.org/article/73b325ca045442d29f422db48ff9cf49/tanzania-seek-german-reparations-over-colonial-acts (February 09, 2017).

33   https://www.icc-cpi.int/mali/al-mahdi/Documents/AlMahdiEng.pdf (May 27, 2016).

34   Amartya Sen, *The Idea of Justice* (London: Penguin Books, 2010), 75, 37.

former colonies played key roles in the formulation of the 1948 UN Declaration of Human Rights.[35] Countries in South America were prominent in setting up the 1970 UNESCO Convention.[36] At the same time, former colonies have rarely used these instruments to support claims to colonial cultural objects.[37] This observation is elaborated later (6.2.1.; 6.2.2.).

The third change concerns a renewed discussion about restitution. After the fall of the Berlin Wall in 1989 and the disintegration of Eastern Europe, the past of this continent had to be redefined and restitution became a key element in his redefinition.[38] Initially restitution concerned confiscated estates, factories and other economic properties that were claimed by their former owners,[39] but soon it also came to cover cultural objects confiscated after the 1917 Russian Revolution or during the division of Germany after the Second World War. It opened up the possibility of returning objects in public collections to private collections. There were also colonial cultural objects among these objects: an example of an assigned claim was the Great Zimbabwe Bird, which the Soviet Union handed over to Germany after 1989, but which Germany transferred back to Zimbabwe in 2004 (see Box: *Incidental returns of colonial cultural objects*). An example of a rejected claim is the refusal to return Benin objects in the University of Leipzig, which had been acquired by professional collector Hans Meyer between 1900 and 1930. After 1989, his descendants had claimed the objects.[40] The museum argued that restitution '*would be almost as tragic as the original removal of the objects of the Oba's palace nearly a century ago*'. At present, the treasures are still in the museum.[41]

During the last decades, cultural objects have incidentally been transferred to their countries of origin. They clearly show diversity in motivation behind such transfers: a gift because of a country's independence, a donation to gain a lucrative industrial contract, a voluntary return by a non-state owner or a long-term or easily renewable loan. The list below (Box: *Incidental returns of colonial cultural objects*) is chronological and does not pretend to be complete.

---

35 Stuurman, *Uitvinding van de Mensheid*, 447 – 449. Also: Drafting Committee: Charles Malik (Lebanon), Alexandre Bogomolov (USSR), Peng-chun Chang (China), René Cassin (France), Eleanor Roosevelt (US), Charles Dukes (United Kingdom), William Hodgson (Australia), Hernan Santa Cruz (Chile), and John P. Humphrey (Canada), http://www.un.org/en/documents/udhr/drafters.shtml (May 23, 2013). Chang was the intellect behind the Declaration. Malik and Roosevelt were the political motor.

36 Prott, *Witnesses to History*, 12.

37 Samuel Moyn, *The last Utopia – Human rights in history* (Harvard: Belknap Press of Harvard University Press, 2010), 85.

38 Ana Vrdoljak, "Restitution of Cultural Property Trafficked During Colonization: A Human Rights Perspective" in *Strategies to Build the International Network for the Return of Cultural Property* (UNESCO, Ministry of Foreign Affairs and Trade of Korea and Korean National Commission for UNESCO, 2011), 200.

39 Elazar Barkan, *The Guilt of Nations: Restitution and Negotiating Historical Injustices* (New/York London: W.W. Norton & Company, 2000), 112, 113.

40 Adam Jones, "The Benin collection of Hans Meyer: An endangered part of Leipzig's heritage", in *Museums and Xenophobia* (Paris: ICME, report Conference Leipzig, 1994). http://icme.icom.museum/fileadmin/user_upload/pdf/1994/Museums_and_Xenophobia_small.pdf: 17 (December 18, 2015).

41 http://afrikanistik.gko.uni-leipzig.de/index.php/en/afrika-in-leipzig (January 15, 2016).

Incidental returns of colonial cultural objects

East Germany to China
To strengthen the ties with China, the then East German Republic (DDR) returned some volumes of the Yongle Encyclopaedia (Ming Dynasty) and ten flags in 1955, confiscated by German soldiers at the end of the 19th century. The ten flags were originally part of a collection of 190 Boxer flags, but the others were lost in Berlin during the Second World War. The DDR did not want to keep objects that had been stolen in the European colonial period. Chinese Prime Minister Zhou Enlai declared that the day that all such objects would be returned was not far (5.1.).[1]

UK to Myanmar
In 1885, the British army confiscated the *Mandalay Regalia* as indemnity after the third Anglo-Burmese war. They were placed in the Victoria and Albert Museum in London. In 1964, after four years of discussions, the museum returned the treasures. In appreciation of the museum's safekeeping, Myanmar donated a gold and jewelled container in the form of a karaweik (mythical bird) that symbolises longevity and had belonged to the last Burmese king, Thibaw, (1878 – 1885).[2]

UK to Ghana
In 1985 descendants of Captain Jackson donated an Ashanti stool, which Jackson had appropriated during the British ransacking of the royal palace in Kumasi in 1874.[3]

United Kingdom/Kenya to Ethiopia
In 1868, British and British-Indian soldiers confiscated, in retaliation for imprisoning a British consul and some European missionaries, 468 items of regalia, religious objects and ancient manuscripts from Emperor Tewodros' palace in Maqdala and some nearby churches (2.3.3.). Most objects ended up in the United Kingdom, but some went to British colonies that had provided soldiers. In 2008, Ethiopia asked for the return of these treasures, stating that '*Ethiopians have long grieved at the loss of this part of their national heritage.... This act of appropriation had no justification in international law.*'[4] Ten objects have been returned from Great Britain at an incidental base.[5] In 1985, the National Museum of Kenya returned a precious shield and other weapons, attributed to Tewodros.[6]

USA to Malawi
In 1989, on the occasion of Malawi's silver jubilee of independence, the Whatcom Museum in Bellingham City, WA, sent the Cox Brothers' Collection of 91 Malawian artefacts to Malawi's National Museum.[7]

UK to Australia
When approving the merging of six British colonies in Australia into a Commonwealth with its own constitution in 1900, the British Parliament kept one folio of vellum of the Constitution Act. Although its return was resisted in the UK as '*it would break an unbroken series of archives stretching back to the thirteenth century*',[8] the folio went back as a '*gift of inestimable value*' in 1990. Australia, however, did not see it as a gift but as a restitution, as the vellum had '*always been Australian*'.[9]

Germany to Namibia
Hendrik Witbooi, resistance leader against German colonialism, lost a number of precious objects. His family bible, which was captured in 1893 and has been in the Linden Museum in Stuttgart since 1902, has been subject of a return-dispute since 2013. Witbooi was a letter-writer, which was rare at the time in Africa. The parts of his letter books that a German trader had captured in 1904 and sold in 1935 to the German Colonial and Overseas Museum in Bremen, were returned

by the German museum to Namibia's National Archive in 1995. Witbooi's letters to a German army officer that had ended up in the ethnological museum in Freiburg have been digitalised.[10]

France to Algeria

To promote reconciliation, French President Jacques Chirac gave the seal of Husseyn Pacha, ceded after his surrender to the French colonial authorities in 1830, to Algeria in 2003.[11]

Germany/South Africa to Zimbabwe

In 2004, the Prussian Cultural Heritage Foundation repatriated the lower half of its Great Zimbabwe Bird. In 1889, a South African trader had taken the sacred object from the ruined city of Great Zimbabwe to Germany, thereby neglecting protests of local Shona people. After the Second World War it was brought to the Soviet Union and after the collapse of that regime it was sent back to the Prussian Foundation. The upper part had always remained in Zimbabwe. When the two were reunited in an exhibition in the Royal Museum for Central Africa in Tervuren in 1997,[12] Zimbabwe's President Mugabe asked for the restitution of the lower half. The Prussian Foundation only agreed when the transfer was not defined as restitution, but as *permanent loan*.[13] In 1981, the South African Museum in Cape Town had already returned some carved birds from Great Zimbabwe.[14]

Japan to South Korea

In 1709, Koreans erected Bukgwandaecheopbi, a stone monument to commemorate the 1593 victory of Korea's general Jeong Mun-bu over Japanese invaders. Japanese forces had taken it during the Russo-Japanese War (1904 – 1905) and offered it to the Japanese Emperor. One hundred years later Buddhist monks mediated its return to North Korea, where it was reinstalled on its original pedestal.[15]

Netherlands to Indonesia

In the 1980s, the Order of the Capuchins in the city of Tilburg began to consider the return of textiles, ritual items and other objects gathered in the colonial era to their place of origin – in Indonesia. '*It was difficult to store them, and after all, they are theirs*', said mission procurator Huub Boelaars.[16] With the help of the Tropenmuseum in Amsterdam, the Order sent objects to two regional museums in Kalimantan and Sumatra, complemented by some objects of the Tropenmuseum, in 2009.

France/Japan to South Korea

In 2010, 297 manuscripts of the Joseon Dynasty (1600 – 1900) were returned by the Bibliothèque Nationale in Paris to South Korea (4.1.). French soldiers had confiscated them in a raid in 1866. As they had become part of French national heritage and were therefore inalienable, the transfer was defined as renewable loan. No one has the illusion that South Korea will ever return them, but the country cannot register them as national heritage. A curious detail is that the French government, when it was seeking a contract for the construction of a high-speed train in South Korea in 1993, had handed over one manuscript, without bothering about its inalienability.[17]

In 1966, Japan returned 1,431 objects and, in 2011, over twelve hundred ancient manuscripts. Of these, 167 were from the Joseon Dynasty.[18] In 1922, the Japanese colonial governor who had taken them donated them to Japan's emperor.[19] Japan wanted to improve relations with the government and the people of South Korea. These relations had been undermined by the unresolved issue of Korean comfort women who had worked for Japanese military during the Second World War.[20] Unlike the French transfer, the Japanese gesture was a return, which enabled South Korea to designate the manuscripts as South Korean national cultural heritage.

US to Costa Rica

In 2011, the Brooklyn Museum in New York sent 4,500 pre-Columbian ceramic and stone objects to the National Museum of Costa Rica. American railroad magnate and United Fruit Company founder, Minor Keith, had taken them to the USA around 1900 and donated them to the Brooklyn Museum in 1934. Their return was part of the culling of the Brooklyn Museum's collection. The objects fill a vacuum in the history of indigenous societies in Costa Rica.[21]

UK to Nigeria

In 2012, a grandson of British Captain H.S. and Josephine Walker brought back a bronze bird, a bronze bell and part of his grandfather's diary in which he wrote about the raid of the Benin Court in 1897.[22]

France to China

In 2013, France announced the return of a rat and a rabbit, part of a set of twelve zodiac symbols looted by British and French soldiers from Beijing's Old Summer Palace in 1860.[23] In 2009, commotion arose when the widower of owner and fashion-designer Yves Saint Laurent wanted to auction them in Paris. A French court rejected the Chinese request to stop the auction. A Chinese bidder won the auction, but he refused to pay. Finally, the French industrial Pinault family, owner of Christie's auction house, offered to pay. It helped the family to open up a Christie's location in China.[24]

Norway to China

In 2014, the Kode Art Museum in Bergen, Norway, deposited seven marble columns taken from the Imperial Summer Palace in 1860 at Beijing University on a long-term basis. The two institutions signed a cooperation agreement. A Chinese real estate developer donated $1.63 million to the Norwegian museum.[25]

The Netherlands to Indonesia

In 2015, descendants of Dutch Governor-General J.C. Baud (1833 – 1836) returned an ancient pilgrim's staff that had belonged to Indonesia's national hero Diponegoro to the National Museum in Jakarta.[26]

Notes

1   Deutsches Historisches Museum, *German Colonialism – Fragments Past and Present* (Berlin: Deutscher Historisches Museum, 2016), 220. Visit to Deutscher Historisches Museum, December 28, 2016. Email Deutscher Historischer Museum, January 12, 2017.

2   Jeannette Greenfield, *The Return of Cultural Treasures* (Cambridge: Cambridge University Press, 2007), 371. Also: http://commons. wikimedia.org/wiki/File:Mandalay_Regalia.JPG (July 03 2014); http://hansard.millbanksystems. com/written_answers/1961/may/16/burma-mandalay-regalia (July 03, 2014).

3   Greenfield, *Return of Cultural Treasures*, 122. Kwame Opoku, "When will Britain return looted golden Ghanaian artefacts? A history of British looting of more than 100 objects" in *Modern Ghana News* (Accra), January 5, 2011.

4   *The Independent* (London), November 23, 2008.

5   Returned were a royal cap and silver seal from Queen Elisabeth II's collection (1965); two objects donated by private owners, one by an Edinburgh church, two were purchased by supporters of the return of Maqdala treasures: The Art Newspaper (London), October 13, 2004; http://www.afromet.org/ (June 21, 2011).

6   The shield (decorated with silver), two swords, four knives and a bayonet. Information provided by National Museum, Addis Ababa, September 26, 2012.

7   Lovemore Mazibuko, Acting Director Malawi Museums, email April 2, 2014. The US consul in

Lilongwe had instigated the negotiations, http://www.worldcat.org/title/forgotten-legacy-of-malawi-african-artifacts-from-the-cox-collection/oclc/48480317 (May 20, 2014).

8 Magnus Magnusson's "Introduction" in: Greenfield, *The Return of Cultural Treasures*, 8.

9 http://pmtranscripts.dpmc.gov.au/browse.php?did=8103 (April 30, 2015).

10 Deutsches Historisches Museum, *German Colonialism*, 221.

11 Jean-Gabriel Leturcq, ''La question des restitutions d'oeuvres d'art : différentiels maghrébins'', in *L'Année du Maghreb* (Paris: CNRS Publications http://anneemaghreb.revues.org/431 [September 11, 2014], 85 – 86).

12 William J. Dewey and Els De Palmenaer, *Zimbabwe – Legacies of Stone: Past and Present* (Tervuren: Royal Museum for Central Africa, 1997), Vol. I, 223.

13 William J Dewey, "Repatriation of a Great Zimbabwe Stone Bird", in *Proceedings of Society of Africanist Archaeologist's 18th Biennial Conference*, (Alberta: University of Calgary, 2006), http://safa.rice.edu/WorkArea/DownloadAsset.aspx?id=2147484153 (May 20, 2014); and https://plone.unige.ch/art-adr/cases-affaires/great-zimbabwe-bird-2013-zimbabwe-and-prussia-cultural-heritage-foundation-germany/case-note-great-zimbabwe-bird (June 30, 2014).

14 Greenfield, *The Return of Cultural Treasures*, 374.

15 Geoffrey R. Scott, "Spoliation, cultural property, and Japan", in *Journal of International Law* (Pennsylvania: University of Pennsylvania Law School, 2008), 29/4, 845. Also: http://english.chosun.com/site/data/html_dir/2005/10/20/2005102061026.html (July 4, 2016).

16 Jos Van Beurden, *Return of Cultural and Historical treasures*, 2012: 38.

17 Corinne Herskovitch and Didier Rykner, *La Restitution des Œuvres d'Art* (Paris: Hazan, 2011), 72, 73.

18 Lee Kyong-hee, "Joseon Royal Books return home after 145 years", in *Koreana, A Quaterly on Korean Culture and Arts*, No. 1851, http://www.koreana.or.kr/months/news_view.asp?b_idx=1576&lang=en (June 5, 2014).

19 Geoffrey R. Scott, *Spoliation, cultural property, and Japan*, 846.

20 http://ajw.asahi.com/article/asia/korean_peninsula/AJ201112080019a (January 15, 2015); http://traffickingculture.org/encyclopedia/case-studies/uigwe/ (May 21, 2014).

21 http://www.nytimes.com/2011/01/01/arts/design/01costa.html?_r=0 (April 17, 2016); http://www.ticotimes.net/2011/10/04/thousands-of-pre-columbian-artifacts-returning-to-costa-rica (April 17, 2016).

22 Peju Laywola, "Walker and the restitution of two Benin bronzes", in *Premium Times* (Lagos, Nigeria), June 20, 2014, https://www.premiumtimesng.com/arts-entertainment/165632-walker-and-the-restitution-of-two-benin-bronzes-by-peju-layiwola.html#sthash.zHmDyYEu.dpbs (August 18, 2014).

23 http://french.china.org.cn/foreign/txt/2013-05/07/content_28750539.htm (May 13, 2013)

24 Kwame Opoku, "Rat and rabbit sculptures returned to China by owner of Christie's", in *Modern Ghana* (Accra), May 5, http://www.modernghana.com/news/462152/1/rat-and-rabbit-sculptures-returned-t.html [May 13, 2013]).

25 https://itsartlaw.com/tag/kode/ (Febnruary 23, 2017); and http://usa.chinadaily.com.cn/china/2014-02/12/content_17278007.htm (February 23, 2017).

26 Harm Stevens, *Bitter spice – Indonesia and the Netherlands from 1600* (Nijmegen: Vantilt, 2015), 158 – 163.

1.3. Main questions

In the 1970s and 1980s, the Netherlands returned a number of colonial cultural objects to its former colonial possessions in the East and the West (none to South Africa). Since then there have scarcely been any others. This hiatus does not differ greatly from the situation in other former colonial powers and colonies, as shown further on in the book. Former colonies long for the return of important cultural and historical objects and, as discussed further on in the book, have their own reasons not to pursue them. The legal path offers no solution, but the maldistribution of cultural and historical treasures that resulted from the European colonial era raises questions about historical injustice and whether this should and can be undone. As the Box: *Incidental returns of colonial cultural objects* has made evident, there have been incidental returns, but they are fragmented experiences.

Can the discussion about the future of colonial cultural objects be raised above the incidental and fragmented? The question seems to be timely. In the global village, former colonisers and former colonised are becoming more equal. The uncovering of what happened in the colonial past and the lasting impact of colonialism and slave trade raise new discussions. The dynamics of the repatriation of colonial human remains might offer lessons in dealing with colonial cultural objects. Some European heritage institutions continue to keep the remains; others are increasingly prioritising the groups of origin above academic research, and de-accessioning them. This is also the case in the restitution of Nazi-looted art. Restitution committees for Nazi-looted art in European countries and the USA apply lenient policies in restitution matters. For both categories guidelines and principles for dealing with them are being formulated.

This leads to the following main questions for this book:

- **How can the loss of cultural and historical treasures during the European colonial era be charted?**

- **What lessons can be drawn from the way other contested categories of such treasures have been handled?**

- **How to devise a model for negotiating the future of cultural objects acquired in colonial times, including the option of their return?**

Answering these questions requires an interdisciplinary approach. The input of history is needed for a periodisation of the European colonial era and for mapping the loss of cultural and historical objects from colonial possessions in each period. History and legal studies help to uncover the formal protection of cultural heritage in the colonial era and the effectiveness of hard law and soft law instruments for dealing with disputes about colonial cultural objects. The discipline of conflict studies is used for developing the model for negotiating the future of colonial objects.

Many authors have influenced me. Their books rarely fit on the shelf of only one discipline. With *The return of cultural treasures*, Jeanette Greenfield has inspired me to look for cases of the disappearance of colonial cultural objects, claims to them and their return. I adopt her decision to define Iceland as a former Danish colony and treat the return of manuscripts to Iceland as one of colonial objects. I prefer the use of the term Parthenon Marbles, as is *usance* in the UNESCO, above her use of Elgin Marbles.[42] In her study *International Law, Museums and the Return of Cultural Objects*, Ana Vrdoljak focuses mainly on restitution claims from minorities and other victims of internal colonialism.[43] My focus is on claims from victims of external colonialism. I add some points of difference and build on her human rights perspective for return issues. Lyndel Prott's *Witnesses to history: Documents and writings on the return of cultural objects* has helped to chart the disappearance and return of objects. To the three instances of bilateral negotiations on the return of colonial cultural objects that she mentions, I add two more. In *Contested Cultural Property: The return of Nazi-spoliated art and human remains from public collections*, Katja Lubina sees few chances for the return of colonial cultural objects. I lift part of the dividing line between the categories of Nazi-looted art and colonial cultural objects and uncover some more chances. I elaborate Amartya Sen's thoughts from *The idea of justice* for colonial cultural objects. Johan Galtung has helped to define the multi-layered violent nature of colonialism: I nuance it slightly. In *Contemporary Conflict Resolution* by Oliver Ramsbotham ea., other introductions into conflict studies and Galtung's texts, I miss profound references to conflicts concerning colonial issues – as things of a distant past – and to conflict resolution methods from outside Europe and North America. I include the latter. Moreover, I expand their work by defining decolonisation as an unresolved conflict with the many lost colonial cultural objects as an aspect of it. I am indebted to Jane Burbank and Frederick Cooper's *Empires in world history – Power and the politics of difference*, Vijay Prashad's *The darker nations – A people's history of the Third World*, and Pankaj Mishra's *From the ruins of empire – The revolt against the West and the remaking of Asia* for insights into the place of European colonialism in the history of our era. I complement their studies with insights into the loss of cultural and historical treasures during colonialism.

It has been hard to find sources for two issues. One is the question whether colonialism was a European phenomenon or one which European nations experienced simultaneously, and connected to this is the question whether the discussion about the future of colonial cultural objects should acquire a European dimension. Susan Legêne offers some clues, on which I build my own answer to this question. The second issue is cultural diplomacy and framing return as a diplomatic instrument. As will be shown, cultural diplomacy runs through many studies about bilateral return negotiations, but is rarely addressed explicitly. I make an effort to do so.

---

42 Jeannette Greenfield, *The Return of Cultural Treasures* (Cambridge: Cambridge University Press, 2007), 41.

43 There is internal colonialism when the dominant group subjugates, exploits and/or looks down upon one or more minority groups inside the same state. When subjugation, exploitation and looking down on groups occur outside a state, there is external colonialism, http://www.sociologyguide.com/references.php (April 19, 2016).

The 1975 agreement between the Netherlands and Indonesia has been thoroughly researched. A description of comparable agreements between Belgium and Congo, Australia and Papua New Guinea, Denmark and Iceland and Denmark and Greenland and of the ongoing dialogue between Western museums and Nigeria is added. Such a comparison is relatively new and helps to find more elements for the model. In each case study, relevant literature is discussed.

My research methodology has been summarised in the Box: *Research methodology*.

Research methodology

Ethical imperative

Dealing with a subject as sensitive as the future of colonial cultural objects burdens me with an *'ethical imperative'*.[1] I have to pursue systematically the *'not-yet-known'*,[2] to scrutinise each finding, to dare to doubt and to challenge my own preconceived ideas. I consider the outcome as a work-in-progress and offer it up for discussion and greater depth.

Qualitative research

Most research for this book has been done through qualitative methods. There is a long-standing debate about the use of quantitative and qualitative methods.[3] The nature of the subject makes the application of purely quantitative methods hard, but, wherever possible, the collected information has been systematised.

Primary sources

Primary research was done in the National Archive of the Netherlands and in archives of museums such as Museum Volkenkunde in Leiden and Museum Bronbeek in Arnhem. Field research[4] consisted of formal and informal interviews with cultural authorities, traders, collectors, and experts, of visits to monuments deprived of statues, looted burial hills, and museum exhibitions, and of observing the course of business at art fairs, in auction houses and in art and antique shops.

Secondary sources

Secondary sources have been used extensively – academic books, articles and blogs, newspaper clippings, relevant websites, incidentally a novel. This raises dilemmas. Sources coming from the former colonisers easily dominate; therefore, wherever possible, valuable voices from the former colonies have been integrated. As evidence of some acquisitions, claims and returns, only newspaper clippings were available and no academic research finding supported them. For these I have looked for confirmation/denial in other media sources or contacted experts by mail.

Case study/micro-history

This book contains case studies/micro-histories of bilateral return negotiations.[5] They are examples of thick description, in which reportage and explanation are followed by analysis and evaluation, and combine the advantage of offering an in-depth analysis and context with the disadvantage that their conclusions cannot necessarily be generalised. The many annotated examples in this book of claims and returns can be considered as mini case-studies/micro-histories or thin description.

Boxes and appendices

Most boxes in this book list acquisitions and returns of, and claims to colonial cultural objects. Some offer a helicopter view of, for example, protective measures or a historical development of, for example, the evolution of conflict studies as a discipline. Three appendices have been added that allow official texts to be checked.

Linguistic dilemmas

A dilemma that emerges regularly is how to name historical events. Was what happened in 1894 in Lombok or in 1897 in Benin City a punitive action, or was it looting and arson? Is the violence in Indonesia between 1945 and 1949 best covered by the term police actions, war of independence or Dutch aggression? These dilemmas are mentioned in the book.

For reasons of convenience, the present names of geographical areas have been used. *Papua* for instance, is the name of an Indonesian province, which early Western seafarers called *Irian* and Dutch colonial administration called *New Guinea*. *European* in European colonial era also covers the USA and Japan, which joined the colonisers at a late stage.

Unless otherwise mentioned, the translations of quotations from other languages into English are mine.

Notes

1   W. Lawrence Neuman, *Understanding Research* (Boston: Pearson – Prentice Hall, Boston, 2012), 62.

2   Arjun Appadurai, *The future as a cultural fact – Essays on the global condition* (London/New York: Verso Books, 2013), 271.

3   Neuman, *Understanding Research*, 2012: 10. Alexander L. George and Andrew Bennet, *Case*

Studies and Theory Development in the Social Sciences (Cambridge MA: MIT Press, 2005), 3.

4   Neuman, *Understanding Research*, 264 ff.

5   Bent Flyvbjerg, "Case Study", in *The SAGE Handbook of Qualitative Research,* ed. Norman Denzin and Yvonna S. Lincoln (Thousand Oaks, CA: Sage, 2011). History News Network 2006. Reykjavik Academy, http://historynewsnetwork. org/article/23720 (October 24, 2013).

Chapter 2

On colonial cultural objects

In the literature one finds many terms that cover the physical, cross-border handover of valued objects that came from colonised places to the Western world – return, restitution, redress, transfer or repatriation. They can have legal implications. They focus on an action by the possessing state or by the claiming state. They presuppose two states as stakeholders or offer room to non-state actors. Which one is most suitable for this study? And what precisely is the meaning of a colonial cultural object?

2.1. Return

A common choice is *return*, a *'fairly neutral', 'catch-all concept'* that is meant for when the removal of a cultural object did not violate a legal obligation.[44] Even then, as we shall see, Western states object to it for fear of being accused that the objects claimed were acquired in a manner open to dispute.[45] For undoing the wrongful act of disputable acquisitions, the term *restitution* is used. The distinction between return and restitution has been codified since the 1976 report of the *Venice Committee of Experts*, convened by UNESCO.[46] An institution in Europe that advises its government about the allotment of Nazi-spoliated art is called a *restitution* committee.

Several terms are close to restitution. *Redress* is meant to correct or compensate a wrong. It is a way of reparatory justice.[47] Nigerian Nobel laureate Wole Soyinka[48] and Latin American and Caribbean countries (1.2.) are asking for *reparation* to undo the injustice of colonialism and slave trade; sending back colonial acquisitions can be part of it. In terms such as *recovery, retrieval* and *recuperation* there is a focus on the requesting party.[49] *Repatriation* indicates that an object or collection has a patria, Latin for fatherland, – a state or an indigenous people or other actor inside a state – and has often concerned human remains. It is interconnected with waiting for objects and echoes of *'kinship, language and history'* and shared identity.[50]

---

44 Prott, *Witnesses to History*, XXI. Lubina, *Contested Cultural Property*, 44, 42.
45 Greenfield, *Return of Cultural Treasures*, 2007: 367. Jos Van Beurden, *Return of Cultural and Historical Treasures*, 2012: 74.
46 Lubina, *Contested Cultural Property*, 127.
47 As in *On the poetics and politics of redress*, http://www.leidenuniv.nl/agenda/item/on-the-poetics-and-politics-of-redress (November 6, 2015).
48 Wole Soyinka, *The burden of memory, the music of forgiveness* (Oxford: Oxford University Press, 1999), 85.
49 Prott, *Witnesses to History*, XXI. Wojciech Kowalski, "Types of Claims for Recovery of Lost Cultural Property", in *Museum International* (Paris: UNESCO, 2005), 85 – 101.
50 Prott, *Witnesses to History*, 17.

Transfer has a broader meaning of moving, carrying or transporting something – be it in real life, virtually or in psychological terms – from one surface, body or person to another. In this study, it is usually a change in governance and control with legal implications – the moment at which property changes hands. Possessing states prefer it, as it carries less risk of association with past wrongs than return.

In this book the open term *return* is mostly used. It can be given more layers and refer to restoration, reconciliation, repair of the integrity of a source country or an instrument of cultural diplomacy.[51]

The return of a precious object often is an instrument in a country's cultural diplomacy. Cultural diplomacy is as old as humanity, but a relatively new topic in academic research. The Soviet Union and France were the first to consider '*the human side of foreign policy*', followed by Great Britain and the USA.[52] For American authors, who dominate the older literature, cultural diplomacy or '*peacetime psychological warfare*'[53] consisted of Cold War propaganda programmes with scholarships, tours, exhibitions and information services. Cultural institutes set up by powerful countries in former colonies and elsewhere, operated between propaganda programmes and genuine exchange.[54]

The Institute for Cultural Diplomacy – initiated by the USA and based in Berlin – defines the present cultural diplomacy as '*a course of actions, which are based on and utilize the exchange of ideas, values, traditions and other aspects of culture or identity, whether to strengthen relationships, enhance socio-cultural cooperation or promote national interests*'.[55] It can be practiced by '*the public sector, private sector or civil society*'. The Netherlands Foreign Ministry sees cultural diplomacy as '*putting in art and culture for the Dutch foreign relations*',[56] others as '*the deployment of a state's culture in support of its foreign policy goals or diplomacy, a government's communication with foreign audiences in order to positively influence them*'.[57]

Having written all this, I define diplomacy as the art and the ability of a country or other entity to arrange, covertly or openly, its foreign policy goals and get things from other countries or entities. Diplomacy has sub-sets such as peace and disarmament negotiations, economic diplomacy and cultural diplomacy. Cultural diplomacy helps to pursue one's foreign policy goals by cultural means. Its potential is often underestimated or remains underexposed and one of its instruments is the return of a colonial cultural object. But, as shall be shown, not every return falls under cultural diplomacy.

---

51 Greenfield, *Return of Cultural Treasures*, 2007: XIII. Soyinka, *Burden of memory*, 1999: 85. Zuozhen Liu, *The case for Repatriation China's Cultural Objects* (Singapore: Springer, 2016), 164.

52 Philip H. Coombs, *The fourth dimension of foreign policy: Educational and cultural affairs* (New York/Evanston: Harper and Row, 1964), 95, 17. Under President John F. Kennedy Coombs became the US first Assistant-Secretary of State for cultural diplomacy.

53 Niall Ferguson, *Kissinger (1923 – 1968) – The idealist* (London: Allen Lane, 2015): 263, 275.

54 Jessica C.E. Gienow – Hecht and Mark Donfried, Mark, eds., *Searching for Cultural Diplomacy* (New York/Oxford: Berghahn Books, 2010), 9.

55 Institute for Cultural Diplomacy, http://www.culturaldiplomacy.org/index.php?en_culturaldiplomacy (January 28, 2016).

56 file:///C:/Users/Jos/Downloads/131014-renilde-steeghs-acs.pdf (February 26, 2016).

57 Simon Mark, *A greater role for cultural diplomacy* (The Hague: Institute Clingendael, 2009). http://www.clingendael.nl/sites/default/files/20090616_cdsp_discussion_paper_114_mark.pdf (January 25, 2016).

2.2. Cultural objects

An object is a tangible thing that one can feel, touch, see and smell. It is made of wood, stone, silver, gold, or any other material or natural resource. Objects have a certain use and social potential and can be a source of information.[58] They are alienable or inalienable. Their inalienability can be perceived in a legal sense, when, for instance, a country's law forbids their sale. When it is considered in a cultural sense, objects become inalienable through their *'exclusive and cumulative identity with a particular series of owners through time'* and are *'to be guarded against all the exigencies that might force their loss'.*[59] Objects can be *'essential connectors with the past',* although their stories are rarely *'unambiguous'.*[60] That objects are primary sources in historical research is not self-evident.[61] Until a few decades ago, historians had *'little or no engagement'* with them.[62] Engagement with (disputed) objects is normal in legal studies and in conflict studies.

The value of cultural objects can be practical (e.g. carved household utensils), spiritual (e.g. voodoo objects or a prayer chair), symbolic (e.g. royal crown), aesthetic (e.g. a still life painting), commercial (after becoming a commodity) or a mix of these.[63] They can cause passion or fear, evoke a memory and bring people together. They are more cultural and social processes, more relational things than physical things. They often tell us more about the present than about the past and are an inherently political practice that performs the cultural work of the present.[64]

There is much to say about the authenticity of cultural objects. There is a *nominal* and an *expressive authenticity.* Nominal authenticity is about an object's origins, creator and provenance. This information is fixed and, if available, relatively easy to agree upon. Expressive authenticity is less in the object and has more to do with an object's *'character as a true expression of an individual's or society's values and beliefs'.*[65] For villagers or monks in Papua New Guinea, DR Congo or Southeast Asia, out-of-use ritual masks or damaged Buddha statues no longer have a ritual value. They have lost their expressive authenticity and are to be replaced with new masks or statues, but the laws of the countries of origin usually protect such out-of-use masks and statues. Traders and collectors acquire(d) them, often to resell them as authentic.

58 Arjun Appadurai (ed.), *The Social Life of Things – Commodities in cultural perspective* (Cambridge: Cambridge University Press, 1986). Igor Kopytoff, "The Cultural Biography of Things: Commoditization as Process", in Appadurai, *The Social Life of Things*, 1986: 64 – 91.

59 Annette Weiner, *Inalienable possessions – The paradox of keeping while giving* (Berkeley: University of California Press, 1992), 65, 33.

60 Susan Legêne, *Spiegelreflex – Culturele sporen van de koloniale ervaring* (Amsterdam: Bert Bakker, 2010), 25, 34.

61 Congress Royal Dutch Historical Society "Voorwerpen maken geschiedenis. Niet-schriftelijke bronnen in historisch onderzoek" (The Hague: Royal Dutch Historical Society, November 27, 2012). Also: Legêne, *Spiegelreflex*, 228.

62 Giorgio Riello, "Things that shape history: material culture and historical narratives", in ed. Karen Harvey, *History and Material Culture: A student's guide to approaching alternative sources* (London: Routledge, 2009), 25.

63 Kopytoff, *Cultural Biography of Things*, 64.

64 Laurajane Smith, *Uses of heritage*, (London: Routledge, 2006).

65 http://denisdutton.com/authenticity.htm (February 18, 2013).

There are *transcending, expressively authentic copies of artworks*. They are popular in fashion, jewellery, design, tattoos and also in art. Two examples explain the relevance of the concept of *transcending, expressively authentic copies of artworks* for this study. One is the bronze and the gold-gilded bronze Circle of Animals/ Zodiac Heads that Chinese artist Ai Weiwei has created. They are copies of the zodiac with twelve bronze animal heads that French and British soldiers took from the Old Summer Palace in Beijing in 1860. With their oversized scale, Ai Weiwei *'focuses attention on questions of looting and repatriation, while extending his ongoing exploration of the 'fake' and the copy in relation to the original'.*[66] The zodiac has been shown in North and South America, Asia and Europe. The other concerns artworks that resemble ancient Benin treasures, created by Peju Laywiola, granddaughter of Oba Akenzua II of the Edo Kingdom and daughter of a sculptress. She considers the works as a *'cultural action for freedom'* through which *'the past seems to be indicting the present... They who once enjoyed the splendour of the palace are now trapped behind glass in foreign lands'.*[67] In 2010, at the occasion of 50 years of independence, her work was shown in Nigeria.

Expressive authenticity has a political overtone, as it influences why and when objects are part of a country's cultural heritage. Whether the objects are or are not a part of cultural heritage is laid down in national legislation and in treaties to which countries have acceded.[68] Defining an object as cultural heritage is also a *'social process of meaning making'*, as it cannot *'unproblematically be identified as "old", grand, monumental and aesthetically pleasing sites, buildings, places and artefacts'.*[69] Its meaning can change through time. The discourse about this meaning is usually controlled by a few, usually powerful, actors. It is an *'authorised heritage discourse'*. The self-appointed universal museums try to dominate it, as did the compilers of the World Heritage List, which was pretended to be *'all-embracing'*, while for a long time it was largely compiled on *'European aesthetic notions'.*[70] Recently listed properties indicate that UNESCO is overtaking this backlog.[71] An authorised heritage discourse also takes place inside a country.[72] The definitions of cultural objects in the national legislation can be too narrow or exclusive for regional populations. Indigenous peoples in the USA, Canada, Australia and New Zealand have been *'the most strident and vocal groups'* to criticise authorised heritage discourses.[73] Going beyond the discourse can offer surprises, as two examples of suitcases show.

Upon the arrival of Holocaust victims in concentration camps, the Nazis took all their belongings – combs, glasses, suitcases and so on. The Auschwitz Birkenau State Museum in Oswiecim has them in large showcases, the suitcases

66   http://www.zodiacheads.com/about_exhibit_bronze.html (February 20, 2015).

67   http://www.pejulayiwola.com/#benin (February 22, 2015).

68   http://www.unesco.org/culture/natlaws/ (June 24, 2013). This database shows legislation, contact details and official websites. Their number differs from one to eighty-five laws per country.

69   Smith, *Uses of Heritage*, 2006: 276, 11.

70   Smith, *Uses of Heritage*, 2006: 98.

71   http://whc.unesco.org/en/newproperties/ (May 13, 2015).

72   Tular Sudarmadi, *Between colonial legacies and grassroots movements: Exploring cultural heritage practice in the Ngadha and Manggarai Region of Flores* (Amsterdam: Free University, PhD, 2014), 90.

73   Smith, *Uses of Heritage*, 2006: 277.

often still displaying the owner's name. In 2004, it loaned Pierre Lévi's suitcase (who had lived in Paris) to the Shoah Memorial Museum in the French capital. When the museum wanted to send it back, Lévi's heirs protested, as they did not want the suitcase to make the same journey as during the War. In 2009, a judge ruled that the suitcase would remain on loan in the Paris museum.[74] In the second example, barack 1B of the Camp Vught National Memorial in the Netherlands shows suitcases of Moluccan soldiers and their families who had to depart from Indonesia, where they had served in the Dutch coloniser's army. These suitcases, perhaps worth a few pence at a flea-market, are symbols of their forced journey and fate as a minority.[75]

Cultural objects are easily linked to *identity*. Without them, a community, people or state is said to suffer identity damage, and this can be an argument in support of a return claim, argues Ana Vrdoljak.[76] She discusses this for victims of internal colonialism and external colonialism alike. But differences between cultures of internally colonised communities and those of externally colonised communities make this problematic. Those of internally colonised people have often remained the same since time immemorial; the disappearance of their cultural heritage damages their identity *and* history. The cultures of many externally colonised possessions were often succeeded by new ones; they became more part of their history than of their identity. When objects are claimed to date back to an old and different cultural period, their link with identity can become a straightjacket, as two examples illustrate.

One is that opponents of a German return of the Nefertiti bust to Egypt argue that a Muslim majority in Egypt no longer adheres to, and even abhors, the religion and customs of Pharaoh Akhenaton and his Great Royal Wife Nefertiti.[77] Although many Egyptians might not consider the bust as part of their identity, it is part of their history. The second example comes from Somaliland. This unrecognised state has over one hundred rock art sites, some thousands of years old. According to former Director of the Department of Antiquities of Somaliland, Sada Mire, many inhabitants considered archaeological objects to be pre-Islamic *'things that you hand over to the white man, be it a scientist, an NGO worker or a looter. They do not link them with their heritage, due to their myth of origin, i.e. an Arab origin, and links with the prophet Mohamed's Quraysh people. At first they gave them free of charge. After 1990 they discovered that they could ask money for it.'* Telling them that the rock drawings were part of their identity made them feel uneasy, but when the Department of Antiquities explained that the drawings are part of their history

74   Anne Laure Bandle, "Auschwitz Suitcase – Pierre Lévi Heirs and Auschwitz-Birkenau State Museum Oswiecim and Shoah Memorial Museum Paris", in *Arthemis database* (Geneva: Art-Law Centre, University of Geneva, 2012) https://plone.unige.ch/art-adr (June 24, 2013).

75   http://www.nmkampvught.nl/english/ (March 22, 2016).

76   Ana Vrdoljak, "Restitution of Cultural Property Trafficked During Colonization: A Human Rights Perspective", in *Ministry of Foreign Affairs and Trade of Korea, Strategies to Build the International Network for the Return of Cultural Property* (Seoul: Korean National Commission for UNESCO, 2011), 202.

77   Stephen K. Urice, "The beautiful one has come – To stay", in ed. John Henry Merryman, *Imperialism, Art and Restitution* (Cambridge: Cambridge University Press, 2006), 153. James Cuno, *Who Owns Antiquity? Museums and the Battle over Our Ancient Heritage* (Princeton: Princeton University Press, 2008), http://press.princeton.edu/chapters/i8602.pdf (April 5, 2013).

Other frequently used concepts

Provenance/biography

Influenced by Kopytoff,[1] I would say that provenance is the history of an object in terms of the context in which it was made and who made it, of its use value and exchange value through time, of the ways in which it has passed from the maker to subsequent possessors. Provenance is also called an object's biography.

Country of origin

Country of origin is a common term for identifying mass products in commerce.[2] In this book it indicates the present day state of the country where an object was made and whence it came. It is a part of an object's provenance. The term source country is also used.

Violence

Galtung defines violence as avoidable insults to basic human needs.[3] Threats of violence are also violence. There are four classes of basic human needs: (1) survival needs, (2) well-being needs, (3) identity or meaning needs and (4) freedom needs. Basic human needs are location- and time-specific. Galtung distinguishes three sub-types of violence: direct, structural violence and ideological violence. Direct violence is an event or an act that threatens people in their survival needs, for instance through killing, war, genocide, maiming or rape. In this study, direct violence insults people's needs to foster their own identity and history, for instance through the expropriation of cultural objects during wars or by confiscation. Structural violence exists in a setting where direct violence becomes systematic, for instance in the form of unnecessary poverty, underdevelopment, exploitation, alienation, identity damage, abuse and other forms of ingrained injustices. Structural violence can cover colonial policies that lead to expropriation of cultural objects or iconoclasm.[4] Galtung has been criticised for using too broad a definition of structural

violence, based on a malleability vision.[5] Galtung's third sub-type, cultural violence, serves to justify, downplay or deny direct and structural violence. It is a constant that changes *'the moral colour of an act from red/wrong to green/right or at least to yellow/acceptable'*. The term is confusing, not only because this book is about cultural objects, but also because Galtung mentions in his own explanation that cultural violence serves as justification and legitimisation.[6] Therefore I prefer the term ideological violence. Conflict researchers have rarely linked ideological violence with Spivak's concept of *'epistemic violence'* or the infliction of harm against marginalised men and certainly also women through discourse, with Said's *Orientalism* and *Culture and Imperialism* or with Mbembe's *Critique de la raison nègre*.[7] One does not have to embrace all Spivak's, Said's and Mbembe's thoughts to understand that they have depicted the depth of the ideological violence committed in the European colonial era and that descendants of former colonisers have difficulty in decolonising their minds.[8]

Legal obligations[9]

The law of war is part of international public law, which sets rules for engaging in war and conduct during war; it covers dealing with disputes about cultural heritage in case of destruction and looting. Laws in times of peace set rules for dealing with disputes about the theft and smuggling of cultural heritage in other times. Relevant for this study are both hard law and soft law. Hard laws are binding legal instruments, laws, treaties and UN Security Council Resolutions; a claim based on these is enforceable in court. Soft laws are non-binding instruments, such as UN Resolutions or Declarations, Principles for dealing with restitution of e.g. Nazi-looted art, Codes of Conduct, etc. They are often vaguely formulated.

Dialogue

Adopting a somewhat schematic presentation, I state that in a dialogue, two or more stakeholders try to come to a common decision and are willing to adjust their own insights. They can engage a third party to help them. A debate, in contrast, is a competition with three participants. Two try to convince each other about their own position and the other's wrong, while the third decides who has won. Debaters do not necessarily have the intention to problematise their own points of view. In practice the term debate is also used as a method to bridge gaps.[10]

--- **Notes** ---

1   Kopytoff, *Cultural Biography of Things*, 64 – 67.

2   Keith Dinnie, *Country-of-origin 1965 – 2004: A literature review* (Tokyo: Temple University Japan, 2003), http://www.brandhorizons.com/papers/Dinnie_COO_litreview.pdf (July 01, 2016).

3   Johan Galtung, "Cultural Violence", in *Journal of Peace Research* (Oslo: Peace Research Institute, 1990), Vol. 27/3: 291 – 305.

4   My master thesis was titled *Economic Structural Violence*, (Utrecht: Utrecht University, May 1971; unpubl.).

5   Hans Achterhuis *Met alle geweld* (Rotterdam: Lemniscaat, 2008), 76, 77.

6   Galtung, *Cultural Violence*, 294.

7   Spivak, Gayatri. "Can the Sub-altern speak?". In: Rosalind C. Morris ed., *Can the Subaltern Speak – Reflections on the history of an idea* (New York: Columbia University Press, 2010). Edward W. Said, *Orientalism* (New York: Vintage Books, [1978] 2003) and *Culture and Imperialism* (London, Vintage, 1994). Mbembe, *Kritiek van de zwarte rede*, 117, 118. Spivak explicitly includes the gender-issue in her analysis.

8   This is the scope of Gloria Wekker's *White innocence: Paradoxes of colonialism and race* (Durham and London: Duke University Press, 2016).

9   The concepts of legal obligations come from: Lubina, *Contested Cultural Property*; Prott, *Witnesses to History*; Patrick O'Keefe and Lyndell Prott, *Cultural Heritage Conventions and Other Instruments: A compendium with commentaries* (Pentre Moel, Crickadarn, Builth Wells, UK: Institute of Art and Law, 2011); Evelien Campfens, *Fair and just solutions? Alternatives to litigation in Nazi-looted art disputes: status quo and new developments* (The Hague: Eleven International Publishing, 2015); https://clg.portalxm.com/library/keytext.cfm?keytext_id=66 (December 18, 2015). Personal communication Katja Lubina, June 02, 2015.

10 This definition is based on what I learnt from courses on debate and dialogue that I followed and on my experience as a facilitator.

and showed their ancestors' '*survival mechanisms, which were similar to their own*', they became willing to help in protecting them.[78]

The term *colonial cultural object* is imprecise. In this book, it is used for reasons of convenience. What I mean with it is *an object of cultural or historical importance that was acquired without just compensation or was involuntarily lost during the European colonial era*. It is an umbrella term that is rather similar to that used e.g. in bilateral agreements between the former colonisers and their former colonies and

---

78   Sada Mire. "Locals and their heritage" (Leiden: Conference *The Heritage Heist*, Leiden University, May 18, 2015, unpubl.).

by UNESCO Director-general Amadou-Mahtar M'Bow.[79] That the objects were acquired without just compensation or were involuntarily lost refers to the unequal colonial situation and the violence in collecting. The expression *involuntarily lost* is used in disputes about Nazi-looted objects. In practice, colonial cultural treasures that are claimed are often *known objects*. They derive fame from their presence in Western collections and/or are missed in their community of origin. With unknown objects, there is less chance that they are claimed. Custom officers in the port of Rotterdam for instance, stored endless quantities of Chinese porcelain smuggled into the Netherlands, as the Chinese embassy in The Hague did not show any interest in these ancient mass-produced, *unknown* objects.[80]

In China known colonial cultural objects are often named '*lost cultural relics*'.[81] Admittedly, China and also Ethiopia were never fully colonised. In 1920, China was among the founding members of the League of Nations, while Ethiopia joined the organisation in 1923.[82] But both countries suffered extensive losses of material cultural heritage during European colonialism. In this study, therefore, objects such as those lost during the 1860 looting of the Summer Palace and the emptying of the Dunhuang caves in China around 1900, and those looted in 1868 from Ethiopian Emperor Tewodros' palace and churches are called colonial cultural objects.

Other concepts, such as provenance, violence, hard and soft law, which also deserve further explanation, are described in the Box: *Other frequently used concepts*.

2.3. Typology of colonial cultural objects

Museums and others develop typologies of objects and collections that are, understandably, adjusted to their needs. Going through these and other typologies uncovers the different startings for it. One is that of the *maker* or *first possessor*, but with respect to colonial cultural objects their names are rarely known, nor do we know much about motivation, skills and the context of creation. Another is that of the *acquirer* in the colonial period. To know whether this was a state or a non-state owner is relevant, as the return of a state-owned object requires government approval, while missionary orders, private collectors and traders can decide for themselves. The *non-material value* is a third starting, keeping in mind a broad definition of cultural heritage and a focus on inalienable objects '*which represent best their culture, ...are the most vital and whose absence causes them the greatest anguish*'.[83] There is the starting of *how* objects were acquired. Did the acquirers consult its makers, original owners or their descendants? Was the transfer voluntary or was pressure exerted and was it an involuntary loss? How (un)equal were the stakeholders? In this study the emphasis is on the *how*, the degree of *equality* among the stakeholders and the *colonial actor* who acquired the object.

---

79   Amadou-Mahtar M'Bow, "A plea for the return of irreplaceable culture heritage to those who created it", in *Unesco Courier* (Paris: UNESCO, July 1978), 4 – 5.
80   Jos Van Beurden, *Goden, Graven en Grenzen*, 47.
81   Liu, *Repatriating China's Cultural Objects*, 145.
82   http://www.indiana.edu/~league/nationalmember.htm (June 1, 2016).
83   M'Bow, "A plea for the return".

Three ways of acquisition are distinguished:

1. Acquisition by normal purchase or barter, at equal level;
2. Acquisition in accordance with colonial legislation, but at unequal level;
3. Acquisition in violation of this legislation and at unequal level.

Five categories of colonial cultural objects have surfaced:

1. Gifts to colonial administrators and institutions;
2. Objects acquired during private expeditions;
3. Objects acquired during military expeditions;
4. Missionary collecting;
5. Archives.

2.3.1. Gifts to colonial administrators and institutions

Why does someone give a present to another person? Gift-giving without any expected reciprocity is exceptional. Many are an instrument in cultural diplomacy. In the literature the exchange of gifts is described as part of a system of services in which obligation and liberty intermingle, and rivalry and reciprocity dominate.[84] A gift can consist of an alienable or an inalienable object. In many languages *'give'* and *'forgive'* are connected.[85] To give is linked to the present, to forgive to a past thing. One can reinforce a request for forgiving with a gift of a precious object.[86] Such gift-giving can be a hidden acknowledgement of a past injustice, and approach the concept of *restitution*.

Colonial gifts require special attention. There was frequent gift exchange between colonial administrators, local rulers and commanders. Certain gifts by rulers on Java and Bali to Dutch colonial administrators were an expression of subjugation.[87] Some rulers were even criticised for exaggerated generosity.[88] Others gave alienable objects or ordered their craftsmen to produce them for foreign visitors and rulers, while keeping the inalienable ones in hiding.[89] To ascertain the nature of a gift-giving requires provenance research.

---

84 Marcel Mauss, *The gift: the form and reason for exchange in archaic societies* (London: Routledge, [1950] 2000), 65.

85 Jacques Derrida, "To forgive: The unforgiveable and the imprescriptible", in eds. John D.Caputo, Mark Dooley and Michael Scanlon, *Questioning God* (Bloomington/Indianapolis: Indiana University Press, 2001), 22.

86 Prott, *Witnesses to History*, 417, 418.

87 Francine Brinkgreve, "Balinese Chiefs and Dutch Dominion: Building a Collection and Politics", in eds. Endang Sri Hardiati and Pieter Ter Keurs, *Indonesia: The discovery of the past* (Amsterdam: KIT Publishers, 2005), 122. Trigganga, Peni Mudji Sukati and Djunaidi Ismail, "Three centuries of collections", in eds. Retno S. Sitowati and John N. Miksic, *Icons of Art – National Museum of Jakarta* (Jakarta, National Museum, 2006), 82.

88 Susan Legêne, *De Bagage van Blomhoff en Van Breugel – Japan, Java, Tripoli en Suriname in de Negentiende eeuwse Nederlandse Cultuur van het Imperialisme* (Amsteram: KIT Publishers, 1998), 273.

89 Francine Brinkgreve and Itie Van Hout, "Gifts, Scholarship and Colonial Rule", in eds. Hardiati and Ter Keurs, *Indonesia: The discovery of the past*, 104.

2.3.2. Objects acquired during private expeditions

The 19th and early 20th centuries witnessed a peak in scientific and commercial collecting expeditions. They were initiated by governments with close contacts with scientists or by enterprises and collectors with contacts in the museum world, such as the German New Guinea Company, to name just one.[90] Collectors uncovered the economic potential, flora and fauna of colonial possessions and collected antiquities and ethnographic objects. With few exceptions, they left no notes about *how* they had acquired objects. Mention of whether they met with difficulties at customs upon leaving the country of origin or on entering the mother country is rare.[91]

Generally, scientists and also missionaries and charitable institutions met no restrictions in colonial possessions of other European countries. Art. 6 of the *General Act of the 1885 Berlin Conference on West Africa*[92] called upon the participating countries to '*protect and favour all religious, scientific or charitable institutions or undertakings*' aimed at '*instructing the natives and bringing home to them the blessings of civilisation*'.[93] As a result, objects were easily spread over public and private collections in Europe.

Some colonial administrators were active collectors and guarded a colony's cultural heritage. Charles Stuart (ca. 1758 – 1828) opposed missionary efforts to convert Hindus to Christianity and acquired one hundred statues, each representing a Hindu deity. After his death they were shipped from Kolkata to London, sold and resold, finally ending up in the British Museum.[94] Lieutenant-Governor William MacGregor (1846 – 1919) purchased objects or exchanged these for such things as iron utensils in British New Guinea between 1888 and 1897. Hubert Murray (1861 – 1940), active in different functions in the same colony, did this between 1904 and 1940.[95]

Colonial soldiers, officials and others, or their descendants, donated their antiquities and ethnographic objects to metropolitan cultural institutions. By not testing how they had been acquired, these institutions released themselves

---

90 Rainer Buschmann, "Exploring tensions in material culture: Commercialising ethnography in German New Guinea, 1870 – 1904", in eds. Michael O'Hanlon and Robert L. Welch, *Hunting the gatherers – Ethnographic collectors, agents and agency in Melanesia, 1870s -1930s* (New York/Oxford: Berghahn, 2000), 61.

91 Hanneke Hollander, *Een man met een speurneus – Carel Groeneveldt (1899 – 1973), beroepsverzamelaar voor Tropenmuseum en Wereldmuseum in Nieuw Guinea* (Amsterdam: KIT Publishers, Bulletin 379 Tropenmuseum, 2007), 63.

92 The 1884 -1885 Berlin Conference is also known as Berlin Congo Conference or the Berlin Conference on West Africa. For reasons of convenience, the term Berlin Conference is used in this book. Thomas Pakenham, *The scramble for Africa – The white man's conquest of the dark continent from 1876 to 1912* (New York: Random House, 1991), 239ff.

93 http://africanhistory.about.com/od/eracolonialism/l/bl-BerlinAct1885.htm (January 14, 2015). Participating countries: Great Britain, Austria-Hungary, Belgium, Denmark, France, Germany, Italy, the Netherlands, Portugal, Russia, Spain, Sweden and Norway, Turkey and the United States of America.

94 Bernard S. Cohn, *Colonialism and its forms of knowledge – The British in India* (Princeton: Princeton University Press, 1996), 101. Neil MacGregor, *A history of the world in 100 objects* (London: Penguin, [1996] 2012), 376, 377.

95 Michael Quinnell, "'Before it is too late' – The making and repatriation of Sir William MacGregor's official collection from British New Guinea", in eds. O'Hanlon and Welch, *Hunting the gatherers*, 83.

implicitly from the duty to do provenance research and discover unpleasant truths.[96] The statement in the 1979 magazine Museum of UNESCO that all objects from Congo in the Tervuren Museum were '*procured through the regular channels*' and that none were obtained '*through extortion, spoliation or theft*' is proof of this attitude, and is nowadays untenable (9.1.).[97] When the Tervuren Museum opened in 1898, 3.008 objects – almost forty percent of the total collection – were war trophies from Congo. The Museum named acquisitions from King Leopold II's period as '*gifts*' from the Congo Free State to the Belgian state, thus exempting itself from the need to conduct research into the often-violent collecting. People in the colonies viewed expeditions differently, varying from inimical invasions[98] to profitable opportunities.

Many fruits of expeditions resulted from normal trade with local craftsmen and dealers who produced some artefacts solely for foreign visitors.[99] In expedition reports about Papua from around 1850 one reads about '*the enthusiasm of Kamoro traders*' in their contact with outsiders.[100] Museum professionals point to the poor condition of ancient monuments from which objects have come and to the disinterest of the local population. Older Hindu and Buddhist stone statues in the Rijksmuseum in Amsterdam were not deliberately removed but taken from abandoned monuments in the Indonesian archipelago, so we are assured.[101] The same institution does suffer, however, from incidental blindness.[102]

---

96   Boris Wastiau, *Exit Congo Museum* (Tervuren: Royal Museum for Central Africa, 2000). Sarah Van Beurden, *Authentically African: African arts and postcolonial cultural politics in transnational perspective (Congo [DRC], Belgium and the USA, 1955 – 1980)* (Pennsylvania: University of Pennsylvania, Ph.D., 2009). Caroline Drieënhuizen, *Koloniale collecties, Nederlands aanzien: De Europese elite van Nederlands Indië belicht door haar verzamelingen, 1811 – 1957* (Amsterdam: University of Amsterdam, Ph.D., 2012).

97   Huguette Van Geluwe, "Belgium's contribution to the Zairian cultural heritage", in *Museum* (Paris: UNESCO, 1979), XXXI/1, 32 – 37.

98   Michel Leiris, *L'Afrique fantôme* (Paris : Gallimard, Paris, [1934] 1981), 450. Anna G. Marangou, *Life & Deeds – The Consul Luigi Palma di Cesnola 1832 – 1904* (Nicosia: Cultural Centre, Popular Bank Group, 2000), 12. Laura Van Broekhoven (ed.), *Kuifje naar de Inca's – Strijdbaar heden, roemrijk verleden* (Leiden: Museum Volkenkunde, 2003), 36.

99   Chris Gosden, "On his Todd: Material culture and colonialism", in eds. O'Hanlon and Welsch, *Hunting the Gatherers*, 228. Joost Willink, *De bewogen verzamelgeschiedenis van de West-Centraal-Afrikaanse collecties inNederland (1856 – 1889)* (Leiden: Leiden University, Ph.D., 2006). Ed. Pieter Ter Keurs, *Colonial Collections Revisited* (Leiden: CNWS Publications, 2007).

100 Karen Jacobs, *Collecting Kamoro-objects, encounters and representation on the southwest coast of Papua* (Leiden: Sidestone Press, Mededelingen van Rijksmuseum voor Volkenkunde 40, 2011), 41, 214.

101 William Southworth, "The Disembodied Human Head in Southeast Asian Art", in *Aziatische Kunst* (Amsterdam: Rijksmuseum, 2013, 43/2/June), 27.

102 The Rijksmuseum never reacted to information that its late 11th or early 12th century Hindu stone statue of a Durga killing a Buffalo demon, was most probably smuggled out of Bangladesh via the diplomatic bag, as mentioned in a 1980 ICOM report (Jos Van Beurden, *Return of Cultural and Historical Treasures*, 67; https://www.rijksmuseum.nl/nl/zoeken/objecten?q=durga+&p=1&ps=12&ii=3#/AK-RAK-1992-1,3 (January 18, 2016); visit to Rijksmuseum January 13, 2016.

2.3.3. Objects acquired during military expeditions

Reference books about French and Dutch trade companies in the East and West Indies focus on military confrontations, the weapons that were used, the indigenisation of the colonial army and the acquisition of exotic products.[103] They deal only marginally with the impact of the loss of war booty on the local population.[104] From details in these reference books and from monographs that give more prominence to plunder and provenance, one learns that colonial generals and soldiers obtained numerous cultural and historical objects in wars and raids.[105] Their confiscation was ordered by higher-ups or occurred at their own initiative.[106] Commanders offered a bonus to soldiers who had captured a flag or standard.[107] In 1765 VOC soldiers looted, against an explicit ban by their commanders, the palace, main temple and city of Kandy in Sri Lanka. A silver and gold holder of a tooth of the Buddha was returned on the spot.[108] By formally capitulating, defeated rulers could limit the plunder, or they hid precious objects. A *punitive expedition* was a justifiable method for colonisers to crush resistance. For victims it was *looting, arson, humiliation or destruction* by a foreign power.[109]

Military confrontations were countless in colonial empires. British victories were '*brought home in the form of its relics and trophies*' to be displayed in the museum of the East India Company or in the Tower of London.[110] As a present for his birthday in 1902, 190 flags and weapons confiscated from the Boxers in China were shown to German Emperor Wilhelm II. In 1955 the East German government returned the ten flags, which had not perished in the World War II violence, to China (2.1.: Box: *Incidental returns of colonial cultural objects*). Only a few of such unique, inalienable objects ended their long and complicated journeys at their place of origin. An institution as the British Museum justifies

---

103 Ed. René Estienne, *Les Compagnies des Indes* (Paris: Gallimard / Ministère de la Défense – DMPA, 2013), 228, 234. Eds. Gerrit Knaap, Henk Den Heijer and Michiel De Jong, *Oorlogen overzee – Militair optreden door Compagnie en Staat buiten Europa 1595 – 1814* (Amsterdam: Boom, 2015), 236 – 239, 194 – 195.

104 E.g. Knaap e.a. *Oorlogen overzee*, 162. Lequin describes the income through smuggling but not through plunder, Frank Lequin, *Het personeel van de Verenigde Oost-Indische Compagnie in Azië in de 18de eeuw, meer in het bijzonder in de vestiging Bengalen* (Alphen aan den Rijn: Canaletto, [1982] 2005), 97 ff.

105 Cohn, *Colonialism and its forms of knowledge*, 1996. Nira Wickramasinghe, "The return of Keppetipola's cranium: The construction of authenticity in Sri Lankan nationalism", in eds. Gyanendra Pandey and Peter Geschiere, *The forging of nationhood* (New Dehli: Manohar, 2003), 129 – 155. Harm Stevens, "The resonance of violence in collections", in eds. Susan Legêne and Janneke Van Dijk, *The Netherlands East Indies and the Tropenmuseum* (Amsterdam: KIT Publishers, 2011), 28 – 37. Harm Stevens, *Bitter spice*, 37, 85.

106 Michael Carrington, "Officers, gentlemen and thieves: The looting of monasteries during the 1903/4 Younghusband Mission to Tibet", in *Modern Asian Studies* (Cambridge: Cambridge University Press, 2003), 37/1, 81 – 109. Adepeju Layiwola, "The Benin Massacre: Memories and experiences" in ed. Plankensteiner, *Benin Kings and Rituals*, 83 – 90. Knaap ea., *Oorlogen over Zee*.

107 Mariska Pool, *Vergeten vlaggen: De trofeeën van het eskader - Van Braam in de Indische archipel, 1784*, http://collectie.legermuseum.nl/sites/strategion/contents/i004530/arma36%20vergeten%20vlaggen.pdf (January 14, 2016).

108 Raven – Hart, R. *The Dutch Wars in Kandy* (Colombo: Government Publications Bureau, 1964), http://www.defonseka.com/ref_dutch_wars02.htm (January 7, 2016).

109 Layiwola, *The Benin Massacre*. Liu, *Repatriating China's Cultural Objects*.

110 Cohn, *Colonialism and its forms of knowledge*, 104.

its continuing refusal to return objects from Benin City, Egypt or Ethiopia with the argument that it stimulates *a worldwide interest in the archaeology, history and culture... which has continued to this day*.[111] It is not the only one that thus justifies some of its possessions.

2.3.4. Missionary collecting

There is ample evidence that missionaries intentionally and massively confiscated and destroyed traditional religious objects and that countless objects were sent to Europe. According to Wole Soyinka, Europeans denied and had no respect for Africa's *own spirituality... The Euro-Christian armies... burnt and smashed priceless carvings, which, from their point of view, were nothing but manifestations of idolatry and satanism*. Soyinka blames Islam for the same: *the cultural and spiritual savaging of the continent... was not by the Christian-European axis alone. The Arab-Islamic dimension preceded it, and was every bit as devastating*.[112] Such disrespect was also observed in South America, while it was less prevalent in colonised Hindu and Buddhist communities in Asia.

John Williams, a talented early-19th century member of the London Missionary Society in the South Sea Islands, described the *how* of collecting. He urged village chiefs to accept Christianity and to win over their fellow villagers. Williams claimed that these chiefs never *employed coercion to induce their subjects to embrace it*. Not infrequently they had to *defend themselves against the fury of... their own subjects, by whom they were so fiercely attacked*. Women could inflict *gashes on their heads* and cry *in tones of the deepest melancholy to oppose their chiefs' transition to the new religion*. When villagers blamed the traditional gods for a relative's death, Williams gave *fish-hooks... pigs and goats... or showed iron... and proved that two pieces could be welded together*. Williams was said not to speak *for* the natives but to allow *them to speak for themselves*. Those who were allowed to speak, however, were converts, who could be more fanatic than he himself in burning the old gods. He saved religious objects for himself, his family and friends and for institutions such as the London Missionary Society.[113]

From the start of colonialism, tens of thousands of European missionaries travelled to the colonies. Their contact with colonial administrators differed. In Ceuta, which the Portuguese captured in 1415,[114] or in King Leopold II's Congo Free State, which he acquired in the second half of the 19th century, the contact

---

111 http://www.britishmuseum.org/explore/highlights/article_index/m/the_maqdala_collection.aspx (February 3, 2015).

112 Soyinka, *Burden of memory*, 42 – 52. In *Contours of the world economy, 1 – 2030* (Oxford: Oxford University Press, 2007), 188, Angus Maddison charts the impact of the Islamic expansion on Africa between 650 and 1400 and of that of Portugal and other European colonial powers from 1500 until far in the 20th century, thus supporting Soyinka's position. So does Achille Mbembe, *Kritiek van de Zwarte Rede*, 141.

113 John Williams, *A Narrative of missionary enterprises in the South Sea Islands* (London: Snow, 1838), 192; 179; 65, 70, 149; 108, 177; 63. Carol E. Mayer, "A green dress, Vanuaatu", in eds. Karen Jacobs, Chantal Knowles and Chris Wingfield, *Trophies, relics and curios? Missionary heritage from Africa and the Pacific* (Leiden: Sidestone Press, 2015), 132.

114 Luís Miguel Duarte, ""Grey hairs to the fore!" The Portuguese Conquest of Ceuta in 1415", in ed. Amândio Barros, *Os Descombrimentos e as Origens da Convergência Global/The Discoveries and the Origins of Global Convergence* (Porto: Câmara Municipal do Porto, 2015), 106.

was very close.[115] In Namibia and other German colonial possessions it varied *'from outright anti-imperialism and criticism of colonial rule to complicity and cooperation'*. Their *'abstinence from violence, their theological anthropology, ... often mediating role in conflicts, and ... organisational autonomy set them apart from political empire'*.[116] Many translated the bible and preached in local languages.[117] They passed their knowledge of vernacular languages to the colonial administration.[118] From around 1900, some missionaries in West Africa questioned forced conversions and confiscation of ritual objects.[119] In China missionaries met with tough resistance from rulers and the population and although there is evidence of destruction and confiscation of religious objects, it happened less than in other regions.[120]

Many missionaries justified their iconoclasm with the *salvage paradigm*, their intention to save people from paganism, bring civilisation, save the material symbols of customs and religion and replace them with their own.[121] It is difficult to assess to what extent converts renounced traditional religious objects and altars voluntarily. Seduction tactics were applied, but there was also a desire for modernisation. Conversion to Christianity could be an expression of *'autonomous local developments with missionaries as ... bystanders'*.[122] Many converts were *'far from naïve and passive recipients of the gospel'*, while many missionaries had *'naïvely entered a world of immense political complexity, becoming pawns as much as players'*.[123]

---

115 Jan Derix, *Brengers van de Boodschap – Geschiedenis van de katholieke missionering vanuit Nederland van VOC tot Vaticanum II* (Nijmegen: Valkhof Pers, 2009), 555.

116 Bernhard Gissibl, "Imagination and beyond: cultures and geographies of imperialism in Germany, 1848 – 1918", in ed. John M. MacKenzie, *European empires and the people – Popular responses to imperialism in France, Britain, The Netherlands, Belgium, Germany and Italy* (Manchester: Manchester University Press, 2011), 174, 173.

117 Eugène Casalis, *My life in Basutoland – A story of missionary enterprise in South Africa* (London: The Religious Tract Society, 1889), 292.

118 Boris Wastiau, *Exit Congo Museum* (Tervuren: Royal Museum for Central Africa, 2000), 21.

119 Harry Leyten, *From idol to art – African 'objects-with-power': A challenge for missionaries, anthropologists and museum curators* (Leiden: African Studies Centre, 2015), 90, 285.

120 Jung Chang, *Keizerin – Het verhaal van de vrouw die bijna vijftig jaar over China heerste* (Amsterdam: Boekerij, 2014). The Royal Ontario Museum houses thousands of oracle bones, bronzes, pottery and jade of Canadian missionary James Mellon Menzies acquired between 1913 and 1936: Liu, *Repatriating China's Cultural Objects*, 40 – 42. Also: https://www.rom.on.ca/en/collections-research/research/world-culture/james-menzies-chinese-research-fellowship (March 20, 2016). The extensive collection of American missionary John Calvin Ferguson, who worked from 1877 onwards in China, was divided over the University of Oregon, Nanjing University and the Shanghai Jiao Tong University, https://library.uoregon.edu/speccoll/photo/warner/40years.html (March 20, 2016) .

121 Clark P., http://www.panya.ca/publication_salvage_paradigm_introduction.php (August 20, 2014); http://www.reichertz.ca/uploads/6/0/2/5/6025669/beyond_salvage.pdf (August 20, 2014). Iconoclasm occurred *'also on the part of Africans themselves'*, e.g. around 1500 in the Kingdom of Congo (Leyten, *From Idol to Art*, 156).

122 Corbey and Weener, "Collecting while converting", 13.

123 Andrew Mills, "Female statuette, Tonga", in ed. Jacobs ea., *Trophies, Relics and Curios?*, 37.

Archives back to Suriname

In 1913, the administration in Paramaribo and the government in The Hague agreed to ship archives from the colony to safer places in the Netherlands. The colony had a lack of storage facilities. Its humid climate damaged paper materials. It was stipulated that the archives would remain *'property of the colony Suriname'*. When in 2010, thirty-five years after its independence, Suriname opened its own archival buildings with trained personnel, the Dutch Keeper of Public Records handed over the first hundred running metres of baptism, marriage and funeral records, notarial archives and the 1921 population census.[1] The repatriation of altogether eight hundred metres archive was completed early in 2017.[2]

Notes

1   Interview Frans Van Dijk, National Archive of the Netherlands, January 25, 2011. Jos Van Beurden, *Return of Cultural and Historical Treasures*, 36.

2   http://www.gahetna.nl/actueel/nieuws/2017/ historisch-geheugen-suriname-gaat-terug-naar- eigen-bodem (January 24, 2017).

The missionary orders put confiscated objects up in display cases at home for the instruction of new missionaries or for fundraising. Missionary museums were set up,[124] exhibitions were organised.[125] Since the 1960s the increasing secularisation, the diminishing number of religious vocations and the competition with secular organisations in developing countries have forced some missionary museums to close their doors. They sent back their collections to the headquarters of their orders in Europe, offered them to other museums, while some were sold to dealers or ended in the dustbin. Only in incidental cases did they send them back to the places of origin.[126]

2.3.5. Archives

Archives have a factual and sometimes symbolic meaning and can also have an aesthetic value. They are decisive in *'how the future will remember the past'*. Possession of archives and power are connected, as there *'is no political power without control of the archives'*.[127] Their power was a driving factor behind the first European ban on looting cultural property in times of war in the Treaty of Westphalia of 1648.[128] During decolonisation, the control of archives became important. Colonial powers wanted to keep archives with economic information

---

124 In *Missionaire collecties in beeld: Een onderzoek naar de omvang en herkomst van verspreide volkenkundige collecties van missionaire oorsprong* (Maarssen, 1992) A.M.C. Van Pesch and H.W. Campbell researched the collections of 29 Roman-catholic missionary museums.

125 In *Missionary exhibitions in the Netherlands* (unpubl., 2010) Frans-Karel Weener counted one hundred exhibitions between 1920 and 1939, and seventy-seven between 1945 and 1955.

126 Jos Van Beurden, *Return of Cultural and Historical Treasures*, 37.

127 Michael Joseph Karabinos, "Displaced archives, displaced history: Recovering the seized archives of Indonesia", in *Bijdragen tot de Taal-, Land- en Volkenkunde* (Leiden: Brill, 2013), 169.

128 Lubina, *Contested Cultural Property*, 51.

or destroy those with incriminating information.[129] Archives are less surrounded with emotions than objects. They were part of the 1975 agreement between the Netherlands and Indonesia, but not of agreements between Belgium and Portugal and their former colonies, as I found.[130] The return of archives by the Netherlands to Suriname between 2010 and 2017 was based on an old agreement (Box: *Archives back to Suriname*).

In conclusion, those who lost colonial cultural objects and those who acquired them, look differently at their continued presence outside the countries of origin. The act of returning such objects has many names and behind each are a reason and an interest. In this study the term return is preferred because of its open, neutral meaning and multi-layered character, which makes it acceptable for many and is more nuanced than other terms such as restitution, repatriation or reparation. Based mostly on *how* they were acquired, five types of colonial cultural objects have been distinguished. Some were acquired under relatively equal circumstances; in the acquisition of many others inequality and the violence triangle of direct, structural and ideological violence played a major role. The confiscation of objects by missionaries has been interpreted as iconoclasm. I argue that, in some instances, the distinction between identity and history in relation to cultural objects can unburden the discussion about their future.

---

129 *The Independent*, November 29, 2013, http://www.independent.co.uk/news/uk/home-news/revealed-how-british-empires-dirty-secrets-went-up-in-smoke-in-the-colonies-8971217.html (December 2, 2013).
130 Belgium – Congo: email exchange with Belgium's General Record Office, July 1, 2014, and the archivist of Belgium's Foreign Ministry, August 27, 2014; Portugal – colonies: email exchange with CIDAC, Lisbon (Centro De Intervenção Para O Desenvolvimento Amílcar Cabral), July 17, 2014.

COLONIALISM AND CULTURAL OBJECTS

Part II - Colonialism and cultural objects

Part II focuses on the massive one-way traffic of cultural and historical objects from colonised societies to Europe. It criss-crosses continents and shows a wide variety of acquisitions. The starting point is the five types of acquisition of colonial cultural objects identified in Part I. They are applied within a periodisation of colonialism that distinguishes between the early colonial trade and territorial expansion, settler and exploitation colonialism and finally, decolonisation. These are three overlapping periods and types of colonialism. Decolonisation, which began years or decades before the actual transfer of sovereignty, is still an unresolved conflict in many cases. Disputes over colonial cultural objects are an expression of this conflict. Part II closes with a discussion on whether conflict studies offer a methodology to bring such unresolved issues to an end.

Photograph previous page: Benin object, National Museum of World Cultures, the Netherlands.

Chapter 3

Colonial expansion

Historical events are often interpreted differently, as the following two battles show. The victory of Ethiopia over Italy near Adowa, in 1896, was the *'symbol of a new era'* in world-history[131] and the *'beginning of the decline of Europe as the centre of world politics'*. Met with disbelief in Europe, in Africa it became *'a meaningful prelude and stimulus to a budding'* anti-colonial struggle.[132] In 1905, Japan's defeat of Russia in the Battle of Tsushima inspired M.K. Gandhi, Sun Yat-sen, Mustafa Kemal and African-American leader W.E.B. Du Bois. The defeat of a white empire by a non-white power *'accelerated an irreversible process of intellectual, if not political, decolonisation'*,[133] whereas at the same time, it led to demonstrations against Tokyo's imperial aspirations in Korea, which Japan had colonised, and in China, which Japan had forcibly opened up and where it had helped Western powers to crush the 1900 anti-foreign Boxer Rebellion.[134] According to Italian historian R.H. Rainero, the Battle of Adowa had more impact than the Battle of Tsushima.[135] Ethiopian historian Abraham does not mention the Battle of Tsushima. With his focus on Asia, Indian scholar Mishra's omits the Battle of Adowa. Burbank and Cooper pay considerably more attention to the Japanese than the Ethiopian achievement.[136]

Diverging views on historical events also exist in relation to the periodisation of European colonialism. Although an obvious one is followed in this book – that of colonial trade and territorial expansion, settler and exploitation colonialism and decolonisation -, problems emerge in its elaboration. The *'almost unstoppable.... Europeanisation of the globe'*[137] started in different places at different moments and, even then, it was a *'creeping colonisation'*.[138] Europe had many types of colonialism. Small or newly-formed European nations such as, initially, Portugal, the Netherlands and Denmark, and, later, Belgium, Germany and Italy needed colonies to strengthen their unity and identity and to strengthen their economies.

---

131 R. H. Rainero, "The Battle of Adowa on 1st March 1896: A Reappraisal", in eds. Jaap De Moor and Henk Wesseling, *Imperialism and War: Essays on Colonial Wars in Asia and Africa* (Leiden: E.J. Brill, 1989), 189.

132 Kinfe Abraham, *Adowa – Decolonisation, Pan-Africanism and the Struggle of the Black Diaspora* (Addis Ababa: Ethiopian International Institute for Peace and Development, 2012), 93, 48, 49.

133 Pankaj Mishra, *From the Ruins of Empire – The Revolt against the West and the Remaking of Asia* (London: Allan Lane, 2012), 7.

134 Burbank and Cooper, *Empires in World History*, 302. Chang, *Keizerin*, 452, 453.

135 Rainero, *Battle of Adowa*, 189.

136 Burbank and Cooper, *ibid.*, 302, 315.

137 MacKenzie, *European Empires and the People*, 1, 2.

138 Burbank and Cooper, *ibid.*, 241.

There are remarkable differences between the expansion by European powers and other powers in the world. One had to do with distance. While the Chinese, Roman, Aztec, Ottoman and Russian empires mostly conquered bordering states and peoples, '*the Ottomans' lock on the eastern Mediterranean*' and '*the Muslim-controlled gold trade across the Sahara*' forced European colonisers to practice long-distance expansion.[139] Moreover, European powers distinguished themselves from other powers in their typical '*propagation of Christian missions*', which aggravated the ideological violence against unknown peoples.[140] Also typical for Europe's colonialism was that each period had independent minds criticising it, some of whom are mentioned throughout the book.[141]

In common with the other empires were the wide-spread slave trade and the colonial taxes on land and its products, which easily resulted in bonded labour.[142] Next to the Trans-Atlantic slave trade for sugar plantations in the Americas,[143] large-scale slave trade existed in Asia.[144] In areas such as British India and West Africa, European traders built on pre-colonial slave trade and bonded labour systems. In most places slaves and servants made the traders' efforts pay.[145]

Early sources indicate that the European colonial powers applied a combination of direct, structural and ideological violence from the start.[146] In its efforts to gain colonial ground in Asia, Portugal remained moderate in the application of violence, as it respected the highly developed '*commercial dialogue*' there.[147] Other European powers had fewer scruples. In the early 16th century, only one out of ten Mexicans survived slaughter and extermination of the Aztec empire at the hand of the Spanish conquistadores.[148] VOC commanders were notorious too.[149] The founder of the Dutch empire in Asia, Governor General Jan Pieterszoon Coen (1587 – 1629), created a bloodbath on the Banda Islands, in which fourteen thousand of the fifteen thousand

139 Ibid., 149, 154.

140 MacKenzie, *European Empires and the People*, 7.

141 Ewald Vanvugt, *Roofgoed: Het Europese museum van overzeese gestolen schatten – met de monumenten voor de dieven* (Soesterberg: Aspekt, 2010), 13.

142 Henri Charles Carey, *The Slave Trade, Domestic and Foreign: Why It Exists, and How It May Be Extinguished* (Philadelphia: A. Hart, late Carey and Hart, 1853).

143 Anton De Kom, *Wij Slaven van Suriname* (Amsterdam/Antwerpen: Contact, [1934] 2009).

144 Burbank and Cooper, *Empires in World History*, 160, 290. Reggie Baay, *Daar werd wat gruwelijks verricht – Slavernij in Nederlands-Indië*, (Amsterdam: Athenaeum – Polak & Van Gennep, 2015). Matthias Van Rossum, *Kleurrijke tragiek – De geschiedenis van de slavernij in Azië onder de VOC* (Hilversum: Verloren, 2015).

145 Burbank and Cooper, *ibid.*, 178 ff.

146 Barthelomé de las Casas, *Brevisima relacion de la destruccion de las Indias* (Sevilla, 1522), http://www.verbodengeschriften.nl/html/zeerbeknoptrelaasvandeverwoesting.html (November 19, 2015).

147 Barros, *Discoveries and the Origins of Global Convergence*, 206.

148 Maria Longhena, *Het oude Mexico: De geschiedenis en de cultuur van de Maya's, Azteken en andere pre-Columbiaanse volkeren* (Lisse: Zuid Boekproducties, 1998), 79.

149 Henk Schulte Nordholt, "A genealogy of violence". In: eds. Frank Colombijn and Thomas Lindblad, *Roots of Violence in Indonesia: Contemporary violence in historical perspective* (Leiden: KITLV Press, KITLV Verhandelingen, 2002), 36, 37.

Bandanese were killed, driven away or sold.[150] King Leopold's assistants *'frivolously'* applied direct violence in Congo.[151] The *'deliberate forgetting'* of the *'holocaust in Central Africa'*, resulting from Leopold's run on rubber, combined ideological violence with extreme direct and structural violence.[152]

The ideological violence towards indigenous peoples in Latin America and Africa was more serious than that in parts of Asia. Columbus reported *'one-eyed men, and others, with the snout of dogs, who ate men'*, although he had never seen one.[153] Dutch slave owners in Suriname disdained their *'cursed blacks, covered with rags'* intensely.[154] Mbembe pinpoints to *'the forced break with the self'* ...*'expropriation'* and *'humiliation'*, resulting from European colonialism, that continue to affect Africans and other colonised peoples up to today.[155]

3.1. Early migration of objects to Europe

In this period, the newcomers were scarcely interested in the cultures and religions that they encountered, although the objects that represented these cultures and religions could make their heads spin. When the Portuguese had captured Ceuta in 1415, one of the first things they did was change mosques into churches.[156] While the conquistadores were impressed by the temple buildings of the Aztec, Maya, Inca and other cultures, they despised the indigenous religions attached to them. They burned mummies, destroyed ritual objects and ancient codices, or melted down the silver and gold.[157] They took stone statues and objects made of precious metals to Europe and built administrative complexes and churches on top of destroyed temple complexes.[158] In Asia, Europeans were mainly interested in botany for medicinal reasons, in coffee, indigo, cane sugar and other cash crops for economic reasons, and in maps and atlases for their military operations. Yet the conclusion that material culture remained *'a stepchild'*[159] is only partially valid.

---

150 http://voc-kenniscentrum.nl/vocbegin.html (01 November 2013). In 1893 a statue of Coen was erected in the Dutch city of Hoorn, later also one in Jakarta. After the arrival of the Japanese in the Dutch East Indies in 1942, that in Jakarta was removed. A Dutch citizens' initiative asked in 2011 for the removal of that in Hoorn. After a public debate the statue remained but with an adjusted text panel. Also: Ewald Vanvugt, *Nestbevuilers. 400 jaar Nederlandse critici van het koloniale bewind in de Oost en de West* (Breda: De Geus, 1996). Joop De Jong, *De Waaier van het Fortuin – De Nederlanders in Azië en de Indonesische Archipel 1595 – 1950* (Den Haag: Sdu, 2000), 51, 52. Stevens, *Bitter Spice*, 23.

151 David Van Reybrouck, *Congo – Een Geschiedenis* (Amsterdam: De Bezige Bij, 2010), 105.

152 Adam Hochschild, *De geest van Koning Leopold II en de plundering van de Congo* (Amsterdam: Meulenhoff, 2000), 295, 226.

153 Miles Harvey, *The island of lost maps – A true story of cartographic crime* (Portland: Broadway books, 2001) 19.

154 De Kom, *Wij Slaven*, 49.

155 Mbembe, *Kritiek van de Zwarte Rede*, 117, 118.

156 Luís Miguel Duarte, ""Grey hairs to the fore!", 106.

157 Maria Longhena and Walter Alva, *De Inca's: Geschiedenis en cultuur van de beschavingen in de Andes* (Lisse: Zuid Boekproducties, 1999), 164 ff.

158 Ed. Laura Van Broekhoven, *Kuifje naar de Inca's – Strijdbaar heden, roemrijk verleden* (Leiden: Rijksmuseum voor Volkenkunde, 2003), 36. Esther Pasztory, *Pre-Columbian art* (London: Weidenfeld and Nicholson, 1998), 7, 8.

159 Hans Groot, *Van Batavia naar Weltevreden: Het Bataviaasch Genootschap van Kunsten en Wetenschappen, 1778 – 1867* (Leiden, KITLV, 2009), 26, 28.

Wherever Europe's trade flow came, curiosities were collected, first as 'souvenirs of contact' or as a 'trophy'.[160] Trophies were a 'tangible means of showing penetration, conquest and domination'.[161] In Europe they found eager customers – the names of many are still known – and received a 'prominent place' in curiosities cabinets.[162] For the sake of completeness: indigenous elites along the coasts of Africa were also collectors; they opted for objects from Europe, but these were alienable objects.[163]

Gifts to colonial administrators and institutions

The literature has several references to gifts in this period. Since Emperor Montezuma II saw Hernán Cortés and the conquistadores as divine beings at first, he welcomed them with gifts in accordance with Aztec customs.[164] In 1542, Bhuvanoka Bahu VII, the monarch of the Sinhala in Sri Lanka, donated two exquisitely carved, gem-studded ivory caskets to Don Juan III, King of Portugal; they are now in Munich.[165] In 1595, some Islamic princes in the Indonesian archipelago offered a kris and a lance to Dutch commanders in exchange for letters and presents from the Dutch Prince Maurits.[166] Whereas gift-giving had some semblance of equality initially, gift-giving by indigenous rulers to the European visitors soon became signifiers of subjugation.

Objects acquired during private expeditions

Objects were confiscated from South and Central America; they are now in museums in Europe and the USA.[167] Their biographies uncover little about their makers. The Spanish Crown issued a regulation stipulating that the graves of kings and nobles were equal to geological gold veins, because of their gold and silver treasures.[168] In Africa and Asia, objects were purchased, exchanged or taken away.[169] British Royal Navy captain James Cook (1728 – 1779) was among the first

---

160 Jacobs, *Collecting Kamoro Objects*, 21.

161 Eds. Enid Schildkrout and Curtis A. Keim, *The scramble for art in Central Africa* (Cambridge: Cambridge University Press, 1998), 21.

162 Roelof Van Gelder, "De wereld binnen handbereik: Nederlandse kunst- en rariteitenverzamelingen, 1858 – 1735", in eds. Ellinoor Bergvelt and Renée Kistemaker, *De Wereld binnen Handbereik* (Amsterdam: Amsterdams Historisch Museum, 1992), 30. Bergvelt and Kistemaker mention Dutch collectors from between the late 16th and late 18th centuries. Also: 8.1., Box: *Evidence of migration of objects in the first period*.

163 Hilario Casado Alonso, "The Geographical Discoveries: New economic Opportunities in a Globalising World", in ed. Barros, *Discoveries and the Origins of Global Convergence*, 196.

164 Longhena, *Het oude Mexico*, 79.

165 P.H.D.H. De Silva, "Sri Lanka", in *Museum* (Paris: UNESCO, 1979), Quarterly review, XXXI/1, 22.

166 Rita Wassing – Visser, *Koninklijke Geschenken uit Indonesië: Historische banden met het Huis Oranje-Nassau (1600 – 1938)* (Zwolle: Waanders, 1995), 164.

167 Random examples are 120.000 objects in the Ethnological Museum of Berlin; most have no or a poor provenance, http://www.smb.museum/en/museums-and-institutions/ethnologisches-museum/about-the-collection.html (December 17, 2015) and the abundance of Mexican treasures in the British Museum, http://www.britishmuseum.org/visiting/galleries/americas/room_27_mexico.aspx (December 17, 2015).

168 Broekhoven, *Kuifje naar de Inca's*, 37.

169 Boris Wastiau, *Legacy of Collecting*. Jacobs, *Collecting Kamoro Objects*, 2011.

who collected objects in the Pacific and North America; some are in the British Museum and in Berlin's Ethnological Museum.[170]

Curiosities that came to Europe are visible on 17th and 18th century paintings, crockery and decorative bowls.[171] Personnel of trade companies bothered little about the people with whom they mingled. They were *'adventurers'* looking for *'accumulation of fortune'*.[172] They felt disdain for ethnographic objects. In some German colonial realms in the Pacific, objects were initially considered *'firewood'*.[173] Most information about the *how* of these acquisitions has been lost.

Objects acquired during military expeditions

European trade companies fought wars to expand and consolidate their colonial power. The VOC did so in the Dutch East Indies, South Asia, the Persian Gulf, the Sea of Arabia, Southern Africa and the western Archipelago.[174] Commanders and soldiers of the companies and conquistadores acquired large-scale war booty, which ended up in museums in the metropolis and in the colony's capital, or disappeared into private collections. Some examples are given in the Box: *War booty during colonial expansion and its present whereabouts.*

Missionary collecting

In response to the 1453 fall of Constantinople/conquest of Istanbul and the increasing Islamisation of Northern Africa, the pope ordered Portuguese explorers to Christianise areas on the African coasts and to consider them *'as their lawful possession'* .[175] Ships of trade companies had *missionaries* on board for the welfare of the crew and the establishment of mission posts. In the early period, destruction of indigenous cultural heritage must have outweighed confiscation by far. In 1531, the first bishop of Mexico reported the destruction of five hundred temples, twenty thousand images and the hieroglyphs of the Aztec library of Texcoco.[176] A few decades later the Spanish missionary Diego de Landa burnt tens of Maya codices and thousands of Maya religious objects, admitting that this was a tragic event for the Maya. De Landa was famous for his knowledge of the Maya culture and language.[177]

Archives

Little evidence was found of the collecting of archives in this early period.

---

170 Raymond Corbey, *Tribal Art Traffic: A Chronicle of Taste, Trade and Desire in Colonial and Post-Colonial Times* (Amsterdam: KIT Publishers, 2000). Jacobs *Collecting Kamoro Objects.* Neil MacGregor, *A history of the world in 100 objects.*

171 E.g. the 2015 *Asia > Amsterdam exhibition* in the Rijksmuseum in Amsterdam and the Peabody Essex Museum in Salem, https://www.rijksmuseum.nl/en/asia-in-amsterdam (November 17, 2015).

172 Carey, *Slave Trade, Domestic.* Lequin, *Het personeel van de VOC.* Leyten, *From idol to art.*

173 Buschmann, "Exploring tensions in material culture", 58.

174 Knaap ea., *Oorlogen over Zee*, 106.

175 Derix, *Brengers van de Boodschap*, 48.

176 Derix, *Brengers van de Boodschap*, 63.

177 Exhibition *Maya's – Heersers van het Regenwoud* (Assen, Drents Museum, 2016), and http://epicworldhistory.blogspot.nl/2012/06/diego-de-landa.html (September 05, 2016).

War booty during colonial expansion and its present whereabouts

1520 Mexico

Spaniards looted the palace and parental house of Aztec Emperor Montezuma Xokoyotzim II.[1] An imperial headdress that consisted of four-hundred bronze-green feathers of the rain forest quetzal bird, which were mounted in gold with precious stones, is surrounded with provenance questions. Was it a gift, or was it loot? Since the late 16th century, it has been in Austria. Mexico has repeatedly asked for its return and several political parties in Austria favour a return.[2] But its holder, the World Museum in Vienna, disputes that it belonged to the Aztec King and argues that the headdress is too fragile to be transported. The museum houses other precious Pre-Columbian or early colonial Mexican feather objects.[3] In 1520, many ancient codices were burned or shipped to Europe, where their names of origin were changed into European names. This can be considered as ideological violence.[4] Few have remained *in loco*.

1533 Peru

Spaniards confiscated golden and silver objects from the Inca Sun temple in Cuzco.[5] Since they melted *'almost all gold and silver... down into bars'*, many objects disappeared, while some ended up in Western and North-American museums.[6]

1550 – 1570 Iceland

After expelling Roman Catholic churches and priests, Danish Lutherans took shipments of medieval Roman Catholic calices, fonts and other religious silver objects to the Royal Palace in Copenhagen, where they were melted down. Among the newly made products were three silver lions, which are currently among the masterpieces of Rosenborg Slot.[7]

1691 India

VOC soldiers, who were fighting the Malabar-rulers in Kerala, seized 16 bronze Hindu statues from a temple. In 1687 they had found five others in a nearby fort. All of them ended up in the collection of the Amsterdam mayor and VOC governor, Nicolaes Witsen, who had them auctioned in 1728. It is unknown where they went from the auction house.[8]

1765 Sri Lanka

Against the instruction of their commander, VOC soldiers plundered the Palace of the King and the city of Kandy. Although there is no precise *'list of the Kandy booty'*, it did definitely contain *'linen, fine furniture and curiosities, with some minted and unminted silver'*,[9] a canon with the King's symbols (sun, half-moon and Singhalese lion) and silver weapons. The canon was given to Stadtholder William V in The Hague and remains in the Rijksmuseum in Amsterdam nowadays, although Sri Lanka had asked for its return through UNESCO in 1980.[10] A silver and gold reliquary for a tooth of the Buddha, seized during the plunder of the city's main temple, was returned on the spot.[11]

1776 Indonesia

VOC soldiers captured manuscripts, seals, a staff and a glass from local princes of Macassar at Sulawesi. They are now in the National Museum, Jakarta.[12]

1784 Indonesia/Malaysia

In the fourth Anglo-Dutch war, Dutch commander J.P. van Braam captured 27 flags and two elephants in Telok Ketapang.[13] In the Netherlands, the flags were shown together with trophies from wars against Spain and England. Due to neglect and poor restoration work some have been lost.[14] The remaining 15 are in the National Military Museum in Soesterberg.[15] The National Maritime Museum in Amsterdam possesses a drawing of the flags, dating from 1784.[16]

Notes

1   Sources: Rudolf Van Zantwijk, *De oorlog tegen de Goden – Azteekse kronieken over de Spaanse Verovering, uit het Nahuatl vertaald* (Amsterdam: Meulenhoff, 1992), 98 – 102, in this book the name of the King is spelled Motecuzoma; Longhena, *Het oude Mexico*, 79, 80; http://www.weltmuseumwien.at/besuchen/sammlungen/nord-und-mittelamerika/die-geschichte-der-sammlung/ (February 20, 2017).

2   http://latino.foxnews.com/latino/lifestyle/2014/11/14/symbol-mexicos-precolonial-grandeur-fades-out-sight/ and http://www.laht.com/article.asp?articleid=384813&categoryid=13003 (February 2, 2015).

3   http://www.weltmuseumwien.at/en/explore/organisation/press/penacho-pomp-passion/ (November 9, 2015).

4   It has been suggested to undo this ideological violence and rename the codices in conformity with the Mesoamerican culture. E.g. the Codex Borbonicus (Library National Assembly, Paris), presently named after the Palais Bourbon in France, would become the Codex Cihuacoatl, named after a goddess. Maarten Jansen and Gabina A. Pérez Jiménez, "Renaming the Mexican Codices", in *Ancient Mesoamerica* (Cambridge: Cambridge University Press, 2004), 15/02, July 2004.

5   Longhena and Alva, *Inca's*, 71, 126.

6   Pasztory, *Pre-Columbian art*, 8.

7   Hallgrímur Helgason, „Warum ist ausgerechnet Island so korrupt?", in *Die Welt*, Berlin, http://www.welt.de/kultur/literarischewelt/article154159974/Warum-ist-ausgerechnet-Island-so-korrupt.html (June 06, 2016). Steinunn Kristjánsdóttir, University of Iceland, discovered the origins of the silver lions (email June 22, 2016). Peter Kristiansen of Rosenborg Slot commented: melting was a '*normal habit*' at the time, as there was no use for these objects anymore, and '*the Crown could always use money*' (email June 06, 2016). http://www.kongernessamling.dk/en/rosenborg/object/silver-lions/ (June 06, 2016).

8   *Asia in Amsterdam – The culture of luxury in the Golden Age* (Amsterdam: Rijksmuseum, 2015): 202, 203.

9   http://www.defonseka.com/ref_dutch_wars02.htm (January 7, 2016).

10 Government of Sri Lanka, *Statement concerning the restitution of significant cultural objects from Sri Lanka*. Paris: UNESCO/ICPRCP, May 1980, 18.

11 Knaap ea., *Oorlogen over Zee*, 142.

12 Groot, *Van Batavia naar Weltevreden*, 133.

13 Knaap ea., *ibid.*, 162. http://resources.huygens.knaw.nl/bwn1780-1830/lemmata/data/Braam (January 8, 2016).

14 Mariska Pool, *Vergeten vlaggen*. http://collectie.legermuseum.nl/sites/strategion/contents/i004530/arma36%20vergeten%20vlaggen.pdf (January 14, 2016).

15 Emails Mariska Pool, January 14, 2016, and Paul Van Brakel (National Military Museum), February 15, 2016.

16 Email Scheepvaartmuseum, January 15, 2016. Inv. No. S.0585(04), http://www.maritiemdigitaal.nl/index.cfm?event=search.getsimplesearch&saveToHistory=1&database=ChoiceMardig&searchterm=S.0585%2804%29&needImages=YES (January 15, 2016).

3.2. Meagre protection

In this first period, the issue of war law and booty was raised only incidentally. In 1625, Hugo Grotius wrote in *De Jure belli ac pacis* that '*things, taken in an unjust war, are to be restored, not only by those, who have taken them, but by others also into whose hands they may have by any means fallen*'.[178] The principle of universal restitution of private property, recorded in the 1648 *Treaty of Westphalia*, is often seen as '*the first sign of an emerging ban*' on looting cultural property.[179] As this principle was focussed on the protection of archival materials that were needed for the administration of states, it cannot be really interpreted '*as providing for the restitution of cultural property as such*'.[180] In his *Second Treatise on Civil Government*, which John Locke published in 1698, he accepted the victor's full right to take an enemy's life but not his property.[181] Swiss lawyer Emeric de Vattel argued around 1750 that a conqueror had to respect private property, but was allowed to take public property, with the exception of cultural properties, such as temples, tombs and other buildings that did not contribute to an enemy's strength.[182] In discussions after the defeat of Napoleon that led to the *Second Treaty of Paris* of November 20, 1815, '*stolen art was a major topic*'. France was pressured to return spoils of war, be it not to the countries of origin, such as Egypt, but to victorious European countries and the Vatican. For some authors, the 1815 treaty contained the basis for later repatriations (6.2.1.).[183]

Principles for dealing with war booty applied only to intra-European state relations and not to those with distant colonial possessions/indigenous entities. The dominating legal discourse did not recognise them as international legal persons. From today's perspective, this discourse is questionable, as it is unclear why kingdoms in the Indian sub-continent, sultanates on Java and Bali[184] and empires along the Niger River in West Africa were considered lesser states than the '*different and non-equivalent forms*' of strong monarchies, merchant republics and confederations in Europe.[185] The European colonisers recognised states in South America, Africa and Asia *de facto* by entering into trade agreements with their rulers, and after their independence, many of them returned as internationally recognised states, albeit with '*continuity and rupture*'[186] and often in new formations. If they

---

178 Campfens, *Fair and just solutions?*, 13.
179 Wojciech Kowalski, "Types of Claims for Recovery of Lost Cultural Property", in *Museum International* (Paris: UNESCO, 2005), 87.
180 Lubina, *Contested Cultural Property*, 51, 52. In accordance with the Treaty of Westpahlia, Sweden returned Bohemian archival records and manuscripts to what was then Austro-Hungary (Prott, *Witnesses of History*, 2).
181 Kowalski, "Types of Claims for Recovery", 87.
182 John A. Cohan, "An examination of archaeological ethics and the repatriation movement – Respecting cultural property", in *Environs* (Berkeley: University of California, 2004), 27. Vrdoljak, *International Law, Museums and the Return of Cultural Objects*, 64, 65.
183 Kowalski, *Types of Claims for Recovery*, 87. Also: Paige S. Goodwin, "Mapping the limits of repatriable cultural heritage: A case study of stolen Flemish art in French museums", in *University of Pennsylvania Law Review*, Vol. 157, 680, 681.
184 The text on the Nagarakertaggama palm-leaf (7.2.) mentions kingdoms explicitly. *Het oud-Javaansche Lofdicht Nagarakertaggama van Prapatje (1365 A.D.)* (Weltevreden: Drukkerij Volkslectuur, 1922), 5 ff.
185 Burbank and Cooper, *Empires in World History*, 183.
186 Vrdoljak, *International Law, Museums and the Return of Cultural Objects*, 200.

are deservedly accepted as states, *'one must qualify the violent contentions with the European powers during the process of colonisation as armed conflict'.*[187] This would make them fall under the regime of war law and impact the protection of their cultural heritage.

There were critics of the colonial violence in Europe.[188] In 1522, Roman Catholic bishop Bartolomé de las Casas brought into the open the horrible bloodbaths and other cruelties that his fellow countrymen committed on the Indians in the Americas.[189] To solve the problem of labour shortage, he proposed to import enslaved Africans.[190] Legal experts in the Iberian empire such as Francisco de Vitoria (1483 – 1546) also expressed doubts about Spain's behaviour in the Americas and deplored the spoliation of goods from indigenous people.[191] In 1623 Dutch poet Joost van den Vondel criticised some Dutch people for undue force and greed:

> *Feel free to travel far lands in foreign places,*
> *But act in righteousness in deed, and in your words,*
> *Neither mark by undue force your Christian greed,*
> *But chase the rightful goal.*[192]

In conclusion, European powers began their colonial expansion at different moments. Trade companies with strong links to the metropolis played a major role. They applied, with differing intensities, large-scale direct, structural and ideological violence. The ideological violence in relation to cultural objects was most extreme in South America and Africa. Although the information about the collecting activities of European colonials is scarce, there is evidence that collecting started in an unsystematic way and then increased. It was done through purchase or exchange, force, coercion and conversion. Force was applied during wars and other types of violent action and through missionary collecting. Initially, destruction outweighed confiscation in missionary activities. There is scarcely evidence of legal protection of indigenous cultural heritage in this early period. Although colonisers recognised the rulers of indigenous states de facto by concluding commercial treaties with them, they did not treat these territories as states, as meant in international law. In Europe, there was moral indignation about the creeping colonisation and forced removals of cultural objects.

---

187 Lubina, *Contested Cultural Property*, 138.
188 In *Nestbevuilers*, Ewald Vanvugt found critics in the first period of Dutch colonialism: L. Reael († 1637), N. de Graaff († 1688), W. van Haren († 1768), W. van Hogendorp († 1784), and his son D. van Hogendorp († 1822).
189 Barthelomé de las Casas, *Brevisima relacion de la destruccion de las Indias*, Sevilla 1522 http://www.verbodengeschriften.nl/html/zeerbeknoptrelaasvandeverwoesting.html (November 19, 2015).
190 Anton De Kom, *Wij Slaven*, 23.
191 Prott, *Witnesses to History*, 2.
192 Copied in this translation from panel about VOC attitudes, Museum Bronbeek, Arnhem (March 24, 2014).

Chapter 4

Settler and exploitation colonialism

Settler colonialism was aimed at the establishment of a branch of the metropolis with its own administrative structures. It could attract subjects from different Europeans nations, who looked for an alternative to unemployment or failed ambitions.[193] The goal of exploitation colonialism was narrower and aimed at getting the maximum out of other peoples' natural resources and workforce. It enabled Europeans to enrich themselves quickly. The speed of the transition to either form differed per continent, coloniser and colony. To impose their will, colonial powers fought ferocious wars, making numerous victims and confiscating extensive war booty.

In South America, the Spaniards soon regularised settlement patterns, organised the collection of tribute, rounded up labour for the gold and silver mines and introduced forced agricultural production, especially of sugar. They saw the indigenous people as *'infidels and inferiors'*.[194] Settler and exploitation colonialism was associated with massive direct, structural and ideological violence. Aztec sources mention massacres.[195]

In Asia, the transition could take years. By 1800, a colonial administration had replaced the bankrupt VOC in the Dutch East Indies, but it was not until 1920, that the archipelago was fully under control of the Dutch. The British were the dominant colonial power. To practice exploitation colonialism, they expelled or exterminated much of the indigenous population in North America and Australia. In other possessions, they set up minority rule with oppressive administrative structures. In the second half of the 19th century, the creeping colonisation, practiced by France, passed into protectorates in Laos, Cambodia and parts of Vietnam, and later also in Tunisia and Morocco.

From the opening of the Suez Canal in 1867 and the 1884 – 1885 Berlin Conference, colonial powers began to occupy Africa's coastal areas, and soon also moved into inland areas to exploit the natural resources. Belgium, Italy, Germany, France and Great Britain established administrative structures in their African possessions, and some also did this in the Pacific. Sweden and Denmark had

---

193 Burbank and Cooper, *Empires in World History*, 319.
194 Ibid., 162.
195 Van Zantwijk, *Oorlog tegen de Goden*, 79, 81, 82 and passim.

given up most tropical trade posts and trade companies in the 17th century. They practiced settler colonialism in the Nordic areas.[196]

4.1. Peak in migration of objects

Influenced by the Enlightenment and the rise of private collections, several European powers opened museums. They showed the conquest and profitability of the colonial possessions. Each collecting institution or individual had his own (mix of) motives, varying from the salvage paradigm and scholarly curiosity to greed and disdain for local people. European collectors sometimes showed more interest in ancient monuments than local people. They wrote enthusiastically about, for instance, the Angkor Wat and the Borobudur temple complexes in Asia, the ancient caravan oasis and city of thousand columns of Palmyra in the Middle East, and the religious, ceremonial, astronomical and agricultural centre Machu Picchu in Peru.[197] All these places are listed as World Heritage sites; some are also on UNESCO's List of World Heritage in Danger.[198] Their violated walls tell stories of neglect, conquest and objects that have been forcibly removed, not only but also in the European colonial period.

Little is known about acquisitions from South America during this second period. There were expeditions, but most that are known took place after the independence of countries (5.1.). European visitors of Asia neglected Islamic and local cultural heritage, while Hindu and Buddhist objects migrated extensively from Asia to Europe. There is even provenance information about some of them.[199] In Africa, the dominance of disdain over admiration for indigenous cultures made '*that the process of documentation has not been properly carried out*'.[200] The objects' biographies are very restricted.[201]

Gifts to colonial administrators and institutions

Most evidence about *gift-giving* in this period that I found comes from Asia, both about those from local rulers to colonial administrators and those exchanged between colonial officials. Princes from Java and Bali confirmed their submission to Dutch colonial administrators with, for instance, a weapon rack that is currently

---

196 Magdalena Naum and Jonas Nordin, eds., *Scandinavian Colonialism and the Rise of Modernity – Small Time Agents in a Global Arena* (New York: Springer, 2013). Gavin Lucas and Angelos Parigoris, "Icelandic Archaeology and the Ambiguities of Colonialism", in: Naum and Nordin, *Scandinavian Colonialism*, 89 – 105.

197 Claude Jacques, *Angkor* (Cologne: Könemann Verlagsgesellschaft, 1999), 158. Endang Sri Hardiati, "The Borobudur temple as a place of pilgrimage" in eds. Hardiati and Ter Keurs, Indonesia: *The discovery of the past*, 49. Robert Wood, *The Ruins of Palmyra* (London: 1753). http://www.silkroadfoundation.org/newsletter/2004vol2num1/Palmyra.htm (November 26, 2015);http://whc.unesco.org/en/list/274 (December 17, 2015).

198 http://whc.unesco.org/en/danger/ (June 03, 2016).

199 Sudarmadi, *Between colonial legacies and grassroots movements*, 75, 91. Mirjam Shatanawi, *Islam at the Tropenmuseum* (Arnhem: LM Publishers, 2014), 31.

200 Francis Musonda, "How accurate are interpretations of African objects in western museums", in ed. Peter R. Schmidt and Roderick McIntosh, *Plundering Africa's Past* (Bloomington: Indiana University Press, 1996), 168.

201 Boris Wastiau, *Exit Congo Museum* (Tervuren, Royal Museum for Central Africa, 2000), 13.

in the Rijksmuseum in Amsterdam.[202] Other such gifts can be found in Dutch ethnographic museums and in the National Museum in Jakarta.[203] During the British interregnum in the Dutch East Indies (1811 – 1816), British colonial officials donated two ancient stones with inscriptions to colleagues in South Asia. The Indonesian government wants both to be returned (Box: *Ancient Indonesian gifts dispersed*).

Objects acquired during private expeditions

Colonial officials and military, private entrepreneurs and collectors gathered antiquities and ethnographic objects during *expeditions*. For the *German New Guinea Company* and other German enterprises in the Pacific and Africa, this was a lucrative side activity. Norway had sea captains and traders in the Pacific, Africa and the Americas, who purchased or exchanged objects for European goods, took them away with coercion, not shunning '*the most brutal atrocities*'.[204] In West-Central-Africa, traders and collectors vied with each other. European museums competed for the best objects.[205] Cecil Rhodes, founder of the British South Africa Company, enabled employees of the *Ancient Ruins Company Ltd.* to exploit all two hundred Rhodesian ruins, of which Great Zimbabwe was the biggest. They took '*gold and everything of value, tearing down structures and throwing away whatever was not valuable to them (pottery shards, pots, clay figurines)*'.[206]

In most Dutch, British, French and German possessions, learned societies were set up to streamline research and collecting. As they began as private initiative of officials of the trade companies and colonial administrations, and despite the fact that at a later stage they gained organisational and financial support from the colonial administrations, their acquisitions are put here under the heading *Objects acquired during private expeditions*.

The *Batavian Society for Arts and Sciences* in Batavia (nowadays Jakarta), established by VOC officials in 1778, soon had a museum and collections. Indonesian authors recognise it as '*a unique and valuable starting point*' for Indonesia's National Museum.[207] In 1784, a British East India Company official set up the *Asiatic Society* in Kolkata with museum and library.[208] It acquired a branch in Colombo with the

202 https://www.rijksmuseum.nl/nl/collectie/NG-BR-554 (November 24, 2015).

203 Brinkgreve, "Balinese Chiefs and Dutch Dominion", 122. Trigganga ea., "Three centuries of collections", 82.

204 Mary Bouquet, *Sans og Samling… hos Universitetes Etnografiske Museum / Bringing it all back home… to the Oslo University Ethnographic Museum* (Oslo: Scandinavian University Press, 1996), 74, 77.

205 Willink, B*ewogen verzamelgeschiedenis*, 2006: 170.

206 Webber Ndoro 2005, "Great Zimbabwe", in http://www.scientificamerican.com/article/great-zimbabwe-2005-01/ (September 6, 2016).

207 Wardiman Djojonegoro, "The evolution of the National Museum", in eds. Sitowati and Miksic, *Icons of Art*, 49, 64. Bambang Sumadio, "Indonesia's Cultural Evolution" in: ed. Haryati Soebadio, *Pusaka – Art of Indonesia* (Jakarta: Archipelago Press with National Museum, 1992), 19 – 24. Amin Sutaarga, "The role of museums in Indonesia: Collecting documents from the past and the present for a better future", in eds. Reimar Schefold and Han F. Vermeulen, *Treasure Hunting? Collectors and collections of Indonesian artefacts* (Leiden: Mededelingen van het Rijksmuseum voor Volkenkunde 30, 2002), 281 – 282.

208 http://www.asiaticsocietycal.com/history/index.htm (November 23, 2015).

Ancient Indonesian gifts dispersed

In 1812, Colonel Colin Mackenzie of the British-Indian forces in Java collected the so-called *Pucangan Stone*. It was shipped to the colonial administration in India and is currently in a storeroom of the Indian Museum in Kolkata. Through the years, the clarity of the inscription on *'the sole known documentary source'* about the reign of King Airlangga (1019 – 1049), has been damaged.

In the same period, Mackenzie collected the 10th century East-Javanese *Sangguran Stone*, which also has a rare inscription. Lieutenant-Governor T.S. Raffles donated it to the Governor-General of India, Lord Minto. Upon his departure, Minto took *'the last* known recorded document issued by the Sailendra rulers of ancient Mataram in Central Java (8th – 10th century)'* to his estate in Scotland, where heavy winds and rain eroded the inscription of what has now become a *'garden ornament'*. The Minto family is willing to return the Sangguran Stone, but wants a high sum as compensation, which Indonesia is unwilling to pay.[1]

——— Notes ———

1 Nigel Bullough and Peter Carey, "The Kolkata (Calcutta) Stone and the bicentennial of the British Interregnum in Java, 1811 – 1816", in *The Newsletter*, (Leiden: IIAS, 2016), No. 74: 4 – 5. Email Peter Carey, November 18, 2014.

Government Oriental Library for ancient palm leaf manuscripts.[209] It operated more independently of the colonial administration than the Batavian Society, and its members were more research oriented.[210] In 1822, a French *Société Asiatique* was established, focussing mainly on manuscripts and books from the Maghreb to East and Southeast Asia.[211] The German *Morgenländische Gesellschaft*, established in 1845, had scientific ambitions and a modest collection.[212]

The tens of thousands of objects that came to Europe overloaded colonial museums and made one museum director fear that they would *'start rotting'* and that his storage space would become a *'rubbish heap'*.[213] Their creators, use and first possessors are rarely known. The origin of the hundreds of objects, for instance, that Dutch female explorer Alexine Tinne and German zoologist Theodor von Heuglin collected along the White Nile in South Sudan in 1863 and 1864, is shrouded in obscurity. They purchased the objects in situ and in Khartoum, but only noted the name of the ethnic group who had produced them. Most objects ended in the storerooms of fifteen European museums, with the curators hardly aware of their existence.[214]

209 Jonathan Sweet, "Colonial museology and the Buddhist chronicles of Sri Lanka: agency and negotiation in the development of the palm-leaf manuscript collection at the Colombo Museum", in *Museum & Society* (Leicester: Leicester University, November 2014), 12/3, 228.
210 Groot, *Van Batavia naar Weltevreden*, 151, 152.
211 http://www.aibl.fr/societe-asiatique/histoire/?lang=fr (November 23, 2015).
212 http://www.dmg-web.de/?page=1 (November 23, 2015).
213 Gert Staal and Martijn De Rijk, *IN side OUT – ON site IN: Redesigning the National Museum of Ethnology* (Amsterdam, BIS Publishers, 2003), 34, 35.
214 Joost Willink, *The Fateful Journey: The Expedition of Alexine Tinne and Theodor von Heuglin in Sudan (1863-1864)*, (Amsteram: Amsterdam University Press, 2011), 305 – 308.

Possessors or their descendants donated or sold objects to museums in the colony and in the metropolis. The receiving institutions rarely investigated the provenance of these donations. It was the time of the *'imperial blind-eye to opportunistic collecting'* in the British,[215] the Belgian[216] and other European empires. The museums, in their turn, dominated the attribution of objects. In 1830, Governor Robert Brownrigg of Sri Lanka gave the 8th or 9th century, gilt bronze statue of Tārā to the British Museum. Sri Lanka has repeatedly asked for its return, the only one of its kind found in the country. While Sri Lanka claims it was war booty,[217] the British Museum informs its visitors that *'nothing is known about how and when the statue was found nor how it came... in the possession'* of the London museum.[218]

In some collection activities, echoes of the salvage paradigm can be found, especially when the lack of storage facilities, absence of experts and other circumstances in the colony made preservation impossible. Two British colonial officials in Papua New Guinea gained fame for it (Box: *Relocating to preserve better: From Papua New Guinea to Australia*).

An example of a controversial expedition is that of Lord Elgin, who acquired the 75 meter long frieze that adorned the Parthenon (5th century BCE), which is now in the British Museum.[219] The poet Lord Byron and archaeologist Richard Payne Knight criticised Elgin for it, while a Parliamentary Committee that had to decide about the British purchase of the Marbles in 1816, was confused over the question of whether Elgin had had the right to take them. In this book, the term 'Elgin Marbles' is avoided for the same reason that people object to naming Aztec codices after the Europeans who confiscated or purchased them. In UNESCO documents they are called Parthenon Marbles. *Elginism* has become synonymous with the pillage of precious works of art in subjugated countries.[220] For decades, the Greek Government has been asking UNESCO's *Intergovernmental Committee for Promoting the Return of Cultural Property to its Countries of origin or its Restitution in case of Illicit Appropriation* to facilitate mediation (6.1.), while it opened a special museum for the Marbles in Athens in 2009. The British Museum, however, rejects mediation, arguing that the Intergovernmental Committee mediates between states and the British Museum is *'not a government body'*.[221] In May 2015, the Greek government made *'an unexpected move'* by rejecting a suggestion of British lawyers to formally request repatriation of the Parthenon Marbles and, in case of a rejection, to take the British Museum to the International Court of Justice in The Hague. Overwhelmed by financial problems, unwilling to make enemies in

---

215 Sweet, *Colonial museology and the Buddhist chronicles of Sri Lanka*, 230.
216 Sarah Van Beurden, *Authentically African*, 137.
217 Greenfield, *Return of Cultural Treasures*, 133, 134.
218 MacGregor, *A history of the world in 100 objects*, 298.
219 Irina A. Stamatoudi, "The law and ethics deriving from the Parthenon Marbles case", in *Parthenon NewMentor* (1997), http://www.parthenon.newmentor.net/legal.htm (November 27, 2015). Merryman, *Imperialism, Art and Restitution*. Greenfield, *Return of Cultural Treasures*. MacGregor, *A history of the world in 100 objects*. Etc.
220 Greenfield, *ibid.*, 54.
221 https://www.britishmuseum.org/about_us/news_and_press/press_releases/2015/unesco_mediation_proposal.aspx (November 26, 2015).

Relocating to preserve better: from Papua New Guinea to Australia

Two British Lieutenant-Governors of Papua New Guinea, William MacGregor (1888 – 1897) and Hubert Murray (1904 – 1940) did much for the preservation of cultural heritage.

MacGregor set rules for collecting: reciprocity, no robberies or taking away without the owners' consent, and confiscation of improperly acquired objects by the colonial administration. His visits to Papua New Guinea's coasts were often the first European contact with indigenous people. He practiced reciprocity himself by exchanging iron articles and coloured cloth for hard-to-find stone axes and other ethnographic objects.[1] In 1889, he agreed with the Queensland Museum in Brisbane that the museum would, as long as necessary, take care of what, by then, had become the official British New Guinean collection of 10,800 objects from 178 different places. The Brisbane museum confirmed the agreement.[2] So far, only part of the collection has been returned (11.2.).

Hubert Murray began to build a museum in Port Moresby and drafted the *Papuan Antiquities Ordinance,* which was aimed at the protection of relics.[3] In 1915, he made a custodian agreement with the Australian Museum in Sydney and had 3,200 objects shipped there. In later archival documents, their temporary stay in Australia is confirmed.[4] The Murray collection remains in Australia in full (11.2.). Both MacGregor and Murray had agreed with the safe-haven museum that it could keep a representative proportion for its own use.

Notes

1   Quinnell, "Before it is too late", 84.
2   Ibid., 91. Mark Busse, "Short history of the Papua New Guinea National Museum", in ed. Barry Craig, *Living Spirits with Fixed Abodes* (Adelaide: Crawford House Publications, 2010), 6.
3   Craig, *Living Spirits*, 112.
4   Ibid., 206.

Europe and not convinced that the International Court would solve the dispute, it dropped the option of '*legal action*' for fear it would lose the case, and opted for '*diplomatic and political channels*'.[222]

Some other major expeditions also stand out in this consolidating phase of European colonialism. One example consists of over one hundred and fifty expeditions carried out in China's Dun Huang area around 1900, led by collectors from six European countries, the USA and Japan.[223] The other example begins around 1870 in Cyprus and consists of three waves. American Consul in Cyprus, Di Cesnola, was responsible for the first, the British Museum for the second and Turkish invaders for the third (Box: *Cyprus and Dung Huang expeditions*).

---

222   The Guardian, May 13, 2015, http://www.theguardian.com/artanddesign/2015/may/13/greece-drops-option-legal-action-british-museum-parthenon-marbles-row (May 27, 2015); http://www.ekathimerini.com/204151/article/ekathimerini/news/greek-govt-changes-course-on-parthenon-marbles (March 14, 2016).
223   Liu, *Repatriating China's Cultural Objects*, 13 ff.

Cyprus and Dun Huang expeditions

Cyprus: Three waves of invasion

In 1960, Cyprus became independent. It is a member state of the European Union, the Council of Europe and the Organisation for Security and Co-operation in Europe.[1] From 1571, it was part of the Ottoman Empire. In 1865 Luigi Palma di Cesnola became American consul. Until his departure in 1877, this amateur antiquarian collected 35,573 archaeological objects from all over the island, dating from 300 BCE onwards. Di Cesnola collected in a crude manner. When shipping the objects away, he lost five thousand of them at sea. While the Louvre museum in Paris, the Hermitage Museum in St. Petersburg and other museums were eager to acquire the remaining objects, the Metropolitan Museum of Art in New York got hold of most of them and offered Di Cesnola the position of director in exchange in 1879.[2] Other objects, collected by Di Cesnola, ended up in museums in Europe and Turkey.

In 1878, the British took over control over Cyprus. Again, archaeological objects were excavated and exported on a massive scale, most of which are now in the British Museum. The British overruled regulations set by the Cyprus Legislative Council, which gave the supervision of excavations and exports to the Cyprus Museum authorities. The indignation that the British created among heritage officials and the public in Cyprus continues today.[3] Cyprus has made no formal restitution claims, as it believes it has little or no chance of success.[4]

The loss of antiquities reached a new peak in 1974, after the Turkish invasion of the northern part of the island. This time Christian treasures also disappeared.[5]

Dun Huang: Aurel Stein, Paul Pelliot and other explorers

Around 1900, Hungarian-British archaeological explorer, Aurel Stein sneaked out thousands of manuscripts, paintings, embroideries and other objects from caves in Dun Huang in Northern central China. They ended up in the British Library, the British Museum and the National Museum in New Delhi. In 1930, Stein was named an insatiable *'thief'* by China. A year after him, French sinologist Paul Pelliot took thousands of items from the same caves, which are now in the Bibliothèque Nationale in Paris. Pelliot cannot expect sympathy in China either.[6] All treasures have been put on a lengthy list of objects that China wants to recover. Western authors complain about the *'criminalisation'* of Stein[7] by China and use derogatory terms as *'scoundrel'* for the local guide, who had swindled Stein and not for the European explorer himself.[8] They do not problematise the provenance of the Silk Road collections.[9] Chinese legal expert, Zuozhen Liu, wonders whether civil litigation against e.g. the United Kingdom can be an effective way for China to retrieve Dun Huang treasures. Her conclusion is negative, as the limitation rules of the three legal systems are inconsistent.[10] Liu does not discuss whether the *International Dunhuang Project*, initiated by the British Library in 1994, in which libraries in the UK, China, Japan, South Korea, Germany and France make manuscripts and other objects virtually accessible, serves to replace their return.[11]

Notes

1   http://www.olc.gov.cy/olc/olc.nsf/
    all/30C0465A694B106BC2257D3100285954/
    $file/SECTION%20I%20-%20

MULTILATERAL%20GENNERAL%20.
pdf?openelement (July 3, 2016).

2   Marangou, *The Consul Luigi Palma di Cesnola*, 118.
    Sharon Waxman, *Loot: The battle over the stolen*

treasures of the ancient world (New York: Times Books, 2008), 181. Also: http://www.metmuseum.org/toah/hd/cesn/hd_cesn.htm (July 3, 2016).

3   Marangou, ibid., 357, 359.

4   Off-the-record communication with official of the National Museum of Cyprus, August 2009.

5   Michael Jansen, War and cultural heritage: Cyprus after the 1974 Turkish invasion (Minneapolis: University of Minnesota, 2005).

6   Liu, Repatriating China's Cultural Objects, 15, 16.

7   Justin M. Jacobs, "Confronting Indiana Jones: Chinese Nationalism, Historical Imperialism, and the Criminalization of Aurel Stein and the

Raiders of Dunhuang, 1899-1944", in eds. Sherman Cochran and Paul G. Pickowicz, China on the Margins (Ithaca, NY: Cornell University Press, 2010), 65.

8   Peter Hopkirk, Barbaren langs de Zijderoute – Op zoek naar de verloren steden en schatten van Chinees Centraal Azië (Baarn: Hollandia, 1991), 121.

9   MacGregor, A history of the World in 100 Objects, 272.

10   Liu, Repatriating China's Cultural Objects, 110, 111.

11   http://idp.bl.uk/ (November 27, 2015). Liu, ibid., 17.

Objects acquired during military expeditions

During numerous punitive actions, raids and wars, colonial rulers deprived local power-holders of inalienable regalia, thereby also violating their dignity and legitimacy.[224] Booty also ended up in the hands of private officials and military. Such military expeditions continued until far into the 20th century.

In 1798, General Napoleon Bonaparte set in motion a major looting campaign, when he sailed with 167 scientists and Constantin Volney's book *Voyage en Égypte et en Syrie* to Egypt to start a '*campaign of looting conducted in the name of diplomacy and cultural inquiry, which soon degenerated into an orgy of destruction, greed, and outright profiteering*'.[225] Although he was soon defeated by the British, Napoleon's campaign had a lasting impact and, not in the least because it was continued by the British. Both took treasures from the temples in Luxor and Karnak, the Rosetta Stone, sarcophagus, obelisks and wagon-loads of other treasures. Most of these are now in the Louvre (former *Musée Napoleon*), the British Museum and other Western museums. Some decorate public squares. European diplomats, amateur archaeologists, visitors and others profited as well. Because of the involvement of scientists and the salvage paradigm as a motive, one can categorise this loot under expeditions. It can be defined as war booty because of the involvement of the French army and because the British captured many treasures from the French, thus definitely turning them into war booty.[226] The entire collection was '*simply shipped to Europe without any recourse or reference to the Egyptian government at all*'.[227] Neither France nor Britain ever questioned their presence within their borders.

---

224 Drieënhuizen, *Koloniale collecties, Nederlands aanzien*, 18.
225 Brian M. Fagan, *The Rape of the Nile; Tomb Robbers, Tourists, and Archaeologists in Egypt* (London: Book Club Associates/Macdonald and Jane's Publishers, 1977), 361.
226 John A. Cohan, "An examination of archaeological ethics and the repatriation movement – Respecting cultural property", in *Environs*, (Berkeley: University of California, 2004), 28/1, 116.
227 Fagan, *The Rape of the Nile*, 81.

There is war booty from numerous other battles – a precious Inca textile,[228] religious objects from the state of Benin[229] and weapons, flags and other dignity symbols of Indonesian rulers, to name a few. Some museums were offered too many flags '*to provide a clue to the probable provenance*' of each.[230] Descendants have often asked for their return (Box: *War booty during settler- and exploitation-colonialism*). The absence of these objects means unhealed scars, incomplete pages of history, insults to ancestors, missing unique objects, or injustice that has to be undone. While admittedly some returns have been made, the current possessors have difficulty in honouring return requests. Although the looting of the Benin Court in 1897 evoked moral indignation in Great Britain about looting as standard practice in colonial warfare, it did not diminish the extent of the looting.[231]

Missionary collecting

Missionary orders continued and even expanded their activities in colonial possessions in this period, although the 1789 French Revolution forced some of them to close down or interrupt their activities temporarily.[232] As missionaries from one European nation moved freely through the colonial possessions of another nation, their collecting of objects got strong European features and reached a peak in the second half of the 19th century.[233] They sent objects to newly established missionary and other museums.[234] As remarked earlier (2.3.4.), in some instances missionaries could leave the collecting and the destruction of objects to local chiefs and actors.

In some instances, such as that of the German Rhenish Missionary Society in Namibia, the cross prepared the ground for the sword.[235] In Congo, King Leopold II had only trusted Belgium-based missionary congregations initially, while later one of every four missionary workers was a non-Belgian European.[236] This was in line with Art. 6 of the *General Act of the 1885 Berlin Conference* (2.3.2.). Scandinavian

---

228 Longhena and Alva, *De Inca's*, 117.
229 Patrick Effiboley, "Les musées béninois: du musée ethnographique au musée d'histoire sociale", in *French Studies in Southern Africa* (South Africa: Association for French Studies in Southern Africa, 2015, Nr. 45), 47.
230 Stevens, *Bitter Spice*, 57.
231 Michael Carrington, "Officers, gentlemen and thieves", 82.
232 Derix, *Brengers van de Boodschap*, 147.
233 Derix, *ibid.* Van Pesch and Campbell, *Missionaire collecties in beeld.* Corbey, *Tribal Art Traffic.* Hari Budiarti, "The Sulawesi collections – Missionaries, Chiefs and Military Expeditions", in eds. Hadiarti and Ter Keurs, *Indonesia: Disocvery of the Past*, 160 – 271. Bernard Gissibl, "Imagination and beyond: cultures and geographies of imperialism in Germany, 1848 – 1918", in MacKenzie, *European empires and the people*, 158 – 194. Jacobs, *Collecting Kamoro-objects*.
234 Lotten Gustafsson Reinius, *Touring Congo – Mobility and materiality in missionary media* (Stockholm: Museum of Ethnography, 2011), 81. Lotten Gustafsson Reinius, "Sacred matter and (post)secular frames in a Swedish Museum", in Valeria Minucciani (ed.), *Religion and museums – Immaterial and material heritage* (Torino: Allemandi & C., Torino, 2013), 39. Email Vivian Baeke, Royal Museum for Central Africa, Belgium, December 19, 2015. Extensive Congolese collections are in Belgium, France, Germany, Switzerland, Great Britain, the Netherlands, Sweden and the USA.
235 Gissibl, *Imagination and beyond*, 173.
236 Derix, *Brengers van de Boodschap*, 734.

War booty during settler and exploitation colonialism

India
During the three Anglo-Maratha wars (1775 – 1818), Britain captured *'swords, shields, daggers and other weapons'*.[1]

Egypt
In 1798, French scientists confiscated numerous objects, among them the Rosetta Stone. The latter was subsequently captured by British soldiers and is presently in the British Museum. The museum in London has turned down an Egyptian request for its return on legal grounds and because of the larger audience that it attracts in its present location.[2]

Indonesia
In 1812, British Lieutenant-Governor T.S. Raffles looted the palace of the Sultan of Yogyakarta and caused him and his followers give up their *kris* and gold ornaments. While the Sultan slept, guards took the diamond buttons from his dress jacket. Raffles sent sword and dagger to Lord Minto in Kolkata as a symbol of the Sultan's submission.[3]

Indonesia
In 1830, Indonesia's national hero, Prince Diponegoro, handed over his kris to Dutch colonial officers. It should have been returned on the basis of a 1975 agreement between the Netherlands and Indonesia. Its absence is still felt in Indonesia.[4]

Algeria
In 1833, French soldiers took a 17th century bronze canon that Algeria's rulers once employed against European forces and pirates. Nowadays, it is in the French city of Brest. In 1962, on the eve of Algeria's independence, France took numerous maps of sewers, gas pipes and electricity lines. On the 50th anniversary of independence Algeria's National Archive and civil society groups asked for the return of the canon and the maps, but France only transferred some Ottoman era documents. It allows Algeria to have copies of other archives.[5]

Indonesia
After Dutch soldiers had occupied Baros on Sumatra's north western coast in 1839/40, they captured the flag of Al-Iskander, the leader of the Aceh troops, who had come to help. It is in the Amsterdam Rijksmuseum.[6]

India
The Second Anglo-Sikh War resulted in the annexation of Punjab and the subjugation of the Sikhs by the British in 1849. The major war trophies, the golden throne of Ranjit Singh and the Koh-i-Noor diamond, were shown at the Great Exhibition in 1851 in London. The throne is nowadays in the Victoria & Albert museum. The diamond became a major jewel in the British crown.[7]

South Asia
After defeating the Sepoy Mutiny (British viewpoint) in Lucknow in 1857 or the ending of the First Independence War (Indian viewpoint), British soldiers ransacked palaces and looted daggers and other treasures. Some are now in the National Army Museum in London.[8] For an Indian visitor in 1862 *'it was painful to see the State chair of gold of the late lion of the Punjab'*.[9]

China
In 1860, at the end of the Second Opium War, in retaliation for the torturing to death of some Westerners, Anglo-French forces pillaged the Yuanmingyuan or Old Summer Palace complex in Beijing. In *'one of the most extreme acts of destruction of the 19th century'*, they pulverised vases and mirrors, damaged paintings, scrolls and the empress's robes, and stuffed their pockets full of rubies, sapphires, pearls and pieces of rock crystal.[10] Gold and silver treasures, secret records

and sacred genealogical tablets of the empire were taken. By now, ten thousand have been identified in collections in the United Kingdom, France and the United States; among them are twelve animal heads that represent the Chinese zodiac. As fire ruined all documentation of the relics, it is unknown precisely how many disappeared. For Chinese people this *'orgy of plunder'*[11] remains an *'unhealed scar, still bleeding and aching'*.[12] Some animals of the zodiac have been returned, but most Western public and private collectors remain reluctant to acknowledge the Chinese claims.[13]

Indonesia

Between 1862 and 1865, Dutch officials took ornaments and symbols dignity from the Sultan of Bandjamarsin in southern Borneo and from the Sultan of Bantan in West Java and transferred them to the Royal Batavian Society. A high-ranking colonial military figure denounced taking a kris and a lance from the Bandjamarsin Sultan.[14]

Korea

In retaliation for a massacre of Christian missionaries, French troops plundered the archives of the Joseon Dynasty in Korea in 1866 (also 1.2.), seizing almost three hundred manuscripts. Fire destroyed six thousand others.[15] Since a Korean researcher discovered the manuscripts in the Bibliothéque Nationale in Paris in 1975, South Korea asked for their return. As they had become part of the French cultural heritage and were inalienable according to French law, requests were turned down. In 1993 however, France returned one of them in order to obtain a contract for the construction of a high-speed railway-line in Korea. In 2011, the remaining manuscripts were transferred to South Korea as a renewable long-term loan.[16]

Ethiopia

In 1868, Ethiopian Emperor Tewodros committed suicide, since he had no chance against the British troops that had come to avenge the imprisonment of a British consul and some European missionaries. The foreign soldiers confiscated 468 items of regalia, religious objects and ancient manuscripts from Tewodros' palace in Maqdala and some nearby churches (1.2.: Box: *Incidental returns of colonial cultural objects*). During an auction, organised to cover the costs of the raid, a special agent of the British Museum succeeded in outbidding *'the gathering of civilians and officers, all eager for souvenirs in this surreal scene on an East African plain with ample funds'*. Four years later, British Prime Minister, William Gladstone, said he was *'deeply regretting'* their removal and suggested the artefacts be returned. Most are now in the British Museum, the Victoria & Albert Museum, the British Library and the Royal Collection. British soldiers kept some for themselves.[17] The Jesuit Société des Bollandistes in Brussels, the Chester Beatty Library in Dublin and the Auckland Free Library possess some manuscripts.[18] Almost unnoticed are the precious crosses in a Pakistani army regiment at the Malakand Pass in Pakistan.[19] In 2008, Ethiopia asked for the return of the Maqdala treasures in the United Kingdom. So far, only few objects have been returned.

Ghana

To liberate non-British Europeans and other Ghanaians from a prison in Kumasi, British soldiers attacked the Ashanti court and confiscated the king's sword, gold masks and other precious objects in 1874. They are in museums in Great Britain. In 1894, British troops returned to punish the Ashanti Court for not paying the indemnities imposed after the invasion of 1874. During the centenary of the invasion, in 1974, the Asante King asked for their return. The proposal of a member of the House of Lords to do so was turned down by the British government and the British Museum. Ghanaian citizens have also asked for their return.[20]

Angola

In 1875, F. Hanken, a representative of the African Trade Society, took two Chokwe statues from a village, left by its inhabitants after a Dutch raid.[21] After the same raid, another representative of this trade society, F.G. Hanken, took a Yombe statue by force. The latter is currently with an art dealer in Amsterdam.[22]

Indonesia

Early in 1876, Acehnese fighters attacked Fort Lembu on Sumatra. Eight of them were killed. First Lieutenant W.D.C. Regensburg and three other Dutch soldiers also died. Among the loot, acquired by the Dutch after the raid, was a shield, which is presently in the Rijksmuseum.[23]

Cameroon

During armed clashes with Douala people in 1884, German consul Max Buchner *'looted from the house'* of chief Kum'a Mbape's his *tange* (boat prow). He presented it to the ethnological museum in Munich.[24]

Mali

After defeating the rebellious Sékou Amadou and his Islamic Tukolor Empire in 1890, French troops confiscated golden jewellery and manuscripts. After much wandering, they have ended up in the Musée du quai Branly in Paris. For Mali, their absence is a *'most burning question'.*[25]

Benin

In 1892, French soldiers dethroned King Béhanzin of Benin, seized a throne, royal sceptres, sacred doors and other treasures. Most of these have come to the Musée du quai Branly in Paris through legacies and donations. The West-African state has repeatedly asked for their return. Since 2005, French Parliamentarian, Christiane Taubira, has supported the claim. In 2006, for the centenary of Behanzin's death, the Paris museum loaned

thirty objects to Benin; they attracted over a quarter million visitors.[26] In 2016, the Benin government opened negotiations about the return of this war booty. As the nature of the claim – is it an official one or more an effort to study reactions in France? – has remained unclear, the Musée du quai Branly can pretend it has not heard of it.[27]

Indonesia

In 1894, the Dutch colonial army seized what has become known as the Lombok treasure (7.4.). Many objects were transferred to and remained in the museum of the Batavian Society in Jakarta; others were shipped to the Netherlands. In 1977, half of the treasures that were still kept in the Netherlands were transferred to Indonesia. The other half remains in Dutch museum collections.[28]

East Timor

To break the resistance of local kingdoms and to avenge the murder of Portuguese military in 1895, Portuguese soldiers, Timorese irregulars and others destroyed the mountain village of Dato-Tolo. The skulls resulting from their action remain in the Coimbra Museum in Portugal.[29]

Nigeria/Benin City

In 1897, British soldiers ransacked the palace of the Oba of Benin and took thousands of ancient bronzes, brasses and ivories. The objects were dispersed over Europe and North America. There have been repeated requests for their return. In the second half of the 20th century more of such requests were honoured than at the start of the 21st century (12.1.).

Nigeria

The Aro in Eastern Nigeria were not only known for their strong judicial and administrative system but also for their continuous resistance against the British coloniser. In the Anglo-Aro war (1901 – 1902) the British blew up their precious Ibini Ukpabi shrine, which served as an oracle where criminal cases and family disputes were settled.[30]

Indonesia

After the violent subjugation of the Gajo and Alas in Aceh in North Sumatra in 1904 (*'over a quarter of the population'* killed), Dutch military collected *'jewellery, clothing, ceremonial weapons'*, although they had been instructed to act properly, to pay for objects and *'not to rob the bodies of the dead'*. Nowadays the objects are in museums in the Netherlands, Germany and Indonesia and with the descendants of the Dutch Lieutenant-Colonel Van Daalen.[31]

Notes

1   Cohn, *Colonialism and its forms of knowledge*, 104.

2   Greenfield, *Return of Cultural Treasures*, 119.

3   Peter Carey, *The power of prophecy – Prince Dipanagara and the end of an old order in Java, 1785 – 1855* (Leiden: KITLV Press, Leiden, 2008), 341.

4   Suwati Kartiwa, "Pusaka and the Palaces of Java", in ed. Soebadio, *Pusaka: Art of Indonesia*, 160. Stevens, *Bitter Spice*, 37.

5   http://www.algerieinfos-saoudi.com/article-canon-de-brest-alger-veut-rapatrier-la-consulaire-109003848.html;(January 26, 2015); http://www.univ-paris13.fr/benjaminstora/la-memoire/57-archives-historiques-dalgerie-la-memoire-restituee- (January 26, 2015); http://www.lematindz.net/news/7609-algerie-france-la-guerre-des-archives-se-poursuit.html (January 26, 2015); http://in.reuters.com/article/2012/07/04/france-algeria-archives-idINDEE86308M20120704 (January 26, 2015).

6   Stevens, *Bitter Spice*, 57. https://www.rijksmuseum.nl/nl/collectie/NG-1977-279-2-A (March 3, 2016).

7   Cohn, *Colonialism and its forms of knowledge*, 104.

8   http://www.nam.ac.uk/search/node/mutiny (December 14, 2015).

9   Cohn, *ibid.*, 105.

10 Louise Tythacott, "Trophies of War: Representing 'Summer Palace' Loot in Military Museums in the UK", in *Museum & Society*, (Leicester: University of Leicester) November 2015, 13/4, 469.

11 Liu, *Repatriating China's Cultural Objects*, 9, 10.

12 Lawyer Liu Yang, quoted in *The New York Times*, February 17, 2009.

13 http://www.ft.com/cms/s/0/d5e0487a-e003-11e2-bf9d-00144feab7de.html#axzz3MA0K4fBC (December 17, 2014). Chang, *Keizerin*. Liu, *Repatriating China's Cultural Objects*.

14 Groot, *Van Batavia naar Weltevreden*, 481, 482.

15 Prott, *Witnesses to History*, 301.

16 Herskovitch and Rykner, *Restitution des Œuvres d'Art*, 72.

17 The Art Newspaper, October 13, 2004; http://www.britishmuseum.org/explore/highlights/article_index/m/the_maqdala_collection.aspx (February 3, 2015).

18 Richard Pankhurst, "Five thousand Ethiopian manuscripts abroad, and the international community", in *Addis Tribune*, December 12, 1999.

19 Aid expert Frans Werter (email May 25, 2015) discovered the crosses in the early 1990s in a display case of the Pakistani regiment at Malakand Pass; the commander had explained how they had come there from Ethiopia.

20 Greenfield, *Return of Cultural Treasures*, 119 – 121. Kwame Opoku, "When will Britain return looted golden Ghanaian artefacts? A history of British looting of more than 100 objects", in *Modern Ghana News* (Accra: January 5, 2011).

21 Willink, *De bewogen verzamelgeschiedenis*, 206, 353. Initially Willink stated that the two were the same as two Chokwe statues in the Amsterdam Tropenmuseum. He withdrew this after the museum had come with new evidence. Email Willink to director Lejo Schenk of the Tropenmuseum, October 01, 2008.

22 Dutch art dealer Michel Thieme in an interview in *Blad bij NRC* (Amsterdam: NRC Media, September 4, 2016), 31.

23 https://www.rijksmuseum.nl/nl/zoeken?v=&s=&q=schild%20van%20een%20Atjee%C3%ABr&ii=0&p=1 (June 03, 2016). Stevens, *Bitter Spice*, 87.

24 Larissa Förster, "Problematic Provenances – Museum and University Collections from a Post-colonial Perspective", in Deutsches Historisches Museum, *German Colonialism*, 156.

25 Samuel Sidibé, "Priver des communautés de leur patrimoine n'est pas justifiable". in *La Recherche – L'actualité des sciences* (Paris : Mensuel 445/Octobre 1, 2010), 82.

26 Hershkovitch and Rykner, *Restitution des Œuvres d'Art*, 77, 78. Also : http://www.fondationzinsou.org/FondationZinsou/Behanzin_English.html (June 03, 2016).

27 http://www.lemonde.fr/afrique/article/2016/08/01/tresors-pilles-la-france-doit-repondre-positivement-a-la-demande-du-benin_4977095_3212.html#vzgEp5BivwHrRcyD.99 (August 25, 2016). The Le Monde article at the beginning shows a picture with objects from Benin City, an unfortunate confusion. http://www.humanite.

fr/benin-des-tresors-culturels-loin-du-pays-natal-613708 (January 12, 2017).

28 Ewald Vanvugt, *De Schatten van Lombok: Honderd Jaar Nederlandse Oorlogsbuit uit Indonesië* (Amsterdam: Jan Mets, 1994). Wahyu Ernawati, "The Lombok treasure", in eds. Hardiati and Ter Keurs, *Indonesia: The Discovery of the Past*.

29 Ricardo Roque, *Headhunting and colonialism – Anthropology and the circulation of human skulls in the Portuguese empire, 1870 – 1930* (Basingstoke: Palgrave – Macmillan, 2010), 19 ff.

30 Mazi Azubike Okoro 2015. *Perspectives on Aro history and civilization: The splendour of a great past, Vol. 2*, Lulu Public Services (self-publishing); *www.aronewsonline.com/files/Articles.doc* (December 16, 2015). The colonial 1919 Lugard Report says: '*The Aro Fetish, whose ramifications extended throughout the eastern portion of the country – a cult of human sacrifice and slavery – was crushed by force of arms.*'

31 Harm Stevens, "Collecting and 'The rough work of subjugation' – Van Daalen, Snouck Hurgronje and the ethnographic exploitation of North Sumatra", in eds. Hardiati and Ter Keurs, *Indonesia: Rediscovering the Past*, 77, 80, 83. Stevens, *Bitter Spice*, 91.

missionaries collected thirty thousand objects from Congo,[237] among these the ten thousand masks, ancestral sculptures, items of jewellery and other objects that the Swedish Missionary Society gathered and which ended up in the ethnographic museums of Stockholm and Gothenburg.[238] In colonised regions elsewhere, there was similar freedom to gather objects.[239] From 1807 onwards, around 115 missionary orders, mostly coming from countries in Europe and the USA, were active in China.[240] The Society of Foreign Missions of Paris, for instance, was active in ten countries in South and Southeast Asia.[241]

237 Peter Tygesen and Espen Waehle, *Congospor: Norden I Congo – Congo I Norden* (Copenhagen, National Museum, 2003), 5.

238 Gustafsson Reinius, *Touring Congo*, 81.

239 E.g. Van Pesch & Campbell, *Missionaire collecties in beeld*, and Derix, *Brengers van de Boodschap*, 149, 150.

240 https://en.wikipedia.org/wiki/List_of_Protestant_missionary_societies_in_China_(1807%E2%80%931953) (Febnruary, 14, 2017).

241 http://www.mepasie.org/rubriques/haut/qui-sommes-nous (January 23, 2015).

Archives

Both archives of the colonial administration and precious local archives and manuscripts were shipped to the metropolises in Europe in the second period at an increasing rate.[242] The Icelandic manuscripts, shipped *en masse* to Copenhagen in 1720, were a special case; part of it was returned (10.3.).

4.2. Protection and preservation measures

People have always searched for general values, virtues and rights that they share. In Europe such rights were formulated in the 1789 *Déclaration des Droits de l'Homme et du Citoyen*. Men are born free and equal in rights (Art. 1). Liberty, property, safety and resistance to oppression are fundamental rights (Art. 2). Liberty is doing anything that does not harm others (Art. 4).[243] These rights, however, were restricted to Europeans and excluded others. European states also excluded other entities in the Congress of Vienna of 1815, which led to measures to be taken for the protection of the cultural property by Napoleon's armies.[244] Following the emperor's defeat, such property had to be returned, which meant a '*greater emphasis on the (territorial) link between a cultural object and its country-of-origin*', be it only within Europe's boundaries.[245] Objects that Napoleon's soldiers and scientists had taken from Egypt were not returned to that country, but remained in France or were passed to the United Kingdom after it had defeated Napoleon. The Rosetta Stone is an example.

European powers considered territories not ruled by Christians as *terra nullius*, no man's land, entitling them to conquer these lands and to take over the sovereignty by concluding treaties with non-Christian rulers. In the General Act of the Berlin Conference of 26 February 1885 they agreed to *notify* each other of *effective occupations*,[246] which other European powers then respected.[247] It was a small step from a *terra nullius* to a *res nullius*, a no man's object. Cultural objects, including those collected by missionaries and collectors, were res nullius and could be taken without difficulty.

Sometimes, occupying powers introduced legislation to protect indigenous cultural heritage against attempts of scientists, collectors, colonial officials and soldiers from other European countries to get hold of it. Following an 1840 request by French researchers to get permission for a trip to Java and Borneo (7.1.), the authorities in the Dutch East Indies formulated rules that declared temples, statues and other antiquities on the government's territory public property. The export of antiquities required the Governor General's permission. From 1844 onwards, lists of monuments were made.

---

242 Birgitte Hvidt and Karen Skovgaard – Petersen show a great many in *Skatte/Treasures* in the Danish Royal Library (Copenhagen: Royal Library, 2003).
243 http://www.assemblee-nationale.fr/connaissance/constitution.asp#declaration (December 1, 2015).
244 http://blogs.cuit.columbia.edu/congressofvienna/files/2015/03/Mark-Jarrett.pdf (Nov 4, 2015).
245 Lubina, *Contested Cultural Property*, 55.
246 General Act of the Berlin Conference, 26 February 1885, Art. 34.
247 Cohan, *An examination of archaeological ethics*, 26.

In Asia and Africa, European powers set up museums.[248] The Museum of the Asiatic Society in Kolkata opened in 1814. It had paintings, manuscripts, sculptures, bronzes, coins and inscriptions in its collection.[249] The museum of the Batavian Society for Arts and Sciences had a budget for purchasing *objects of essential cultural importance*. It sent less essential objects to institutions like the Museum Volkenkunde in Leiden.[250] France centralised materials collected in its West-African colonies in Dakar, Senegal.[251] King Leopold II ordered the systematic collecting of cultural objects in Congo Free State, after which they had to be shipped to a new museum in Tervuren, which was the central authority in the study and preservation of '*all objects relating to ... history and not being used by any particular body*'.[252] When Congo became a colony of the Belgian State in 1908, the Tervuren Museum decided which objects it would keep for itself, which ones it would allocate to other museums in Belgium or send back to Kinshasa or a regional museum in Congo.[253] The National Museum in Copenhagen had a similar function with respect to colonial objects from Danish colonies (10.2.). Many national museums in former colonies are continuations of colonial museums.[254]

Some European voices criticised the vast amassing of colonial objects. The controversy surrounding the Parthenon Marbles has been mentioned (4.1.). The destruction of the early 18th century Summer Palace complex in Beijing in 1860 met with severe criticism by French writer Victor Hugo[255] and Lieutenant-colonel Garnet Wolseley, who had participated in the looting and had noticed that soldiers '*in body and soul... were absorbed in one pursuit, which was plunder, plunder*'.[256]

In conclusion, the one-way traffic of cultural objects to Europe reached a peak during the consolidation of European colonialism. Admittedly, normal barter and exchange also occurred. Some colonial officials arranged for the preservation of collected objects. Many objects would not have been preserved now, had they not been taken then. Colonial administrators began to set up a museum infrastructure. Yet the overall evidence of collecting through scientific expeditions, missionary iconoclasm, war booty and smuggling by private people and institutions shows that, within the context of European colonialism, the indigenous cultural heritage

---

248 Anne Gaugue, "Musées et colonisation en Afrique tropicale", in: *Cahiers d'études africaines* (Paris: École des hautes études en sciences sociales, 1999), 39/155 – 156: 727 – 745.

249 http://www.asiaticsocietycal.com/museum/index.htm (December 7, 2015).

250 "Annex of a Memorandum on Indonesian Cultural Objects", The Hague: *National Archive*, Archives Dutch Ministry of Foreign Affairs 1975 – 1984, Inv. No.10266.

251 Effiboley, *Musées béninois*, 30.

252 Maarten Couttenier, "Between Regionalization and Centralization: The Creation of the Musée Léopold II in Elisabethville (Musée national de Lubumbashi), Belgian Congo (1931 – 1961)", in *History and Anthropology* (London: Routledge, London, 2014), 25/1:80.

253 Wastiau, *Legacy of Collecting*, 3.

254 John M. MacKenzie, *Museums and empire, natural history, human cultures and colonial identities* (Manchester: Manchester University Press, 2010).

255 Tythacot, *Trophies of War*, 469; Liu, *Repatriating China's Cultural Objects*, 8. At the 150th anniversary of the looting, a statue of Victor Hugo was unveiled ('*Un jour, deux bandits sont entrés dans le Palais d'été. L'un a pillé, l'autre a incindié.*' – One day two thieves entered the Summer Palace, the one looted, the other burned), *China Daily*, October 18, 2010, http://www.chinadaily.com. cn?china/2010-10/18/content _11425824.htm (March 27, 2013).

256 Chang, *Keizerin*, 51.

was in danger and that all three types of violence – direct, structural and ideological – were extensively applied.

Those acquiring cultural objects showed little consideration for the needs of local possessors. The more ideological violence that they applied, the less we know about the biographies of objects. Especially in the provenance of objects from ancient African kingdoms and South American empires, the histories of colonial acquirers and their successors dominate. There is more information about those from Hindu and Buddhist temple complexes in Asia. In addition to well-known violent confrontations between colonial armies and local rulers, there have been numerous smaller, lesser researched raids, in which war booty was captured. Missionaries destroyed many religious objects and confiscated a few, to be used for instruction or collected out of curiosity. The ideological violence led to the denial of the nature of colonial possessions as occupied states and the subsequent justification of the taking of cultural objects by implicitly regarding them as *res nullius*, no man's objects.

The first measures to protect indigenous cultural heritage were taken, even if this was not to the advantage of the indigenous population but to that of the empire and museums in the metropolis. As in the previous period, that of colonial trade and territorial expansion, there were civil society critics of colonialism and certain acquisitions of cultural objects.

Chapter 5

Decolonisation, the first claims and the ongoing seepage of objects

History is called '*a wonder of continuity as well as an orgy of discontinuity*'.[257] The years prior to the transfer of sovereignty in colonies were '*often violent*' and an '*intermittently intense period of crisis*'.[258] Decolonisation therefore swings to discontinuity. In South Asia, the period led to Partition in 1947 and was characterised by extreme violence, '*a human tragedy at the very moment of triumph over colonialism*', which continues to reverberate in the Kashmir conflict.[259] In Algeria, it included cruel fighting against France between 1954 and independence in 1962. In Indonesia the struggle lasted from 1945 until 1949.[260] Yet independence movements had sprung up much earlier; they made decolonisation part '*of some bigger picture*',[261] which includes the dissolution of European colonial empires.

In South America, two factors set this longer process in motion. One was the Haitian Revolution (1791 – 1804). This slave revolt, inspired by the ideals of the French Revolution, was directed against the French colonial administration and the creoles[262] and ended with independence in 1804. It made a deep impression in South America and Europe.[263] The other was the decline of the Spanish empire, Napoleon's occupation of Spain in 1808 and a revolt by creoles against the Spanish, the French and the British domination.[264] Factors in Africa and Asia were the victories of Adowa (1896) and Tsushima (1905) and the emergence of an educated class and anti-colonial movements.

The outcome of the 1914 – 1918 Great War made Europe's decline inevitable. Post-war treaties downgraded Germany. By taking its colonial possessions in Africa and the Pacific, the winners forced Germany back into the position of an imperial power without colonies. At the same time, they did not offer self-determination to these colonies or to the mandatory territories that had been part

---

257 Eelco Runia, "Presence", in *History and Theory* (Middletown, Wesleyan University, Feb. 2006), No. 45, 8, 9.
258 Martin Shipway, *Decolonisation and its impact: A Comparative approach to the end of colonial empires* (Malden: Blackwell, 2008), 1.
259 Burbank and Cooper, *Empires in World History*, 419.
260 William H. Frederick, "The killing of Dutch and Eurasians in Indonesia's national revolution (1945 – 1949): a 'brief genocide' reconsidered", in *Journal of Genocide Research* (Abingdon: Taylor and Francis, 2012), 14/3 – 4, Sept.-Nov., 359 – 380.
261 Shipway, *Decolonisation and its impact,* 2.
262 Creoles are descendants of Europeans in colonial settings in Latin America.
263 Burbank and Cooper, *Empires in World History*, 228. Mbembe, Kritiek van de Zwarte Rede, 29.
264 Burbank and Cooper, *Empires in World History,* 245.

of the then also dissolved Ottoman Empire.[265] Europe continued to consider all them as backward.[266] The League of Nations, set up in 1920, helped the Western powers maintain peace in Europe and keep their global power, but obstructed the aspirations of the colonies and of China and Ethiopia.[267]

In reaction, socialist, communist and nationalist movements arose in colonies. In 1927, they began their own *League against Imperialism*, with headquarters in Brussels.[268] Anti-colonial pamphlets were published. In 1913, Indonesia's education pioneer Soewardi Soerjaningrat criticised the colonial administration for double standards, when it celebrated the centenary of the independence of the Netherlands from France but denied its colony the same right.[269] Anti-colonial forces felt strengthened by US President Woodrow Wilson's idea of self-determination.[270]

The Second World War had even more far-reaching consequences for the political status of colonies. In Asia, it functioned as a '*catalyst*' for rapid independence. In African colonies, it became a '*cause*' for it.[271] Their path to independence was longer.[272] During that War, Italy had been deprived of its colonial possessions – Libya, Eritrea, and Italian Somalia. After the War, Japan lost Indonesia and other possessions in Asia. The British, the French and the Dutch saw their empires crumble – the British Empire breaking up into sixty-four countries. The War had shattered their economies and they became dependent on loans from the USA.

The world entered the bipolar Cold War. The former colonial powers did not want their former possessions to shift to the communist side and minimalised the chances of new countries to set up their own, unifying Third World project. This project with its own ideology and institutions had to enable '*the powerless to hold a dialogue with the powerful, and to try to hold them accountable*'. [273] To extend their hold and safeguard their interests, either formally or informally, the powerful applied extreme violence. Portugal did so in its African colonies, the Netherlands in Indonesia and France in Algeria.[274] With their support for the secession of the province of Katanga, which was rich in raw materials, Belgium, Britain and France showed disrespect for Congo's newly gained independence. The legitimate Kinshasa government saw no other way than to ask the Soviet Union for military assistance,

265 Henk Wesseling, *The European Colonial Empires 1815 – 1919* (Harlow UK: Pearson, 2004), 231, 233. Gissibl, "Imagination and beyond", 162.

266 Vrdoljak, *Return of Cultural Treasures*, 84).

267 Prashad, *Darker Nations*, 21. Mishra, *From the ruins of empire*, 205.

268 Prashad, ibid., 12, 21.

269 R.M. Soewardi Soerjaningrat, *Als ik eens een Nederlander,...* (Bandoeng: Inlandsch Comité tot Herdenking van Neêrlands Honderdjarige Vrijheid, 1913), Vlugschrift No. 1.

270 https://www.mtholyoke.edu/acad/intrel/doc31.htm (December 5, 2015).

271 http://www.activehistory.co.uk/ib-history/extended-essay-history-samples/empire.pdf (December 5, 2015).

272 Shipway, *Decolonisation and its impact*, 233.

273 Prashad, *Darker Nations*, XVIII.

274 The violence against Algerians extended to Paris, where, on October 17 1961, mostly Algerian demonstrators died in clashes with the French police. The estimates of the number of death vary from 48 to 325. Henk Wesseling, *De Man die nooit nee zei – Charles de Gaulle 1890 – 1970* (Amsterdam: Bert Bakker, 2013), 181. Daniel A. Gordon, "World Reactions to the 1961 Paris Pogrom", in: *University of Sussex Journal of Contemporary History* (Sussex: University of Sussex, 2000), 1.

which in turn appalled the USA.[275] France went to great lengths to continue to control Algeria's oil. Britain did the same Malaysia, which was rich in tin and rubber. The high costs of settler colonialism in e.g. South Asia, combined with the increasing resistance, became a reason to grant independence. The Belgium – Congo case especially shows the intertwining of minerals and return negotiations (9.2.).

5.1. Whimsicalities in collecting

Since discontinuity dominated the third period of the European colonial era, it is hard to offer a bird's-eye-view of the collecting of colonial cultural objects in this period. Generally, the peak in collecting of the previous period continued, since there were still wars and raids and expeditions were undertaken on a large scale. But missionaries in West Africa began to question the forced conversions, destruction of indigenous religions and confiscation of ritual objects.

Gifts to colonial administrators and institutions

There is evidence of initial continuity in the passing of gifts by local rulers to colonial administrators.[276] This changed in the run up to the independence of colonies. From then on, gifts became instruments of cultural diplomacy between heads of state.

Objects acquired during private expeditions

Expeditions to unknown and well-known areas, ethnic groups and economic potential continued. There is sufficient evidence of collecting activities. German scholars shipped, under dubious circumstances, the bust of the 14th century BCE Queen Nefertiti from Egypt, which is now in the Egyptian Museum in Berlin, and the blue Ishtar Gate in Babylon from Iraq, dedicated to the goddess of love and beauty (around 575 BCE), which is now in the Pergamon Museum in the same city. In 2002, Iraq urged Germany for the return of the gate,[277] and in 2010 Egypt asked Germany to hand over the bust.[278] Neither request was honoured. In 1929, British geologist E.J. Wayland sent the 17-cm-high, terracotta Luzira Head from Uganda, the country's most important pre-colonial item (Iron Age, 1000 BCE – 800 AD), to Great Britain to be studied. Since 1931, the object has been in the British Museum, which claims it was *'donated'* by Wayland. Requests for its return have remained unsuccessful and the Uganda Museum has to do with a cast.[279]

---

275 Susan Williams, *Who killed Hammarskjöld? The UN, the Cold War and white supremacy in Africa* (London: Hurst, 2013), 36.

276 Rita Wassing-Visser, *Koninklijke Geschenken uit Indonesië,* 94 ff.; Brinkgreve, "Balinese Chiefs and Dutch Dominion", 124, 125.

277 https://www.theguardian.com/world/2002/may/04/iraq.babylon.

278 http://www.nbcnews.com/id/36280732/ns/technology_and_science-science/t/egypt-museums-return-our-stolen-treasures/#.Vl3uY_kvehc (December 1, 2015).

279 Andrew Reid and Ceri Z. Ashley, "A context for the Luzira Head", in *Antiquity* (Cambridge, Cambridge University Press, 2000), 82 (315), 99 – 112. The Monitor, Kampala, October 17, 2004. http://www.britishmuseum.org/research/collection_online/collection_object_details. aspx?objectId=593988&partId=1%20&searchText=buganda&page=1 (December 3, 2015).

Examples of loot and arson/punitive expeditions during decolonisation

China

During the Boxer Rebellion in 1900, soldiers of the Eight-Nation Alliance (Austria-Hungary, France, Germany, Italy, Japan, Russia, the United Kingdom and the United States) seized flags, weapons, gold and silver treasures and money from Boxer troops, palaces and Chinese residences. This *'carnival of loot'* was comparable with that of the ransacking of the Summer Palace in 1860, although fewer items taken in 1900 have surfaced in public collections or at auctions. The Imperial Library was burned down, but it is unknown who started the fire: British or Boxer soldiers.[1] Earlier, in 1898, under the pretext of the murder of German missionaries but in fact *'to stabilize its economic and strategic interests in China'*, Germany had forced China into a 99-year lease agreement of the Bay of Jiaozhou. During military confrontations, German soldiers confiscated parts of the Yongle Encyclopaedia (Ming Dynasty) and 190 flags from the Boxers. In 1955 ten flags and the encyclopaedia were returned (1.2.).[2]

China/Tibet

During an expedition in 1903/4, officers and soldiers of the British-Indian Army killed thousands of Tibetans and looted, against instructions from above, so many manuscripts and other objects from monasteries that hundreds of mules were needed to carry them to India. An unknown quantity of loot ended up in private luggage.[3]

Korea

In 1922, a Japanese governor gave over fourteen hundred objects and over one thousand ancient manuscripts to Japan's emperor. Of these, 167 came from the Joseon Dynasty. During Japan's colonisation of Korea (1905 – 1945), colonial officials amassed large collections of cultural objects, amongst these numerous objects of celadon, bronze Buddhas, a gold crown, works of calligraphy and ancient books. Most have remained in Japan; but a few were returned in 2006.[4]

Notes

1 Chang, *Keizerin*, 378. Liu, *Repatriating China's Cultural Objects,* 10, 11.

2 Deutsches Historisches Museum, *German Colonialism,* 220. Visit to Deutscher Historisches Museum, December 28, 2016. Email Deutscher Historischer Museum, January 12, 2017.

3 Carrington, "Officers, gentlemen and thieves", 102, 104. Also: John Powers, *History as Propaganda: Tibetan exiles versus the People's Republic of China* (Oxford: Oxford University Press 2004), 88.

4 Geoffrey R. Scott, *Spoliation, cultural property, and Japan,* 845 – 847.

Expeditions *'crisscrossed'* the Dutch East Indies to return with *'tools, weapons, articles of clothing and jewellery, which were distributed among Dutch ethnographic museums'*.[280] The trade and exchange in objects, smuggling, broken promises and confiscation do not differ from previous periods.

The fact that countries in South America had gained their independence at the beginning of the 19th century and set up their own museums and scientific societies did not prevent foreign collectors from smuggling thousands of archaeological objects. But what they justified with the salvage paradigm caused a *'redistribution and relocation of antiquities from Peru and Chile to North America and Europe...*

---

280 Ed. David Van Duuren, *Oceania and the Tropenmuseum* (Amsterdam: KIT Publishers, 2011), 97, 99.

where the large collecting museums absorbed them.[281] An example is the four thousand artefacts that Hiram Bingham took over for study from Machhu Pichu in Peru to Yale University in the USA between 1912 and 1916. The condition was that he would send them back, whenever Peru would ask for them.[282] Formal Peruvian requests for restitution in 1918 and 1920 were neglected. In 2001, Peru and Yale University resumed negotiations. Through mediation of a US senator and pressure by Peruvian President Alain Garcia, the Bingham collection was returned in 2011.[283]

The Second World War and subsequent independence struggles stopped expeditions and private collecting activities.[284] Newly independent countries adopted the existing colonial legislation to ban the illicit trade in and smuggling of cultural heritage, but it was not always their priority. Later they enacted new legislation and some acceded to UNESCO Conventions. In those decades, lack of capacity and funds, inequality, poverty, corruption and other factors caused painful peaks in illicit trade and smuggling.[285] ICOM's Red Lists, meant to stop the one-way traffic, offer an indication of the losses.[286]

Objects acquired during military expeditions

To modernise and industrialise the country, Japan's new Meiji dynasty went on the warpath from the late 1860s onwards. It attacked Korea and gained full control over it in 1910. After defeating China in 1895, it annexed Taiwan. After its victory against Russia in 1905, it annexed Manchuria. The whole of China was too big, and there were also many European competitors.[287] In the violent confrontations with Korea, Taiwan and China, Japan confiscated massive war booty. Britain, Germany and other European powers also captured war booty in East Asia in this period (Box: *Examples of loot and arson/punitive expeditions during decolonisation*).

Missionary collecting

Missionary collecting continued in some areas and diminished or intensified in others. Because of the close links between the cross and the sword in South America – i.e. between Spanish conquistadores, Portuguese colonisers, colonial administrators, slave owners and church dignitaries – secularisation started early.[288] In China many Protestant and Roman Catholic missionaries were killed,

---

281 Stefanie Gänger, *Relics of the past: The collecting and study of pre-Columbian antiquities in Peru and Chile, 1837 – 1911* (Oxford: Oxford University Press, 2014), 12.

282 http://www.npr.org/2010/12/15/132083890/yale-returns-machu-picchu-artifacts-to-peru (December 14, 2015).

283 https://plone.unige.ch/art-adr/cases-affaires/machu-picchu-collection-2013-peru-and-yale-university/ case-note-2013-machu-picchu-collection-2013-peru-and-yale-university (December 11, 2015).

284 Corbey (*Tribal Art Traffic*, 31) mentions many 19th century and early 20th century missionary and scientific collectors, and only one for the 1950s.

285 Jos Van Beurden, *Goden, Graven en Grenzen.*

286 http://icom.museum/resources/red-lists-database/ (December 16, 2015).

287 Burbank and Cooper, *Empires in World History*, 302.

288 Roberto González-Casanovas, "Religious-Secular Politics of Jesuit Frontier Missions as Colonies in Ibero-America", in ed. Christopher Hartney, *Secularisation: New Historical Perspectives* (Cambridge: Cambridge Scholars Publishing, 2014) 34 – 57; Hilary M. Carey, "Secularism versus Christianity in Australian history", in Hartney, *Secularisation*, 15.

e.g. in Tianjin in 1870 and during the Boxer Uprising. Freedom of religion, introduced in 1912, led to a fresh influx of missionaries. Although they fought local traditions and images vigorously,[289] I found little evidence of confiscation or destruction of objects.[290] Africa became a continent where missionaries competed to get converts.[291] In the Dutch East Indies missionaries shifted their focus from the Europeans in the colony to converting the local population. They sent back *'thousands of ethnographical objects'* to the Netherlands.[292] Between 1920 and 1970, some 250 missionary exhibitions were organised in the Netherlands (2.3.4.).[293]

In the second half of the 20th century, many a European missionary changed from a *'heroic adventurer'* into a *'sober hard-working pragmatist'*. Local churches were established and destruction and confiscation of religious objects diminished.[294] Due to the secularisation in Europe, from the 1960s onwards, and the decrease in the number of vocations and financial resources, several missionary museums had to close down. They sent back their collections to the headquarters of their congregations or passed them over to nearby regional or national museums, private collectors, the attic or the dustbin.[295] They rarely considered the possibility of returning them to the places of origin.

Archives
In this period, the political nature of holding certain archives became more visible. They contained strategic or incriminating information. King Leopold II ordered the burning of all archives, as he thought that it was nobody's business to see what he had done in Congo Free State; it took his assistants eight days to finish the job.[296] In the 1950s and 1960s, the British government organised *'hundreds'* of operations in *'at least 23 countries and territories'* to make documents that *'might embarrass members of the police, military forces, public servants'* in colonial service literally go up in smoke.[297] As shown later, the Netherlands and Indonesia quarrelled about the possession of archives with incriminating information about the violent 1945 – 1949 period, but finally came to an agreement.

In the negotiations about postcolonial cultural relations between Belgium and Congo, the ownership of archives with information about mineral resources played a crucial role, be it at the background. In 1962, on the eve of Algeria's

---

289 Derix, *Brengers van de Boodschap*, 301, 508.
290 Chang, *Keizerin*. Liu, *Repatriating China's Cultural Objects*.
291 Derix, *Brengers van de Boodschap*, 542.
292 Corbey and Weener, *Collecting while Converting*, 11.
293 Weener, *Missionary exhibitions in the Netherlands*. Interview F-K Weener, May 27, 2011.
294 Leyten, *From Idol to Art*, 140, 142.
295 Weener, *ibid.*, 5, 7.
296 Hochschild, *Geest van Koning Leopold*, 295.
297 The Independent, November 29, 2013, http://www.independent.co.uk/news/uk/home-news/revealed-how-british-empires-dirty-secrets-went-up-in-smoke-in-the-colonies-8971217.html (December 2, 2013).

independence, France took archives about Algeria's infrastructure and has so far ignored return requests of Algeria's National Archive and civil society groups.[298]

5.2. Early (calls for) returns

Long before transfers of sovereignty came into sight, politicians, educated elites and religious leaders in colonies had begun to claim lost cultural heritage. The first that come to my mind are claims from Denmark's Nordic colonies. In the 1830s, the bishop of Iceland asked Denmark to repatriate ancient manuscripts. In the first half of the 20th century, the Icelandic Parliament repeatedly did the same.[299] In 1913, Greenlandic poet and catechist Josva Kleist requested the repatriation of archaeological material from Denmark.[300]

A second claim was formulated in the *Treaty of Versailles* of 1919, which stipulated that '*Germany will hand over to His Britannic Majesty's Government the skull of the Sultan Mkwawa which was removed from the Protectorate of German East Africa and taken to Germany*' (Art. 246). In 1898, a German soldier had taken the skull of Mkwawa, who had helped the British to fight the Germans in what is now Tanzania: but nobody knew where it was.[301] In 1954, seven years before Tanzania's independence, the Überseemuseum in Bremen transferred a skull, said to be Mkwawa's, to a museum in Mkwawa's village, where it remains to this day.[302]

There were returns at the occasion of a country's independence, and instances of colonial rulers and nationalist leaders who searched together for the emblems for the future state. In most instances, traced in this research (there might be many others), the British government, a British museum or a British subject was involved (Box: *(Pre-)independence returns)*. Their erstwhile flexibility contrasts with the rigidity in return matters that characterise many British heritage institutions nowadays.

---

298 http://www.algerieinfos-saoudi.com/article-canon-de-brest-alger-veut-rapatrier-la-consulaire-109003848.html;(January 26, 2015); http://www.univ-paris13.fr/benjaminstora/la-memoire/57-archives-historiques-dalgerie-la-memoire-restituee- (January 26, 2015); http://www.lematindz.net/news/7609-algerie-france-la-guerre-des-archives-se-poursuit.html (January 26, 2015); http://in.reuters.com/article/2012/07/04/france-algeria-archives-idINDEE86308M20120704 (January 26, 2015).

299 Greenfield, *Return of Cultural Treasures*, 19 – 21.

300 Gabriel, *Objects on the Move*, 106.

301 In 1933 the answer to a question in the British House of Commons about the whereabouts of the skull was, that it had not yet been traced, http://hansard.millbanksystems.com/commons/1933/may/24/treaty-of-versailles-sultan-mkwawas-skull (March 05, 2015).

302 Lubina, *Contested Cultural Property*, 200. John Wilson, *Failed Hope: The Story of the Lost Peace* (Toronto: Dundurn Books, 2012), 12.

(Pre-)independence returns

The Netherlands to Indonesia[1]

The loot from the South Celebes Expedition for subjugating the Bone, Gowa and Luwu kingdoms (1905 – 1906) was shipped to the museum of the Batavian Society in Jakarta and Museum Volkenkunde in Leiden. After a special exhibition in 1907, the Leiden museum returned the treasures from Gowa to the kingdom, while the Batavian Society followed with the return of various collections in 1938.[2]

United Kingdom to Sri Lanka

In 1934, the UK returned a throne and footstool of the last kings of Kandy and the crown of King Sri Vikrama Raja Simha. His sceptre, ceremonial sword and cross belt followed in 1936. In this same period a British private citizen sent back an 18th century Kandyan Kastāne sword, acquired by her husband around 1930.[3] Shortly after the country's independence (February 1948), the cranium of Keppetipola, a leader of the 1818 Great Rebellion of the Kandyan people, was returned and put on display in what was then called the Colombo Museum, and now the National Museum.[4] Since 1954 the skull has been kept in an underground glass box in a tomb.[5]

United Kingdom to India

In 1939, the Victoria & Albert Museum in London acceded to the requests of Buddhist worshippers from India and Sri Lanka, who were concerned about the exhibition of the relics of two disciples of the Buddha. Interrupted by the Second World War, the return of the relics occurred in 1947, two years before the Subcontinent's independence. A few years later, the British Museum returned another set of relics.[6]

United Kingdom to Nigeria/ Benin City

In 1938, a British citizen returned regalia of Oba Ovonramwen (sent into exile in 1897) to his grandson Oba Akenzua II. In the 1950s, the British Museum sold thirteen Benin bronze and brass plaques to Nigeria to raise money for the purchase of other African and American ethnographic objects. In 1957, Josephine Walker, widow of Captain Herbert Sutherland Walker (who was involved in the capture of Benin), donated a six-foot-tall Benin ivory tusk to the museum in the city of Jos, Nigeria.[7]

France to Laos

In 1950, France and the semi-autonomous Laos (independent in 1953) agreed on the restitution of Laotian art objects (unspecified).[8]

United Kingdom to Uganda

In 1908, the Reverend John Roscoe had donated the umbilical cord, part of his skin, and a leather case with part of the genital organs (decorated with cowries and glass beads) of Kibuka, the War God of the Baganda, to the Museum of Archaeology and Anthropology at Cambridge University. Shortly before its 1962 independence, Uganda received the relics from the museum. Nowadays such a return would meet with more obstacles, the museum says.[9]

United Kingdom to Ghana

At the occasion of Ghana's independence in 1957, the UK donated an ancient Ashanti stool.[10]

France to Algeria

In 1962, a short time after its independence, Algeria asked France to repatriate 300 paintings and drawings, which had been made by mostly French artists. The colonial authorities had taken the artworks from the *Musée National des Beaux Arts* in Algiers to protect them against the French dissident OAS that wanted to keep Algeria for France. Their repatriation took place in 1969.[11]

Notes

1 Other early returns by the Netherlands to Indonesia are dealt with in 7.2.

2 Budiarti, "The Sulawesi collections", 168, 170.

3 De Silva, *Sri Lanka*, 23.

4 Wickramasinghe, "The return of Keppetipola's cranium", 146. Greenfield, *Return of Cultural Treasures*, 371.

5 http://www.sundayobserver.lk/2012/12/09/fea08. asp (December 18, 2015).

6 Himanshu Prabha Ray, *The Return of the Buddha: Ancient Symbols for a New Nation* (Abingdon, Taylor and Amp, etc., 2013), 120 – 122. Torkel Brekke, "Bones of Contention: Buddhist Relics, Nationalism and the Politics of Archaeology", in *Numen*, (Leiden: Brill, 2007), 54/ 3: 270 – 303.

7 Layiwola, "Benin Massacre", 88, 89.

8 Greenfield, *Return of Cultural Treasures*, 371.

9 Museum of Archaeology and Anthropology at Cambridge University, Inv. Nos. 112078, 112079 and 112080. According to Rachel Hand of the Museum (email February 7, 2014) academics in the 1960s likely '*did not value material culture as much as today*'.

10 Sarah Van Beurden, *Authentically African*, 166.

11 Leturcq, "La question des restitutions d'œuvres d'art", 82. Andrew H. Bellisari, "The art of decolonization: The battle for Algeria's French art, 1962 – 1970" (Cambridge: Cambridge University, conference *Looted Art and Restitution in the Twentieth Century*, unpubl, 2014).

5.3. Drain of cultural objects before and after independence

After 1945, the erstwhile '*Europeanisation of the globe*'[303] turned irreversibly into Europe's '*provincializing*'.[304] The USA and the USSR took over the initiative, followed after 1989 by some of the BRICS countries (Russia, India, and China), two of which had been affected by European colonialism. They felt strengthened by the increase in global and regional institutions and legal instruments and utilised their position inside the United Nations family.

There was continuity through re-colonisation and informal empires.[305] Uruguayan writer Galeano noticed that in his continent the '*goddess of technology does not speak Spanish*' and wondered '*which flags wave above our machines?*'.[306] New countries with mineral resources, such as DR Congo, initially evaded the underdog role in the informal empires, but not for long. A few years after the nationalisation of the copper and cobalt mines in Katanga,[307] the boom in the economy diminished and DR Congo became dependent on international moneylenders.[308] New countries without oil or other mineral wealth, such as Indonesia, were forced to accept donor-led aid consortia.

303 MacKenzie, *European empires and the people*, 1.

304 Dipesh Chakrabarty, *Provincializing Europe* (New Yersey: Princeton University Press, 2000). Mbembe, *Kritiek van de zwarte rede*.

305 John Gallagher and Ronald Robinson, "The Imperialism of Free Trade", in *The Economic History Review* (Chichester: Economic History Society, 1953), 6/1, August: 2 – 15.

306 Eduardo Galeano, *De aderlating van een continent – Vier eeuwen economische exploitatie van Latijns-Amerika*, (Amsterdam: Van Gennep, 1976), 300, 266.

307 Jef Van Bilsen, *Kongo – Het Einde van een Kolonie*, (Leuven: Davidsfonds, 1993), 209. Sarah Van Beurden, *Authentically African*, 136.

308 Van Reybrouck, *Congo*, 397.

There was also continuity in the one-way movement of historical and cultural treasures, albeit with some changes. Like the independence of most colonies in South America at the beginning of the 19th century, the independence of colonies in Asia and Africa after 1945 led to new national borders that restricted the movement of objects from within European empires into their movement within the now independent parts of them. The successor states set their own rules, which built on the colonial legislation initially, as *the total renunciation of colonial law was not conceivable*,[309] but gradually developed into new national legislation for the protection and preservation of cultural heritage.[310] In spite of this, the rise of informal empires in the art and antiquities trade created continuity with the colonial period.[311] New states in Africa and Asia were confronted with sometimes rapidly increasing pillage and smuggling of their cultural properties to the art markets, collectors and museums in Europe, North America and Japan, while they were, and often still are, inadequately equipped to protect and preserve this heritage. Compared with the past, the main change was that Western art and antiquity dealers and their collaborators in former colonies replaced colonial administrators, missionaries and traders.

Several stakeholders and authors separate the tainted flow of objects in colonial times from that in post-independence times. An example is the 2002 *Declaration on the Importance and Value of Universal Museums*, also mentioned earlier, which is intended to end discussion about objects acquired before 1970 as they would have become an inalienable part of their museum's own history. Another is Harry Leyten's suggestion that two Yoruba masks that had left Nigeria after twenty years of existence and subsequently spent another eighty years in a Dutch or missionary context, do not necessarily qualify for return.[312] His suggestion raises the question as to who is to decide about this. Colin Renfrew, like Leyten an outspoken opponent of the *on-going* illicit trade, wishes to *'separate'* the return of recently looted or smuggled antiquities from those that left their country of origin *'more than thirty to fifty years ago'*, which thus includes colonial appropriations.[313]

For the new states, the consequences of the pre- and post-independence contestable flows of objects are quite similar, and I agree with Jim Specht that in the *'neo-colonial relationship the world's art market has assumed the right to treat the culturally significant artefacts of other people as commercial goods to be traded for profit'*,[314] with Kwame Appiah that *'the modern market... in art from much of the*

---

309 Folarin Shyllon, Vincent Négri and Marina Schneider, M. 2009. "The role of national and international legal instruments in the protection of African cultural goods" (Addis Ababa: paper *2nd Pan African Cultural Congress*, 5 – 7 October, 2009).

310 http://www.unesco.org/culture/natlaws/ (January 12, 2016).

311 Jos van Beurden, *Goden, Graven en Grenzen*.

312 Leyten, *From Idol to Art*, 11.

313 Colin Renfrew, "Museum Acquisitions: Responsibilities for the Illicit Traffic in Antiquities", in eds. Neil Brodie, Morag M. Kersel and Kathy Tubb, *Cultural heritage, and the antiquities trade* (Gainesville: University Press of Florida, 2006), 246.

314 Jim Specht, *Pieces of Paradise* (Sydney: Australian Museum Trust, Australian Natural History, Supplement 1, 1988), 5.

global south, is often a dispiriting sequel to … earlier imperial expropriations,[315] and with Kwame Opoku that such a dividing line is to the detriment of the countries of origin, where the unjust nature of the flow back then is '*still intensively felt today*'.[316]

Some source countries have suffered substantial involuntary cultural heritage losses during the European colonial era and have at the same time, appropriated heritage from countries subjugated by them. An example is China. It wants three groups of objects – those looted by French and British soldiers in 1860, those taken by soldiers of the Western Eight Nation Alliance around 1900 after the Boxer Uprising, and those objects – '*at least ten million*', while only 18 of the '*37 large museums in China…survived the war*' – that Japanese soldiers took during the Second World War.[317] It has listed one million objects, distributed over two hundred museums in 47 countries that it wants to retrieve. Liu mentions '*the destructive Cultural Revolution*' (1966 – 1976) during which many objects disappeared,[318] but does not report the disappearance of treasures from Tibetan monasteries and the Potala winter palace in Lhasa.[319] In 1982 some were sent back to Tibet. Numerous others, which were made of gold or silver, were melted down or disappeared otherwise.

5.4. Decolonisation, an unresolved conflict

It has not been hard to find evidence that the decolonisation continues to impact the present. African leaders stated in the *Abuja Declaration* of 1993 that '*the damage sustained by the African peoples is not a "thing of the past" but is painfully manifest in the damaged lives of contemporary Africans*' and '*in the damaged economies of the Black World*.'[320] In 2014, fifteen Caribbean nations unveiled a plan for demanding reparations from former colonial powers for the enduring suffering inflicted by the Atlantic slave trade. They were '*not exclusively concerned with financial transactions*' but '*more with justice for the people who continue to suffer harm at so many levels of social life*'.[321]

The massive disappearance of cultural and historical treasures echoes in former colonies, among heads of state, heritage professionals and ordinary inhabitants. A recent echo comes from the state of Benin, which wants to negotiate with France about the return of war booty and other objects acquired in the French colonial

---

315 Kwame A. Appiah, *Cosmopolitanism: Ethics in a World of Strangers* (Hammondsworth: Penguin, 2007), 116, 117.

316 Kwame Opoku, "Can we condemn contemporary looting of artefacts without condemning colonial loot and plunder? Comment on Lord Renfrew's Statement on Looted Artefacts" in: *Modern Ghana* (Accra: 2008), http://www.modernghana.com/news/193144/50/can-we-condemn-contemporary-looting-of-artefacts-w.html (December 3, 2008).

317 Liu, *Repatriating China's Cultural Objects*, 11, 12.

318 Ibid., 20.

319 E.g. http://tibet.net/2001/01/china-loots-the-potala-again/ and http://tibet.net/wp-content/uploads/2015/04/OFFICIAL-TIBETAN-AND-CHINESE-POSITIONS-ON-THE-ISSUE-OF-TIBET-1994.pdf (January 15, 2016).

320 http://www.ncobra.org/resources/pdf/TheAbujaProclamation.pdf (April 12, 2013).

321 http://www.theguardian.com/world/2014/mar/09/caribbean-nations-demand-slavery-reparations (December 10, 2015).

Five generations of conflict researchers, a critical review

The discipline of conflict studies emerged after the Great War of 1914 – 1918. The *first generation* of researchers (1918 – 1945) was motivated by the horrors of the war and linked itself to peace movements. They developed a multidisciplinary *science of peace* and influenced governments to set up the League of Nations.[1] When conflicts in the labour market increased with the economic crisis of the late 1920s, they also studied these. American pioneer, Mary Parker Follett, appealed to all stakeholders in a conflict to show leadership and serve the common purpose, which was to be the *'invisible leader'* in the solution.[2] She distinguished three ways of dealing with conflicts – (1) domination, (2) compromise and (3) integration. Integration is the most sustainable solution and has as a basis the bringing of *'differences into the open'*. Integration returns in the model for negotiating the future of colonial cultural objects (14.2.).

Parker Follett's three ways of dealing with conflicts[3]

Domination	One party imposes his will upon the other
Compromise	Parties agree, but remain unsatisfied
Integration	Desires of both parties find a place in a solution

The *second generation* (1946 – 1970) set up its own institutions and spread the discipline.[4] Norwegian scholar Johan Galtung defined violence as avoidable violations of basic needs and subdivided these violations into *direct*, *structural* and *ideological violence* (2.2.).[5] The generation was influenced by the Second World War, the Cold War and the continuous arms race. *Peace research* focussed on the prevention of nuclear war, more through negotiations (compromise) than through deterrence (domination).[6]

The *third generation* (1970 – 1989) witnessed rapprochement between the USA and China and Perestroika in the Soviet Union, as well

as the emergence of the women's movement, civil rights and students organisations, and the anti-Vietnam war movement.[7] Its researchers expanded their scope to domestic politics, family conciliation, and labour and community mediation. Galtung elaborated conflict as a triangle with (1) a *contradiction*, an underlying conflict situation or (perceived) incompatibility of goals, (2) an *attitude* or the parties' (mis)perceptions of each other and of themselves, and (3) a *behaviour* that can involve cooperation, coercion or gestures signifying conciliation or hostility.[8] The *Harvard Program on Negotiation*[9] was launched. It is based on four guidelines: (1) separate the people from the problem; (2) focus on interests, and not on positions; (3) look together for fair and creative options; and (4) use objective standards.[10] Some of these return in our model (14.2.).

With the breakdown of the Soviet Union and the Eastern Bloc, several states disintegrated (for instance, the Soviet Union and Yugoslavia) or experienced regime-change (for instance, Ethiopia, DR Congo and Cambodia). The *fourth generation* (1989 – 2001) helped to define the new order and the rapidly increasing intra-state and regional conflicts in Central America, Southeast Asia, the Horn of Africa and the Great Lakes Region in Africa. It prioritised *'the local and indigenous in the peace-building model'*[11] and created space for trans-national and non-governmental organisations.[12] It emphasised *'the communicative and dialogic aspect of conflict resolution'*,[13] which is akin to Parker Follett's integration. This approach also impacts our model (14.2.).

After the attacks on the Twin Towers in New York and the Pentagon in Washington DC in 2001, Western governments lost their interest in conflict studies; they were too soft and irrelevant. A *fifth generation* (2001 – present) has set itself the task of developing a *'cosmopolitan* conflict resolution… that is not situated within any particular state, society or established site of power, but rather promotes constructive means of handling conflict at local through global levels in the interest of humanity'.[14] The model presented later (14.2.) is also cosmopolitan.

Although this last generation is aware of the 'deep logic' of 'full engagement with emerging non-western and non-northern practices and norms',[15] they mostly pay lip-service to it. Their handbooks mention the names of other approaches or simply leave them out. The African Ubuntu is mentioned, but not integrated.[16] One becomes a person through other persons. Ubuntu replaces the Western (Descartes) I think, therefore I am with I am, because we are. African conflict resolution theories emphasise reconciliation and restoring social harmony and have little 'obsession with the punishment of the guilty party'.[17] In others, such as in Deep Democracy the need to face contradictions is prioritised.[18] 'Rather than avoiding or trying to transcend conflict, we steer our craft directly into the issues at the heart of it'. It uses the 'wisdom of the minority' to strengthen majority's solutions.[19] Muslim scholars are re-examining 'Islamic belief-systems' and 'identifying a rich tradition of non-violent conflict management ideas and practices'.[20] The Indonesian Musyawarah-mufakat, which negotiates until a unanimous consensus has been reached, is not mentioned, while it is practiced in villages and in the national parliament. Children learn about it at primary school.[21]

All in all, a wide range of approaches exists and each dispute requires its own approach. This is why the model for negotiating the future of cultural objects has to be open and broad.

Notes

1   Louise Kriesberg, "The Evolution of Conflict Resolution", in eds. Jacob Bercovitch, Victor Kremenyuk and I. William, The SAGE handbook of conflict resolution (Los Angeles: Sage, 2009), 18.

2   Nanette Monin and Ralph Bathurst, "Mary Follett on the Leadership of 'Everyman'", in Ephemera, theory & politics in organization, http://www.ephemerajournal.org/sites/default/files/8-4monin-bathurst.pdf (2008), 8/4, 457.

3   H. Metcalf and L. Urwick, Dynamic Administration – The Collected Papers of Mary Parker Follett (London: Sir Isaac Pitman & Sons, [1941] 1963), 36, 31.

4   Morgan Brigg, The New Politics of Conflict Resolution (Palgrave: Macmillan, 2008), 9. Kriesberg, Evolution of Conflict Resolution, 22. Eds. Oliver Ramsbotham, Tom Woodhouse and Hugh Miall, Contemporary Conflict Resolution: The prevention, management and transformation of deadly conflicts, (Cambridge/UK, Malden/USA: Polity Press, 2011), 50.

5   Johan Galtung, "A Structural Theory of Imperialism", in Journal of Peace Research (Sage Publications, 1971), 8/2; "Cultural Violence", in Journal of Peace Research (1990), 27/3.

6   Ramsbotham ea., Contemporary Conflict Resolution, 42. In the Netherlands, Bert Röhling, judge in the International Military Tribunal for the Far East after the Second World War, belonged to this generation (I was his student). He founded the Polemological Institute in Groningen (polemos = war [ancient Greek]). In De rechter die geen ontzag had – Bert Röling en het Tokiotribunaal (Amsterdam: Wereldbibliotheek, 2014), 225, 363, son Hugo confirms his father's preoccupation with nuclear war.

7   Kriesberg, "Evolution of Conflict Resolution", 21.

8   Ramsbotham ea., Contemporary Conflict Resolution, 10.

9   http://www.pon.harvard.edu/about/ (March 13, 2015).

10 Roger Fisher and William Ury, Getting to yes – Negotiating agreement without giving in (London: Penguin Books, [1981] 2011).

11 Ramsbotham ea., Contemporary Conflict Resolution, 236.

12 Bercovich ea., *SAGE handbook of conflict resolution*, 3.

13 Ramsbotham ea., *Contemporary Conflict Resolution*, 57, 376.

14 Ibid., 55, 265.

15 Ibid., 267.

16 Ibid., 425, 426.

17 Jannie Malan, "Indigenous dispute resolution and reconciliation: Past, present and future" (Gaborone: *University of Botswana*, Centre for Culture and Peace Studies, International Conference on Indigenous Peace building and Dispute Resolution, September 23 – 24, 2010). Meron Zeleke. "*Ye Shakoch Chilot* (the court of the sheiks): A traditional institution of conflict resolution in Oromiya zone of Amhara regional state, Ethiopia", in *African Journal on Conflict Resolution* (Mount Edgecombe, South Africa: 2010), 63 – 84.

18 http://www.deep-democracy.net/view-page.php?page=About%20Lewis%20Deep%20Democracy (January 18, 2015).

19 Myrna Lewis, *Inside the No – Five steps to decisions that last* (Johannesburg: 2008), 73, 42.

20 Mohammad Abu Nimer, in: Ramsbotham ea., *Contemporary Conflict Resolution*, 243.

21 Musyawarah stands for deliberation, mufakat for consensus. During the Sukarno and the Suharto government (1965 – 1998) musyawarah-mufakat was invoked to silence the opposition, K. Kawamawura, *Consensus and democracy in Indonesia: Musyawarah-mufakat revisited*, IDS Discussion paper No. 308 (Tokyo: Japan External Trade Organization, 2011), 4, 6. http://ir.ide.go.jp/dspace/bitstream/2344/1091/1/ARRIDE_Discussion_No.308_kawamura.pdf (February 29, 2016). Personal communication with Wim Manuhutu, March 31, 2016; email with Hasti Tarekat, June 6, 2016.

era (4.1). These and so many other objects that ended up *en masse* in curiosity cabinets, museums and private collections in colonial empires represent a painful past in the present of many a former colony. Considering the many unanswered calls for their return and the lack of preparedness of many Western museums and private owners to study how the objects left their countries of origin and ended up in their possession, one can conclude that the decolonisation has remained an unresolved conflict.

In the conflict research studies mentioned in the box above (Box: *Five generations of conflict researchers, a critical review*), I have found no references to this unresolved conflict and the objects that are part of it. Some consciously omit everything that has to do with culture, arguing that it is too difficult and that culture changes too slowly, is too specific to a region or population, and covers too much.[322] Researchers of fragile states do not touch this unresolved conflict either.[323] Afghan president and economist Ashraf Ghani omits the potential of the repair of damaged monuments and the recovery of lost treasures for peace and development.[324] A frequently mentioned example of this potential is the reconstruction of the bridge of the city of Mostar in Bosnia-Herzegovina.

---

322 Gert Junne and Willemijn Verkoren, eds., *Postconflict development: Meeting new challenges* (London: Boulder, London, 2005), 11.

323 In e.g. *Fixing Fragile States: A New Paradigm for Development*, Seth D. Kaplan (Santa Barbara: Praeger, 2008) mentions social cohesion as recipe to mend failing states but ignores the social cohesion potential of dealings with material cultural heritage.

324 Ashraf Ghani and Clare Lockart, *Fixing Failed States: A Framework for Rebuilding a Fractured World* (Oxford: Oxford University Press, 2008).

In conclusion, by defining three, sometimes overlapping, periods in the European colonial era and applying the typology of colonial cultural objects of Part I, Part II has offered the start of an overview of the massive one-way traffic of cultural and historical objects from colonial possessions to Europe. It shows that during the period of settler and exploitation colonialism the first legal measures to protect material cultural heritage in colonial possessions were taken, but these were more to the advantage of the colonial empire, its museums and elites than to that of local rulers and people, whose heritage needed protection. Decolonisation, defined as a longer period that started with the first signs of the crumbling of the traditional European empires and the increasing calls for self-determination in colonies, is a period that, in most instances, is not over and shows both continuity and discontinuity. The chaos and instability of this third period is reflected in the colonial collecting of the time. The educated elite in colonies began to issue calls for returns. Missionaries and others began to question their views on indigenous religions and collecting methods. For the first time, a European colonial power, Germany, was forced to relinquish objects that finally went back to Africa. After their independence most new states were confronted with a continuing drain of cultural and historical treasure, in which only the actors had changed, with traders and collectors in the lead. The chapter asks conflict researchers' attention for this unresolved conflict and colonial cultural objects.

COLONIAL CULTURAL OBJECTS AND THE LAW

Part III - Colonial cultural objects and the law

Throughout the three periods of the European colonialism, legal protection measures for colonial cultural objects increased, as shown in Part II. Today, this initially empire-based protection has become a major obstacle on a legal route for national claimants of colonial cultural objects. There are big gaps in the provenance information of most objects, and claims are time-barred. This Part lists the contents and the history of the creation of existing hard and soft law instruments, which are available to negotiate the future of colonial cultural objects. It charts what a human-rights and a justice perspective can contribute. Soft law instruments related to other categories of contested heritage – think of colonial human remains and Nazi-looted art – are studied for their relevance to disputes about colonial cultural objects. This part investigates whether the 1998 Washington Conference Principles for Dealing with Nazi-looted Art can be translated for application to colonial cultural objects.

Photograph previous page: Temple Wall (fragment), Angkor Wat, Cambodia.

Chapter 6

Increasing protection?

It requires big leaps from the 1648 and the 1815 limitations on the looting of cultural property during war-time (3.2.) to the *Hague Conventions on the Laws and Customs of War on Land* of 1899 and 1907, and the *Hague Convention for the Protection of Cultural Property in the Event of Armed Conflict* and its *Protocols* (1954 and 1999).[325] Since these conventions are agreements between states, and colonial possessions were never recognised as states, and since they are not retroactive, the measures taken until early in the 20th century have little legal relevance for former colonies and, as far as I know, no former colony has ever invoked them. Further on in this chapter the non-state status of former colonial states is discussed. First there is a consideration of whether there are hard law instruments that are relevant for a discussion of the future of colonial cultural objects.

6.1. Hard law international instruments

This relevance is investigated for two conventions – the 1970 *UNESCO Convention on the Means of Prohibiting and Preventing the Illicit Import, Export and Transfer of Ownership of Cultural Property* and the 1995 *UNIDROIT Convention on Stolen or Illegally Exported Cultural Objects* – henceforward the 1970 UNESCO Convention and the 1995 UNIDROIT Convention. The two offer no legal remedy for disputes about colonial objects. Many present possessors have pedigrees of their objects and made their acquisitions in good faith. The time to claim such objects has been barred, so their relevance is limited. That the conventions are not retroactive deserves further consideration for two reasons. One is the history of their making which shows the urge among former colonies to claim treasures looted or otherwise removed in the colonial era. China tried to include a retroactivity clause in the 1970 UNESCO Convention, but failed due to the resistance of former colonising powers. The other is that both conventions mention the option of bilateral agreements on return of cultural objects removed *before* the convention came into force of thus in principle covering colonial cultural objects (Box: *The relevance of two conventions*).

---

325 Vrdoljak, *International Law, Museums and the Return of Cultural Objects*, 66. Prott, *Witnesses to History*, 180. Lubina, *Contested Cultural Property*, 138, 139.

The relevance of two conventions

1970 UNESCO Convention

Two former Spanish colonies, Mexico and Peru, played a decisive role in the making of the 1970 Convention. The proposal of China and some other states to include *'in the interest of international goodwill'* a retroactive clause that covered colonial cultural objects was unacceptable for art market countries.[1] This observation raises the question whether, given the present global power relations, China's proposal would have met a different fate now. Art. 15 of the Convention opens up the possibility for bilateral agreements on the return of cultural objects removed *before* the convention came into force of. Many of such agreements have been concluded, although none covers the return of colonial cultural objects.[2]

According to a 2012 report,[3] the Convention has led to few court cases, but has enabled police and customs officers to act more decisively in case of suspicion of import of contestable cultural objects. The year of its acceptance, 1970, has become the standard for many in the heritage sector as the year from when one has to apply due diligence in the acquisition of objects. In chapters per region, written by regional experts, the report offers insight into the functioning of the Convention.

Only half of the *African countries* have acceded to the 1970 Convention. Many countries have developed national legislation but have no faith that international regulations can help. They are anxious about the costs and duration of pursuing cases in foreign courts. Tanzania and the Musée Barbier-Müller in Geneva needed years before a Makonde Mask was handed back. Rapporteur Folarin Shyllon calls upon the continent to *'put her house in order'* and to join the Convention.[4]

Asia offers a better picture, with the remarkable exception of countries in Southeast Asia, which suffer under extensive losses of cultural objects. The growth of the art market in China and other countries has serious consequences for the vulnerability of art and antiques. For Asian countries, concludes Keun-Gwan Lee, the Convention has remained something between *'a clarion call'* and *'a set of common rules accepted and implemented in good faith'*.[5] China, for instance, rarely uses multilateral channels and relies on itself.

Although fourteen of the seventeen states in the *Arab world* are states parties, their flourishing art market and large private collections, as well as their weak national legislation, obstruct effective protection of cultural heritage and control of the trade, reports Ridha Fraoua.[6]

According to Kevin Farmer, the *Caribbean* region – with exceptions such as the Bahamas, Trinidad, Jamaica and Barbados – has done little to enforce concepts contained in the Convention.[7] There was no report about Central and South American countries; most of these are states parties, though.[8]

The United States of America and Canada were among the first Western-market countries to join the Convention, writes Patty Gerstenblith. It has led to significant changes in import laws for cultural objects, closer cooperation between states parties through bilateral agreements and *'potential reforms in acquisition practices by private institutions'*.[9]

Most European states have joined the Convention, but *'very few have adopted incorporation laws'*, concludes Marie Cornu. Some states focus on legal aspects, while others highlight operational features and the need for more cooperation in combating the illicit trade.[10]

1995 UNIDROIT Convention

Many former colonies that participated in the making of the Convention faced large-scale losses of cultural heritage, both in the past and in the present. The UNIDROIT Convention was the private international law answer to loopholes in the 1970 UNESCO Convention. It arranged the status of the good faith or *bona fide* private acquirer and the issue of time limitations of claims.[11] Art. 4.4. requires the possessor to prove his due diligence, if he wants to be compensated. Art. 9.1. mentions the possibility of bilateral agreements about the return of cultural property – thus including colonial cultural objects – removed from the country of origin before its implementation. Art. 10.3 states that the absence of a retroactivity provision does not mean that previous theft and smuggling are whitewashed and offers the option of retroactivity. Patrick O'Keefe and Lyndel Prott consider this *'a favourable evolution'*, be it the maximum achievable.[12] Next to some Scandinavian, East and South European countries, most states parties to the Convention are former colonies, all in all thirty-seven.[13] The convention only offers a chance to former colonies if more major colonial powers become State party and are willing to conclude bilateral agreements.

Notes

1   Vrdoljak, *International Law, Museums and the Return of Cultural Objects*, 207. Lubina, *Contested Cultural Property*,124. Patrick J. O'Keefe, *Commentary on the 1970 UNESCO Convention – Second Edition* (Crickadarn, Builth Wells: Institute of Art and Law, 2007), 9.

2   The USA and China each concluded bilateral agreements with over ten countries, mostly former colonies, http://eca.state.gov/cultural-heritage-center/cultural-property-protection/bilateral-agreements (December 21, 2015) and http://icom.museum/uploads/tx_hpoindexbdd/RedListofChineseCulturalObjectsatRisk-English.pdf (July 4, 2016). Colombia concluded one with Ecuador, Lithuania and the Russian Federation (O'Keefe 2007: 90). One between Thailand and Cambodia led to the return of a Cambodian temple wall, trucked to Thailand in 1999.

3   The reports were presented at the Second Meeting of States Parties to the 1970 Convention, Paris, 20 and 21 June, 2012: http://www.unesco.org/new/en/culture/themes/illicit-trafficking-of-cultural-property/meeting-of-states-parties/2nd-msp-2012/ (January 20, 2015).

4   http://www.unesco.org/new/fileadmin/MULTIMEDIA/HQ/CLT/pdf/Shyllon_en.pdf, 32 (January 18, 2016).

5   http://www.unesco.org/new/fileadmin/MULTIMEDIA/HQ/CLT/pdf/Lee_en.pdf, 16 (January 18, 2016).

6   http://www.unesco.org/new/fileadmin/MULTIMEDIA/HQ/CLT/pdf/Fraoua_en.pdf, 19 (January 18, 2016).

7   http://www.unesco.org/new/fileadmin/MULTIMEDIA/HQ/CLT/pdf/Farmer_en.pdf, 19 (January 18, 2016).

8   http://www.unesco.org/eri/la/convention.asp?ko=13039.

9   http://www.unesco.org/new/fileadmin/MULTIMEDIA/HQ/CLT/pdf/Gerstenblith_en.pdf, 15 (January 18, 2016).

10 http://www.unesco.org/new/fileadmin/MULTIMEDIA/HQ/CLT/pdf/Cornu_en.pdf, 2 (January 18, 2016).

11 Patrick O'Keefe and Lyndel Prott, *Cultural Heritage Conventions and Other Instruments: A compendium with commentaries* (Pentre Moel, Crickadarn, Builth Wells, Institute of Art and Law, 2011), 110.

12 Ibid., 112.

13 http://www.unidroit.org/status-cp (December 21, 2015).

UNESCO Intergovernmental Committee for return and restitution (ICPRCP)
In order to fill the vacuum, which had been created by the absence of a
retroactivity clause in the 1970 UNESCO Convention, UNESCO installed the
*Intergovernmental Committee for Promoting the Return of Cultural Property to its
Countries of origin or its Restitution in case of Illicit Appropriation* – henceforward
the ICPRCP – in 1978. The ICPRCP discusses objects of fundamental significance
that were lost as a result of colonial or foreign occupation or as a result of illicit
appropriation. Return or restitution of colonial cultural objects was thus a central
task. Using this opportunity, Sri Lanka submitted a remarkably detailed *Catalogue
of Antiquities and other Cultural Objects from Sri Lanka (Ceylon) Abroad* to the
ICPRCP in 1975. It covered 27 countries and 140 institutions. I have not found
evidence that the submission led to returns.[326]

There are concerns about the effectiveness of the ICPRCP. Given *'the ideological
gulf between participants of opposed political persuasions',*[327] its mandate remained soft
and became a *'forum for the amicable resolution'.*[328] In its nineteen sessions so far,[329]
it has advised formally in about five cases and helped informally as a facilitator
between member states and public and private stakeholders (Box: *Cases dealt with
by ICPRCP*).[330] Discussions about colonial treasures have largely disappeared
and been replaced by disputes about cases of recent theft and smuggling. Former
colonies rarely use the ICPRCP road, although enough opportunities seem to
present themselves. Peru, Guatemala, Mexico, and Costa Rica could have invoked
the ICPRCP's services recently, but have chosen not to do so.[331] This fairly overall
reluctance surprises many.[332] Shyllon criticises Nigeria for never formally requesting
the return of the Benin treasures, when it was selected in the ICPRCP committee
(12.2.).[333]

---

326 P.H.D.H. de Silva, *A Catalogue of Antiquities and other Cultural Objects from Sri Lanka (Ceylon)
     Abroad*, (Colombo: Government of Sri Lanka, 1975).

327 Jim Specht of the Queensland Museum, Brisbane, after attending a meeting of experts in Senegal in
     1978, in Prott, *Witnesses to History*, 28.

328 Maria Vicien-Milburn, Asoid García Márquez and Fouchard Papaefstratiou, "UNESCO's role in
     the resolution of disputes on the recovery of cultural property", in *Art and Heritage Disputes in
     International and Comparative Law, Transnational Dispute Management* (5/2013), 1.

329 http://www.unesco.org/new/en/culture/themes/restitution-of-cultural-property/sessions/19th-
     session-2014/ (December 27, 2014).

330 http://www.unesco.org/new/fileadmin/MULTIMEDIA/HQ/CLT/pdf/3_Report_Secretariat_19_
     ICPRCP_en.pdf (December 27, 2014).

331 In 2013, Peru (67) , Guatemala (13), Mexico (51) and Costa Rica (number unknown) claimed individually
     tens of objects, illegally exported from their territories, acquired by the Barbier-Müller museum since
     the 1920s and prepared for auction by Sotheby's in Paris, https://chasingaphrodite.com/2013/03/19/
     red-flags-in-paris-half-of-sothebys-barbier-muller-pre-colombian-sale-lacks-provenance/ (June 8, 2016).
     All in all, three hundred objects were auctioned for over €10 million. http://www.sothebys.com/en/
     auctions/2013/collection-barbier-mueller-pf1340.html (August 25, 2016).

332 Lyndel Prott, *Strengths and Weaknesses of the 1970 Convention: An Evaluation 40 years after its adoption*
     (Paris: UNESCO, Background paper (2nd edition) for Second Meeting of States Parties in the 1970
     Convention, 20 – 21 June 2012), 5. Kwame Opoku, "Will Nigeria finally raise restitution of Benin
     Bronzes at UNESCO Governmental Committee" in: http://www.museum-security.org (August 17,
     2013).

333 Folarin Shyllon, "Museums and universal heritage: Right of return and right of access" in: http://
     www.blackherbals.com/museums_and_universal_heritage.htm (August 21, 2014).

In 2011, over three decades after the establishment of the ICPRCP, the International Commission of Museums ICOM launched, in cooperation with the Arbitration and Mediation Centre of the World Intellectual Property Organisation (WIPO), its *Art and Cultural Heritage Mediation*. It differs from ICPRCP in that the UNESCO Committee offers procedures for mediation and conciliation, whereas ICOM-WIPO offers only mediation.[334] The ICPRCP focuses on return and restitution of cultural objects; ICOM-WIPO includes issues of insurance of artworks, loans, and even misappropriation of traditional cultural expressions.[335] The ICPRCP operates at intergovernmental level. ICOM-WIPO goes further: private parties can also apply for mediation. So far, ICOM-WIPO has offered its services in one case, that of the transfer of a Makonde Mask from the Barbier-Müller Museum of Geneva to the National Museum of Tanzania (Box: *Cases dealt with by the ICPRCP*); it then cooperated with the ICPRCP.[336]

Experts disagree whether international customary law can help former colonies. Wojchiech Kowalski claims that the development of the principle of unconditional restitution of cultural property looted in war was completed in 1815, and that restitution and a ban on looting have become '*generally accepted international customs*' since then.[337] Katja Lubina admits that there have been returns of colonial cultural objects, but this '*does not mean that one can speak of state practise as is required for the existence of customary rules*'; an accepted state practice means: sufficient duration, uniformity and spread. International public law and customary rights therefore do not '*provide a basis for claims for the restitution of cultural objects removed during the colonial era*'.[338] According to Evelien Campfens, developments are so rapid that '*the obligation to return cultural property looted in war*' and its '*counterpart... the prohibition of pillage... today have acquired the status of international customary law*'.[339] The disagreement makes it doubtful whether international customary law can effectively be invoked for involuntary lost colonial objects.

6.2. Soft law international instruments

Among soft law instruments that are relevant to colonial cultural objects, are UN resolutions and declarations, codes of conduct and guiding principles. Some are meant for dealing directly with claims of colonial cultural objects, others for disputes about (colonial) human remains and Nazi-looted art.

Initially, former colonies felt encouraged in their claims for colonial cultural objects by the 1970 UNESCO Convention.[340] In December 1973, DR Congo submitted General Assembly Resolution 3187 (XXVIII) on the *Restitution of works*

---

334 Sabrina Urbinati, "Alternative Dispute Resolution Mechanisms in Cultural Property Related Disputes: UNESCO Mediation and Conciliation Procedures", in eds. Vadia and Schneider, *Art, Cultural Heritage and the Market*, 2014: 113.
335 http://www.wipo.int/amc/en/center/specific-sectors/art/icom/ (March 25, 2015).
336 http://archives.icom.museum/press/MM_PressFile_eng.pdf (March 25, 2015).
337 Kowalski, "Types of Claims for Recovery", 86, 87.
338 Lubina, *Contested Cultural Property*, 134, 140.
339 Campfens, *Fair and Just Solutions?*, 13.
340 E.g. Quinnell, "Before it is too late", 95.

Cases dealt with by the ICPRCP

Parthenon Marbles

Earlier (4.1.), the case of the Parthenon Marbles was explained. The ICPRCP has done much to get Greece and the United Kingdom together to solve their dispute about these. So far there is no solution, and prospects for it remain meagre.

Boğazköy sphinx

The ICPRCP helped to solve the dispute about two sphinxes and ten thousand four hundred cuneiform tablets, taken from Boğazköy excavations in Anatolia in Turkey to Germany for restoration and study in the early 20th century (5.3.). Between the 1920s and the 1930s, one sphinx and three thousand tablets were returned. In 1987, the then German Democratic Republic returned the remaining 7,400 cuneiform tablets. In 2010, the ICPRCP advised to return the other sphinx. In 2011, it was handed over to the Turkish authorities.[1]

Makonde mask

Together with ICOM (International Council of Museums), the ICPRCP mediated the transfer of a Makonde mask by the Barbier-Müller museum in Geneva to the Republic of Tanzania in 2010. It was one of seventeen artefacts that had been stolen from the National Museum of Tanzania in 1984. For a long time, both parties had claimed to be its rightful and bona fide owner. Finally, the two agreed that the Geneva museum would *donate* the mask to Tanzania. The whereabouts of the other sixteen artefacts remain unknown.[2]

Kneeling Khmer attendants

The ICPRCP informally facilitated discussions between Cambodia and the Metropolitan Museum of Art in New York about two 10th century Koh Ker stone statues of kneeling attendants, which had been looted around the country's civil war in the 1970s. They were donated to the American museum in four separate gifts between 1987 and 1992. The intervention led to their return in 2013.[3]

Khurvin treasure

Iran accused the widow of the physician of the Shah of having smuggled out 349 clay and bronze archaeological objects from the necropolis of Khurvin and dating from around 1.000 BCE, via the Belgian diplomatic bag in 1965.[4] The ICPRCP suspended the preparation of an advice, as litigation was pending. In a Belgian court, the possessor argued that she did not want the objects to end in the *'hands of the ayatollahs'.*[5] At the end of 2014, the Court of Appeal in the Belgian city of Liege ruled in favour of Iran; the widow's daughter had to pay the costs of sequestering the objects in Belgium during the long period. A few days later, the objects were flown home from a university museum in Brussels to Teheran.[6]

Notes

1   http://www.unesco.org/new/en/culture/themes/
    restitution-of-cultural-property/committes-
    successful-restitutions/bilateral-agreement-on-
    the-bogazkoy-sphinx/ (December 27, 2014).
    Today's Zaman, 27 November 2011, http://
    www.todayszaman.com/news-264110-bogazkoy-
    sphinx-back-home-after-94-years-from-germany.
    html (23 September 2013). Boz, Zeyneb B.
    "Bogazkoy Sphinx and Turkey's policy on return
    and restitution cases", paper Conference on the
    Return of Cultural Property, South Korea, 2012,
    https://www.academia.edu/6644263/Bogazkoy_
    Sphinx_and_Turkeys_Policy_on_Return_and_
    Restitution_Cases (September, 23, 2013).

2   Personal communication with Caroline Mchome,
    Ministry of Natural Resources and Tourism,
    Tanzania, June 21, 2015.

3   http://whc.unesco.org/en/news/1029 (July 6, 2015); http://www.nytimes.com/2013/05/04/arts/design/the-met-to-return-statues-to-cambodia.html?_r=0 (July 12, 2016).

4   Prott, *Witnesses to History*, 40, 407.

5   Daily *Le Soir* of October 4, 1988. "L'Iran voudrait bien récupérer des objets d'art", http://archives.lesoir.be/tribunal-civil-de-bruxelles_t-19881004-Z010L0.html (August 21, 2013).

6   http://www.iran-daily.com/News/57999.html (June 28, 2015) ; http://archaeologynewsnetwork.blogspot.nl/2014/12/belgium-to-return-stolen-artefacts-to.html#.VY-yxvntlBc (June 28, 2015) ; http://en.mehrnews.com/news/105220/Stolen-Iranian-antiques-returned-from-Belgium (June 29, 2015); http://www.lambrechtlaw.be/en/news/2015/8/31/the-khurvin-case (January 8, 2016).

of art to countries victims of expropriation, which was meant to alleviate the absence of a retroactivity clause in the Convention. The Assembly explicitly deplored '*the wholesale removal, virtually without payment, of* objets d'art *from one country to another, frequently as a result of colonial or foreign occupation*' and affirmed '*that the prompt restitution*' of them, '*without charge, is calculated to strengthen international cooperation inasmuch as it constitutes just reparation for damage done*'. The resolution recognised '*the special obligations*' of former colonial powers. In 1975, DR Congo submitted a watered-down Resolution 3391, with the same title as the one of 1973: instead of covering '*all objects*' it was limited to '*small representative collections, where such did not exist*'.[341] Comparable resolutions have been accepted in the following years. The item has been kept on the UN agenda but has produced little effect.

6.2.1. Instruments for the repatriation of human remains

Especially from the second half of the 19th century onwards, human remains – skulls, foetuses, pelvises, bones, hair and blood samples – were massively collected from battlefields, hospitals and other places in colonial possession. The same occurred in internally colonised areas. In some places, for instance Dutch-controlled Papua, collecting continued until after 1945. The human remains that were collected did not always stay within the borders of the colonial empire, but could be spread throughout Europe.[342]

From the 1930s onwards, indigenous groups and civil society organisations in the USA, Canada and Australia have claimed ancestral lands, human remains and funerary objects. They have shifted the balance in the control over these from universities, museums, scientists and heritage professionals to source communities. Because of the horror of the Nazi racial policies, such policies were also brought into question for colonies, and this led to a shift in, for instance, West-Africa.[343] Hard and soft law instruments came into being for dealing with human remains.

The 1990 Native American Graves Protection and Repatriation Act (NAGPRA) stands out as a hard law instrument. NAGPRA enables native groups in the USA to recover human remains and funerary objects from federal agencies and federally

---

341 Prott, *Winesses to History*, 14.
342 Fenneke Sysling, *De onmeetbare mens – Schedels, ras en wetenschap in Nederlands-Indië* (Nijmegen: Van Tilt, 2015), 25, 26, 29, 42.
343 Leyten, *From Idol to Art*, 342.

Incidental returns of colonial human remains

Germany/Great Britain to Tanzania

After the death of the anti-colonial Sultan Mkwawa in 1898, a German soldier took his skull. The Treaty of Versailles of 1919 that made Tanzania part of the British Empire stipulated that Germany passed it to the United Kingdom. In 1954, the Überseemuseum in Bremen transferred a skull, which was said to have been of Mkwawa, to Tanzania, which was still a British colony then. Since then, it has been kept in a museum in Mkwawa's village.

Great Britain to Kenya

In 1981, the Natural History Museum in London returned the skull of the *Proconsul Africanus*, an ape over fourteen million years old, to Kenya. After discovering the skull in 1948, Mary Leaky had taken it to London for detailed study.[1]

France to South Africa

In 1810, a British businessman smuggled Khoikhoi woman *Saartjie Baartman* aboard a ship to Europe. She was the female slave of Dutch farmers, who had captured her in a raid, in which her other family members had been killed. The businessman exhibited her as the *Hottentot-Venus* at fairs in London and Paris. In 1815, she died of an infectious disease. Her remains ended up in the Museum of Natural History in Paris. From the 1940s onwards, there had been claims for her repatriation. After a formal request by President Nelson Mandela in 1994, it took another eight years of debates in the French National Assembly and a special Act to let Saartjie cease to be part of a French public collection (her inalienability was lifted). After this she could rest in peace in her native area.[2]

Spain to Botswana

A comparable case is that of a deceased Tswana warrior. When a French collector and trader witnessed this warrior's burial in 1830, he secretly dug up the dead body. After preparing it with metal, wood and newspaper as stuffing materials, he took it to Paris, from where it travelled to the world exhibition in Barcelona of 1888, and ended up in the nearby Darder Museum in Bayoles in Spain. In 1992, when the Olympic Games in Barcelona were to be held, a Spanish doctor of Haitian origin suggested that the remains were removed from the museum. He got wide support for this. Taken from the public view in 1997, the body was returned to Botswana in 2000 and reburied there.[3]

The Netherlands to Ghana

In 1838, *King Badu Bonsu II* killed two Dutch emissaries. His subjects handed this apparently unpopular ruler over to Dutch traders, who hanged him and took his head to the Netherlands. Informed by Dutch novelist Arthur Japin, Ghana formally requested the repatriation of the King's head. In 2009, the Dutch government honoured this request with the argument that the head no longer had any scientific or cultural value for the Netherlands.[4]

France to New Zealand

In 2006, the re-opening of the municipal museum of Rouen led to a discussion about a decorated Maori head that had been in Rouen since 1875. While the deputy mayor favoured repatriation for ethical reasons, the museum and the French Ministry of Culture and Communication referred to the inalienability of the head, which had become part of France's national collection. It took several court cases and a special Act in the French Parliament, before this (and other decorated Maori heads) was returned in 2010.[5]

Austria to South Africa

The well-known Austrian anthropologist, Rudolf Pöch, collected colonial human remains for the Natural History Museum in Vienna. From 1907 to 1909, he sought San remains. Among what he brought back, were those of *Klaas and Trooi Pienaar*. Recent research has, however, damaged his charisma, because of his *'systematic grave robbery and of clandestine deals for newly dead corpses'*. It appeared that the Pienaar couple had been exhumed three or four months after their death. From 2008 onwards, efforts to bring the two bodies back to South Africa were finally successful, and the couple was reburied in Kuruman, South Africa, in 2012. Earlier the Natural History Museum of Vienna had returned Aboriginal remains to Australia.[6]

Germany to Namibia

In 2011, a Namibian delegation took twenty skulls – eleven from Nama and nine from Herero people – from the Charité university hospital in Berlin back to Namibia. German race science researchers had taken them *'under exceedingly dubious circumstances'* in the early 20th century from Namibia. The delegation's proposal, that Germany formally acknowledged the colonial injustice wreaked upon the Namibians, was rejected. This occurred only in 2015.[7]

Australia to Papua New Guinea

In 2012, the Maclea Museum of Sydney University repatriated five skulls, which originated from communities in the Sepik River, the Western Province and the Gulf Province and were said to be more than a hundred years old. They had been acquired before Papua New Guinea's independence in 1975 and were part of a private collection. When descendants of the collector offered them for sale, the Australian authorities stopped this. As it was difficult to establish their place of origin, the National Museum and Art Gallery in Port Moresby has given them a home.[8]

France to New Caledonia

Part of the Nouméa Accord on self-determination between France and New Caledonian political parties of 1998 was the repatriation of the head of Kanak chief *Atai*. He had been the leader of an anti-colonial insurrection in 1878, in which two hundred Europeans and one thousand Kanaks had died. Atai's head had been cut off and taken to the National Museum of Natural History in France then. The repatriation took place in August 2014.[9]

Notes

1   ICOM, *Illicit traffic of cultural property in Africa*, (Paris: ICOM, 1995), 79.

2   Prott, *Witnesses to History*, 288/9. Hershkovitch and Rykner, *Restitution des Œuvres d'Art*, 99/100. Ciraj Rassool, "Human remains, the disciplines of the dead and the South African memorial complex", in eds. D. Peterson, K. Gavua and Ciraj Rassool, *The politics of heritage in Africa* (Cambridge: Cambridge University Press, 2015), 134.

3   Frank Westerman, "The man stuffed and displayed like a wild animal", *BBC Magazine* (London: BBC, September 16, 2016), http://www.bbc.com/news/magazine-37344210 (December 21, 2016). Frank Westerman, *El Negro en ik* (Amsterdam: Atlas, 2004), 237.

4   Jos Van Beurden, *Return of Cultural and Historical Treasures*, 26.

5   Hershkovitch and Rykner, ibid., 96 – 98.

6   Rassool, ibid., 151.

7   Deutsches Historisches Museum, *German Colonialism*, 146.

8   http://sydney.edu.au/museums/research/repatriation.shtml (August 26, 2016).

9   https://news.artnet.com/in-brief/france-returns-new-caledonian-rebel-chiefs-skull-89168 (April 27, 2015); http://www.theguardian.com/world/2014/nov/03/france-museums-restitution-colonial-objects (December 23, 2015).

Return-refusals for colonial human remains

Great Britain to Zambia

In 1921, workers of the Broken Hill Mines in Northern Rhodesia found the skull of the *Homo Rhodensiensis*. The General Manager gave it to the British Museum, although this was *'contrary to the existing regulations'* that *'prohibited export of Bushman relics without a permit'*.[1] From around 1975, Zambia has pursued its restitution. The 125,000-year-old, almost complete skull and accompanying bones remain *'the most single important hominin find'* in Zambia. Zambians consider its smuggling as a wrong. *'At the local level, there is great demand for the skull by museum visitors, who consider its absence a real loss'*.[2] On its website, the Natural History Museum in London, where it currently is, does not mention the skull's disputed provenance.[3]

Italy to Papua New Guinea

In 1877, Italian explorer Luigi D'Albertis met the Boazi ethnic group in the Little Fly region of Papua New Guinea. Fearing they were cannibals, D'Albertis killed headman Kasikanawa, had his head sawn off, put it in a glass, filled with alcohol, and took it to Italy. When British traveller-writer Redmond O'Hanlon visited the descendants of the headman in 2014, Kasikanawa's successor asked for the head's whereabouts, as he wanted it to be returned. O'Hanlon discovered it in the attic of the Natural History Museum of Florence, which was reluctant to put it on display for fear of a return-claim.[4]

France to Senegal

Senegal has been asking France for the repatriation of the remains of Sihalebé, the last King of the Casamance (Senegalese region south of the Gambia). The King had died in starvation in 1903. France continues to hesitate as long as the people of the Casamance fight for independence.[5]

Notes

1   ICOM, *Illicit traffic of cultural property in Africa*, 193.

2   Francis B. Musonda, "Decolonising the Broken Hill Skull: Cultural loss and a pathway to Zambian archaeological sovereignty", in *African Archaeological Review* (New York: Springer, 2013), Vol. 30, 195 – 220. Emails F.B. Musonda, University of Zambia, January 24, 2014, February 22, 2014.

3   http://www.nhm.ac.uk/nature-online/collections-at-the-museum/museum-treasures/broken-hill-skull/index.html (January 13, 2015)

4   http://historiek.net/redmond-ohanlon-ontdekt-lang-verdwenen-kannibalenhoofd/39723/ (January 13, 2015).

5   Jordi Tómas, "The traditional authorities cross the border: Opposing views on the role of the religious leaders of the Jola Huluf and Ajamaat of the Lower Casamance", in *Africana Studia*, 9 (Porto: University of Porto, 2006), 73 – 97. http://www.theguardian.com/world/2014/nov/03/france-museums-restitution-colonial-objects (December 23, 2015).

funded museums. These institutions have to inventory and repatriate remains and objects, which they acquired before 1990. NAGPRA criminalises the trafficking of human remains and objects and provides guidelines for their excavation. The act has made the debate about human remains *'truly international'*.[344] It shows the importance of legislative measures and has strengthened the right of native groups to reclaim human remains and related objects.

---

344 Lubina, *Contested Cultural Property*, 194.

Successful repatriation of Maori heads

In 2003, the *Museum of New Zealand Te Papa Tongarewa* began a campaign for repatriating tattooed ancestral Maori heads and other remains. In addition to the fifty-four that it possessed already, over seventy heads have been repatriated. They come from (university) museums and collections in Great Britain, Scandinavia, Switzerland, France,[1] Germany, Ireland, the Netherlands, the USA, Canada, Australia, Hawaii and Argentina.[2] An estimated one hundred are still thought to be overseas.[3] In 2015, the Swedish Karolinska Institute promised to return several heads. The Viennese World Museum returned the remains of a child.[4] In 2016, following five years of negotiations, the National Museum of Natural History in Washington returned four heads. Two other institutions in the USA and three in the United Kingdom returned one each.[5] In 2017, the Pitt Rivers Museum in Oxford will follow. From 1987 onwards, Maori heads on permanent display were removed and replaced with an explanation of their meaning and the reason for their removal.[6]

The success of the campaign is due to a firm commitment of Maori communities, the museum and the government of New Zealand and to new views in the Western heritage institutions. *'These items being stolen or traded is an example of historical practices we're now deeply ashamed of'*, said an expert of the University of Birmingham. *'To keep them would be wrong'*. Roseanna Maxwell of New Zealand expressed her gratitude: *'This shows others… how to take a look in their own closets and repatriate to culturally affiliated tribes'.*[7] Museum Volkenkunde in Leiden applied two principles to justify the return of a Maori head in its collection: for dealing with human remains *'the current practice in countries of origin'* is determinative, and the *'title of direct descendants'* outweighs *'the formal property rights of the State of the Netherlands'.*[8]

On their homecoming in New Zealand, remains are ceremonially welcomed and go into quarantine. The Te Papa Tongarewa museum takes care of them, until they can be returned to their kith and kin.[9]

Notes

1   It took court cases and a special Act before this and other decorated Maori heads in public collections were repatriated, Hershkovitch and Rykner, *Restitution des Oeuvres dearth*, 96 – 98.

2   http://www.noodls.com/view/CDBE9440 BE782FEDAC65C1EEE857DB859 246DE42?7428xxx1425303769 (May 28, 2015); http://www.nzherald.co.nz/nz/news/article. cfm?c_id=1&objectid=11392177 (May 28, 2015) 532http://www.tepapa.govt.nz/AboutUs/ Repatriation/toimoko/repatriation/Pages/ HowmanyToimokohavealreadybeenrepatriated fromoverseas.aspx (June 11, 2013).

3   http://www.tepapa.govt.nz/AboutUs/Repatriation/ toimoko/repatriation/Pages/Howmany Toimokohavealreadybeenrepatriated fromoverseas.aspx (June 11, 2013).

4   http://www.tepapa.govt.nz/AboutUs/Media/Pages/

vienna-repatriation-may2015.aspx (May 28, 2015).

5   https://www.tepapa.govt.nz/international-repatriation (January 27, 2017). https://www. theguardian.com/world/2016/may/27/new-zealand-repatriation-remains-maori-indigenous-people-mummified-heads (January 27, 2017).

6   https://www.prm.ox.ac.uk/human.html (February 15, 2017). Email January 30, 2017, Director Laura van Broekhoven of Pitt Rivers Museum.

7   http://www.bbc.com/news/uk-england-birmingham-24939696 (May 29, 2015)

8   Steven Engelsman, "De Toi Moko van Volkenkunde", in ed. Hanna Pennock ea., *Erfgoedverhalen voor Charlotte van Rappard-Boon* (Den Haag, Erfgoedinspectie, 2007), 132, 133.

9   http://www.tepapa.govt.nz/ SiteCollectionDocuments/Media/2014/questions-and-answers.pdf (May 28, 2015).

Soft law instruments can be found in UN documents, such as the 2007 UN *Declaration on the Rights of Indigenous Peoples*. Art. 12 recognises the right of indigenous people *'to maintain, protect, and have access in privacy to their religious and cultural sites; the right to the use and control of their ceremonial objects; and the right to the repatriation of their human remains'*.[345]

The thinking about colonial human remains in former European colonial powers is in transition. Most institutions allow their return, but a return is not mandatory, as provided in NAGPRA. Yet, in 2003, the *British working group on human remains* argued against the non-retroactivity of many regulations by stating that retention can be *'a continuing wrong'* for individuals and groups.[346] In 2013, the *German Museum Association* issued Recommendations for the Care of Human Remains in Museums and Collections, favouring a proactive and reactive return of human remains.[347]

In the Netherlands, the discussion began relatively late. In 2002, the Amsterdam Tropenmuseum retrieved colonial human remains, acquired between 1906 and 1969 and given on loan to the Medical Faculty of the University of Amsterdam, and began to de-accession this rather *'disparate accumulation… of human remains'* of limited scientific value.[348] In 2009, the Netherlands was pressured into returning the remains of King Badu Bonsu II to Ghana (Box: *Incidental returns of human remains*). The Code of Conduct of ethnological museums in the Netherlands requires them to provide information to the communities concerned and to deal *'in an open and balanced way'* with return requests. Museums have to actively register and document existing collections of human remains and to equip their staff with sufficient expertise.

So far, returns of colonial human remains by European countries and heritage institutions have been fragmented. There have been also refusals (Box: *Some return-refusals for colonial human remains*). While, for instance, Uganda got back the human remains of a national hero from Great Britain, the Zambian requests for an ancient skull that only went to the same country to be studied, were turned down. That many European countries have returned tattooed Maori heads to the former British colonial possession New Zealand, is the result of a concerted effort on the side of the source community and country (Box: *Successful repatriation of Maori heads*).

---

345 http://www.un.org/esa/socdev/unpfii/documents/DRIPS_en.pdf (January 13, 2016).

346 Department for Culture, Media and Sport, *Working group on human remains report* (London: November 14, 2003; updated February 9, 2007), http://webarchive.nationalarchives.gov.uk/20100113212249/ http://www.culture.gov.uk/reference_library/publications/4553.aspx (November 28, 2012), 123 – 125; 116.

347 German Museum Association, *Recommendations for the Care of Human Remains in Museums and Collections* (Berlin, 2013), http://www.museumsbund.de/fileadmin/geschaefts/dokumente/ Leitfaeden_und_anderes/2013__Recommendations_for_the_Care_of_Human_Remains.pdf, (September 8, 2015), 60; 48.

348 David Van Duuren (ed.), *Physical Anthropology Reconsidered: Human Remains at the Tropenmuseum* (Amsteram: KIT Publishers, 2007), 38- 41. Jos Van Beurden, *Return of Cultural and Historical Treasures*, 26.

6.2.2. Instruments for the restitution of Nazi-looted art

There exist several soft law instruments for dealing with disputes about Nazi-looted art: the 1998 Washington Conference Principles on Nazi-Confiscated Art; Resolution No. 1205 concerning Looted Jewish Cultural Property of the Parliamentary Assembly of the Council of Europe of 1999; the Vilnius Principles, accepted in 2000; and the Terezin Declaration on Holocaust Era Assets and Related Issues of 2009 (Box: *Four soft law instruments for dealing with Nazi-looted art*). These instruments have lifted the issue of Nazi looted cultural properties to an international level. They appeal to public and private possessors of such properties to take their responsibility, to do '*active provenance research*' and publish the results. The possessors should help to solve claims in a just and fair manner. The instruments favour '*alternative dispute resolution mechanisms*'. Most of these instruments handle a concept of cultural heritage that goes '*beyond a concentration on high-profile objects of significant monetary value*'.[349] The Council of Europe Resolution of 1999 suggests the removal of '*restrictions on the inalienability of cultural objects*'.[350]

Whereas most attention has gone to contestable artworks in public collections since 1998, the 2012 discovery of over 1,400 artworks by painters such as Chagall, Matisse, Munch, Picasso and Klee, in the private collection of the late German art dealer Hildebrandt Gurlitt in Munich has brought up the issue of Nazi-looted artworks in private possession. The Dutch Advisory Committee on the Assessment of Restitution Applications for Items of Cultural Value and the Second World War – henceforth Dutch Restitutions Committee – refers to this issue in its Annual Report on 2013, where it noted that the restitution problem is only fully solved if private owners are involved.[351] There is an important parallel here with tainted colonial objects, since many colonial objects are in private possession or they have been transferred by private owners to museums without passing on provenance information.

The four instruments certainly offer inspiration for dealing with colonial cultural objects. As was argued at the conference of European and North American Restitution Committees, organised by the Dutch Restitutions Committee in 2012, the emphasis on confiscation, forced sale and sale under duress[352] and of involuntary loss can be relevant for retrieving colonial cultural treasures.[353] Too few Western museums and private owners do active provenance research to identify contestable colonial cultural objects, while such research might yield much. Inalienability of objects is often presented as argument against return – think of the Austrian refusal to consider the return of Benin objects (12.2.) – while it can also hide the reluctance of possessing states to consider a return.

---

349 Patrick O'Keefe, "A comparison of the Washington and Vilnius Principles and Resolution 1205", in Prott, *Witnesses to History*, 158.
350 Campfens, *Fair and Just Solutions?*, 38, 31.
351 Dutch Restitution Committee, Annual Report 2013, 5, 6.
352 Ibid., 37.
353 Dutch Restitution Committee, *Fair and just solutions: Alternatives to litigation in Nazi-looted art disputes: Status quo and new developments* (The Hague: conference, November 27, 2012).

Four soft law instruments for dealing with Nazi-looted art

In 1998, forty-four countries adopted the *Washington Conference Principles on Nazi-Confiscated Art*. Relevant are the stipulations that consideration should be given to *'unavoidable gaps or ambiguities in the provenance'* of confiscated objects and that steps should be taken *'to achieve a just and fair solution'*, depending upon each case (VIII). The principles recommend *'alternative dispute resolution mechanisms'* (XI).

In 1999, the Parliamentary Assembly of the Council of Europe issued Resolution No. 1205 concerning *Looted Jewish Cultural Property* about the most significant *'private and communal Jewish property'* (2). The Resolution declares that restitution should enable *'the reconstitution of Jewish culture in Europe'* (8); in other words, it promotes a cultural revival for victims. Restitution should be facilitated by *'removing restrictions on alienability'* (13 II). The Resolution favours out-of-court approaches (16).

In 2000, during the Vilnius International Forum on Holocaust-Era Looted Cultural Assets, thirty-eight governments adopted the *Vilnius Principles*. Governments are to maximise efforts *'to achieve the restitution of cultural assets looted during the Holocaust era'* (1). They ask *'governments, museums, the art trade and other relevant agencies to provide all necessary information'* (2).

In 2009, forty-seven countries adopted the *Terezin Declaration on Holocaust Era Assets and Related Issues*. It does not only mention confiscations, but also *'forced sales and sales under duress of property'* and applies a broad concept of cultural property, including *'sacred rolls, synagogue and ceremonial objects as well as the libraries, manuscripts, archives and records of Jewish communities'*. Worried about the slow progress, it favours *'intensified systematic provenance research'* and *'the establishments of mechanisms to assist claimants and others in their efforts'*.

Throughout the research, the possibility of a 'translation' of the 1998 Washington Principles into principles for dealing with colonial cultural objects has puzzled me. Although the 1998 Washington Principles are non-binding, they have strengthened the position of claimants and influenced dealing with disputes about Nazi-looted art in Germany and in countries that belonged to the Allied Forces in the Second World War. While discussing the translation with experts,[354] several obstacles and differences popped up: the definition of the objects concerned, the nature of the acquisitions and of the recipients of objects to be returned. One expert warned of the risk that such principles might lead to endless court cases.

The differences between Nazi-looted art and contestable colonial cultural acquisitions are substantial indeed. The looting by the Nazi's was part of a systematic extermination policy of peoples during a clearly defined, relatively brief period in history. Nazi-looted art covers any category of objects, including colonial cultural objects. Looting is broadly defined and ranges from *'destruction and seizure of monuments and public collections, systematic expropriation of property belonging to Jews and other persecuted groups and forced sales – in occupied territories and in*

---

354 Susan Legêne (personal communication, February 18, 2015), Wouter Veraart (personal communication, February 16, 2015), Lyndel Prott (email June 23, 2015), Katja Lubina (email July 09, 2015).

Germany itself'.[355] Former owners or their descendants are usually identifiable individuals and sufficiently organised to hire specialised lawyers.[356] The Dutch Restitutions Committee has shifted the burden of proof to the current possessor by considering all sales of art objects by private Jewish individuals during the German invasion as '*forced sales*', unless '*clear evidence*' is found '*to the contrary*', while '*the heirs of previous Jewish owners would no longer have to prove that the sale was involuntary*'.[357] The fear that such a lenient policy and focus on involuntary sales would open the floodgates never materialised. In only slightly over half of the cases, for which the Dutch Restitutions Committee's advice was asked, did it fully endorse the wishes of the claimants.[358]

It is harder to define the category of contestable colonial acquisitions. It covers objects of cultural or historical importance that were acquired in a contestable manner during the European colonial era. This era lasted over five centuries and Europe's colonial possessions covered an extensive, capricious geographical area. Because of the time span and the scarcely known circumstances under which most objects disappeared, it is difficult to discover their full provenance and it can be hard to identify who in a former colony is entitled to an object: the national government, the national museum, a regional museum, the descendants of a former local prince or a certain community.

An important argument in favour of a translation of the 1998 Washington Principles is that both categories represent acts of historical injustice and that principled reasons to omit options for colonial cultural objects that exist for Nazi-looted art are hard to find. Another is that such principles can help to break the impasse in the discussion about colonial objects. The 1998 Washington Principles have been accepted by countries and their inhabitants, who themselves possess contested artworks and their acceptance has contributed to the foundation of national restitution committees in Europe and North America.[359]

The last Washington Principle mentions the option of alternative dispute resolution mechanisms. Although these have long been an accepted way of dealing with disputes in other sectors, including the art trade, they are rarely invoked by heritage institutions. The ICOM Code of Ethics of 2004 does not mention them.[360] However, in 2011, ICOM launched in cooperation with the Arbitration and Mediation Centre of the World Intellectual Property Organisation (WIPO) its Art and Cultural Heritage Mediation (6.1.).

ICOM has been sparing in its attention for colonial cultural objects. This might be due to the fact that it has to keep together the richly endowed, self-declared universal museums and museums in former colonies with poor collections. Art.

---

355 Campfens, ibid., 15.

356 Barkan, *Guilt of Nations*, 9.

357 Ekkart Committee, *Origins Unknown – Final report* (Zwolle: Waanders, 2006), 28, 29.

358 Of its 118 advices to the Dutch Government until early 2015, 62 were to the advantage of the claimants, 39 fully rejected, while the outcome of the remaining 17 was mixed. http://www.restitutiecommissie.nl/ sites/default/files/RES_JV2014_NL_web_nieuw.pdf: 19 (December 22, 2015).

359 Annemarie Marck and Eelke Muller, "National panels advising on Nazi-looted art in Austria, France, the United Kingdom, the Netherlands and Germany", in Campfens, *Fair and Just Solutions?*, 41 – 89. Douglas Davidson, "Just and fair solutions: A view from the United States", in Campfens, *ibid.*, 91 – 101.

360 http://icom.museum/fileadmin/user_upload/pdf/Codes/code_ethics2013_eng.pdf (March 25, 2015).

6.2. and Art. 6.3. of its Code of Ethics mention return and restitution; this can cover colonial cultural objects. They are similar to Art. 4.4. of the 1986 first Code.[361] In both versions, museums – *'if they are legally free to do so'* – are asked to initiate dialogues about return and restitution in an *'open-minded attitude'* (1986) or in an *'impartial manner'* (2004), based *'on scientific and professional principles'* (1986) and also *'humanitarian principles'* (2004). As to human remains, the 1986 version does not mention the return option, while in 2001 an amendment was added that the return of *'human remains and material of sacred significance'* must be addressed *'expeditiously with respect and sensitivity... Museums policies should clearly define the process for responding to such requests'.*[362] The amendment has been adopted in Art. 4.4. of the version of 2004.

All in all, the 1998 Washington Principles and other declarations with principles for dealing with Nazi-confiscated artworks together offer the base material for the formulation of non-binding principles for dealing with colonial cultural objects. The final chapter presents *Principles for Dealing with Colonial Cultural and Historical Objects* (14.2.)

6.2.3. A human rights and a justice perspective

Can human rights further the discussion about the future of colonial cultural objects? That they are mostly non-binding and rarely retroactive makes them irrelevant for dealing with disputes about colonial objects along a strictly juridical path. Moreover, it has been argued earlier (1.2.) that many in the former colonies consider the United Nations and human rights as white, Western inventions. Although this was put into perspective, one cannot deny a discrepancy between human rights and decolonisation matters. Colonies rarely used human-rights to support their independence claims. They associated these with *individual* self-determination, while colonies were more familiar with the idea of *collective* self-determination. The 1944 Dumbarton Oaks Conference that led to the establishment of the United Nations had been aimed more at consolidating Western power than at decolonisation.[363]

However, in the early 1960s, the UN became a force in support of decolonisation[364] and the aversion to human rights dwindled further in the 1970s, when these rights emerged *'seemingly from nowhere'* to fill the vacuum that had arisen when the two main ideologies – capitalism and communism – began to lose their lustre. [365] Arguments in favour of a human rights perspective for dealing with colonial objects can be found in UN declarations and academic sources. They centre on the human right to self-determination and development, and the right to belong to an organised community.

The 1960 Declaration on the Granting of Independence of Colonial Countries and Peoples provides that *'All people have the right to self-determination; ... they freely determine their political status and freely pursue their economic, social and*

---

361 http://archives.icom.museum/1986code_eng.pdf (March 25, 2015).
362 Lubina, *Contested Cultural Property*, 212.
363 Samuel Moyn, *The last Utopia*, 85; 118; 93, 86.
364 Williams, *Who killed Hammarskjöld?*, 35.
365 Moyn, ibid., 3.

cultural development'.[366] Although the self-determination right '*was firmly tied to the control of natural resources*' it can be linked to cultural matters.[367]

In the 1980's, Dorothee Schulze elaborated a '*right to development*', including a right to restitution. Unwillingness to return can infringe on development chances.[368] The objective of the UNESCO Convention on the Protection and Promotion of the Diversity of Cultural Expressions of 2005, is '*to create the conditions for cultures to flourish*', and '*to reaffirm the importance of the link between culture and development* [...], *particularly for developing countries*' (Art. 1). Art. 4 is about the principle of international solidarity and co-operation, and the enabling of especially developing countries to create and strengthen their means of cultural expression. Art. 7 asks for '*equitable access to a rich and diversified range of cultural expressions*'.[369] It echoes in Kwame Opoku's plea for the countries of origin's '*fundamental human right to keep their cultural artefacts for the development of their culture in their own way and at their own pace.*'[370] A right to development conflicts with the systematic exploitation and underdevelopment practiced during European colonialism.

With the increasing statelessness, lack of rights and systematic extermination of '*unwanted people*' in mind, which had resulted from the 1914 – 1918 War and the 1939 – 1945 War, Hannah Arendt advocated '*a right to have rights*' and a right '*to belong to an organised community*' as the most fundamental human right. This '*right of every human individual to belong to humanity*' resounds in several declarations and conventions.[371] The Declaration on the Rights of Persons Belonging to National or Ethnic, Religious and Linguistic Minorities of 1992, declares in Art 2.1. that persons belonging to minorities '*have the right to enjoy their own culture, to profess and practise their own religion, and to use their own language, in private and in public, freely and without interference or any form of discrimination*'.[372] The UN Declaration on the Rights of Indigenous People of 2007 establishes a framework with minimum standards for the survival, dignity, well-being and rights of the world's indigenous communities. Art. 11.2 opens the option of restitution: '*States shall provide redress through effective mechanisms, which may include restitution, developed in conjunction with indigenous peoples, with respect to their cultural, intellectual, religious and spiritual property taken without their free, prior and informed consent or in violation of their laws, traditions and*

---

366 http://www.un.org/en/decolonization/declaration.shtml (December 23, 2015).

367 K. Chamberlain and Ana Vrdoljak, "Controls on the Export of Cultural Objects and Human Rights", in eds. J.A.R. Nafziger and R.K. Paterson, *Handbook on the Law of Cultural Heritage and International Trade* (Cheltenham: Edward Elgar, 2014), 532 – 570.

368 Dorothee Schulze, *Die Restitution von Kunstwerken: Zur Völkerrechtlichen Dimension der Restitutionsresolutionen der Generalversammlung der Vereinigten Nationen* (Bremen: Ganslmayr, 1983).

369 http://portal.unesco.org/en/ev.php-URL_ID=31038&URL_DO=DO_TOPIC&URL_ SECTION=201.html (December 23, 2015).

370 Kwame Opoku, *What are they really celebrating at the Musée du quai Branly, Paris?* (Wantage Oxon: Pambazuka News, May 5, 2016) http://www.pambazuka.org/arts/what-are-they-really-celebrating-mus%C3%A9e-du-quai-branly-paris (June 8, 2016).

371 Hannah Arendt, *The Origins of Totalitarianism* (Orlando: Harcourt, Inc., [1950] 1968), 267; 295, 296; 298.

372 http://www.ohchr.org/Documents/Publications/GuideMinoritiesDeclarationen.pdf (June 8, 2016).

customs'.[373] O'Keefe and Prott warn that having this principle work in practice '*is a very different matter*'.[374]

In conclusion, especially the human right to belong to an organised community with its own culture as most fundamental right offers a foundation on which a dialogue about the future of colonial objects can be based. Taking away cultural objects against the will of the community diminishes the possibilities of the deprived communities and its members to be a complete human or community.

There is another perspective that is even harder to get around: justice. Discussing justice raises several interrelated issues: equality, capabilities to realise justice and trust. First, I consider justice. Some authors, such as Amartya Sen, argue that it so hard to define justice that they shift their focus to the identification of redressable injustice, of injustice than can be undone.[375] From childhood onward, humans are aware when a grave injustice has taken place. Sen himself, Mbembe, Said, Soyinka, Galeano and other writers, who have been mentioned through these pages, show that they are fully aware of the injustices of the European colonial era. Injustice resounded in the words of the Minister of Culture of Mali, Aminata Traoré, at the occasion of the opening of the Musée du quai Branly in France in 2006. She was touched by the contrast between the beauty of the building and its objects as proof of Africa's orchestrated decline under the French colonial yoke. The objects belong to the people of Mali, Benin, Guinea, Niger and other African countries, '*Vous nous manquez terriblement – We miss you terribly*', she said.[376]

Aristotle, or Aristu in Arabic, – he was important for the Western/Christian, *and* the Arabic/Islamic world[377] – did define justice. In his *Nicomachean Ethics* (Book V) he describes it as one of many virtues, a condition of character that enables people to act justly and to choose the just. Justice makes people law-abiding and enables them to promote equality. The ancient Greek philosopher's remarks were about (in)justice in the *polis* or city-state, a clearly demarcated area, where inhabitants were divided into free citizens and enslaved people, a division that existed in the European colonial era too. Aristotle never questioned slavery. For the free citizens, he distinguished between *distributive* justice and *corrective* justice. The first is about the proportional distribution of goods and wealth inside the city-state. Corrective justice restores the unequal distribution of gain and loss, and involves involuntary transactions of goods or money. It is aimed at undoing injustice; both goods and the way of acquiring them are relevant.[378]

Aristotle's city-state has had many successors: nation-states, colonial empires, the global village. Are his concepts of distributive and corrective justice for the polis of his time applicable to its scaled-up successor, today's global village? They

---

373 http://www.un.org/esa/socdev/unpfii/documents/DRIPS_en.pdf (December 23, 2015).

374 O'Keefe and Prott, *Cultural Heritage Conventions and Other Instruments*, 335.

375 Amartya Sen, *The Idea of Justice* (London: Penguin Books, 2010), VII.

376 http://www.africultures.com/php/index.php?nav=article&no=4458%23sthash.GOV3MWAQ. dpuf%20%20 (June 10, 2016).

377 http://www.muslimphilosophy.com/ip/rep/H002 (June 14, 2013).

378 Wouter Veraart, *Ontrechting en rechtsherstel in Nederland en Frankrijk in de jaren van bezetting en wederopbouw* (Deventer: Kluwer, 2005), 34.

are to a great extent. Although many objects were collected in a law-abiding way, their maldistribution reached such heights that an institution such as the Tervuren Museum has 120,000 ancient ethnographic objects from DR Congo, Rwanda and Burundi,[379] while these three countries themselves have considerably less.[380] Public museums in the West-African state of Benin together own less than 4,500 objects, while the Musée du quai Branly alone has more than 5,500 ancient ones.[381] This maldistribution is felt both in Benin City and the state of Benin. The Benin Court has regularly appealed for the return of war booty (12.2.). The state of Benin claims from France thousands of objects that were taken in the European colonial era (4.1., Box: *War booty during settler and exploitation colonialism*). Considering the dubious provenance of many objects in Western heritage institutions, this is a problem of corrective justice.

Aristotle links justice with equality, as does Sen.[382] Equality is as hard to define. One can use the term in a descriptive form, in which case it points to a fact or an observation or in prescriptive form, where it has a normative connotation and becomes '*a constitutive feature*' of justice.[383] How equal are parties with a relationship to a colonial cultural object? The one is possessor, the other a claimant. The one belongs to a former coloniser, the other to a formerly colonised nation. The one is better equipped and has stronger capabilities to realise justice than the other.

Amartya Sen and Martha Nussbaum have written about justice and equality, Sen in the context of international cooperation, Nussbaum in that of gender. They argue that, if one side – e.g. the recipient country vs. an aid consortium, women vs. men – lacks the capabilities to realise justice, discussing justice is of little use. To counter this, the two developed a '*justice and capabilities approach*'. Capabilities are about what a person *wants* to do, what he or she is *able* to do and what he or she *is enabled* to do; realising justice requires an enabling environment.[384] Their approach raises new questions: who decides, and how, about the weight of differences in capabilities between stakeholders, and whether and how they are to be handled? The answer to these questions differs with each case. As to colonial cultural objects, both sides might have to strengthen capabilities. The party that claims an object is easily considered the weaker one, that does not have certain capabilities, but the possessing party often lacks the capability to open up for injustice that was committed in the past, and for dialogue and mediation.

An essential element of this discussion is trust. Trust is needed, when two sides discuss the future of colonial cultural objects and want to come to an agreement that satisfies both sides. Trust has to do with a balance between what one gives and expects to receive, with willingness to give up part of one's control over actions,

---

379 http://www.africamuseum.be/museum/collections/general/index_html (January 14, 2016).

380 See e.g. Kanimba Misago Célestin and Lode Van Pee, *Rwanda – Its cultural heritage, past and present* (Institute of National Museums of Rwanda, 2008).

381 Patrick Effiboley, "Musées béninois", 48.

382 Sen, ibid., 232.

383 Descriptive and normative equality, see: Stefan Gosepath, "Equality", in ed. E.N. Zalta, *Stanford Encyclopaedia of Philosophy* http://plato.stanford.edu/archives/spr2011/entries/equality/ (April 30, 2014), §2.

384 Sen, *ibid.*, 235. Martha Nussbaum, *Creating capabilities: The human development approach* (Cambridge, Massachusetts and London: Belknap Press, 2011), 20.

with confidence that the other will not harm one's interests. One can argue that in exchange for dependency and vulnerability, a stakeholder gains the prospect of a better outcome.[385] Trusting the other stakeholder includes the risk of his unreliability; part of the trust is one's own capability to assess the reliability of the other. The unequal treaties and treatment, the underdevelopment and other direct, structural and ideological violence of the European colonial era have heavily eroded the trust of former colonies in former colonisers.[386]

In conclusion, European colonialism resulted in an unbalanced division of cultural heritage over the globe, whereby the countries of origin are poorly endowed. Many more objects in public and private possession are tainted than has long been accepted. These can be considered as historical injustices. There are no hard law instruments to deal with claims to tainted colonial cultural objects. They are time-barred. The relevant conventions are non-retroactive. The history of the making of some conventions shows the desire of former colonies to retrieve their cultural heritage. For different reasons – trust being one, lack of initiative another – these countries have hardly used the ICPRCP. Former colonies can gain inspiration from the fundamental human right to belong to an organised community and from the concepts of distributive and corrective justice to strengthen their return claims. One can argue that this right, although it is non-binding, has become international customary right. Soft law instruments for colonial human remains and Nazi-looted art offer several lessons for discussing the future of colonial objects. Like the return of colonial cultural objects, that of human remains has remained a fragmented, piecemeal experience. What can be learnt from them is the need for heritage institutions in the West to conduct active provenance research and the primacy of source communities above outside scientists and collectors, and above property of the state. The translation of the 1998 Washington Conference Principles for dealing with Nazi-Confiscated Art into principles for dealing with colonial cultural objects is a step to raise this discussion to a higher level. They offer a form of embedding. If endorsed, they require commitment. They urge stakeholders to avoid the legal path and to look for non-judicial alternative dispute resolution mechanisms. In Part VI these principles come back as part of the model for negotiating the future of colonial cultural objects. Before that, a number of case studies of bilateral negotiations about colonial objects will be studied to gather information about the migrations of objects to Europe and to find elements for a model for negotiating the future of these objects.

---

385 Jack Barbalet, *A characterisation of trust and its consequences* (Canterbury: University of Kent, 2006), https://www.kent.ac.uk/scarr/publications/Barbalet%20Wk%20Paper(2)%2013.pdf (June 13, 2016).
386 Mbembe, *Kritiek van de Zwarte Rede*.

PART IV

AMBIGUITIES BETWEEN THE NETHERLANDS AND INDONESIA

Part IV - Ambiguities between the Netherlands and Indonesia

Part IV, a case study of the negotiations between Indonesia and the Netherlands about new cultural relations and the return of objects (1949 – 1975), builds strongly on the previous Parts. The investigation offers clues to what disappeared from the Dutch East Indies – based on the typology of objects (Part I) and the periodisation of the European colonial era (Part II) – and how and why the Netherlands returned objects after Indonesia's independence, and Indonesia accepted them. It provides elements for a model for negotiating the future of colonial cultural objects. The history of the negotiations is described twice, first in a historical reconstruction, based on archival sources of the time and literature needed to explain the context at that time, and is then followed by a revisit on the basis of more recent research findings. The differences in outcome are clearly marked.

Photograph previous page: Indonesian krisses or daggers, National Museum of World Cultures, the Netherlands.

Chapter 7

The 1975 Joint Recommendations

In a confidential report on Indonesian cultural objects of 1975, the Dutch Government wrote convincingly that the Netherlands had always preserved and protected Indonesia's cultural heritage relatively well.[387] The VOC (Dutch East India Company) did so in the 17th and 18th century. The colonial administration created a framework of protective laws and enabled the *Batavian Society for Arts and Science* to preserve objects in the 19th and early 20th century.[388] Admittedly, in the chaos during and after the Second World War, some disappeared. In spite of this, Indonesia submitted a wish list for returns with ten thousand objects.[389]

7.1. Cultural heritage policy until 1949

Since the foundation of the VOC in 1602, says the report, there has been an *'absolute ban'* on the transfer of objects not officially ordered from the Netherlands.[390] In the first period of Dutch colonialism this cannot have been a big problem, since VOC officials had little regard for local material culture and were more interested in botany, agricultural products, maps and atlases. This was still so in 1778, when they founded the Batavian Society for Arts and Science.[391] From the early 19th century onwards, antiquities from Java, Sumatra and Dutch settlements in Sri Lanka and Decima in Japan arrived in the museum of the Society.[392] The King of the Netherlands appointed the director and gave financial support. Many colonial administrators, army personnel, private entrepreneurs and missionaries, who all

---

387 "Report on Indonesian cultural objects (excluding documents) in Dutch public collections (undated, but probably part of a file for the Dutch Team of Experts in 1975)", in The Hague: *National Archive*, Archives Dutch Ministry of Foreign Affairs 1975 – 1984, Inv. No. 10266. Given its place in the file, it was submitted end May/beginning June, 1975. No author is mentioned.

388 Bataviaasch Genootschap van Kunsten en Wetenschappen. Batavia is nowadays Jakarta. The museum is the present National Museum in Jakarta.

389 "Memorandum Head of Culture and Public Education of the Foreign Affairs Ministry to Minister for Culture, Recreation and Social Affairs", October 22, 1974, in The Hague: *National Archive*, DCV/CS-243378-4084GS. "Historische voorwerpen uit het voormalige Nederlands-Oost-Indië afkomstig", in The Hague: *National Archive*, Inv. No.2.27.19, file 4193.

390 Obviously excluded were objects from China, Japan and South Asia, modelled to European tastes and produced for export to Europe: porcelain, textiles, lacquer, objects of precious metals, etc. Jan Van Campen and Ebeltje Hartkamp-Jonxis, *Aziatische Weelde – VOC-kunst in het Rijksmuseum* (Zutphen: Walburg Pers, 2011), 12, 24, 74.

391 Groot, *Van Batavia naar Weltevreden*, 26, 28; 135. Djojonegoro, "Evolution of the National Museum", 39, 45.

392 Groot, ibid., 129; 137, 215). Sudarmadi, *Between colonial legacies and grassroots movements*, 66.

became members, were more driven by the need for social status and contacts than by cultural curiosity.[393] From 1826 onward, Indonesians could join the Society.

As a safeguard against Indonesian claims, the Dutch Government summed up the rules and the measures it had prepared to protect the archipelago's heritage. The first rule came in 1840, when French researchers requested permission for a scientific trip to Java and Borneo. Temples, statues and other antiquities located on Government's territory were declared public property. Local authorities were responsible for them and were ordered to keep an inventory of antiquities in their region. Export of antiquities required the Governor-General's signature. Soon, the Society asked for lists of antiquities in the residences of colonial administrators and selected a number to be purchased.[394] In 1844, a list of monuments was made. Throughout the colonial period, it was refined and more stringently formulated.[395] An 1855 Law of Treasure Trove stipulated that archaeological finds be reported to the Government.[396]

The confidential report of 1975 mentions an 1858 Regulation that made the Batavian Society responsible for objects and collections of the colonial administration. It included tokens of homage and gifts such as *krisses* (daggers), lances and clothing from native rulers to the Governor-General that he did not want to keep himself.[397]

Ordinance no. 146 of 1878 decentralised the responsibility for cultural objects to regional administrators. People had to report antiquity finds to them and they, in turn, had to forward the information to the Batavian Society. The Society had a budget for purchasing *objects of essential cultural importance* for its own museum. It complemented public collections in the Netherlands with the less essential objects. Museum Volkenkunde in Leiden, which had been founded in 1837, benefitted most from this.

By 1923, 2,600 archaeological sites had been registered. Ordinance No. 238 of 1931 stipulated that pre-Islamic antiquities had to be registered, including those in private ownership. Their export was forbidden. During the final years, regional museums were established in Yogyakarta, Denpasar, Surabaya, Surakarta and Banda Aceh.

Between the start of the Japanese occupation of Indonesia in 1942 and the transfer of sovereignty in 1949, instability and lawlessness reigned. The authorities no longer controlled the export of objects by individuals and families who left the country. From the confidential report and other sources, it is known that private Dutch citizens, Japanese and Indonesians inflicted damage, looted and smuggled out cultural objects.[398] In Yogyakarta, the capital of the Indonesian Republic, Dutch troops seized archives at ministries and at the home of Mohammed Hatta

---

393 Lequin, *Het personeel van de VOC*, 183. Drieënhuizen, *Koloniale collecties, Nederlands aanzien*, 6.
394 Pauline Lunsing-Scheurleer, "Collecting Javanese Antiquities: The appropriation of a newly discovered Hindu-Buddhist civilization", in ed. Pieter Ter Keurs, *Colonial Collections Revisited*, 2007, 90.
395 "Report on Indonesian cultural objects (excluding documents) in Dutch public collections", *National Archive*, ibid.
396 Djojonegoro, ibid., 53.
397 Brinkgreve and Van Hout, "Gifts, Scholarship and Colonial Rule", 101.
398 Email Louis Zweers, March 10, 2014.

and other leaders. Later, papers of Sukarno and Abdoel Gaffar Pringgodigdo, who was Minister of Justice in 1950, emerged in the National Archive of the Netherlands.[399] With these Yogya archives, the Dutch substantiated accusations that the independence war was funded with illicit opium sales and linked the leaders of the Republic to communists in neighbouring Malaysia. The accusations, however, did not bring the international community to their side.[400]

7.2. Negotiations between 1949 and 1975

After the unilateral declaration of independence in 1945, Indonesia was eager to cut ties with its coloniser. In President Sukarno's vision, the *dark colonial period* was sandwiched between the *glorious past* of the Çrivijaya kingdom on Sumatra and the Majapáhit kingdom on Java and a *promising future* for all.[401] Shattered by the Second World War, the Netherlands wanted to restore the pre-war situation. Fresh troops, including soldiers from the Moluccas, who were promised autonomy for their islands, carried out large-scale military interventions. In the Netherlands, they were called police actions, in Indonesia, aggression against the struggle for independence. During a period of four years both sides committed extreme direct and ideological violence at various times and at specific locations; suffering was immense.[402] Those Dutch, who could, left for the Netherlands or for Papua, which remained under Dutch control.[403] The formal transfer of sovereignty finally took place on December 27, 1949.

The talks about future relations were difficult. While Sukarno was the father of the nation for Indonesians, he was associated with Japan and Nazi-Germany in the Netherlands. Dutch Prime Minister, Willem Drees, later admitted to have underestimated the '*major role in the relationship*'[404] of Sukarno's popularity and the anti-Dutch sentiment in Indonesia.[405] For the new Republic, the return of cultural objects had priority. The Dutch, haunted by UN Security Council Resolution 67 (1949) to cancel the Dutch '*occupation*' of Indonesia and to release political prisoners,[406] wanted to polish its damaged image, to ensure the survival of the Dutch culture and language in Indonesia and to keep the cultural treasures it had acquired.

---

399 Undated note, Iris Heidebrink, *National Archive*, The Hague.
400 Karabinos, "Displaced archives, displaced history", 287.
401 Sudarmadi, *Between colonial legacies and grassroots movements*, 78.
402 William H. Frederick, "The killing of Dutch and Eurasians in Indonesia's national revolution".
403 Dirk Vlasblom, *Papoea – Een geschiedenis* (Amsterdam: Mets & Schilt, 2004), 187.
404 Willem Drees, *Zestig jaar levenservaring* (Amsterdam: Arbeiderspers, 1962), 198 – 199.
405 Possibly due to this friction, President Sukarno's role in claiming back colonial cultural objects remained less visible than that of his successor, President Suharto, although both leaders were persistent in their return claims. Also see: Cynthia Scott, *Negotiating the colonial past in the age of European decolonization: Cultural property return between the Netherlands and Indonesia* (Claremont, Claremont Graduate University, PhD, 2014), 109. Sukarno collected paintings by Indonesian and European artists. His plan for a new national museum never materialised, Louis Zweers, "Sukarno's art collection", in *The Newsletter* (Leiden: International Institute of Asian Studies, 2014), 67/Spring, 7. Email Zweers March 10, 2014.
406 http://www.un.org/en/ga/search/view_doc.asp?symbol=S/RES/67(1949)&referer=http://www. un.org/en/sc/documents/resolutions/1949.shtml&Lang=E (July 11, 2014).

Some voices in the Netherlands favoured returns. In May 1949, a citizen suggested to the Government to give back, on the occasion of the transfer of sovereignty, crown jewels that had been taken during military confrontations in Lombok, Bali and Java. Within two weeks the Minister for Overseas Territories, J.H. Van Maarseveen, replied that the suggestion was '*worth considering*', but it was not the '*appropriate moment*'. Two days later, the Council of Ministers decided '*to consider a return in the final phase of the constitutional reforms in Indonesia*',[407] Minister Van Maarseveen informed the Dutch High Representative in Indonesia, Tony Lovink, that if a return were to take place, it had to occur '*spontaneously*' creating the impression of a '*generous gesture*', and not in reply to suggestions from political or press circles.

Lovink supported an '*unsolicited giving back to Indonesia*' as proof of '*the Dutch desire to establish the relationship... on a new basis of friendship*'. It should occur '*at short notice*' so that it could not be viewed as '*a remorseful restitution of illicitly acquired colonial loot*'.[408] He suggested making an inventory of Indonesian crown jewels in state-owned collections first, and proposed to return them to the familiar National Museum in Jakarta, and not to the Sukarno Government or the offspring of traditional regional rulers. Returning objects to traditional rulers went against Jakarta's efforts to centralise the administration.

When the Minister raised the issue in the Council of Ministers on August 23, 1949 again, he met with opposition. The Government wanted the inventory first, and the outcome of this was that there were only few contestable jewels, since most had been acquired '*by purchase or as a gift*' and, therefore, they could not be claimed. That the number was small was due to art-protection officer, Dr J.L.A. Brandes, who had accompanied the Lombok punitive expedition of 1894 to prevent looting. Such careful dealing was '*not an isolated incident*', but had also occurred during military expeditions to Bali, Sumatra and Celebes.[409] '*In this way the truly valuable cultural treasures remained in Indonesia and did not go to the Netherlands or fall into the hands of dealers, who might have acquired articles from individual soldiers, which the latter had taken as loot, and put them on the market.*'[410] Crown jewels from the Gowa and Bene Kingdoms in Bali had been sent back

---

407 "Secret memorandum of the Dutch Foreign Minister to the High Representative of the Crown in Indonesia" dd. April 9, 1968, in: Archive Foreign Affairs – Netherlands Embassy Indonesia 1962 – 1974, Inv. No.2.05.188, file number 863, in The Hague: *National Archive*, Inv. 2.27.19 – file 4194 – Ministry of Culture, Recreation and Social Welfare 1965 – 1982. The document mentions D. Schurink in the city of Winschoten as sender. In "Isn't it all culture? Culture and Dutch development policy in the post-colonial period" (in eds. Nekkers and Malcontent, *Fifty Years of Dutch Development Cooperation*, 358), Susan Legêne and Els Postel-Coster write about a railway employee '*of Christian persuasion*' without mentioning a name. Considering what they write about the Government's reaction, it must be D. Schurink.

408 Ministry of Culture, Recreation and Social Welfare 1965 – 1982, Letter of the High Representative of the Crown, A.H.J. Lovink to Minister J.H. van Maarseveen for Overseas Territories dd. August 1, 1949, No. 14, in The Hague: *National Archive*, Inventory 2.27.19 – file 4194.

409 In 1847, for instance, assistant-librarian R. H. Th. Friedrich was sent along with the military to Bali to collect manuscripts (Lunsingh Scheurleer, "Collecting Javanese Antiquities", 91).

410 "Report on Indonesian cultural objects (excluding documents) in Dutch public collections", *National Archive*, ibid.

in 1913. The result was that the citizen's return suggestions faded away. Other suggestions met with the same fate.[411]

While continued fighting made the Netherlands even consider a third military intervention,[412] that same August 23, 1949, a UN sponsored Round Table Conference (RTC) between the two countries began. The Dutch delegation included three Papua observers.[413] According to one of them, Nicolaas Jouwe, the observers were only there to impress the Indonesian delegation and were not even allowed '*to attend the meetings. They read, mostly afterwards, what had been discussed and decided.*'[414] A sub-committee of the RTC drafted a Cultural Agreement. Art. 19 stipulated that cultural objects of Indonesian origin in the hands of the Dutch or former Dutch East Indies authorities acquired '*by means other than as specified in private law for the acquisition of property*' – an explicit reference to tainted objects – were to be handed over to the Indonesian Government.[415] The article provided for a possible '*exchange of objects of cultural or historical values*', which a '*mixed commission*' was to prepare. For the Netherlands, the provision opened the possibility of the return of archives of the VOC. The RTC led to the formal transfer of sovereignty to Indonesia. Fearing a continuing Dutch economic dominance, the young country did not dare pursue the return issue.[416]

After the quiet death of the draft Cultural Agreement of 1949,[417] every now and then the talks were reopened, albeit to little effect. In February 1952, the two governments agreed to deal with return matters in ad hoc committees and to exchange letters about them, which they never did.[418] In 1954, Indonesia suggested the maintaining of Art. 19 of the 1949 draft Cultural Agreement. The Dutch Ambassador in Jakarta was in favour and suggested to link Dutch willingness to return certain treasures to the Indonesian willingness to pay for a new Dutch chancellery in Jakarta.[419] The proposal led to nothing. In 1956, Indonesia waited in vain for a reply to its complaint that no information had been received about objects of art-historical value in the Netherlands.[420]

Relations remained tense. The continuing Dutch control over Papua irritated the former colony. Three times, in 1954, 1956 and 1957, it had the Papua issue scheduled for the UN General Assembly, but it never gained sufficient support.[421]

---

411 Mrs. H.A.M. Wurth, city of Brouwershaven, suggested in a letter to the Foreign Ministry (September 8, 1963) the return of Javanese stone statues during a planned visit of Indonesia's President, in The Hague: *National Archive*, Inv. No.2.27.19, file 4194.

412 Hans Daalder, *Vier jaar nachtmerrie. Willem Drees 1886 – 1988. De Indonesische kwestie* (Amsterdam: Balans, 2004), 383, 377.

413 Vlasblom, *Papoea*, 177.

414 Interview Nicolaas Jouwe, Jakarta, November 24, 2014.

415 Legêne and Postel-Coster, "Is it not all culture?", 272.

416 De Jong, *Waaier van het Fortuin*, 611.

417 Legêne and Postel-Coster, "Is it not all culture?", 273.

418 The Hague: *National Archive*, Inv. No.2.27.19, file 4193, Letter of Prime Minister to Minister of Foreign Affairs (number U 18940) dd. November 6, 1968.

419 The Hague: *National Archive*, Inv. No.2.27.19, file 4193, Coded message dd. August 21, 1974 to Ministers for Foreign Affairs, Culture, Recreation and Social Welfare, and Education and Sciences.

420 Legêne and Postel-Coster, "Is it not all culture?", 274.

421 Vlasblom, *Papoea*, 181, 265.

Papua culture in safety

Due to the increasing interest in Papua's material culture, heritage officials feared that cultural objects would disappear after a Dutch departure. In 1959, Pieter Pott, director of Museum Volkenkunde in Leiden, proposed, therefore, that the Dutch Government should *'try and arrange to introduce some system of control of the export of objects of major cultural value and importance... as well as the planning of a regional museum'* in Papua.[1] Colonial officers, researchers and private persons brought together objects. Civil servant, G.W. Grootenhuis, in turn was worried that *'Dutch civil and marine servants took everything with them'*, as they could earn big money by doing so.[2] Upon his departure at the end of 1962, he took three-hundred and eighty objects, mostly ethnographic,[3] all labelled with information.[4] In July 1963, he deposited them in the museum in Leiden.

In October 1974, the Indonesian Embassy in The Hague informed the Dutch Government that, as *'part of the Indonesian Government's efforts to develop museums as important educational institutions'*[5], the capital of Papua, Jayapura, had a museum and that there were no obstacles for the transfer of the objects.[6] When handing them over in July 1975, Pott said that the objects *'could not be accepted to form part of the collection of the museum, while at the same time their return could not be effected due to the then prevailing circumstances. The only possibility was to keep the objects in custody and to return them, when the situation had been cleared up.'*[7]

Notes

1 Leiden: *Museum Volkenkunde*, Correspondence Archive 1975, Box number 61, Cover 118, No. 887.

2 Ben van der Velden in: *NRC* (Amsterdam: national daily), March 22, 1974.

3 Curator Simon Kooijman mentions the help of Papua-leader Nicolaas Jouwe ("Report over the 3rd quarter of 1976" in Leiden: *Museum Volkenkunde*, Archief P. Pott – Kwartaal + Jaarverslag 1975 – A 17, 2). Pott omits Jouwe's contribution in the 1975 annual report of the museum. Interviewed on November 24 in Jakarta, 2014, Jouwe said he did not remember the shipment to the Netherlands. He had collected for the Michael Rockefeller Foundation, which was willing to finance a Papua museum.

4 Letter of Pieter Pott to Mr. Soemarmo, Cultural department of the Indonesian Embassy, The Hague, October 16, 1974, in Leiden: *Museum Volkenkunde*, Correspondence Archive, Box No. 58, cover 113, No. 1504.

5 Indonesian Ambassador Sutopo Yuwono at the occasion of the transfer. Leiden: *Museum Volkenkunde*, Correspondence Archive, Box No. 61, Cover 118, No. 877.

6 Letter of October 4, 1974 by Mr. Soemarmo, c/o Indonesian Embassy – Cultural Department, The Hague, in Leiden: *Museum Volkenkunde*, Correspondence Archive, Box No. 58, Cover 112, No. 1458.

7 Press release Ministry of Culture, Recreation and Social Work, The Hague and speech Pieter Pott, June 13, 1975 (both untitled), in Leiden: *Museum Volkenkunde*, Archive P. Pott – Kwartaal + Jaarverslag 1976 – A 17.

Indonesia stopped radio broadcasting in the Dutch language in 1954. To pressure the Dutch to give in on Papua, it ordered Dutch nationals to repatriate and nationalised Dutch companies in 1957.[422] The Netherlands tried all means to keep Papua,[423] but finally had to give in. In the New York *Agreement between the Republic of Indonesia and the Kingdom of the Netherlands concerning West New Guinea (West Irian)*, signed in 1962,[424] it handed over the sovereignty over Papua to the United Nations, which would pass it to Indonesia. In five years, the Papuans would decide in an *Act of Free Choice* about their relationship with Indonesia. On their departure, the Dutch shipped a collection of cultural objects meant for a new museum in Papua to the Netherlands (Box: *Papua culture in safety*).

The signing away of Papua created the room that was needed for negotiations about new cultural relations between Indonesia and the Netherlands. Indonesia remained explicit about its interest in the return of cultural objects and archives and its dislike of the Dutch emphasis on the strengthening of museum and archival infrastructure. On July 14, 1963, Deputy Minister for People's Welfare, Muljadi Djojomartono, ventilated his views via the Indonesian news agency *Antara* that manuscripts and books *'that are historically important for Indonesia'* were better returned. Dutch officials had studied them during colonialism, but they *'now no longer had any practical value for the Dutch'*. Their return *'would certainly be of good influence on the development of friendly relations'*.[425] A Dutch diplomat in Jakarta supported the minister's suggestion.[426] Although it was not a formal request, the Dutch Coordination Group Cultural Relations with Indonesia discussed the Indonesian suggestion on August 19, 1963. It distinguished between manuscripts that were Indonesian cultural achievements and those related to Dutch and Dutch East Indian authorities, and it favoured *'an inventory and a gradual exchange'*.[427]

In September 1963, Indro Soegondo of the Department of Cultural Affairs of Indonesia's Ministry of Education and Culture argued before the *Agence France de Presse*, that the Netherlands should return authentic antiquities, *'of which there was no second specimen and many of which were very valuable'*. To *Antara* he said that *'the Indonesian cultural articles now kept in Holland are not many in number but they consist of the choicest and authentic ones that have no doubles.... As a matter of*

---

422 Vlasblom, *Papoea*, 266. Sudarmadi, *Between colonial legacies and grassroots movements*, 88.

423 When Michael Rockefeller, son of New York's Governor Nelson Rockefeller, disappeared during an art collecting expedition in 1961, the Dutch Government purposely hid information that he had been killed in revenge for the killing of Asmat leaders by a Dutch man in 1958. To show their control of Papua, it provided the Rockefeller family facilities to look for their relative. It did not change Washington's position. Michael's objects, found after his death, are in the Metropolitan Museum of Art in New York. Derix, *Brengers van de Boodschap*, 693. Carl Hoffman, *Savage harvest – A tale of cannibals, colonialism, and Michael Rockefeller's tragic quest*, [New York: HarperCollins,2014], 173, 223.

424 http://en.wikisource.org/wiki/New_York_Agreement (July 5, 2013).

425 The Dutch Minister for Culture, Recreation and Social Welfare asked government servants about the statement for *Antara* on July 17, 1963, No. 17849, in The Hague: *National Archive*, Inv. No.2.27.19, file 4193.

426 A brother of Dutch Prime Minister Jan De Quai, also teacher at the Gadjah Mada University in Yogyakarta, had tipped off Minister Djojomartono, Letter to Dutch Foreign Minister by Temporary Chargé d'Affaires, C.D. Barkman, July 20, 1963, No. 1324/141, in The Hague: *National Archive*, , Inv. No. 2.27.19, file 4193.

427 A report of the meeting is in The Hague: *National Archive*, Inv. No.2.27.19, file 4193.

*fact, some ... items in our museums are only duplicates of those in the Netherlands....
Indonesia has the full and detailed list of the Indonesian cultural items now still kept
in the Netherlands'.*[428]

The Dutch Government ordered civil servants to undertake some tracking
work. Within half a year they felt sure that there were no grounds for a claim,
nor had they found a list of contestable objects.[429] The Netherlands did not feel
bound by Art. 19 of the 1949 Cultural Agreement on the return of objects, as
Indonesia had declared the Agreement void in 1956.[430] It felt that it was in a strong
position, as it had, with the transfer of sovereignty, handed over all possessions
of the Batavian Society to the newly established National Museum in Jakarta.[431]
In 1964, there was some rapprochement between the two countries, when they
signed an agreement for technical cooperation, which was based on the principle
of reciprocity, but it obviously had no reference to return issues.[432] As shown later,
the reciprocity principle would play a role in the return negotiations too.

New tensions, however, blocked progress.[433] The Netherlands was worried about
the hundreds of thousands suspected of membership of the Indonesian communist
PKI, who were killed or imprisoned in the aftermath of a 1965 coup d'état, and
about the way in which President Sukarno was marginalised and General Suharto
was becoming the country's new leader. The Jakarta Government was upset by
Moluccans in the Netherlands, who kept hammering on self-determination for
their islands. Nevertheless, in the Cold War, Suharto's Indonesia opted for the
Western camp, and when, in 1966, it was in great need of foreign funding, the
Dutch Government reacted immediately. In exchange for the repayment of DFL
600 million (€ 272 million) as compensation for Dutch properties, which had
been nationalised and confiscated in the 1950s,[434] it invited bilateral donors to
join the IGGI (Inter-Governmental Group on Indonesia) in 1967.[435] Indonesia
disliked the IGGI yoke and especially the criticisms on human rights violations
during and after 1965 of the lead country.[436]

---

428 Telegram Dutch Consul-General in Singapore, September 7, 1963, to Dutch Foreign Minister, J.
     Luns, in The Hague, *National Archive*, Inv. No. 2.27.19, file 4193.
429 The Hague, *National Archive*, Inv. No. 2.27.19, file 4193: (1) Letter of Foreign Affairs Minister
     (DBI/PL-133098) to Minister of Education, Arts and Sciences, October 3, 1963, in which the latter
     is asked whether he knows of such a claim. (2) Memorandum to both Ministers by the Deputy Chief
     of Department of International Cultural (ICB 63078), December 17, 1963, that the tracking has not
     yielded anything. (3) Letter by the same to Foreign Minister (ICB 61739), March 12, 1964.
430 Letter Prime Minister to Minister of Foreign Affairs (number U 18940), November 6, 1968, in The
     Hague: *National Archive*, Inv. No. 2.27.19, file 4193.
431 Legêne and Postel-Coster, "Is it not all culture?", 274.
432 Ibid., 275.
433 Note of the Directorship for Asia and Oceania dd. October 26, 1983, DOA/IN, No. 149/83 in: The
     Hague, *National Archive*, Ministry of Foreign Affairs 1975 – 1984, Inv. No. 10146.
434 The end of the payments in 2003 aroused indignation in Indonesia and shame among some in
     the   Netherlands,   http://www.historischnieuwsblad.nl/nl/nieuws/3064/einde-indonesische-
     herstelbetalingen-aan-nederland.html (April 28, 2014).
435 G.A. Posthumus, "An 'ideal form of aid'" in: eds. Nekkers and Malcontent, *Fifty Years of Dutch
     Development Cooperation*, 150.
436 Note of the Directorship for Asia and Oceania dd. October 26, 1983, DOA/IN, No. 149/83, in The
     Hague: *National Archive*, Ministry of Foreign Affairs 1975 – 1984, Inv. No.10146.

The issue of Papua caused irritations again, but now on the Dutch side. When the Indonesian Government began to make people from Java migrate to Papua, Papuans feared marginalisation. Moreover, Indonesia manipulated the Act of Free Choice. Papuans in the Netherlands were allowed to continue their anti-Indonesian protests.[437] Then there was East Timor. After the 1974 Carnation Revolution and the abandonment of East Timor by Portugal, a civil war broke out on the half-island and in November 1975, the East Timorese Fretilin unilaterally declared independence. One week later Indonesian troops invaded and annexed the new country. The Netherlands offered Portugal its services to represent its interests in Jakarta. Indonesian human rights violations in East Timor were widely discussed in the Dutch media, Parliament, trade unions and civil society organisations. Indonesia's occupation lasted until 2002.

Despite the tensions, Indonesia and the Netherlands signed a Cultural Agreement on sciences, culture and arts on July 7, 1968. It resulted in intensified archival cooperation and the establishment of a Dutch cultural centre, Erasmus House, in Jakarta.[438] The Agreement stipulated that '*the question of cultural objects of Indonesian origin remaining in the Netherlands*' had to become topic of consultation between the two states.[439] The improved relations made visits from both sides easier. Dutch development aid became available for cultural programmes.

The Agreement fitted in with Indonesia's policy for strengthening national unity and identity, and the Dutch were willing to support this goal with the return of some treasures. Halfway through 1969, Chairman of the Dutch House, Frans-Jozef van Thiel, wrote to Dutch Prime Minister, Piet de Jong, that during a Dutch parliamentarian visit he had spoken privately with Suharto. The Indonesian President had urged the return of documents and manuscripts from the Library of the University of Leiden, which had been confiscated during the Lombok expedition (1894) and Aceh Wars (1873 – 1914).[440] The Dutch embassy in Jakarta suggested returning the late 14th century Hindu-Javanese manuscript Nagarakertagama. It was a most precious palm-leaf manuscript seized in Lombok, which was interpreted as proof that Indonesia, including Papua and Timor, had been a pre-colonial entity.[441] As to other manuscripts, Indonesia accepted that, because of its own weak archival infrastructure, it was better off with microfilms.[442] De Jong informed the House Chairman confidentially of his '*principled willingness*'

---

437 Vlasblom, *Papoea*, 447, 448.
438 http://erasmushuis.nlmission.org/erasmus-huis (July 11, 2014).
439 Memo 93/78 d.d. May 25, 1978 by Deputy chief DOA to chief DOA for cultural relations with Indonesia, *in* The Hague: *National Archive*, Foreign Ministry 1975 – 1984, Inv. No. 10146.
440 Letter of the Chairman of the House, Van Thiel, to Prime Minister d.d. May 21, 1969, number 67843, in The Hague: *National Archive*, Inv. No. 2.27.19, file 4193. In these years, Theo Pigeaud prepared in *Literature of Java – Catalogue raisonné of Javanese manuscripts in the Library of the University of Leiden and other public collections in the Netherlands* (Leiden: Bibliotheca Universitatis Leidensis – Codices Manuscripti, 1967 – 1970) an extensive overview of manuscripts in Leiden and elsewhere in the Netherlands.
441 *Het oud-Javaansche Lofdicht Nagarakertaggama van Prapatje*, 12.
442 Letter of Ambassador H. Scheltema to Chairman of the House, Van Thiel, dd. May 17, 1969, in The Hague: *National Archive*, Inv. No. 2.27.19, file 4193.

to support the exchange of archives, as it enabled the Netherlands to regain the VOC archive from Indonesia's Arsip Nasional, but he waited for the right moment to hand over the Nagarakertagama and the exchange was to be 'at the basis of reciprocity'. De Jong was averse to any 'obligation to transfer' objects, based on claims from a rather distant past and favoured 'maintaining the status quo', as otherwise, 'the unity of a collection' in the Netherlands could be impaired.[443]

In June 1970, President Suharto again asked a visiting Dutch Minister, this time Mrs. Marga Klompé (Culture, Recreation and Social Welfare), for the manuscripts and included the option of sending microfilms instead of original copies.[444] The Dutch Government estimated that ten thousand original documents were 'traceable'.[445] It repeated that Indonesian cultural objects and archives in the Netherlands could be 'complementary' to 'the much bigger volume of authentic cultural goods', which had remained inside Indonesia. The Netherlands was willing to help fill the gaps.[446]

During this time a new view seeped through the recent years in the archipelago and the dealing with cultural objects. Former Dutch conscripts began to talk about the extreme violence.[447] The Dutch weekly Nieuwe Revue questioned the right of the Netherlands to hold colonial objects. In 1974 the Dutch national daily Nieuwe Rotterdamse Courant[448] and again the Nieuwe Revue[449] published reports about Indonesian claims and wondered, whether the Netherlands had a legal or moral duty for restitution. A researcher suggested that 'an objective Dutch – Indonesian commission investigates which Indonesian art-treasures... qualify for return to the country-of-origin'.[450] Dutch museum officials accused these pro-return voices of insufficient understanding and played down the importance of their colonial

---

443 Letter Prime Minister to Chairman of the House Van Thiel, July 9, 1969, number 184244, in The Hague: National Archive, Inv. No. 2.27.19, file 4193.

444 Report Minister of visit to Indonesia, June 14 – 25, 1970, in The Hague: National Archive, Inv. No. 2.27.19, file 4193. From the report it was clear that Mrs. Sumartini, Director of Indonesia's Arsip Nasional, actively endorsed President Suharto's proposal.

445 Coded message, August 5, 1970, Dutch Foreign Affairs Ministry to the Dutch Embassy in Jakarta, in The Hague: National Archive, Inv. No. 2.27.19, file 4193.

446 "Nota inzake de zich in Nederlandse rijksinstellingen bevindende etnografica, kunstobjecten, manuscripten en archiefonderdelen van Indonesische oorsprong", in The Hague: National Archive, Ministry of Foreign Affairs 1975 – 1984, Inv. No. 10266.

447 After a 1968 TV interview with former conscript J.H. Hueting, Dutch parliamentarians asked for an investigation. An Excesses Report made them aware of extreme violence and neo-colonialism. Two other former conscripts, J.A.A. Van Doorn and W.J. Hendrix, published Het Nederlandsch/Indonesisch Conflict – Ontsporing en Geweld (Dieren: De Bataafsche Leeuw, [1970] 1983), about the Dutch abuses.

448 Nieuwe Rotterdamse Courant, March 22 and 29, 1974, in Ger Van Wengen, "'Wat is er te doen in Volkenkunde?' De bewogen geschiedenis van het Rijksmuseum voor Volkenkunde in Leiden" (Leiden: Museum Volkenkunde, 2002) and November 8, 1974 (in The Hague: National Archive, Inv. No. 2.27.19, file 4193).

449 De Nieuwe Revue, date unknown, deducted from letter by P. Pott dd. May 19, 1974.

450 A.W. Vliegenthart, submitting in 1969 a dissertation at Utrecht University about Michelangelo Buanarotti, in: Aad Van der Toorn, 'Peyton Place dient op de lijst van soft drugs te worden geplaatst' (Paris: Manteau, 1973).

collections. Dutch collectors had only gathered objects of minor quality.[451] An Indo-Dutch journalist criticised Suharto and his generals for appropriating public artworks for private use.[452]

In 1970, the nine member states of the European Community – all former colonial powers, except for Greece and Ireland – set up the European Political Co-operation.[453] In July 1973, they agreed to 'consult each other on all important foreign policy questions', if 'the purpose of the consultation is to seek common policies on practical problems' and the subject dealt with concerned 'European interests whether in Europe itself or elsewhere where the adoption of a common position is necessary or desirable'.[454] The keeping of colonial cultural objects was such a common interest. Fearing claims from DR Congo and Greece (Parthenon Marbles), Belgium and the United Kingdom refused to ratify the 1970 UNESCO Convention. European countries brought constitutional and legislative obstacles forward against it, especially the insufficient protection of private property and complications for customs officers. Their opposition was based on the wrongly assumed retroactivity of the Convention.[455] In the European view, ratification required 'far-reaching adjustments', while it was 'wholly unrealistic to establish precise and systematic guidelines to cope with each and every case in point'.[456]

That European countries acted jointly to minimise return claims also became visible in years thereafter. In a 'speaking note'[457] for a 1981 intergovernmental meeting, the British representative asked the Netherlands how it proposed 'to reply to the Sri Lankan claim' in the report, which Sri Lanka had submitted to the ICPRCP (6.1.) with detailed descriptions, including the inventory numbers of 'significant cultural objects' in the United Kingdom, France, the Federal Republic of Germany, the Netherlands and Belgium. A Dutch delegation to a United Nations consultation about restitution had 'consistently avoided recognising a generally

---

451 Letter of Pieter Pott of May 19, 1974 to Mr. Holzhaus, editorial office of the weekly Nieuwe Revue. Leiden, *Museum Volkenkunde*, Archief P. Pott – Kwartaal + Jaarverslag 1975 – A 17. Museum Volkenkunde, Leiden, Annual report, in *Nederlandse Rijksmusea 1975* (Den Haag: Staatsuitgeverij, 1977), Deel XCVII, 262.

452 Ernst Utrecht, http://www.iisg.nl/archives/nl/files/u/ARCH01507full.php (July 16, 2014). Imprisoned in 1965, he escaped from Indonesia in 1969.

453 http://eur-lex.europa.eu/legal-content/EN/TXT/?uri=URISERV:a19000 (January 25, 2016).

454 *Second report on European political cooperation in foreign policy matters (Copenhagen), 23 July 1973*, http://www.cvce.eu/content/publication/1999/1/1/8b935ae1-0a38-42d4-a97e-088c63d54b6f/publishable_en.pdf (July 16, 2014). This position was strengthened in the *Declaration on European Identity by the Nine Foreign Ministers, Copenhagen, 14 December 1973*, http://hist.asu.ru/aes/EFP_Documents_0415158222.pdf (July 16, 2014).

455 Susan Legêne, *Ratification/Implementation/Commitment – What is the problem for our Governments?* (Copenhagen: unpubl. lecture for Danish UNESCO Committee, 2007). Also: Report of the Dutch delegation: "Bespreking te Kopenhagen op 8 en 9 juli 1982 van delegaties van de E.G.-staten over het Unesco verdrag cultuurgoederen -Verslag van 13 juli 1982", in The Hague: *Archief Ministerie van Buitenlandse Zaken*, DVE/1945 – 1984/4034.

456 Willem Van Gulik, "Holding or losing: The return of cultural property", in ed. Rob Van Zoest, *Generators of Culture: The museum as a stage* (Amsterdam: AHA Books, 1989), 50.

457 The Hague: *National Archive, Archive of the Ministry of Culture, Recreation and Social Work (1910) 1965 – 1982 (1990)*, Archive bloc number XII, Inv. No. 2051.

applicable origin and property principle, but limited itself to recommendations related to specific objects or categories.[458]

The return issue created frictions inside the Dutch Council of Ministers. One was mentioned: in 1949, some Cabinet members had successfully stalled a return of crown jewels. Another occurred in 1964, when the Minister for Education, Arts and Sciences, Theo H. Bot, opposed any return to Indonesia with the so-called floodgate-argument: *'There is no telling where it will end if such a precedent is created'*.[459] Jan Pronk, Dutch Labour Party Parliamentarian from 1971 until 1973, remembers these frictions. The return issue and the accession to the 1970 Convention were raised several times in the Parliament. *'The Foreign Ministry was in favour of accession, whereas other ministries were against and high-ranking officials often delayed and came up with pretexts not to do it'*.[460] Archival evidence confirms this. In May 1972, the Deputy Director-general for Cultural Affairs of the Ministry of Culture, Recreation and Social Work, warned his Minister that Dutch accession might offer Indonesia and the Dutch Antilles – which had also raised the restitution issue – a handle, and *'then the quarrel starts again'*.[461] In February 1974, an official at the same Ministry wrote to his minister that Indonesia could point to Art. 15 of the 1970 Convention, which states that nothing prevents States Parties *'from concluding special agreements... regarding the restitution of cultural property removed, whatever the reason, from its territory of origin, before the entry into force of this Convention for the States concerned'*.

The risk of retroactivity and the fear that Indonesia would call the colonial era *'occupation'* and invoke wartime agreements for the protection of cultural property to give restitution claims a legal basis, were quickly set aside by colleagues.[462] A Comment on UN Resolution 3187 (XXVIII) *Restitution of works of art to countries victims of expropriation* for Minister Harry van Doorn for Cultural, Recreation and Social Work warned that it covered, in principle, all objects that had been transferred to the metropolis. They would have to be returned.[463] There were some civil servants who favoured returns, if these would help to repair the premature rupture of the late 1940s.[464]

Although internationally the silence about colonial cultural treasures *'was slowly being broken'*[465] and the atmosphere was becoming more *'return-friendly'*,[466] the Dutch Government did not adjust its policy. While it remained pro-active

---

458 Note for the Council of Ministers, August 30, 1976, in The Hague: *National Archive*, Ministry of Foreign Affairs 1975 – 1984, Inv. No. 10268.

459 Legêne and Postel-Coster, "Is it not all culture?", 275.

460 Interview Jan Pronk, The Hague, October 13, 2014.

461 The Hague: *National Archive*, Inv. No. 2.27.19, file 4193, Memo Deputy Director-general for Cultural Affairs, Ministry of Culture, Recreation and Social Welfare to Minister dd. May 21, 1972 about UNESCO Convention.

462 Confidential memo dd. February 12, 1974, IB/BS 102.356-1, in The Hague: *National Archive*, Inv. No. 2.27.19, file 4193.

463 Director for Culture and Public Education to Minister for Foreign Affairs dd. October 22, 1974, DVC/CS-243378-4084GS, "Historische voorwerpen uit het voormalige Nederlands-Oost Indië afkomstig", in The Hague: *National Archieven*, Inv. No. 2.27.19, file 4193.

464 Cynthia Scott, *Negotiating the colonial past*, 133.

465 Vrdoljak, *International Law, Museums and the Return of Cultural Objects*, 197.

466 Lubina, *Contested Cultural Property*, 478.

in the exchange of archives and other documents, based on reciprocity, it was increasingly reluctant to return cultural objects, unless Indonesia came up with concrete requests.[467]

Two developments helped to reach a breakthrough. One was the taking office of a centre-left cabinet (1973 – 1976) in the Netherlands. It did not cause *'a break'* in the cultural relations with Indonesia, but *'raised delays'* in their improvement, remembers Jan Pronk, Minister for Development Cooperation. There was *'no change in the attitude towards the UNESCO Convention'*, but an agreement with Indonesia about cultural relations and transfer of objects *'was not a bone of contention'* in the cabinet.[468] Pronk and his fellow party-member, Minister of Foreign Affairs Max van der Stoel, clashed about Indonesia. Pronk openly criticised the Suharto Government for human rights violations and imposed conditions on development aid, while Van der Stoel favoured silent diplomacy and a rapprochement. After Indonesia's invasion of East Timor, Pronk saw his position being strengthened due to public calls to suspend aid to Indonesia.[469] In hindsight, he argues, his position had not *'hindered an agreement on cultural affairs'*.[470]

The second development consisted of Indonesian surprise searches for missing treasures. In 1970, the Military Attaché of the Indonesian Embassy in The Hague visited incognito the Royal Home for Soldiers in Bronbeek and the Armies and Weapons Museum in Leiden, and looked for military objects that would qualify for return.[471] On August 2, 1970, the acting head of the Yogyakarta Inspection Office for Cultural Affairs, Dahlan Maksam, told a journalist that *'during the last war'* (1945 – 1949), members of the Dutch army had taken *'cultural valuables'* from the *'Yogyakarta Museum Sana Budaja and other museums'*.[472] The Dutch Defence Minister, responsible for military museums, ordered a search immediately. In a confidential note to his Foreign Affairs colleague of August 6, 1970, he concluded that no such objects or documents had been traced. He promised a more thorough investigation, if Mr. Maksam could hand over a list of missing objects, also those in non-army museums. Probably feeling uneasy about it, he did not exclude the possibility that individually committed thefts had evaded his observation and, on August 8, 1970, he urged Museum Bronbeek to report immediately to his Secretary-General, in case of *'direct requests from Indonesian side'*.[473]

---

467 See e.g. report of discussion between Minister for Education, Arts and Sciences with three Members of Parliament dd. November 8, 1968 in The Hague: *National Archive*, Inv. No. 2.27.19, file 4193, Document 43 of the Coordination Commission International Cultural Policy ICB/F/12880/68.

468 Interview Jan Pronk, October 13, 2014.

469 Margriet Brandsma and Pieter Klein, *Jan Pronk – Rebel met een missie* (Utrecht: Scheffers, 1996), 60.

470 Interview Jan Pronk, October 13, 2014.

471 Letter E.L.C. Schiff, Secretary-General of the Ministry of Foreign Affairs, March 20, 1970, in The Hague: *Archives Ministry of Foreign Affairs*, DCV/CS-43609/979GS, to Director Cultural Cooperation and Information Abroad. Also: Cynthia Scott, *Negotiating the colonial past*, 166.

472 Letter Minister for Defence to the Minister for Foreign Affairs, August 6, 1970, in The Hague: *Archives Ministry of Foreign Affairs*, DCV/CS-148316-30760CS.

473 Confidential note of Secretary-General of the Ministry of Defence, G.H.J.M. Peijnenburg, to the Chairman of the Advice and Assistance Committee for Bronbeek, August 8, 1970, in Arnhem: *Museum Bronbeek*, Dossier Diponegoro, 347373.

In October 1974, under a technical cooperation agreement between the Jakarta and Amsterdam municipalities, former mayor Sudiro of Jakarta and two other representatives of the Historic Buildings Foundation (*Yayasan Gedung2 Bersejarah*) came to the Netherlands '*to examine, study and collect Indonesian historic items*' to be used in some historic buildings in Jakarta.[474] The Ministry of Internal Affairs let them dig into secret documents and to photograph authentic messages of Mohamed Hatta, who, together with Sukarno, had proclaimed Indonesia's independence in 1945. After visiting twenty-one institutions, speaking to thirty-eight dignitaries and loaded with photocopies, reproductions and photographs, the delegation was '*impressed that the Netherlands feels obliged to return historic objects, which are unlawfully in its possession, to Indonesia.*' The outcome of their surprise searches was a list of ten thousand claimable items, including objects from a museum in Aceh, the Lombok treasure, ornaments of the Luwu court, the equipment of Indonesia's national heroes Pangeran Diponegoro and Pattimura, and the Wadjak skull. The archives offer no evidence for why director Pott of the Leiden museum, who had known about this visit from Mohamed Amir Sutaarga of the National Museum in Jakarta beforehand, had not mentioned it to the Dutch Government.[475]

Irritated by the visit and the long list,[476] the Foreign Ministry ordered a charting of the history of Dutch acquisitions. It was discovered that some Dutch dignitaries had had Javanese antiquities, coming from the Buddhist Borobudur or the Hindu Javanese Prambanan temple complexes, in their residencies.[477] To the *Nieuwe Rotterdamse Courant* Indonesia's Foreign Minister, Adam Malik said that '*Indonesia wants everything back*', but added that '*we should not think that it comes now*'. A spokesperson of the Indonesian Embassy in The Hague claimed four Hindu-Javanese stone sculptures in Museum Volkenkunde in Leiden from the temple complex in Singasari in Java. They are the property of the whole world, '*so there is no objection if copies are made. But the originals belong in Indonesia.*'[478]

Indonesia was not the only party that made surprise visits though. An official of the international cultural relations desk at the Ministry of Culture, Recreation and Social Welfare visited Indonesia in June 1974. Miss Ans Kalmeijer wanted to get to know the country better, but she did not do it as a government employee, but rather as member of the Commission International Relations of the Netherlands Association of Housewives. She would use the experience that she had gained then during the negotiations that would start in 1975.[479]

---

474 Memorandum Head of Culture and Public Education of the Foreign Affairs Ministry to Minister for Culture, Recreation and Social Affairs, October 22, 1974, DCV/CS-243378-4084GS "Historische voorwerpen uit het voormalige Nederlands-Oost-Indië afkomstig", in The Hague: *National Archive*, Inv. No. 2.27.19, file 4193. The memo was a reaction on a telex message of the Dutch Ambassador in Jakarta, October 16, 1974.

475 Leiden: *Museum Volkenkunde*, Archives "Klapper op Agenda 1974 (436)", 1399.

476 Harald Van Straaten, "Terug of houden zo? Restitutie van cultuurschatten", in *Verre Naasten Naderbij* (Leiden: Museum Volkenkunde, April 1, 1985), 31.

477 Jos Van Beurden, *Return of Cultural and Historical Treasures*, 32.

478 Despite protests by the newspaper and pressure by the Dutch Government, Museum Volkenkunde refused to pass on pictures of the Singasari sculptures. The article showed therefore an empty spot. NRC-Handelsblad, November 8, 1974 in The Hague: *National Archive*, Inv. No. 2.27.19, file 4193.

479 Personal archive A.M. Kalmeijer 1975 (via Susan Legêne). Kalmeijer told Legêne about the visit (June 27, 2014).

In 1974, Minister Van der Stoel discussed an Indonesian memorandum about return matters in Jakarta. Indonesia wanted to educate its youth in cultural and historical matters. The hiatuses in museums and archives had been caused by what the Dutch had taken to the Netherlands. Back home, he reported that return was a hot subject in Indonesia and that he had assured his hosts of the Dutch willingness to exchange documentation and knowledge. He considered an immediate solution necessary in order to not damage the relationship.[480] Through the years, there were fears in Government circles that the constant postponement of returns would make Indonesia lose interest in the return issue, which, in turn, would endanger the Dutch relationship with the country.[481]

Early in 1975, the Dutch Government declared that it was ready to intensify the cooperation to build up archives and museums in Indonesia. In reply, the Indonesian Government proposed that both sides set up a team of experts to work on cultural relations and the return of objects. This was accepted by the Dutch. The brief that was prepared for the Dutch team of experts showed minimal cracks in sturdiness of the assertion about the good care of the Dutch and the return of Indonesia's cultural heritage. *'The statement... that individual Dutchmen "rifled" Indonesia... is not based on research or knowledge of the facts....'* and *'important objects or collections were not brought to the Netherlands, although there were, of course, exceptions.'* It was admitted that museums had acquired *'the really valuable objects from the better sort of collections but since this happened throughout the world, returning any of these objects seems out of the question. This would mean depriving museums of their collections in a completely arbitrary way, and making any museum policy impossible.'*[482]

Before the two teams met, some transfers of objects of cultural or historical importance helped to diminish tensions between the two countries (Box: *Early returns to Indonesia*).

7.3. Towards an agreement

The first meeting of the teams of experts took place in Indonesia and lasted two weeks. Both teams were headed by the Director-general for Culture of the Ministry of Education and Culture (Indonesia) and the Director-general of the Ministry of Culture, Recreation and Social Work (the Netherlands). The meeting consisted of formal declarations, defining competencies, presentation of Indonesian wishes and Dutch intentions, visits to Indonesian sites, monuments and museums and, unexpectedly, an agreement on recommendations. During the site visits, the

---

480 The Hague: *National Archive*, Inv. No. 2.27.19, file 4193, "Nota inzake de zich in Nederlandse rijksinstellingen bevindende etnografica, kunstvoorwerpen, handschriften en archiefonderdelen van Indonesische oorsprong".

481 Coded message from Netherlands Embassy Jakarta to Minister for Foreign Affairs, July 12, 1982, Ref. No. 15198/72; Memorandum from DOA/IN to ACS M.J.J. van Loosdrecht, April 26, 1983, No. 66/83. Both in The Hague: *National Archive*, Archives of the Ministry of Foreign Affairs 1975 – 1984, Inv. No. 10146.

482 "Report on Indonesian cultural objects (excluding documents) in Dutch public collections", in The Hague: *National Archive*, Ministry of Foreign Affairs 1975 – 1984, Inv. No. 10266: 13.

Early returns to Indonesia

Two paintings by Raden Saleh

During a short visit to the Netherlands in 1970, President Suharto offered Queen Juliana a golden evening bag and Prince Consort Bernard a smoking set of Yogya silver.[1] The Dutch Royal couple gave him *two paintings of the Javanese artist Raden Saleh Sjarif Bastaman* (1811 – 1880). At young age, this talented artist had been entrusted to the Belgian landscape painter Antoine Payen. In 1829, he had come to the Netherlands, where the King supported his study and painting. In appreciation of his decades in the Netherlands and other European countries, Raden Saleh donated several paintings to the Royal family. One, showing a fighting lion, a lioness and a buffalo, was exhibited in the Dutch pavilion of the 1931 World colonial exhibition in Vincennes near Paris, and there destroyed by fire. A second depicted a buffalo hunt. A third showed the arrest of Prince Diponegoro on March 28, 1830; it would be returned later. The subject of a fourth one was a fight between a man and a lion.[2] The second and fourth were given to President Suharto. As they had come from the Queen's own collection and went to the President's collection, these were, legally viewed, gifts by a private person to a private person.[3]

Nagarakertagama manuscript

On behalf of the Dutch Government, Queen Juliana offered this 14th century palm-leaf manuscript during a state visit to Indonesia in 1973. It came from the library of the University of Leiden and had been part of the 1894 Lombok treasure. Currently, it is in the National Library of Indonesia.

Ethnographic collections from Papua

On July 13, 1975, Museum Volkenkunde in Leiden handed over 380 ethnographic objects from Papua, which it had kept since early 1963 (7.2., Box: *Papua culture in safety*).

Archival cooperation

Since the 1968 Cultural Agreement, the Indonesian Arsip Nasional and the Netherlands National Archive have exchanged and duplicated various archives and documents.[4]

Notes

1   Marie-Odette Scalliet (Leiden, University Library), email May 2, 2014.

2   Wassing-Visser (*Koninklijke Geschenken uit Indonesië*, 86 – 93) describes these four donated paintings. According to Scalliet, the painter donated at least twelve works to the Kings William I, II and III. Through the time most have been auctioned. The low profile sale in 2014 to the National Gallery in Singapore of the last painting that had remained in the royal collection, the large *Boschbrand* (Forest fire) that Raden Saleh had donated to King III in 1860, aroused, when disclosed two years later, public outcries. Although private property, the painting should have remained inside the Netherlands. The royal family was blamed for neglecting art historical sensitivities (NRC Handelsblad, 8 & 9 October, 2016).

3   *De Tijd* (September 4, 1970) reported a third
    Dutch Royal gift, a painting by the Dutch J.H.
    Weissenbruch. The magazine also wrote about
    a first visit by the International Red Cross to
    political prisoners, strong anti-Suharto protests of
    Moluccan and Dutch activists. These forced the
    Government to curtail the visit,
    http://kranten.delpher.nl/nl/view/index?query=
    raden+saleh+koningin&coll=ddd&image=

    ddd:110612060:mpeg21:a0098&page=30&
    maxperpage=10&sortfield=date (May 2, 2014).

4   Koesnadi Hardjasoemantri, "Een overzicht
    van activiteiten, causerie voor de jaarlijkse
    vergadering van het Genootschap Nederland-
    Indonesië", 17 november 1978, in The Hague:
    *Archives Dutch Ministry of Foreign Affairs 1975
    – 1984*, Inv. No. 10267: 2.

Indonesian hosts confronted the Dutch delegation members with what had gone missing in, for instance, the Singasari area during the colonial era.[483]

In his opening address in the National Museum in Jakarta on November 10, 1975, Indonesian delegation leader, Prof. Mantra – who refused to speak Dutch and kept his distance from the Dutch team[484] – expressed his country's appreciation of the Dutch *'warm response... to our request for returning some of our works such as Nagarakertagama, the paintings of Raden Saleh and... the archives and cultural objects of Irian Jaya'*. In the *Statement of the Indonesian Delegation on the Return of Cultural Objects*, he put Indonesia's claim in a context of cultural development, strengthening national identity and improving the *'overall economic, political and social condition of the country... which enables the Government of Indonesia to pay more attention to... cultural development'*. Indonesia needed cultural objects to improve existing museums and establish new ones. Mantra praised the Netherlands for its cooperation in the archival field. The preservation of philological materials had been better *'than would have been the case if these manuscripts and inscriptions had remained in their land of origin'*.[485]

The transfer of a considerable number of objects under colonial rule to the Netherlands and other foreign countries had made them inaccessible to nearly all Indonesians, whereas they should be their principle beneficiaries. The *Statement*, read by Mantra, did not ask for all objects: *'It is... understood that not all Indonesian cultural objects located in foreign countries ought to be returned.... Many... are, perhaps, specimens which are comparable, or similar, to specimens already available in Indonesia.... It is desirable to have collections of Indonesian cultural objects which are accessible to interested individuals in certain foreign countries.'* Indonesia asked for objects that were *'unique'*, a *'source of national pride'* and a *'fundamental contribution to the development of national consciousness of the very diverse population of the Indonesian archipelago'*. The Indonesian Statement listed three categories:

483 Pott, "Kort verslag", November 16 and 23.

484 Ans Kalmeijer, "Verslag van de reis naar Indonesië van de Nederlandse delegatie van het 'Team of Experts' betreffende de culturele samenwerking tussen Indonesië en Nederland op het gebied van archieven en musea – 10 t/m 22 november 1975", in The Hague: *National Archive*, Archive Foreign Ministry 1975 – 1984, Inv. No. 10266, 1.

485 Opening address Prof. I.B. Mantra and Statement Indonesian Delegation on the Return of Indonesian Cultural Objects 1975: 4, in The Hague: *National Archive*, Archive Foreign Ministry 1975 – 1984, Inv. No. 10266.

1. *Cultural objects*, regarded as significant creations of Indonesian thinkers and artists and as tangible manifestations of Indonesian people's cultural heritage;
2. *Historical objects* as evidence of momentous or memorable historical events in the past of the Indonesian peoples;
3. *Objects of aesthetic value* or with a special appeal to the aesthetic feelings of Indonesians.

A lengthy description of the desired archaeological objects, manuscripts and inscriptions, ethnographical materials and all public records mentioned explicitly the '*Ganesh, Durga, Nandicwara and Mbakala statues*' (the ones removed in 1804 from the Singasari temple) and the Prajñaparamita statue from the same region, all in Museum Volkenkunde, Leiden.

The Dutch delegation leader, Rob Hotke, reiterated the Dutch willingness '*to make available to Indonesian researchers material from Dutch archives and museums... of cultural and historical importance*', but made the restriction that, as '*our common history and the relations between our countries are cultural facts which cannot be denied nor erased..., it is essential that there should be a certain distribution of cultural objects throughout the world.*' He pointed to UNESCO, which never demanded '*that all countries should return artistic treasures to their land of origin*' but '*simply recommended that any particular wishes should be dealt with in bilateral discussions*'.[486] According to team member and director of the Museum Volkenkunde, Pieter Pott, Hotke had given Indonesia '*the clear warning not to expect that all its wishes could be met*' and emphasised the limited ability of the State of the Netherlands to hand over objects of non-state owners.[487] Working with the list of ten thousand objects, which had been created by the Indonesian surprise delegation in 1974, would cause endless difficulties, and it was better to look for solutions for concrete problems.[488]

The many objects that were considered during the first day's discussions were in both state owned and non-state owned collections in the Netherlands, or it was unclear where they were. In its reaction to Indonesia's *Statement*, the Dutch delegation mentioned a state-owned crown and other Lombok treasures, the ancient Prajñaparamita statue, manuscripts of specific historical value such as Nagarakertagama, and the Yogya-archives (taken during the last days from the Yogyakarta and other museums to the Netherlands). The Dutch did not refer to the four Singasari statues in the Leiden museum. In an article published for the 125th anniversary of the museum in 1962, Pott had written about these statues that, although there were many of them, the ones in his museum belonged to the finest.[489] In a 1969 note, he had put these and the Prajñaparamita '*on a par*

---

486 Speech Rob Hotke dd. November 10, 1975, in Leiden: *Museum Volkenkunde*, Archive of delegation-member P. Pott, Serie-archief NL-LdnRMV 360-1.
487 Pieter Pott, "Kort verslag van de missie van deskundigen naar Indonesië ter bespreking van problemen en mogelijke oplossingen terzake van de overdracht van voorwerpen en archieven in het kader van de culturele samenwerking tussen Nederland en Indonesië, 10 – 22 november 1975", in Leiden: *Museum Volkenkunde*, 1975, Seriearchief NL-LdnRMV 360/1, 1, 2.
488 Pott, "Kort verslag", November 10.
489 Pieter Pott, "The Wonder of Man's Ingenuity" in: *Mededelingen van het Rijksmuseum voor Volkenkunde* (Leiden: Brill, No. 15, 1962).

with the Elgin Marbles in the British Museum and the Mona Lisa in the Louvre' and neither these marbles nor this painting would be returned either to their country of origin.[490]

Concerning non-state owned objects, the Dutch mentioned objects that had belonged to Diponegoro, the sword of Pattimura, and the insignia of the state of Luwu in Sulawesi, taken at the beginning of the 20th century. If Indonesia could provide information about their location, the Netherlands was willing to establish contact with their holders. As to collections with unclear provenance, the Dutch mentioned extensive prehistoric materials as the Wadjak skull, collected by Dutch military physician and paleoanthropologist Eugene Dubois, and objects from the army museum collection from Aceh. They needed further research, as Pott wrote in his report of the meeting.[491]

When the Indonesian team did not move from its long list to one acceptable to the Dutch, the Dutch team elaborated a proposal and presented this at the end of their visit.[492] In their reports about the negotiations, both Kalmeijer and Pott mention a visit on the last day to Minister for Education and Culture, Sjarif Thayeb, which was probably decisive in the Indonesian delegation accepting this proposal. *'To the annoyance of some and the surprise of all'*, the Minister *'pronounced as his opinion, that he was not in any need to retrieve "all", as he did not know where he could leave it and what he could do with it'.*[493] Pott found it *'striking'.*[494] Kalmeijer noted that pushing for large quantities of objects had stood no chance from the start, especially not *'as long as Indonesia misses a decent museum infrastructure'.*[495] Pott felt annoyed by the fact that *'on the one hand collections are being claimed, while on the other large collections are being put together and exported almost unchecked'* to the National Museum of Ethnology in Osaka in Japan.[496] At the time, however, Indonesia's relationship with Japan differed from that with Pott's own country.

On November 22, 1975, the teams of experts agreed upon *'Joint Recommendations by the Dutch and Indonesian Team of Experts, Concerning Cultural Cooperation in the Field of Museums and Archives Including Transfer of Objects'*[497] (in: Appendix, at end of the chapter). The Council of Ministers of the Netherlands approved them on August 20, 1976 and informed the Indonesian Government about it on December 9, 1976.[498] Most probably the Indonesian Government had done so earlier.

---

490 Pieter Pott, "Nota inzake het probleem van zgn. teruggave aan Indonesië van voorwerpen van cultureel belang uit Nederlandse openbare verzamelingen" (The Hague, Rijkscommissie voor de Musea, vergadering 5 maart 1969, agendapunt 297) in: Seriearchief NL-LdnRMV 360, Leiden, *Museum Volkenkunde*, 1969.

491 Reaction Dutch delegation dd. November 10, 1975, in The Hague: *National Archive*, Archives Dutch Ministry of Foreign Affairs 1975 – 1984, Inv. No.10266.

492 Pott, "Kort verslag", November 21.

493 Kalmeijer, "Verslag van de reis naar Indonesië", 8.

494 Pott, "Kort verslag", 15.

495 Kalmeier, ibid., 2.

496 Pott, "Kort verslag", 12.

497 The Joint Recommendations were written in English.

498 Letter December 9, 1976 Minister Van Doorne for Culture, Recreation and Social Welfare to Indonesia's Minister for Culture and Education, Sjarif Thayeb, in: The Hague *National Archive*, Ministry of Foreign Affairs 1975 – 1984, Inv. No. 10267.

Luwu insignia

In 1905 and 1906, the colonial army organised the so-called South Celebes Expedition to subjugate the local kingdoms of Bone, Gowa and Luwu. The loot of the three kingdoms was divided between the museum of the Batavian Society in Batavia (Jakarta) and Museum Volkenkunde in Leiden. In 1907, the latter organised a special exhibition to show jewellery and weapons. Because of a request of the eldest son of the King of Gowa, who had died in battle, the Leiden museum returned the Gowa treasures soon for *'reasons of fairness'*. In 1938, the Batavian Society returned various other collections from Gowa to the former kingdom. The Luwu insignia that the Dutch had captured, however, remained missing.[1] In 1978, Indonesia asked again for their return, showing the official minutes of their seizure in 1946 and pointing to slides of the insignia, which someone had seen in the Netherlands. The slides, however, were said to be unreliable

evidence and did not help to find the regalia. When members of the two teams of experts visited the treasury of the ruler of Luwu in the town of Palopo, it was empty. Possibly members of the royal family kept them in their homes.[2] The Netherlands Government was convinced that these treasures were lost in the period 1945 – 1950.[3]

Notes

1. Hari Budiarti, "The Sulawesi collections – Missionaries, Chiefs and Military Expeditions", in eds. Hardiati and Ter Keurs, *Indonesia – The Discovery of the Past*, 168; 170.

2. Ans Kalmeijer, "Verslag reis Indonesië 8 april – 6 mei 1978", private archive (through Susan Legêne), 2, 3.

3. Note for Council of Ministers, April 1976: 3, in The Hague: *National Archive*, Archive of the Ministry of Foreign Affairs 1975 – 1984, Inv. No. 10266.

In the context of the argument, which have been developed in Parts I, II and III, several elements in the Joint Recommendations stand out. In the Introduction, the delegations declared their willingness to make *'cultural objects such as ethnographical and archival material available for exhibition and study in the other country in order to fill the gaps in the already existing collections of cultural objects in both countries to promote mutual understanding and appreciation of each other's cultural heritage and history'*. The wording implies that the two countries treated each other on an equal footing and that there would be no large-scale remigration of objects.

The first recommendation of paragraph II on Museums and Archaeology about return issues requires some comment. One is about a *transfer in stages*. It implied that the return would be implemented in several stages, and that only the first stage was elaborated. According to Recommendation II.2, it *'consists of the transfer of state-owned objects'*, among them the Prajñaparamita and Lombok treasures. The Conclusion states that the implementation of the Recommendations would take five years.

A second comment is that the word 'return' was no longer used and was replaced by 'transfer'. In a 1980 retrospective, Indonesia's Cultural Attaché, Koesnadi Hardjasoemantri (1980: 8),[499] also adopts *transfer (penyerahan* in Bahasa). Whereas the starting point for the Indonesian delegation had been (1) the return of (2) thousands of cultural objects, the Dutch team had focussed all the time on (1) the

499 Koesnadi Hardjasoemantri, "Penyerahan Benda Budaya kepada Indonesia", 45.

transfer of (2) a limited number. Return was only used in relation to the Luwu insignia, captured by the Dutch army during raids in 1905 and 1906 on South Celebes (nowadays Sulawesi) (Box: *Luwu insignia*). If these could be located in the Netherlands, the Dutch Government was prepared *'to establish contact with their holders and to further arrangements for their* return*'*.

A third comment is that the category of objects, proposed by the Indonesians, *'of aesthetic value or with a special appeal to the aesthetic feelings of Indonesians'* remained unmentioned. The Netherlands had objected to it. Eligible for transfer were only objects *'directly linked with persons of major historical and cultural importance or with crucial historical events in Indonesia'*.

In Joint Recommendation II.3, the Dutch Government expressed its willingness to render assistance *'within the limits of its competence'* in establishing contacts with non-state owners of Indonesian objects. Among them were lower governmental bodies, institutions such as the Royal Tropical Institute in Amsterdam, the Dutch royal family and private individuals. The Dutch Government promised to contact holders of objects discovered afterwards, and to investigate their provenance in cooperation with Indonesian experts. The addition *'within the limits of its competence'* seriously weakened Indonesian wishes, as it discharged the Netherlands from the obligation to search intensively after objects in private possession.[500] As a consequence, the Netherlands Government never went after, for instance, Buddha heads from the Borobudur temple,[501] which it considered as *'very scattered'* and *'mostly privately owned'*,[502] although they admittedly belonged to the *'categories of controversial objects... exported in clear transgression of the law, particularly of the Monuments Ordinance'*. But there was *'no documentation available'* on them, *'nor has the Dutch Government any power to enforce the return of such objects; the only possibility would be for the present owners to return them voluntarily.'*[503] Acknowledging the Borobudur's importance, the Dutch royal couple had visited the site in 1971, while Prince Consort Bernard had become the patron of the Dutch Saving Borobudur Foundation. To sugar the pill, the Netherlands offered financial and technical support to save the Borobudur from further damage.[504]

The Netherlands declared itself to be willing to find ways of transferring military objects *'of historical-emotional value... such as those belonging to Diponegoro'* (II.4). The demand for the unconditional return of the saddle and other *'emotionally loaded objects'* of Diponegoro in Museum Bronbeek was turned into a softer formulation

---

500 Ans Kalmeijer, "Verslag reis Indonesië 8 april – 6 mei 1978", 8.
501 Of 504 Borobudur stone heads, 90 have disappeared. Of the eight in the Tropenmuseum linked to the temple, only one certainly comes from there. Email Ben Meulenbeld, November 14, 2011. Even if a head was returned, it would be hard to find the torso on which it fitted. "Letter Saving Borobudur Foundation to HRH Prince Bernard", November 29, 1973, in Leiden: *Museum Volkenkunde*, Seriearchief (NL – LdnRMV) 2364 – 2.
502 Letter DOA to DGPZ on 'Transfer of cultural objects', January 30, 1976, No. 7/76, in The Hague: *National Archive*, Archive Ministry of Foreign Affairs 1975 – 1984, Inv. No. 10267.
503 Report on Indonesian cultural objects (excluding documents) in Dutch public collections.
504 Martijn Eickhoff and Marieke Bloembergen, "Decolonizing Borobudur: Moral Engagements and the Fear of Loss. The Netherlands, Japan and (Post)Colonial Heritage Politics in Indonesia", in: eds. Susan Legêne ea., *Sites, Bodies and Stories: Imagining Indonesian History* (Singapore: NUS Press, 2015), 34, 53, 54.

about the Dutch Government's willingness to find ways of transferring them to Indonesia.[505] The text did not limit these to those of Diponegoro, but to objects *'such as those'* belonging to Diponegoro.

The Lombok treasures that had to be transferred were *'to be selected together'* (II.2). Pott had downplayed the importance of Lombok objects in the Netherlands in a document, which he had written in 1949: the Museum in Jakarta had most *'golden jewellery'* and *'a much richer collection'* than his Museum Volkenkunde, which had received its golden and silver jewellery either through the Batavian Society, as gifts, from the collection of the Dutch royal family, or by purchase. Some were admittedly *'very fine objects'*, but none *'of exceptional importance'.*[506]

Each team of experts had a sub-team for archives. The Indonesian team noted that the presence of manuscripts and inscriptions in the Netherlands made it *'rather difficult for interested Indonesians to study them'*.[507] In spite of the Dutch effort to get VOC archives to the Netherlands, the two sub-teams agreed that those in the Indonesian National Archive would remain in Jakarta and those in the Dutch National Archive in the Netherlands (V.1.). Both sides would make microfilms available. If the documents known as the Yogya archives were to be found, however, they would be transferred to Indonesia.

Concerning Indonesia's request for four hundred *'manuscripts with historiographical information, such as the various babads* (chronicles) *of Java, Madura, Bali and Lombok, various historical accounts of other regions of the country, and manuscripts on customs'*,[508] the Dutch delegation continually pointed out the weak archival infrastructure. Finally, Indonesia contented itself with the transfer of only one original, the Nagarakertagama – already transferred in 1973 – and with duplicates or microfilms of others. Their request for the return of some manuscripts *'because of their special aesthetical qualities'*[509] remained unfulfilled. The delegations agreed about the reproduction and exchange of archival material and continued cooperation between their archives (Appendix: Joint Recommendation V.4 and V.7).

7.4. Dynamics of the agreement's implementation

With the Joint Recommendations as outcome, the first meeting was the most decisive. In June 1977, the second meeting followed, this time in the Netherlands. It was meant to implement the first stage of transfers. The third meeting, one year later in Indonesia, coincided with the 200th anniversary of the National Museum in Jakarta. On this occasion, the Prajñaparamita was handed over and the teams agreed on a five year plan for cultural cooperation.[510] A closer look at the objects that were transferred helps uncover the dynamics of acquisition and return.

---

505 Ans Kalmeijer, "Verslag reis Indonesië 8 april – 6 mei 1978", 8.
506 Pieter Pott, "Overzicht gouden sieraden in bezit van het museum"(Leiden: *Museum Volkenkunde*, September 15, 1949, Archive Pieter Pott, file 'divers-divers').
507 "Statement of the Indonesian Delegation on the Return of Indonesian Cultural Objects 1975" in The Hague: *National Archive*, Archive Foreign Ministry 1975 – 1984, Inv. No. 10266: 6.
508 Ibid., 7.
509 Ibid., 7.
510 Koesnadi Hardjasoemantri, "Penyerahan Benda Budaya kepada Indonesia", 1978.

Lombok treasure

The island of Lombok was an attractive colonial target because of its rice export to Australia, the Philippines and China.[511] The Lombok treasure was the result of what colonisers named a *punitive expedition*. The Dutch administration disagreed with King Anak Agung Gde Ngurah Karangasem of Mataram-Cakranegara about the rule of his kingdom. When in skirmishes during a first expedition (July and August 1894), a Dutch army general and some soldiers were killed, the Governor General ordered five thousand troops to move to Lombok and attack the king's palace. In battles in October and November 1894, several thousand Indonesians were killed, as opposed to one hundred and seventy-five Dutch colonial military dead. Plundering the palace, Dutch soldiers took more than one thousand krisses, betel sets and other golden objects, 230 kilograms in gold money and 7,199 kilograms of silver coins. They also took 400 Javanese manuscripts, including the Nagarakertagama. From another captured palace, rings, spearheads, golden tobacco-boxes and opium-pipes and headdresses were taken.

The Batavian Society, which had sent art-protection officer Dr Brandes to safeguard the war booty, kept most items in its museum in the colony, and put the rest in 75 boxes for shipment to the Netherlands. Most of them were delivered to the National Bank in Amsterdam. Simple objects and duplicates were sold to cover the cost of the expedition and to support the widows of the Dutch soldiers, who had been killed.[512] The Dutch royal family and some dignitaries saw the treasures. Twenty-three thousand visitors came to the Amsterdam Rijksmuseum to gaze at them. In July 1898, some of them were sent back to the Batavian Society. In 1937, the Rijksmuseum handed most of its Lombok treasures to Museum Volkenkunde in Leiden and more in 1977. It also kept some.[513] Other objects that had been looted from Lombok but lacked a clear provenance, ended up in private collections or in other museums in the Netherlands.[514]

During the second meeting, the teams of experts asked Md. Amin Sutaarga and Pieter Pott to jointly select 243 Lombok treasures. Among them was the Crown of Lombok: a dancer's headdress set with rubies. Museum Volkenkunde in Leiden delivered 122 of the 243 objects[515]; the other 121 were from the Rijksmuseum's shipment to Leiden.[516] Together, they formed about half of the Lombok treasures in the Netherlands. Sutaarga and Pott signed the minutes of the transfer in Museum Volkenkunde on July 1, 1977. The latter handed them over on September 12, 1977 to cultural attaché Hadjasoemantir of the Indonesian Embassy in The Hague.[517] Their departure was said to mean a loss for the Leiden museum and a '*substantial*

511 Wahyu Ernawati, "The Lombok treasure", in eds. Hardiati and Ter Keurs, *Indonesia: The Discovery of the Past*, 151.
512 Ibid., 155.
513 https://www.rijksmuseum.nl/nl/zoeken?v=&s=chronologic&q=lombok%20schat&ii=0&p=1 (July 17, 2013).
514 Vanvugt, *De Schatten van Lombok*, 99. Drieënhuizen, *Koloniale collecties, Nederlands aanzien*, 207.
515 Part of Series 2364, consisting of 411 objects of the Leiden museum.
516 Part of Series 4905, consisting of 150 objects of the Rijksmuseum. Leiden: *Museum Volkenkunde*, "Series Archive [NL-LdnRMV] 2364-1".
517 Leiden: *Museum Volkenkunde*, Series Archive [NL-LdnRMV] 2364-2.

interference' in the setting-up in its treasure-room, but – as that year's Annual Report noted -, pieces of comparable quality of most types had remained.[518]

Prajñaparamita

The Indonesian team considered the 13th century stone statue of the goddess of the highest wisdom, Prajñaparamita, *'one of the most beautiful cultural remains of the cultural heritage created by Indonesian artists in the ancient past'* and was explicit about its wish to recover it.[519] It became *'the most important transfer'*.[520] Assistant-administrator of Malang, D. Monnereau had found it in ruins near Singasari in 1818. He had transferred it to his residence and handed it over to the Batavian Society in 1822. The Society had it shipped to the Netherlands, where it arrived in 1824.[521]

Pott, who had compared the statue with the Parthenon Marbles and the Mona Lisa, now wrote about *'comparable pieces'* in the museum in Jakarta. He saw no legal grounds for a claim, as the acquisition had not been based on theft. A claim could only rest on an *'emotional background of a possible identification'* with the wife of the founder of the Singasari dynasty. The Dutch Secretary of State for Culture praised Pott's relinquishing his *'favourite daughter'* and one of the *'most costly possessions'* of the museum.[522] Before its departure, Pott had four plasters casts made,[523] later on called *'the tears of Pott'*.[524] The transfer of the original on the occasion of the 200th birthday of the National Museum in Jakarta created press coverage and enthusiasm there.[525]

Equipment of Prince Diponegoro

Javanese nobleman Diponegoro instigated a rebellion against the Dutch, which is known in history books as the Java War (1825 – 1830). In 1829, a Dutch major captured his red saddle and lance. They were sent as war trophies to the Dutch King William I and ended up in Museum Bronbeek in Arnhem. The museum claims that the saddle with stirrups and the bridle, which it had in its possession, had been donated by Mr. A. Ver Huell – who had most probably inherited it

---

518 Museum Volkenkunde, Leiden, Annual Report 1977, in: Ministerie van Cultuur, Recreatie en Maatschappelijk Werk, *Nederlandse Rijksmusea 1977* (Den Haag, Staatsuitgeverij, 1979), Deel XCIX: 308.

519 "Statement of the Indonesian Delegation on the Return of Indonesian Cultural Objects" (1975), 4, in The Hague: *National Archive*, Archive Foreign Ministry 1975 – 1984, Inv. No.10266.

520 Pieter Pott and Amin Sutaarga, "Arrangements concluded or in progress for the Return of Objects: the Netherlands – Indonesia", in *Museum* (Paris: UNESCO, 1979), XXXI, 42.

521 Pieter Pott, "Nota inzake het probleem van zgn. teruggave aan Indonesië van voorwerpen van cultureel belang uit Nederlandse openbare verzamelingen" (Den Haag: Rijkscommissie voor de Musea, vergadering 5 maart 1969, agendapunt 297), in Leiden: *Museum Volkenkunde*, Seriearchief NL-LdnRMV 360, 1969, 3.

522 Letter dd. June 8, 1978 of G.C. Wallis de Vries, State Secretary of Culture, Recreation and Social Work to P.H. Pott (Leiden: *Museum Volkenkunde*, Correspondence Archive, Box No. 73, Cover 142, No. 894).

523 Ministerie van Cultuur, Recreatie en Maatschappelijk Werk, *Nederlandse Rijksmusea 1977*, Deel XCIX: 300.

524 They remain in the museum's storerooms. Leiden: Museum Volkenkunde, *Annual Report 2005*, 9. Interview Steven Engelsman, Museum Volkenkunde, Leiden, March 22, 2011.

525 *Indonesian Observer*, April 25, 1978. Interview with Prof. Edi Sedyawati (Universitas Indonesia), Jakarta, November 24, 2014.

from his father[526] – and the lance by Major General W.A. Roest, who had been present at Diponegoro's arrest.[527] The donor of Diponegoro's *pajong* (umbrella) is unknown.[528]

In 1830, Dutch army commander De Kock invited Diponegoro for negotiations under a flag of truce. Instead of discussing peace, however, De Kock had the Javanese rebel arrested. Many in the Netherlands considered it a cunning stratagem,[529] but not all people did so. Prince Hendrik, son of the Prince of Orange (the later King William II), visited Prince Diponegoro in Fort Rotterdam at Celebes, where the prisoner welcomed him warmly. In his personal diary and in a letter to his father,[530] the Prince was critical about the arrest – a *'disgrace'* to Diponegoro's loyalty and a breach in the relations with Javanese chiefs. However, he was not allowed to say this in public.

On October 7, 1977, the Dutch State-inspector for Moveable Monuments handed over the red saddle with stirrups, the bridle, the *pajong* and a spear of Diponegoro to Indonesia's Ambassador in The Hague. Museum Bronbeek had tried in vain to keep the objects until the end of the five-year implementation of the Joint Recommendations.[531] The whereabouts of the kris that Diponegoro had to hand over upon his arrest and any other objects that had belonged to national heroes of Indonesia remain unknown and the Netherlands never made any great effort to find them.

Archives

The sub-teams for archives discussed two types of materials. The first was the earlier mentioned Yogya archives, which the Dutch had captured between 1945 and 1949. They were war booty with fragmentary information about the violent behaviour of both Indonesians and Dutch in the period 1945 – 1949.[532] The transfer of the Yogya archives had been set in motion years before the first meeting in 1975 and would last until 1987. The Netherlands considered it a *'unique gesture'*, since transfer of original archival materials was *'certainly uncommon in the international archival world'*, and expected that the Indonesian authorities *'would appreciate this gesture on its merits'*.[533] The Dutch retained photocopies of some originals.[534]

The second and most bulky were archives of the VOC and of the colonial administration. Sailors had kept journals of their trips. Businessmen had exchanged letters about their work. Afraid to lose these, they had sent them on different ships to the Netherlands. The information that colonial archives contained was archipelago-

---

526 *Museum Bronbeek*, Inv. No. 1865/05/13-1-1.
527 *Museum Bronbeek,* Inv. No. 1869/02-4-2.
528 Without inventory number. Email Pauljac Verhoeven, director Bronbeek Museum, May 30, 2011.
529 J.G. Kikkert, *Geheimen van de Oranjes IV – Minder bekende episodes uit de geschiedenis van het Huis Oranje Nassau* (Soesterberg: Aspekt, 2010), 176.
530 Wassing-Visser, *Koninklijke Geschenken uit Indonesië*, 70, 71.
531 Letter J. van der Leer to P. Rodenhuis, Chairman Assistance and Advise Committee for Bronbeek, January 28, 197, in Arnhem: *Museum Bronbeek* Dossier Diponegoro.
532 Frederick, "The killing of Dutch and Eurasians in Indonesia's national revolution", 360.
533 Letter Dutch Foreign Minister to the Extraordinary, plenipotentiary Ambassador in Jakarta, October 28m, 1975, in The Hague: *National Archive*, Archive Foreign Ministry 1975 – 1984, Inv. No. 10266.
534 Karabinos, "Displaced archives, displaced history", 281.

wide, regional and local. Until 1880, these records had been shipped to the metropolis. That year, the colonial administration set up a *Landsarchief* (nowadays Arsip Nasional) in Batavia.[535] In Joint Recommendation IV.1., the teams accepted the general principle that archives were to be kept by the administration that had originated them. Consequently, archival material produced by the Dutch Colonial Administration, the Japanese Military Government and the National Government and regional administrations of Indonesia, but located in the Netherlands, was to be returned to the successor state, Indonesia. The Dutch National Archive in The Hague and the National Archive in Jakarta were to arrange their transfer.

In practice, the territory principle often dominated: archives became the property of the state on whose territory they were. It meant that all archives that had been shipped to the Netherlands until 1880 remained in the Netherlands and that after 1949, some 10,000 meter of colonial records, including those of the VOC and Dutch colonial administrators, remained in Indonesia. The national archives of both countries began to busily exchange microfiches. There were some exchanges of records, among these documents of the Netherlands and other allied forces from immediately after the Japanese occupation.[536]

In conclusion, following independence, Indonesia was outspoken about the urgency of retrieving cultural and historical treasures from the Netherlands. It made lists and prepared negotiations, but instability and excessive violence between 1945 and 1949, anti-colonial sentiments in Indonesia, mounting tensions regarding the future of Papua, disappointment in the Netherlands and criticism of the violence applied by Indonesian military and militia hindered an early agreement. Although some Dutch officials and citizens favoured a more generous return policy, the Dutch Government was reluctant to acquiesce to many requests. A proposed return of crown jewels did not materialise. Although Indonesia had cancelled the 1949 Cultural Agreement with the Netherlands, it wanted to maintain Art. 19 of the agreement about the transfer of cultural objects, but the Netherlands did not feel obliged to honour it. After the Dutch departure from Papua and a regime change in Indonesia, a new round could begin. Indonesia's joining of the Western camp paved the way for foreign funding and new relations and dependences. The frictions that this created were smoothed in the Cold War ideology.

---

535 Intan Lidwina, *Het Landsarchief – The history of the Landsarchief in Indonesia (1892 – 1942)* (Leiden: Leiden University, Master thesis, 2012), 11, 12, 14; 69.

536 Roelof Hol, "A shared Legacy", congress-paper for '*Archives without Borders*', The Hague: August 30 – 31, 2010. Roelof Hol, "Gedeelde historie & archieven", in *Vitruvius*, Rotterdam: No. 18, January 2012, 26 – 29.

The Netherlands was rather complacent about its protection and preservation of Indonesia's cultural heritage. In the negotiations in 1975, the Netherlands broadened the focus from returns to strengthening Indonesia's museum infrastructure. The benevolent aid, which it offered for this, would enable the Netherlands to continue its presence in Indonesia. The issue of UNESCO's magazine *Museum* of 1979 considered the Joint Recommendations, which Indonesia and the Netherlands agreed upon in 1975, as one of three successful bilateral return agreements in the post-independence era; the other two were the agreement between Belgium and DR Congo, and the one between Australia and Papua New Guinea.

Appendix[1]

JOINT RECOMMENDATIONS BY THE DUTCH AND INDONESIAN TEAM OF EXPERTS, CONCERNING CULTURAL COOPERATION IN THE FIELD OF MUSEUMS AND ARCHIVES INCLUDING TRANSFER OF OBJECTS

I. Introduction

In view of the mutual desire to promote cultural cooperation in the field of museums and archives between the Kingdom of the Netherlands and the Republic of Indonesia, a series of meetings between a Dutch Delegation, consisting of Mr. R. Hotke (Chairman), Miss A.M. Kalmeijer, Mr. P.W.A.G. Cort van der Linden, Prof. dr. P.H. Pott, Mr. A.E.M. Ribberink and Mr. A.L. Schneiders, and an Indonesian Delegation, consisting of Prof. dr. I.B. Mantra (Chairman), Haraja W. Bachtiar, PhD., Prof. dr. Koentjaraningrat, Mrs. Rudjiati Muljadi, Mr. Noegroho Notosoesanto, Prof. dr. Haryati Soebadio, Mr. P.J. Soejono, Mr. Soemarmo, Miss Soemartini, Mr. Ilen Surianegara and Mr. Amir Sutaarga, were held in Jakarta between November 10 and November 22, 1975.

The two delegations recognize that specific objects and specimens which are directly linked with persons of major historical and cultural importance or with crucial historical events in Indonesia should be transferred to the country-of-origin.

The two delegations also recognize the desirability to make cultural objects such as ethnographical and archival material available for exhibition and study in the other country in order to fill the gaps in the already existing collections of cultural objects in both countries to promote mutual understanding and appreciation of each other's cultural heritage and history.

The two delegations also express the wish that a programme of visual documentation be established in mutual cooperation to the direct benefit of museums of ethnology and archaeology of both countries.

It is within this general framework that the two delegations reached the following conclusions:

II. Museums and Archaeology

Both delegations recommend that:

1. Concerning the transfer of historical and archaeological objects a programme should be implemented in stages;
2. The first stage consists of the transfer of state owned objects which are directly linked with persons of major historical and cultural importance or with crucial historical events in Indonesia. The transfer should be executed as early as possible. These objects comprise in the first instance the Prajnaparamitra statue, the crown of Lombok and other specimens, the transfer of which should be selected together.
3. As far as objects are involved which are directly linked with persons of major

historical and cultural importance or with crucial historical events in Indonesia and which are not state owned, the Dutch Government render assistance within the limits of its competence in establishing the necessary contacts.

4. With regard to the objects kept in Museum Bronbeek at Velp of historical emotional value, such as those belonging to Diponegoro, the Dutch Government be willing to find the ways for their transfer to Indonesia.

5. In the case that the Luwu insignia could be located in the Netherlands the Dutch Government be prepared to establish contact with their holders and to further arrangements for their return to Indonesia.

6. Investigation toward the ownership of particular specimens like the Dubois collection (comprising the Pithecanthropus skull and femurs from Trinil the two skulls from Wadjak, the army museum collection from Aceh and other specimens of possibly unclear ownership, will be performed by experts of both parties.

III. <u>Visual documentation</u>

1. Both parties recommend that a programme of visual documentation be established in mutual cooperation about specific subjects to be selected in consultation by experts from both sides, which should be fruitful for museums of ethnology and archaeology in both countries.

2. Both parties further recommend that the programme mentioned above should not be restricted to objects, but it should consider in particular the ways in which the objects are (were) made, how they are (were) used and how they were evaluated within the cultural group they belong to, in order that in the course of such an activity of visual documentation the results are likely to show that a number of objects kept in collections in one country, for their proper use in study, research and display, could be transferred to the other country.

3. Both parties recommend that cooperation in scientific documentation, which includes photographic and descriptive activities of archaeological objects, should be established.

IV. <u>Archivology</u>

1. It is acknowledged that it should be the general principle that archives ought to be kept by the administration that originated them. Consequently original archival material produced by the functionaries of the Government of the Netherlands Indies, the Japanese Military Government in Indonesia during World War II, the Government of the Republic of Indonesia, the Governments of the various member states and the territories of the United States of Indonesia and the Governments of the United States of Indonesia and currently located in the Netherlands should be returned to the Republic of Indonesia in accordance with the Netherlands legislation concerning archives. The Algemeen Rijksarchief in The Hague and the National Archives in Jakarta assume the task of arranging for the transfer of such material to the rightful parties.

2. Both parties recommend to continue and develop the cooperation already existing in the field of archives between the Algemeen Rijksarchief and the Arsip Nasional R.I.

3. It is the opinion of both parties that the documents on the so-called "overgebrachte brieven" (Lit: Transferred letters - JvB) – the archives of the "Procureur-Generaal" and the "Algemeene Secretarie" (Attorney General and General Secretariat of the colonial administration - JvB) – concerning Dutch individuals and groups be left with the Algemeen Rijksarchief and documents originated by Indonesian organizations and Government institutions in Indonesia be transferred to Indonesia.

4. Both parties recommend to facilitate the reproduction in microform of archival material as might be needed by the other party and to arrange for the transmission of the resulting microforms to the other country.

5. It is understood that this exchange of microfilm shall cover archives of the Dutch East Indies Company as deposited in the Algemeen Rijksarchief and the Arsip Nasional R.I.

6. The Netherlands Delegation will recommend that the Dutch Government render all possible assistance to the Indonesian side in its endeavour to obtain copies of visual records, documentary photographs and motion pictures, particularly but not exclusively material of historical value.

7. Both parties support the cooperation between the Algemeen Rijksarchief and the Arsip Nasional R.I. with regard to the exchange of specialists and to the training programmes as already agreed upon, the details of which are to be elaborated in direct contact between the two national archives concerned.

V. <u>Manuscripts</u>

Apart from programmes of exchange regarding the content of manuscripts and inscriptions in the form of reproduced material, such as microfilms and microfiches, both delegations recommend that manuscripts and inscriptions which are directly linked to persons of major historical and cultural importance or with crucial historical events in Indonesia be transferred to the country of origin.

VI. <u>Conclusion</u>

Both delegations are of the opinion that in order to achieve the aforementioned aims, a time-schedule should be followed lasting for the next five years.

In the next meeting of the delegations to be held within one year, a programme shall be outlined to meet the time-schedule.

Signed in Jakarta on November 22, 1975.

For the Indonesian Delegation: For the Dutch Delegation:

Prof. Dr. I.B. Mantra   Mr. R. Hotke

Note

1   English text in The Hague: *National Archive*, Archive of the Ministry of Foreign Affairs
     1975 – 1984, Inv. No.10266. Copies were found in other archives as well. The text has
     been retyped literatim.

Chapter 8

The Joint Recommendations revisited

After signing the Joint Recommendations and the transference of objects, Dutch officials breathed a sigh of relief: *'This phase in the relationship... has been practically finished'*.[537] *'All wishes of Indonesia have been met. This operation is over.... New wishes can come up, which then have to be considered in mutual agreement'*.[538] The Introduction to the Joint Recommendations echoed the reciprocity that the Dutch had been after so much. It provided that, if certain objects were better in place in the one country than in the other, they would be transferred to that country with mutual consent. This provision could also lead to a *'transfer to the Netherlands'*.[539]

Until far in the 1980s, post-independence issues such as the return of objects mostly concerned academics in the Netherlands. Other than some media coverage and individual initiatives (7.2.), there was little public debate.[540] With the generation of Dutch people that had been active in colonial Indonesia still alive, there was a sentiment that emphasised the colonial assets – the unity of Indonesia, the religious tolerance, the promotion of science, culture and arts, infrastructural works, primary education and health care.[541]

8.1. New research findings

In the last quarter century, research into the biographies of colonial objects has expanded greatly and much more is known about the migration of the sort of state owned objects that were reviewed during the 1975 deliberations, such as crown jewels, Hindu-Javanese and Buddhist stone and bronze statues, ancient manuscripts and so on, and also of non-state or privately owned objects, which were donated, sold or lent to state owned institutions. Most scholars who have contributed to this research and who will pass by soon, are Dutch or Western. Only some of them are Indonesian.

---

537 Memo 104/78, November 16, 1978 of DCV/CS to DOA/IN about "Culturele betrekkingen Nederland – Indonesië", in The Hague: *National Archive*, Ministry of Foreign Affairs 1975 – 1984, Inv. No. 10146.

538 Letter R. Hotke to P.W.A.G. Cort van der Linden, Ministry of Foreign Affairs, March 31, 1980, ibid.

539 Memo 29/1978, June 7, 1978, of Chef DCV to DGPZ about Culturele relaties Netherland – Indonesië, ibid.

540 Ulbe Bosma, "Why is there no Post-colonial debate in the Netherlands?", in ed. Ubo Bosma, *Post-Colonial Immigrants and Identity Formations in the Netherlands* (Amsterdam: Amsterdam University Press, IMISCOE Research, 2012), 193 – 212.

541 Lodewijk Van Gorkom, *Door Europa en de wereld: Een trektocht in Buitenlandse Dienst* (Amsterdam: Boom, 2009), 200.

Thomas Raffles and Indonesia's heritage

In 1812, Raffles looted the large *kraton* (palace) of the Sultan of Yogyakarta. The Sultan and his relatives had to hand over their krisses, other weapons and gold ornaments. Guards cut off the diamond buttons of the Sultan's dress jacket, while '*he lay asleep*'.[1] Raffles also collected numerous antiquities. Two Borobudur Buddha heads, fragments from Borobudur and some Hindu and Islamic artworks from the Raffles Collection are in the British Museum. In their description, director MacGregor does not dwell on their problematic origin, but adopts Raffles' description of the poor condition of monuments at Java.[2] '*Neighbouring peasants*' used lost stones and fragments '*to their own purposes*'.[3] The exhibition '*Adventures, travels and collecting in Southeast Asia*' of 1999 portrayed Raffles '*as a progressive colonial reformer*'.[4] Under his supervision, two ancient stones with rare inscriptions disappeared to Kolkata and Scotland (4.1.). Possibly motivated by feelings of competition, Raffles considered the Dutch narrow-minded and criticised their divide-and-rule approach in the colony.[5]

Raffles acquired ancient books and manuscripts and made natural history drawings. In 1824, on his way home, his ship, the *Fame*, caught fire and two and a half thousands of these and his research notes were lost. He immediately began to make new drawings.[6] In 2007, the British Library purchased over one hundred fifty natural history and topographical drawings related to Indonesia and Malaysia from the Raffles Family Collection.[7]

Notes

1   Peter Carey, *Power of prophecy*, 334; 341.

2   MacGregor, *A history of the world in 100 objects*, chapter 59.

3   Thomas S. Raffles, *The History of Java* (Oxford: Oxford University Press, 2 Volumes, [1817] 1978), Vol. II, 7.

4   http://www.theguardian.com/books/1999/ mar/13/books.guardianreview6 (July 16, 2014). Victoria Glendinning, *Raffles and the golden opportunity* (London: Profile Books, 2012).

5   '*By corrupting and bribing the chiefs, and sowing disunion among them*' the Dutch had '*dismembered an empire*' already shaken by '*wars which attended the establishment of Mahometanism*' (Raffles, *History of Java*, Vol. I, 297). The Dutch cultural policy was '*narrow*' and '*denied to other nations facilities of research*' into Java's treasures. Apparently the Dutch '*devotion to the pursuits of commerce was*

too exclusive to allow of their being much interested by the subject' (ibid., Vol. II, 5, 6). That Dutch experts delivered contradictory information caused him to rely on skilled Indonesians (Bastin, J. in introduction to Raffles' *History of Java*). One Dutch man gained Raffles' respect: Governor Nicolaus Engelhard of *Semárang*. His collection was the '*only one…, which appears to have been made by Europeans… previously to the establishment of the British Government in 1811*' (ibid., Vol. II, 55). Raffles noticed the Ganesha and Durga stone statues from Singasari in his compound, claimed by Indonesia in 1975 and presently in Museum Volkenkunde in Leiden.

6   http://www.bl.uk/learning/langlit/texts/ship/ raffles/stamfordraffles.html (July 11, 2014).

7   http://www.bl.uk/onlinegallery/onlineex/ spicetrail/raffles.html (July 11, 2014).

The reader *Treasure Hunting? Collectors and Collections of Indonesian Artefacts* focuses on collectors who made their acquisitions for a *public* goal and who *'used not only their powers of persuasion and glass beads, but also trickery and sometimes even violence'* to appropriate objects.[542] Several findings contradict the positive briefing for the Dutch team of experts. Between 2,500 and 3,000 of the 36,000 Indonesian objects that Museum Volkenkunde in Leiden possessed around 1910 resulted from military interventions in areas as Aceh, Bali, Bone and Lombok.[543] The establishment of regional museums in the archipelago was motivated by the need *'to prevent the drain of cultural objects and to provide training in arts and handicrafts'.*[544] Confronted with photographs of *'magnificent carvings from a chief's house'* on the island of Nias, which a Danish doctor appropriated in the 1920s and which is currently in Copenhagen, villagers rejected these pieces of paper and asked for the house to be returned.[545] Inequality plays a role in the destination of collections, as the example of the Stammeshaus collection shows. Around the year 1900, F.W. Stammeshaus, colonial official and private collector, lent 1,350 objects to the museum in Banda Aceh, of which he was curator. When the museum had no funds to pay for the objects upon his return to the Netherlands, Stammeshaus sold all of them to the then Colonial Museum (nowadays: Tropenmuseum) in Amsterdam, which subsequently employed him.[546] Presently, his descendants are considering whether to return the collection.[547] *Treasure Hunting* deals mildly with Sir Thomas Raffles, British Governor-general of the Dutch East Indies from 1811 until 1816, although there is so much more to write about Raffles' role in passing Indonesian war booty and other objects to the British Museum and the Indian Museum in Calcutta (Box: *Thomas Raffles, the Dutch and Indonesia's cultural heritage*).

In *Indonesia: The Discovery of the Past*, a catalogue for an exhibition in Jakarta and Amsterdam with *'the two largest and most beautiful collections in the world of the Indonesian legacy'*, Dutch and Indonesian contributors offer information about the tainted origin of objects in state owned collections in the Netherlands.[548] Yet they avoid the return issue by redirecting their *'concerns with unfinished business of the colonial past, into more present-oriented ones'* of cooperation.[549]

Colonial Collections Revisited has insights into collecting after punitive actions. Without offering extensive evidence, its editor, Pieter Ter Keurs, states that the number of objects thus acquired *'was considerably smaller than in many other colonial*

---

542 Schefold and Vermeulen eds., *Treasure Hunting?*, 4.
543 Van Wengen, "Indonesian collections in the National Museum of Ethnology in Leiden", 100.
544 Amin Sutaarga, "The role of museums in Indonesia: Collecting documents from the past and the present for a better future", in eds. Schefold and Vermeulen, *Treasure Hunting?*, 283, 284. Schefold and Vermeulen, *Treasure Hunting?*, 16.
545 Schefold, *Treasure Hunting?*, 1, 2.
546 Coos Van Brakel, "Hunters, gatherers and collectors: Origins and early history of the Indonesian collections in the Tropenmuseum in Amsterdam", in eds. Schefold and Vermeulen, *Treasure Hunting?*, 175.
547 Personal communication with grandson, Fred Stammeshaus, October 2, 2014.
548 Eds. Hardiati and Ter Keurs, *Indonesia: The Discovery of the Past.*
549 Cynthia Scott, "Sharing the divisions of the colonial past: an assessment of the Netherlands-Indonesia shared cultural heritage project, 2003 – 2006" in *International Journal of Heritage Studies* (London: Taylor & Francis Online, 2012), 3.

collecting contexts'.[550] Collecting for colonial exhibitions was a *'balanced activity'.* Objects were specially ordered and paid for.[551] Lunsingh Scheurleer emphasises that the Dutch laws on the archipelago's cultural heritage were motivated by the need to protect it against the deplorable ways in which Europeans collected and preserved statues and other archaeological objects in their gardens for themselves, brought them home or sold them.[552]

Icons of Art – National Museum of Jakarta contains many provenance details.[553] Djojonegoro offers the history of the Batavian Society and the National Museum.[554] Trigangga ea. study the museum's acquisitions; many findings coincide with the ones in this study.[555] Budiarti expands the concept of cultural heritage in the country beyond the Hindu and Buddhist scope.[556]

The authors of other studies deal with specific subjects. In *De schatten van Lombok*, Vanvugt spares neither side. He criticises Dutch museums for their unwillingness to communicate about this war booty and the National Museum in Jakarta for poor preservation after their return. His surprise visits in Jakarta might look unacademic, but it is possible that he had little choice. Since the renovation and expansion of the National Museum, many objects are safely shown, possibly also those that he had wished to see.[557]

Hanneke Hollander emphasises the role of a professional collector: Carel Groenevelt (1899 – 1973). A focus on the activities of private collectors is much needed to map a bigger part of the flow of objects. Driven by a mix of the salvage paradigm and self-interest, Groenevelt provided the Tropenmuseum in Amsterdam and the World Museum in Rotterdam with ethnographic objects. Incidentally he was caught for bypassing export laws.[558]

In his 2009 study of the Batavian Society, Hans Groot reveals contestable acquisitions. The Society used euphemisms, noting that regalia had been *'found'*, when in fact they had been captured. There were internal thefts of regalia and atlases that had been taken during the conquest of Goa in 1780 and given to the

550 Pieter Ter Keurs, *Colonial Collections Revisited*, 1.
551 Francine Brinkgreve and David Stuart-Fox, "Collections after Colonial Conflict – Bandung and Tabaman 1906 – 2006", in ed. Ter Keurs, *Colonial Collections Revisited*, 145-179. Hari Budiarti, "Taking and Returning Objects in a Colonial Context – Tracing the Collections acquired during the Bone-Gowa military expeditions", in eds. Schefold and Vermeulen, *Colonial Collections Revisited*, 123 – 144.
552 Lunsing – Scheurleer, "Collecting Javanese Antiquities: The appropriation of a newly discovered Hindu-Buddhist civilization", in ed. Ter Keurs, *Colonial Collections Revisited*, 89.
553 Eds. John Miksic and Retno Sulistianingsih Sitowati, *Icons of Art – National Museum of Jakarta* (Jakarta: National Museum, 2006).
554 Djojonegoro, "The evolution of the National Museum", in eds. Miksic and Sitowati, *Icons of Art*.
555 Trigangga, Peni Mudji Sukati and Djunaidi Ismail, "Three centuries of collections", in eds. Miksic and Sitowati, *Icons of Art*.
556 Hari Budiarti, "Heirlooms of an Archipelago", in eds. Miksic and Sitowati, *Icons of Art*.
557 Ewald Vanvugt, *De Schatten van Lombok: Honderd Jaar Nederlandse Oorlogsbuit uit Indonesië* (Amsterdam: Jan Mets, 1994), 116, 108. My own visit, November 22, 2014.
558 Hanneke Hollander, *Een man met een speurneus – Carel Groeneveldt*, 66, 69; 62, 63. Jacobs, *Collecting Kamoro-objects*, 68.

Batavian Society in 1781. The line between administration and private property often remained unclear.[559]

In his study about the Royal Dutch Cabinet of Curiosities and Museum Volkenkunde in Leiden, Rudolf Effert demonstrates the importance of colonial cultural objects for the Dutch national identity. Collecting was not neutral, but an expression of a unified kingdom with heroes, commercial successes and an emphasis on '*the superiority of the Western civilisation*', combined with '*a genuine curiosity regarding foreign cultures*'.[560]

According to Karen Jacobs, the discovery of new regions and people on the southwest coast of Papua led to the collecting of curiosities as concrete proof of conquest and domination. In *Collecting Kamoro-objects*, she rightly emphasises the interest of coastal people in selling artefacts to Western visitors.[561]

In her study of four elite families in the Dutch East Indies, Caroline Drieënhuizen argues that much collecting by the Dutch was '*purposely*' meant to rob, buy or trick out *pusaka* (heirlooms) with a ritual value from local rulers. Many had passed from generation to generation. Their loss implicated a loss of their identity, ancestors and history. '*It was a political act, in which appropriation, spiritual subjugation and oppression of the population were central*', the aim being a '*double surrender*'. In the families' collections, she found '*numerous objects... acquired in war circumstances*' – batiks from Sumatra, textile and paintings from Bali, flags, weapons and Korans from Aceh and treasures from Lombok. Many ended up in museums without proper provenance information.[562] Another researcher investigated the provenance of twenty krisses in the collection of the Dutch Royal Family and discovered that more were colonial loot than gifts.[563]

Rijksmuseum historian Harm Stevens has written extensively about violence in collecting in the colonial period and the contestable origin of objects. He published documents about the last King of the Batak, who was killed in 1907 and whose kris was donated to the Batavian Society.[564] In a recent publication about the Rijksmuseum's Indonesia collection, he uncovers the provenance of arms, flags and other war booty and adds a chapter to an object in the Netherlands that had belonged to Diponegoro – his pilgrim's staff. Descendants of a former Dutch elite family decided to return it to the National Museum in Jakarta (Box: *Return of Diponegoro's pilgrim's staff to Indonesia*).[565]

---

559 Groot, *Van Batavia naar Weltevreden*, 133.
560 Rudolf Effert, "The Royal Cabinet of Curiosities and the National Museum of Ethnography in the nineteenth century: From the belief in the superiority of western civilization to comparative ethnography", in eds. E. Bergvelt, D.J. Meijers, L. Tibbe, and E. Van Wezel, *Museale Spezialisierung und Nationalisierung ab 1830. Das Neue Museum in Berlin im internationalen Kontext, Berliner Schriften zur Museumsforschung* (Berlin: G + H Verlag Berlin, Band 29, 2011), 164, 163, 153.
561 Jacobs, *Collecting Kamoro-objects*, 21; 42.
562 Drieënhuizen, *Koloniale collecties, Nederlands aanzien*, 12; 305; 50 – 55, 135, 156, 207, 239.
563 Tessa Ver Loren van Themaat, *Royaal geschenk of koninklijke buit? Een onderzoek naar de krissen die door het koninklijk Kabinet van Zeldzaamheden verzameld zijn tussen 1817 en 1835* (Amsterdam: Free University, Bachelor thesis, 2010, unpubl.).
564 Harm Stevens, *De laatste Batakkoning – Koloniale kroniek in documenten 1883 – 1911* (Arnhem: Museum Bronbeek, 2010).
565 Stevens, *Bitter Spice*, 19, 37, 57; 157 ff.

Return of Diponegoro's pilgrim's staff[1]

The 1.4 metre long wooden staff with silver and metal elements and paper with a text was possibly two hundred years old, when Diponegoro acquired it. He used it on pilgrimage to holy places. Governor-General J.C. Baron Baud[2] acquired the staff in 1834.

There is something mysterious with this object. In 1959, one of the great-grandsons of Baud asked the Rijksmuseum and Museum Volkenkunde, in which of the two museums the staff and some other objects that had belonged to Diponegoro would fit best. It is unknown whether he received a reply. In 1964 a curator of the Amsterdam museum inquired of him what had happened to the staff. Nothing had happened and further correspondence fell into oblivion. The mystery is that none of the two museums has annexed this precious object. One cannot believe that the acquisition of such historical treasures was not a collection priority. Did the museums want to keep the object out of the wind, so that it would not become part of the return negotiations with Indonesia?

Anyhow, in 2014, Baud's descendants decided to return the staff to Indonesia and contacted history curator Harm Stevens of the Rijksmuseum. Stevens approached Peter Carey in Indonesia, who was preparing the exhibition *A Prince for all Seasons: Diponegoro in the Memory of the Nation, from Raden Saleh to the Present*, to be held in the refurbished National Gallery in Jakarta early in 2015. The Bauds visited both the National Museum in Jakarta and the Diponegoro Museum in Magelang. That the staff did not end up in the latter had to do with its poorer infrastructure and lower number of visitors.[3]

During the handover '*to the Indonesian people*', the descendants said: '*The staff was given to our forefather in 1834 and has been in the possession of our family ever since. Nevertheless, over time and between the different generations the real significance of the staff was lost.... As heirs of J.C. Baud, who, in a very different historical era, played such an important role in what was then a Dutch colony, we realised the importance of this finding and the responsibility it bestowed upon us. We discussed its significance and the context in which it was given to our forefather. Quickly the possibility of giving the staff back to the Indonesian people emerged. The decision was taken and this exhibition dedicated to the life and memory of Prince Diponegoro seemed a most appropriate moment to hand the heirloom over.*'

Notes

1 Personal communication with Harm Stevens, February 7, 2014. Stevens at conference *New futures for (post)colonial collections and research* (Leiden: RCMC, October 14 – 15, 2014). Email exchanges with Peter Carey, November 2014 – March 2015. Harm Stevens' *Onderzoeksverslag* (unpubl.) dd. January 28, 2015.

2 http://www.parlement.com/id/vg09lkxrbnwk/j_ch_baud (October 15, 2014).

3 Email Erica Baud, June 21, 2015.

Cynthia Scott's *Negotiating the colonial past in the age of European decolonization: Cultural property return between the Netherlands and Indonesia* comes close to my analysis in this Part.[566] She focuses on the role of Dutch officials in the negotiations. They did play an important role, although their differing views often made them act differently. The focus in my study is on the process of the negotiations, from different sides and with the views of more stakeholders. Scott sees the return of the Lombok treasures as

566 I read Cynthia Scott's study after finishing an advanced draft of this Part.

the most prominent transfer, while I follow Pott and Sutaarga, who point to the Prajñaparamitra statue as the one with the most impact.[567] We share the conclusion that in the 1975 Joint Recommendations the Netherlands minimalised returns and wanted to forget a painful past and enlarge its goodwill as a country that acted *'liberally'* and *'generously'* and as *'an example'* for other countries,[568] while the newcomer needed self-esteem and cultural objects to strengthen its national unity and identity. Though she regularly echoes or even uses such concepts as *'diplomatic model'* and *'expression of goodwill'*, she does not frame the return negotiations explicitly as an instrument of the cultural diplomacy for both countries.[569]

All research efforts of the last quarter century offer several insights. To begin with, during the period of colonial expansion there was more collecting than was thought earlier and such was the case for other European colonisers as well.[570] Compared to botany, agricultural crops and minerals, culture might have been a stepchild but, as shown below (Box: *Evidence of migration of objects in the first period*), it was less so than often assumed.

The Dutch government archives rarely give a glimpse of the circumstances of the second period of settler and exploitation colonialism that necessitated the curbing of the smuggling of ancient objects. Yet there was large-scale appropriation of war booty and many more colonial cultural objects were tainted, as their provenance reaches further back than was realised in 1975. This raises new questions. Why did the Netherlands never consider a return of the Ganesh, Durga, Nandicwara and Mbakala statues from the Singasari temple complex, which Indonesia repeatedly requested? The 2013 book of Museum Volkenkunde about its masterpieces or the captions to these objects in the exhibition spaces do not mention the 1975 Indonesian claim to these.[571] Why did the Netherlands not do more to encourage non-state owners to reconsider their possession of contestable objects? Pieter Pott of Museum Volkenkunde, who was a member of the Dutch Team of Experts, for instance, must have known about Diponegoro's pilgrim's staff that was in possession of the Baud family and about the willingness of the family to relinquish the object. Why were the reins of Diponegoro's horse not part of the 1977 transfer?[572] Why did the Netherlands not enquire after the whereabouts of the kris of Diponegoro (Box: *The missing kris of Diponegoro*)? Questions such as these offer evidence to the conclusion that decolonisation has remained an unresolved conflict.

---

567 Cynthia Scott, *Negotiating the colonial past*, 183, 232.

568 Memo 25/1978, May 10, 1978, of Chief DCV to Minister of Foreign Affairs, in: *National Archive*, The Hague, "Ministry of Foreign Affairs 1975 – 1984, Inv. No. 10146".

569 Cynthia Scott, ibid., 192; 232, 236.

570 Hilario Casado Alonso, "Geographical Discoveries: New economic Opportunities in a Globalising World", 196.

571 Museum Volkenkunde, *Masterpieces of Rijksmuseum Volkenkunde* (Amsterdam: KIT Publishers, 2013), 100.

572 They remain unmentioned in the transfer of objects dd. September 2, 1977 (Arnhem: Museum Bronbeek, Dossier Diponegoro). When, in 2015, the Erasmus House in Jakarta was preparing a small exhibition about Diponegoro, the issue of whether Bronbeek might lend the reins came up and was eventually rejected because of time pressure, email Peter Carey, March 18, 2015.

Evidence of migration of objects in the first period

Paludanus of the city of Enkhuizen collected ethnographics from China, Japan and the East Indies (1596).[1]

The Library of **Leiden University** acquired an ancient manuscript from the Southeast Asian islands (1597).[2]

Rembrandt was one of the many artists who collected objects from all corners of the world.[3] In 1628 he depicted a Javanese kris on his painting of Samson and Delilah (presently in Gemäldegalerie, Berlin) and made drawings of royal persons based on Indian miniatures (some are in the Amsterdam Rijksmuseum).[4]

Rijklof van Goens, 17th century VOC-merchant, collected golden jewellery from Islamic graves and Hindu-Buddhist temple sites.[5]

Nicolaes Witsen, a mayor of Amsterdam and VOC governor, acquired bronze Hindu statues from a temple in Malabar, India, captured by VOC soldiers in 1691. He had them auctioned in 1728. It is unknown where they went.[6]

Jan Albert Sichterman (1692 – 1764), a VOC-director in Bengal, needed two ships to transport all his treasures from Asia to Groningen in the Netherlands. It is unknown, how many of these treasures were inalienable objects and how many had been created for foreign visitors.[7]

Notes

1 Roelof Van Gelder, "Liefhebbers en geleerde luiden: Nederlandse kabinetten en hun bezoekers", in ed. Bergvelt and Kistemaker, *De Wereld binnen Handbereik*, 263 – 266. Claudia Swan, "Collecting naturalia in the shadow of early modern Dutch trade", in eds. Londa Schiebinger and Claudia Swan, *Colonial botany: science, commerce, and politics in the early modern world* (Philadelphia: University of Pennsylvania Press, 2005), 224.

2 http://media.leidenuniv.nl/legacy/omslag-2010-3-lage-res.pdf (April 7, 2015).

3 https://hetrariteitenkabinet.wordpress.com/2014/01/16/rembrandt-van-rijn-3/ (January 29, 2016).

4 http://www.smb-digital.de/eMuseumPlus?service=direct/1/ResultLightboxView/result.t1. collection_lightbox.$TspTitleImageLink. link&sp=10&sp=Scollection&sp=SfieldValue& sp=0&sp=2&sp=3&sp=Slightbox_3x4&sp=24& sp=Sdetail&sp=0&sp=F&sp=T&sp=32 (April 7, 2015); https://www.rijksmuseum.nl/nl/zoeken? p=1&ps=12&f.classification.iconClassDescription sort=historical+person+(SJAH+JAHAN)+-+ historical+person(SJAH+JAHAN)+portrayed (January 29, 2016).

5 Lunsingh Scheurleer, 2007: 76.

6 *Asia in Amsterdam – The culture of luxury in the Golden Age* (Amsterdam: Rijksmuseum, 2015, catalogue): 202, 203.

7 Lequin, *Het personeel van de VOC*, 185. https://www.deverhalenvangroningen.nl/alle-verhalen/de-koning-van-groningen-jan-albert-sichterman-1692-1764 (February 20, 2017).

The missing kris of Diponegoro

Streets in Indonesia and a university are named after him. He has a statue near the country's National Monument and a museum in Central Java. Indonesia attaches importance to him and his disappeared kris.[1] The archives of the 1970s and 1980s offer almost no hints about where the kris can be found that Diponegoro's surrendered in 1830 to General De Kock. But there are a few hints.

One is a '*confidential code message*' of 1983, in which Dutch ambassador Lodewijk van Gorkom in Jakarta informed the Dutch Foreign Ministry to have received information from a Dutch source that the kris was in the cellar of the Rijksmuseum in Amsterdam. As it made little sense to keep it in the Netherlands, since it had much more value for Indonesia, the ambassador suggested to '*consider a transfer of the kris to Indonesia*'[2] and mentioned the coming visit of Minister Nugroho Notosusanto of Education and Culture to the Netherlands as an excellent occasion to transfer the precious object.[3] But nothing was done with the message.

Van Gorkom's successor, ambassador Frans van Dongen, also thought that the kris was in the Netherlands, be it not in Amsterdam but in Leiden. He told me that, on the occasion of the 40th anniversary of the Republic Indonesia in 1985 and being aware of Indonesian sensitivities, he '*wrote to Director Pieter Pott of the National Museum of Ethnology.... and also suggested that the Foreign Ministry in The*

Hague should make a large gesture and return Diponegoro's kris. It would have a symbolic meaning for the whole of Indonesia and a special meaning for its President. But Pott sent me a note that a return was undesirable. I know for sure from my correspondence with Pott that at that moment the kris was in the Museum in Leiden.'[4]

Recently, Museum Volkenkunde in Leiden has looked for the kris but found no trace of it.[5] Earlier it declared that it was willing to join an international enquiry and to open its archives and depots. Inquiries at Museum Bronbeek in Arnhem and the World Museum in Vienna did not help either.[6]

Notes

1   Suwati Kartiwa, "Pusaka and the Palaces of Java", in ed. Soebadio, *Pusaka – Art of Indonesia*, 160. Interview with Catrini P. Kubontubuh, BPPI Indonesian Heritage Trust, June 22, 2011.

2   The Hague: *National Archive*, Archive Ministry of Foreign Affairs 1975 – 1984, Inv. No. 10268.

3   Van Gorkom, *Door Europa en de Wereld*, 214.

4   Jos Van Beurden, *Return of Cultural and Historical Treasures*, 59, 61. Van Dongen does not refer to it in his memoirs, *Van Timor naar Jakarta: Bestuursambetnaar in diplomatieke dienst* (Amsterdam: Boom, 2009).

5   Personal communication with Francine Brinkgreve, Leiden, Museum Volkenkunde, November 15, 2015.

6   Jos Van Beurden, ibid., 59, 61.

8.2. The 1975 agreement: lessons for other bilateral negotiations

This case study has made clear that the transfer of objects was, to a great extent, part of both countries' cultural diplomacy. The negotiations certainly were about objects, but also about other, more covert, interests and foreign policy aims. The Netherlands used the transfer to resume its relationship with Indonesia and to improve its image internationally. Indonesia used the negotiations to present itself as a country that could stand up to its former coloniser and was entitled to and able to retrieve important cultural and historical objects.[573] Some early returns – state owned or from the private collection of the Dutch royal family – facilitated the take-off of the talks. Both countries entrenched themselves beforehand in order to have to acquiesce to as little as possible. Indonesia did so with its long list of tainted objects in Dutch museums, the Netherlands with its continuing prioritisation of strengthening its former colony's museum infrastructure.

With its emphasis on equality between the countries and the need for reciprocity, the Netherlands showed little awareness of the direct, structural and ideological violence that had been committed in its name in the colonial era, and what this had meant to Indonesians. Reciprocity was observed in the exchange of archival materials and in the stipulation in the Joint Recommendations that if either country needed an object from the other, they would talk about it. The outcome was a package deal in which Indonesia's demands were only partially met and the Netherlands lost little. The museums that held the Prajñaparamita statue and Diponegoro's equipment felt some pain releasing them. By accepting the transfer of half of all Lombok treasures from Dutch museums, the possession of the other half was cleared. Indonesia's persistent return claims had confronted the Dutch unpleasantly with discrepancies with their self-image of 'ethical colonialists, enlightened scholars and stewards of Indonesian material culture'.[574]

What does a closer examination of the process that led to the Joint Recommendations contribute to a model for negotiating the future of colonial cultural objects? How can five generations of conflict researchers contribute to this examination (Box: *Five generations of conflict researchers, a critical view*, 5.4.)? Their input has to do with ways of dealing with conflicts (compromise or integration), the area of contestation in a conflict (colonial cultural objects), the stakeholders (state and non-state), their commitment, underlying interests and issues of (in)equality.

The Netherlands and Indonesia negotiated in a period in which other countries did so too, and in which an anti-colonial wind was blowing. As a member of the Non-Aligned Movement, Indonesia participated in a process that 'enabled the powerless to hold a dialogue with the powerful and to try to hold them accountable'.[575] The Dutch were aware of negotiations between Belgium and DR Congo and Greek claims for the Parthenon Marbles from Great Britain, and felt encouraged by other European Community members not to give in too much to demands of former colonies.

The contested area was known: the possession of cultural and historical objects in Dutch collections, acquired in a dubious manner during the colonial era. The two parties certainly included provenance discussions in the negotiations, but for the Dutch, these exchanges were less oriented towards compiling biographies of objects than towards downplaying or denying the number of contestable

---

573 Cynthia Scott, ibid., 192.
574 Cynthia Scott, ibid., 122.
575 Prashad, *Darker Nations*, XVIII, XIX.

acquisitions in state collections. With more provenance research, the number of contested or tainted objects that left Indonesia might further increase. [576]

Lengthiness

What is striking is the length of the negotiations (1949 – 1975). The quarter century can be split up into three rounds. In 1949, the first began with the Round Table Conference and an agreement with a return provision, which was, however, never implemented. Until the 1960s, a time of estrangement followed. In 1968, the second round started with the Cultural Agreement, which mentioned the need to discuss new cultural relations and the transfer of objects. Again, not much happened. In 1975, two teams of experts began the third round. Factors that caused the negotiations to last this long were the widespread violence between 1945 and 1949, the stiff relationship between President Sukarno and the Dutch authorities, tensions around Papua, the economic interconnectedness of the two countries and the difficulty of return negotiations. Negotiations about political and economic issues were much more familiar than negotiations about cultural objects.

Compromise

The negotiations were aimed at a compromise – the parties reached an agreement, without being satisfied – and not at integration with a merging of the desires of both stakeholders in the final outcome. The informal talks and extensive socialising during the 1975 and later negotiations, *'were essential to learn and understand ideas, arguments and general feelings, and to try and find a basis where both delegations could meet'*, commented two participants.[577] Pictures found in the personal archive of Dutch team member, Miss Ans Kalmeijer, do not offer a clue about the atmosphere that had prevailed. To word it somewhat schematically, if socialising is focussed on integration, it serves to create trust and makes a relationship sustainable. If it is focussed on compromise, it is part of a lobby and aimed at convincing the other party.[578]

The consultations could be tense and the delegations occasionally behaved as *'quarrellers'*.[579] The outcome was presented as the final word on all claims of the former colony to treasures present in the former metropolis. In the upper echelons of the Dutch heritage world, it is still considered as such.[580] The warm reactions to the recent return by a private Dutch family of a Diponegoro attribute and other developments reveal different desires in Indonesia.

---

576 Legêne, *Spiegelreflex*, 226.
577 Pott and Sutaarga, "Arrangements concluded or in progress for the Return of Objects", 40.
578 To 'convince' comes from the Latin 'convincere', which is winning or conquering and supposes a winner/conqueror and a loser/conquered.
579 Van der Straaten, *Terug of Houden Zo?*, 33.
580 Interview with Steven Engelsman, then Leiden, Museum Volkenkunde, March 23, 2011.

Stakeholders

There were only two parties that participated in the negotiations: two states. Indonesia had excluded princes, regional rulers and other non-state actors from its Team of Experts. Although the Netherlands had close relations with some traditional rulers, they accepted this exclusion and turned down repeated requests of, for example, the descendants of King Singamangaraja XI on Sumatra for the return of the King's regalia.[581] The stakeholders thus simplified the question, to whom the objects should be returned. With more stakeholders involved, the outcome might have been different.

For other potential stakeholders in Indonesia, cultural heritage embraced more than the dominant heritage discourse allowed. The dominant discourse offered little room for prehistoric and proto-historic cultures, Islamic culture, regional and local cultures, and modern, living cultures.[582] Why were these not part of the negotiations? In the USA, Australia, and Canada claims of regional peoples for this sort of cultural heritage are dealt with in legislation.[583]

The exclusion of non-state stakeholders did not mean that there were no internal frictions inside each Team of Experts. The head of the Dutch Team, Rob Hotke, had to persuade Pieter Pott, who wanted to minimise returns, '*to be more reasonable*'.[584] Indonesia's Minister of Education and Culture brushed aside his team's extensive return claims. Dynamics, caused by internal frictions in one stakeholder, are normal,[585] as team members have divergent backgrounds and interests. Such frictions can be productive in finding solutions.

There were also the media. In Indonesia, they had served as a channel for government officials to voice return claims and to prepare the ground for formal negotiations. In the Netherlands, they had helped to clear the way for this by questioning the presence of colonial cultural objects.

(In)equality

During the negotiations, the Dutch emphasised that Indonesia and the Netherlands were equal to each other. But did the two have equal chances and comparable capabilities to run the negotiations? Was their commitment sufficient and of comparable level? One was the possessor of objects, the other claiming them; one was an experienced international negotiator, the other a relative newcomer. The unresolved conflict that they had to discuss was asymmetric. There is no evidence whether and how this asymmetry was considered.

---

581 Letter Director-general for Culture, R. Hotke of the Ministry of Culture, Recreation and Social Welfare to the Dutch Minister of Foreign Affairs dd. August 4, 1980; and letter R. Hotke of July 7, 1980 to Dutch Foreign Ministry, No. DAZ/JZ 184598, reference 210.282, both in The Hague: *National Archive*, Archives of the Foreign Ministry, 1975 – 1984, Inv. No. 10267.

582 Sudarmadi, *Between colonial legacies and grassroots movements*, 92. Another indication is that only 470 (or 1,2 percent) of the 39.300 items from Indonesia in the Tropenmuseum are associated with the Islam (Shatanawi, *Islam at the Tropenmuseum*, 216).

583 Vrdoljak, *International Law, Museums and the Return of Cultural Objects*, 302.

584 Ans Kalmeijer in a 2005 interview with Susan Legêne.

585 Fisher and Ury, *Getting to yes*, 49.

In retrospect, Sutaarga and Pott emphasised that some experts in the two teams *'had already known their "counterparts" from the delegation of the other country for a long time'*.[586] Sutaarga, who had studied in the Netherlands under Pott at Leiden University, was *'certainly not opposed to cooperation with the Dutch'*.[587] From their correspondence – in Dutch – they emerge as friends.[588] Indonesian and Dutch colleagues who had known both, explain that Pott was rather *'standoffish'* and *'focussed on his own interests'*, while Sutaarga was *'more modest'*.[589] Did their relationship influence the outcome of the negotiations or the selection of Lombok treasures to be returned? The archives do not offer a clue, but the question about a hidden hierarchy remains.

Equality is a sensitive issue. Questioning (in)equality carries a risk of paternalism and abuse. If there is much inequality between stakeholders, what should one do? Earlier (6.2.2.), it was suggested to consider the *justice and capabilities approach* developed by Sen and Nussbaum. The issue of equality will be elaborated later (14.2., Box: *Address [in]equality*).

Underlying interests

In conflict studies underlying interests are those that stakeholders do not openly share. They remain hidden, but influence the negotiations. Stakeholders can be unaware of them, while it is essential to know one's own hidden interests and those of the other side.[590]

Whilst open about its desire for aesthetic, historical and cultural objects, which were needed for more national unity and identity, Indonesia was less open about other interests. One such interest was to be seen as equal to the Netherlands. It explains Indonesia's difficulty with the Dutch being patronising about the strengthening of Indonesia's museum and archival infrastructure. Did the Dutch hammer on the weakness of the museum and archival infrastructure of Indonesia to evade discussing large-scale returns and was the Dutch offer to help strengthening this infrastructure motivated by the desire to resume the relationship with Indonesia or was it genuine?

Indonesia's interest in the transfer of Lombok gold and silver treasures was not so much that it did not have any, or that gaps had to be filled in existing collections – a large number had remained in the country or had come back earlier – but rather their high financial value and splendour and the implicit recognition of injustice committed by the Netherlands.

The Netherlands hid its fear of losing many objects, collections and archives and made concessions to serve another interest, that of doing away the damage to its reputation during the decolonisation. It presented itself, therefore, as a

---

586 Pott and Sutaarga, "Arrangements concluded or in progress for the Return of Objects", 40.
587 Cynthia Scott, *Negotiating the colonial past*, 115.
588 Leiden: *Museum Volkenkunde*, Archives, Box number 222, Covers 1975 – 1978, Cover on Agenda 1978, No. 440; Cover on Agenda 1980, No. 442; and Cover on Agenda 1981, No. 443.
589 Personal communication with insiders Museum Volkenkunde (February 28, 2014).
590 Lewis, *Inside the No*, 27.

liberal and generous giver of colonial cultural objects.[591] But the transfer of the Prajñaparamita – the Grand Prize of the negotiating process – enabled Museum Volkenkunde in Leiden to keep four other Hindu-Javanese statues that had been high on Indonesia's wish list.[592] The Dutch acquiesced to certain demands in order to keep other objects. A Dutch interest in the transfer of Lombok treasures was that it made it harder to raise the issue of war booty again and that the remaining treasures could stay in the Netherlands.

It is difficult to envision the Netherlands' underlying interest in doing so little to discover the kris and other parts of Diponegoro's equipment, while Museum Volkenkunde had some details and Dutch diplomats had hinted at where the kris might be. Why did the Netherlands do so little to establish contacts with non-state possessors of objects, as Joint Recommendation II.3 stipulated? Think of Borobudur Buddha heads and other objects that had left Indonesia in violation of the colonial laws. As stated earlier (7.3.), in Dutch law the protection of private property has priority and it would be hard and costly to trace such objects. Moreover, it might have played a role that many of those who would have to implement the search and the possessors of contestable objects belonged to the same elite. As written before (6.2.2.), the Dutch Restitutions Committee for Nazi-looted art has raised the issue of Nazi-looted objects in private possession. Only if private owners of such works are willing to think about the future of these works, '*the end of the restitution issues comes into view*'. The return by the Baud family of in a constructive manner Diponegoro's pilgrim's staff to Indonesia shows that returns of colonial cultural objects by non-state actors can be very welcome.

Two more underlying interests are discussed – that behind the use of the term *transfer* and that behind *gifts*, such as made by the Dutch royal family to Indonesia's presidential couple.

Transfer

Initially, Indonesia employed the term 'restitution', which implied that wrongful acts had to be undone. It shifted during the 1975 deliberations to the neutral 'return'. Both terms appear in the Netherlands Government archives,[593] but only to say that they were not supposed to be used.[594] '*The Netherlands delegation has always opposed such vocabulary, because "return" implied unlawful acquisition of*

---

591 The Netherlands even feared that Indonesia would lose all interest in it: Coded message Embassy Jakarta to Minister for Foreign Affairs, July 12, 1982, Ref. nr. 15198 / 72; Memorandum of DOA/ IN to ACS M.J.J. Van Loosdrecht, April 26, 1983, No. 66/83. Both in The Hague: *National Archive*, Archives Ministry of Foreign Affairs 1975 – 1984 – Inv. No. 10146.

592 Leiden: *Museum Volkenkunde*, Inv. No. 1403-1681.

593 Two exceptions have been found. In July 1975, Pieter Pott of the Leiden museum used 'return', when speaking at the occasion of the transfer to Indonesia of the Papua treasures kept in the museum since early 1963; it was a slip of the tongue as the museum had never considered the objects as its property: Leiden: *Museum Volkenkunde*, Archives, Box number 61, Cover 118, Agenda 1975, numbers 764, 765, 766. In the 1975 Joint Recommendation II.5, the Dutch Government is asked to find the whereabouts of the Luwu insignia and to 'return' them to Indonesia.

594 E.g. Kalmeijer, Verslag van de reis naar Indonesië van de Nederlandse delegatie, 2.

property, or at least supposes it'.[595] That is why the Dutch team pushed for 'transfer' as the main term in the final document.[596]

There is little archival evidence of awareness on the Dutch side of the inequality and injustices of the colonial past. Some Cabinet ministers showed more sensitivity than others, but none expressed explicitly that the Joint Recommendations served to rectify injustice. There is evidence of efforts to hide or deny the colonial past with euphemisms. Colonial officials who knowingly removed or robbed statues from temple sites had rarely been reprimanded.[597] The Dutch team was instructed to give in to Indonesian demands, if necessary, and not to challenge the relationship with the Government of Indonesia. The Indonesian team was *'aware that cooperation should not only benefit one party'* and hoped that the transfer of objects *'to Indonesia would increase and strengthen the cultural cooperation between the two countries'.*[598] This echoes the spirit of *Musyawarah-mufakat*, the habit to continue negotiations until consensus has been reached.

Gifts

The Dutch royal family gave paintings to Indonesia that it had received from painter Raden Saleh in appreciation of their support for his stay and study in the Netherlands and Europe. There was no obligation behind it. What can have motivated the Royal Family? The Netherlands had never welcomed Indonesia's first president, Sukarno. The visit in 1970 of his successor, Suharto, had been intended to normalise relations. In the preparations for the visit, the head of the household division of Suharto's palace and experienced diplomat, Dutchman Joop Ave,[599] had asked after the wishes of Queen Juliana and Prince Consort Bernhard and informed the Dutch ambassador that the Indonesian presidential couple would be delighted to accept the Raden Saleh's paintings.

At that time, the Dutch royal family brought together two slightly jaded archetypes in the Dutch self-image – that of the trader and of the preacher. I know them from the sector of international development aid. Queen Juliana was known for her pacifism and urge to diminish the gap between the rich and the poor in the world.[600] Prince Consort Bernard was close to Dutch multinational companies. His visits to heads of state such as President Mobutu and Emperor Haile Selassie were also meant to pave the way for Dutch commercial interests. He and Suharto

---

595 Note for the Council of Ministers, April 1976: 3, in The Hague: *National Archive*, Archive of the Ministry of Foreign Affairs 1975 – 1984, Inv. No. 10266. Note of Director for Asia and Oceania to Director for Culture and Information on transfer of cultural objects, in The Hague: *National Archive*, Archive Ministry of Foreign Affairs 1975 – 1984, Inv. No. 10267.

596 Memo of the Cabinet of the Prime Minister No. U 18940, November 6, 1968 to Minister for Culture, Recreation and Social Welfare, in The Hague: *National Archive*, Archive Ministry of Foreign Affairs, Inv. No. 2.27.19, 4193, CRM 1965 – 1982.

597 Groot, *Van Batavia naar Weltevreden*, 133. Scheurleer, "Collecting Javanese Antiquities", 86, 89.

598 Statement of the Indonesian Delegation on the Return of Indonesian Cultural Objects 1975: 10, in The Hague: *National Archive*, Archive Foreign Ministry 1975 – 1984, Inv. No. 10266.

599 http://www.thebalidaily.com/2014-02-10/former-minister-joop-ave-cremated-nusa-dua.html (May 7, 2014).

600 Cees Fasseur, *Juliana & Bernard – Het verhaal van een huwelijk. De Jaren 1936 – 1956* (Amsterdam: Balans, 2008), 268. Wetenschappelijke Raad voor het Regeringsbeleid, *Minder pretentie, meer ambitie – ontwikkelingshulp die verschil maakt* (Amsterdam: Amsterdam University Press, 2010), 37.

Returns to Indonesia 1949 – 1978

Two paintings of Raden Saleh
Gift by the Dutch royal family to President Suharto during his visit to the Netherlands in 1970.

Nagarakertagama palm-leaf manuscript
Transferred by the Library of Leiden University to the Government of Indonesia before the first meeting in 1975; currently in the National Library, Jakarta.

380 ethnographic objects from Papua
After they had been held in deposit since 1963, Museum Volkenkunde returned these to the Government of Indonesia on June 13, 1975; efforts to verify their present whereabouts have been in vain.

Painting Capture of Pangeran Diponegoro by Raden Saleh
Donated on behalf of the Dutch royal family by Museum Bronbeek to the Government of Indonesia in 1977; presently in the National Palace, Jakarta.

Equipment of Diponegoro
Objects transferred by the Minister of Defence from Museum Bronbeek to the Government of Indonesia in 1977; now in National Museum, Jakarta.

Prajñaparamita statue
Transferred by the Minister of Education, Arts and Sciences from Museum Volkenkunde to the Government of Indonesia in 1978, at the occasion of the 200th anniversary of the National Museum in Jakarta, where it is presently being held.

Lombok treasure
Transferred by the Minister of Education, Arts and Sciences from Museum Volkenkunde to the Government of Indonesia in 1977; now in the National Museum, Jakarta.

Archives and documents à Several exchanges from 1968 onwards, mostly authorised by the Minister of Education, Arts and Sciences, e.g.:

- The 25-million-page *archives of the Dutch East India Company* remained where they were, either in Jakarta or in The Hague; they have been included in the UNESCO Memory of the World Register in 2004.
- A large number of the *Yogya-archives* were returned to Indonesia. This continued until 1987.[1]
- In 1983, the transfer of a Bahasa Indonesia copy of the 1946/7 *Linggadjati Agreement* between the Netherlands administration and the unilaterally declared Republic of Indonesia took place, on condition that it would be sent back, if Indonesia retrieved its own copy.[2]
- The national archives of both countries have continued to cooperate through the years.[3]

1   In 1983, Indonesia asked for more Yogya-archives. Although the Netherlands thought that this transfer had been finalised in 1970s (Letter Deputy Chief of the Directorate Asia and Oceania to Netherlands Ambassador in Jakarta dd. March 25, 1983, DOA/IN-85479, in The Hague: *National Archive*, Ministry of Foreign Affairs 1975 – 1984, Inv. No.10268), the return went on until 1987.

2   Letter State Archivist to Deputy Secretary-General of the Ministry of Foreign Affairs,

December 21, 1982, CD/A82.1536. Letter Netherlands Ambassador International Cultural Cooperation to General to State Archivist, February 8, 1983, ACS-33442. Both in The Hague: *National Archive*, ibid.

3   Louisa Balk, Frans Van Dijk, Diederick Kortlang, Femme Gaastra, Hendrik Niemijer, Pieter Koenders, *The archives of the Dutch East India Company (VOC) and the local institutions in Batavia (Jakarta)* (Jakarta: Arsip Nasional Republik Indonesia and Leiden: Brill, 2007).

were personal friends.[601] Linking giving with forgiving, one cannot exclude that an implicit request for forgiveness played a role in the Queen's motivation, while the Prince was motivated by the thought that such a gift would bring economic profit in return.

In conclusion, this Part shows that provenance research helps to uncover the nature of the acquisition of colonial cultural objects. In many more instances than thought before, the acquisition was contestable. The number of colonial cultural objects handed back (Box: *Returns to Indonesia 1949 – 1978*) and the way the Netherlands did this, do not justify the label of a generous returner. The Dutch did not meet all Indonesia's wishes by any means. The return of objects was not so much relevant in itself but served, on both sides, other aims.

The lengthiness of the negotiations makes clear that there are ups and downs in negotiations and that one should not give up quickly. The choice for a compromise created difficulties at the time, as well as later. Although, understandably, only two stakeholders were involved, today the engagement of more stakeholders would be preferable and make solutions more sustainable. In two recent instances – the hand-over of a pilgrim's staff of Diponegoro by a Dutch private possessor (8.1., Box: *Return of Diponegoro's pilgrim's staff*) and the transfer of part of the Nusantara museum collection (13.2., Box: *Objections against return offers*) – the Indonesian stakeholder was the National Museum in Jakarta. Now a voice is increasingly being given to minorities and indigenous peoples, non-state stakeholders such as these and regional and local authorities should be more involved. Internal disagreements in one stakeholder can be used to further the process. Inequality in asymmetric conflicts has to be faced.

The formulation in the Joint Recommendations of the transfer of objects as '*a programme*' to be '*implemented by stages*' offers, in my view, the possibility of additional deliberations about:

601 Jan G. Kikkert, *Bernard – Een leven als een prins* (Utrecht: Aspekt, 2004), 248.

1. Joint search for the missing equipment of national heroes such as Diponegoro, especially Diponegoro's kris.
2. The future of four stone statues in the Museum Volkenkunde in Leiden – a Ganesh[602] (located in the museum's entrance), a Durga,[603] a Nandiswara gatekeeper,[604] and a Mahakala gatekeeper[605] from Singasari.[606]
3. Dutch Government efforts to locate cultural objects in non-state owned collections.

One question remains, and it is a question that concerns all former colonies. Why did Indonesia never claim more objects? How eager was and is it to retrieve colonial treasures? What is the position of these treasures in the Indonesian cultural heritage field?

Like any country, Indonesia has creators and preservers of art and heritage, and the socially and politically committed among them have several subjects that inspire them. The colonial past is only one of them. The coup d'état of 1965 and the role of Islamic fundamentalism are two others. Another one is the on-going dispute with Malaysia about shared heritage. Emotions can mount high about the performance of temple-dances or shadow-puppet theatre in Malaysia, which Indonesia claims to be Indonesian.[607]

The Government, regional and local authorities and civil organisations show increased interest for cultural heritage, including monuments from the colonial period and traditional weapons as krisses, batik textiles and musical instruments. Local and community-based museums and non-traditional museum spaces and heritage societies are a departure from the traditional Western museum or the type set up in the colonial period.[608] This trend is broader and noticeable in the whole of East and Southeast Asia,[609] and possibly also elsewhere. In the post-Suharto era, national unity and identity receive less emphasis and people show more attention to regional and local history, identity and interests.

The country has inscribed the Borobudur Temple Compounds and the Prambanan Temple Compounds (since 1991), the Sangiran Early Man Site (since 1996), the Cultural Landscape of Bali Province (since 2012) and some national parks in UNESCO's World Heritage List and put eighteen cultural and natural sites on the tentative list.[610] A 2010 law for cultural heritage protection increases

---

602 Leiden: *Museum Volkenkunde*, Catalogue No. 1403-1681.

603 Ibid., No. 1403 – 1622.

604 Ibid., No. 1403 – 1624.

605 Ibid., No. 1403 – 1623.

606 In an interview (Leiden, April 16, 2014), archaeology professor Inajati Adrisijanti remembered that she exclaimed upon the return of the Prajñaparamita: *'Thank God, it has come back home. But what about the others?'* She thought it *'inappropriate'* that they had remained in the Netherlands.

607 J.W. Chong, "'Mine, Yours or Ours?': The Indonesia – Malaysia Disputes over Shared Cultural Heritage", in *SOJOURN: Journal of Social Issues in Southeast Asia* (Singapore: ISEAS – Yusof Ishak Institute, 2012, 27/1), 1 – 53.

608 Hasti Tarekat, "Monumentenzorg in Indonesië", in *Vitruvius/Indonesië-special* (Rotterdam: Educom, 2012/1), 9 – 13.

609 Conclusion from the conference *'Museum of our own – In search of local museology in Asia'*, Yogyakarta: Gadjah Mada University, November 18 – 20, 2014.

610 See also: http://whc.unesco.org/en/statesparties/ID/ (July 12, 2015).

rewards for finders of artworks and increases the punishment for illicit trade and smuggling. Local authorities get a bigger role in registration and preservation of cultural heritage.

This is sufficient evidence to show that there certainly is an interest in colonial cultural objects. Officials of the Ministry of Culture and the National Museum and academics in the heritage sector were and are still open about their desire to see certain authentic objects return to Indonesia.[611]

---

611 Personal communications with museum officials and academics in Yogyakarta and Jakarta, November 2014.

APPROACHES IN OTHER BILATERAL AGREEMENTS

Part V - Approaches in other bilateral agreements

To continue charting the one-way flow of cultural and historical objects and finding elements for a model for negotiating the future of colonial cultural objects, this Part describes four bilateral negotiations that are comparable with that between the Netherlands and Indonesia: those between Belgium and DR Congo, between Denmark and Iceland and Greenland, and between Australia and Papua New Guinea. They raise questions about the existence of a Nordic and a Melanesian model and about the influence of geographical and cultural distance between stakeholders on negotiations. As the dialogue between Western museums and Nigeria on the future of Benin objects is the only such larger-scale event at the moment and since Benin objects have long featured in return discussions, this is also studied. First the negotiations between Belgium and DR Congo are discussed. From 1815 until 1830, the Netherlands and Belgium were part of the same Kingdom. Their colonial practices had similarities and important differences. The Dutch colonial expansion started early and took two centuries. Belgium was a late-comer and quickly entered the period of settler and exploitation colonialism.

Photograph previous page: Masks, DR Congo.

Chapter 9

The 1970 agreement between Belgium and Congo

For his part in the defeat of French Emperor Napoleon Bonaparte in 1815, Prince William (1792 – 1849), the later King William II of the Netherlands, was rewarded with a summer palace in Tervuren, Brussels. Its location in what is now Belgium resulted from the decision of the 1815 Vienna Congress to merge the Low Countries – Belgium, the Netherlands and Luxemburg – into the United Kingdom of the Netherlands as a buffer against a French revenge. Unlike the United Kingdom at the other side of the North Sea, that of the Netherlands never worked. In 1830, the Belgians broke away and established their own state and Prince William left the palace. In 1898, Belgium's King Leopold II (1835 – 1909) built the Royal Museum for Central Africa on the ruins of the palace, henceforward the Tervuren Museum.[612] It was a follow-up of the 1897 Brussels International Exhibition about economic potential, ethnographic objects and stuffed animals from Congo Free State, which had attracted over one million visitors.

Leopold had carefully guided the decision of the Berlin Conference in 1884 – 1885, which allotted him territory in Africa around the river Congo. In 1876, British explorer Verney Cameron had made public information about abundant minerals in the Congo area, especially the south eastern plateau of Katanga. Other European players had neglected it at the time.[613] Soon after the Conference, however, Cecil Rhodes obtained concessions for mining rights from local rulers in areas adjacent to Katanga. It brought Britain and Belgium together in their colonial adventures in Africa, and their cooperation would continue until far after the independence of their colonies.[614] For over two decades, Congo Free State remained King Leopold's private initiative. The run on rubber that he organised caused an immense burden of direct, structural and ideological violence; it was called the '*worst bloodshed*' and a '*holocaust in Central Africa*' with death, disease, malnourishment and a sharply declining birth-rate.[615] Upon his death in 1909, the Belgian State adopted Congo Free State as Belgian Congo. After the 1914 –

---

612 Jeroen Van Zanten, *Koning Willem II 1792 – 1849* (Amsterdam: Boom, 2013), 284 (illustration: 283). King Leopold II named it Congo Museum. The Belgian State changed it into the Museum of Belgian Congo. In 1960 it was renamed Royal Museum for Central Africa, http://www.africamuseum.be/museum/about-us/museum/history/Congomuseum (July 29, 2014).

613 Pakenham, *Scramble for Africa*, 12, 399.

614 Williams, *Who killed Hammarskjöld?*, 57.

615 Hochschild, *Geest van Koning Leopold*, 227.

1918 Great War, Belgium was allocated the nearby German colonies, Rwanda and Burundi as mandated territories.

In recent decades, the interest in Belgium's colonial past and the violence following the decolonisation has increased. Scholarly and popular writers enhance the debate[616] and detect new backgrounds. As in the case of the Netherlands and Indonesia, more Belgian and non-Congolese writers than Congolese people have joined the discourse, and very few of them deal with colonial cultural policies.[617]

The statement in the 1979 issue of UNESCO's *Museum* that objects in the Tervuren Museum were '*procured through the regular channels*' and not '*through extortion, spoliation or theft*', is untenable.[618] Schildkrout and Keim have produced evidence of pillaging cultural heritage in Central Africa and the coercion that was applied during expeditions at the start of the 20th century.[619] Former Tervuren curator, Boris Wastiau, also found substantiation of coercion in the acquisition of many objects.[620] Shaje'a Tshiluila, director of the Institute of the National Museums of Congo, wrote about Congo's problems in preserving its heritage in the 1990s.[621] Maarten Couttenier describes the role division between the Tervuren museum and other museums in Belgium and Congo.[622] Most useful has been Sarah van Beurden's '*Authentically African: African arts and postcolonial cultural politics in transnational perspective (Congo* [DRC]*, Belgium and the USA, 1955 – 1980*'.[623] There are many parallels between her analysis of the Belgian – Congolese negotiations and my findings and those of Cynthia Scott about the Dutch – Indonesian negotiations. I explicate the link between return and commercial interests. Placide Mumbembele of the University of Kinshasa points to the fate of 199 Congolese objects that Congo had requested in the 1960s, but – as in the case of the kris of Diponegoro – nobody knows where they are. They are not known to have left Belgium.[624]

9.1. Cultural policies up to independence

In 1876, Congo did not exist as a nation state nor was there 'Congolese' art. Both were King Leopold's invention. In order to underline mineral and natural prospects in the colony, he had cultural objects systematically collected. In the beginning, traders and collectors haphazardly gathered '*souvenirs of contact*'. After the Berlin Conference, a period of '*trophy collecting*' followed; trophies were weapons, other

---

616 Hochschild, ibid. Van Reybrouyck, *Congo*. Williams, ibid.
617 To relate the latter to '*the poor situation of historical research*' in DR Congo, as Idesbald Goddeeris and Sindani E. Kiangu do in "Congomania in Academia. Recent Historical Research on the Belgian Colonial Past" (in: *BMGN – Low Countries Historical Review*, The Hague: KNHG, 2011/4, 64; 67), might be insufficient. Possibly Congolese and Indonesian researchers have other priorities, whereas their European colleagues might feel more the need to come to terms with colonialism.
618 Van Geluwe, "Belgium's contribution to the Zairian cultural heritage", 33.
619 Schildkrout and Keim, *Scramble for art in Central Africa.*
620 Wastiau, "The Legacy of Collecting". Currently, Boris Wastiau is Director of the Museum of Ethnography in Geneva.
621 Shaje'a Tshiluila, "Measures for the Protection of Cultural Heritage in Developing Countries", in *Illicit traffic of cultural property in Africa* (Paris: ICOM, 1995).
622 Maarten Couttenier, "Between Regionalization and Centralization".
623 Sarah van Beurden, *Authentically African.*
624 Placide Mumbembele, email May 5 and 7, 2014 and April 1, 2015.

artefacts, animal skins, horns and tusks. They were the *'tangible means of showing penetration, conquest and domination'* that the Conference had asked for, and were displayed *'as propaganda for continuing the campaigns'*.[625] In 1898, when the Tervuren Museum opened, 3,008 objects, almost forty percent of a total of 7,598, were related to military campaigns.[626]

In 1910, a Royal Decree made the museum the central authority in collecting, studying and preserving of *'all objects from Belgian Congo relating to ... history and not being used by any particular body'*.[627] The museum researched new finds and decided which ones to hold and which to allocate to other museums in Belgium or send back to Kinshasa and regional museums in Congo.[628] That museums in the colony were denied a scientific function, could lead to frictions and to diminished supply of objects with scientific value for Tervuren.[629] In 1911, this resulted in a short-lived discussion about *'the possibility of returning collections to Congo'* after being documented and analysed in Tervuren.[630]

Tervuren director Lucien Cahen separated collecting in the period of Congo Free State from that under supervision of the Belgian State and named acquisitions from Leopold's period *'gifts'* from the Congo Free State to the Belgian state. He thus exempted himself from research into their provenance. His hand-written notes show that he was unaware of irregularities committed by his own institute: *'all the objects acquired by the Museum of Tervuren were* [done] *so according to the regulations, and plundering and theft is out of the question'*.[631] Instead, he blamed inhabitants of Leopoldville (Kinshasa) for selling museum objects and UN blue berets for looting the Museum of Elizabethville (Lubumbashi) in 1961.[632] Blaming them should be seen in the context of contradictions between, on the one hand, Belgium and other European colonial powers that supported – to safeguard their mineral interests – an independent Katanga, and, on the other, the government in Kinshasa that wanted, with the support of the United Nations, to keep the country united.[633]

The collecting activities have filled storerooms and showcases of the Tervuren Museum with over one hundred thousand shields, spears, masks, musical instruments and other, mostly Congolese, objects.[634] Although Wastiau discovered little evidence of acquisition practices in 1,200 files, he rejects the conclusion of Cahen and the 1979 issue of UNESCO's *Museum* about the museum's collecting practices. It is impossible *'to establish* what *level of coercion'* there was in collecting,

---

625 Schildkrout and Keim, ibid., 21.
626 Wastiau, ibid., 7.
627 Couttenier, ibid., 80.
628 Wastiau, ibid., 3.
629 Couttenier, ibid., 90, 92.
630 Couttenier, ibid., 79.
631 Sarah Van Beurden, 141, 142; 137.
632 Some mineralogical and ethnographic collections were stolen, zoological specimens destroyed, wooden objects used as firewood. The Elizabethville museum's Friendship Association saved half the ethnographic collection and thirty percent of the prehistoric collection. It brought it back in 1963. The library and all scientific documents were plundered (Couttenier, ibid., 93, 95).
633 Williams, ibid., 34.
634 Visit to the underground storerooms of the Tervuren Museum, May, 1996; http://www.africamuseum. be/museum/collections/general/index_html (January 14, 2016).

Lucien Cahen, director with two hats

After his technical studies and military service, Lucien Cahen (1912 – 1982) joined the Geological and Geographic Service in Katanga. Between 1937 and 1941, he made maps of the province. When he was mobilised for the *Force Publique* of Congo, he continued geological research in his leisure time. In 1946, he was employed as researcher at the Tervuren Museum. The *Mining Research Union of Lower and Middle Congo* (BAMOCO) and the *Société Forminière* in Kasai province profited from his findings and the collection of geological materials. He soon became curator for Geology, Mineralogy and Palaeontology and was director of the Tervuren Museum from 1958 until 1977. In all these years, he produced 186 publications and geological maps, mostly on Congo, Burundi and Rwanda. To guarantee the continuation of research, he helped to set up a museum in Congo and became its first director, spending three months per year in Kinshasa, and nine in Tervuren. Some sources omit his directorship in Kinshasa.[1]

Notes

1   Sarah Van Beurden, "The art of (re)possession: Heritage and the cultural politics of Congo's decolonization", in *The Journal of African History* (Cambridge: Cambridge University Press, 2015, 56/1), 143 – 164; http://www2.academieroyale.be/academie/documents/FichierPDFNouvelleBiographieNational2104.pdf#page=69 (December 31, 2014); http://www.bestor.be/wiki_nl/index.php/Cahen,_Lucien_Simon_%281912-1982%29 (December 31, 2014); this source omits his Kinshasa-work.

but much direct, structural and ideological violence was applied. The context was unbalanced, with educated whites in uniforms, in cassocks or plain clothes facing the local population. The confiscation of objects, such as circumcision masks or fetishes remains sometimes unmentioned, but can be understood from the context.[635]

Missionaries were major suppliers of objects. They converted Congolese people in great numbers, asked them to renounce their religious objects and practices and carried out large-scale iconoclasm. Objects that were not destroyed went to Europe. Congo was a '*textbook example*' of the triangle of colonial administration, private companies and missionary orders. The Belgian government gave these the '*monopoly in the field of education*'.[636] In 1939, over forty missionary orders with two thousand priests, brothers and nuns from all over Europe worked among the two million Roman Catholic converts. The European dimension of colonialism was expressed in their presence, as well as that of non-Belgian European collectors and traders.[637] Congo collections can be found in many European countries.[638]

635   Wastiau, ibid. 20, 22.
636   Derix, *Brengers van de Boodschap*, 555.
637   Derix, ibid., 556, 734.
638   France, Germany, Switzerland, United Kingdom, Sweden, Norway, the Netherlands and Hungary. Viviane Baeke, Tervuren Museum, email December 19, 2014. Peter Tygesen and Espen Waehle, *Congospor: Norden I Congo – Congo I Norden*. Espen Waehle, *Entrepreneurs in the Congo? Two case studies on possibilities for making money among Norwegians in the Congo Free-state*, http://www.uib.no/en/rg/colonialtimes/78215/entrepreneurs-congo (April 13, 2016).

The data about Congo's minerals and natural wealth in the Tervuren archives was of strategic importance.[639] An inventory of two hundred and eighty private archives from officials, who worked in Congo between 1858 and 1960, offers information about the colonial police, military and administrators, about veterinary and medical affairs, about trade, mining and rubber, but scarcely anything about local material cultural heritage.[640] At the moment, the museum still receives requests for the consultation of these archives *'at least twice per month'*.[641] In 1910, the first exposition was held in Congo itself. It was characteristic that it did not take place in the colony's capital Leopoldville (Kinshasa), but in Elisabethville (Lubumbashi) in Katanga, by then the centre of the copper, cobalt and uranium mining industry, and that the *Union Minière de Haut Katanga* was co-financer. Congo was also promoted at the Colonial World Fair in Vincennes in 1931 and at other events to *'convince both Belgian and South African industrialists and consumers of Congo's economic potential'*.[642]

The combination of two types of collecting – economic data and material culture – is reflected in Tervuren's leaders, Frans Olbrechts (1947 – 1958) and Lucien Cahen, the first an ethnologist-anthropologist[643] and *'very influential in the organization of the department of ethnography'*,[644] the second a civil engineer (Box: *Lucien Cahen, director with two hats*).

9.1. Deliberations and transfer of objects

Although a Belgian entrepreneur welcomed, financed and advised the Congolese delegation for the Round Table Conference in Brussels on the eve of Congo's independence, the leaders of the new country rejected the friendship treaty that Brussels offered *'as some sort of an independence-present'*, as they feared that it was a form of neo-colonialism.[645] When Belgium transferred the sovereignty on June 30, 1960, Joseph Kasavubu became Congo's first president and Patrice Lumumba its first prime minister. The relations were tense. Like Britain did in the adjacent area, Belgium wanted to continue its economic hold at any cost and supported efforts in Katanga to secede from Congo.[646] In the chaotic and sudden transition, many of the thirteen museums set up in colonial times, *'were looted'*.[647]

---

639 The 1944 agreement between Belgium, the USA and Great Britain about the sale of uranium from the Shinkolobwe mine enabled the US to develop the two atomic bombs that were later dropped in Japan. http://www.11.be/artikels/item/dossier-belgische-betrokkenheid-in-de-ontwikkeling-van-de-atoombom (April 1, 2015). Sarah Van Beurden, ibid., 65.

640 http://www.africamuseum.be/collections/museum/collections/docs/memoiredesbelges.pdf: 93 (January 2, 15). An exception was J. Thiriar, who worked in Congo between 1920 and 1935 and wrote about Congolese art for the *Bulletin du Palais des Beaux-Arts de Bruxelles*.

641 Director Guido Gryseels, email February 26, 2015.

642 Couttenier, ibid., 77; 73.

643 http://www.olbrechtsgenootschap.be/wie.html (April 1, 2015).

644 Sarah Van Beurden, ibid., 86.

645 Jef Van Bilsen, *Kongo – Het Einde van een Kolonie*, 141, 191.

646 Williams, ibid., 34.

647 Van Geluwe, ibid., 34.

Soon, Lumumba and Kasavubu presented restitution claims, on which Mobutu Sese Seko would later build.[648] The Congolese people went even further than claims that applied to objects only. In 1961, the periodical *Notre Congo* (Our Congo) questioned, very interestingly, the legality of the Belgian ownership of the Tervuren Museum and its collections. Did the museum, despite its location on Belgian ground, now not also belong to the Congolese state? Its building had been paid for with Belgian and Congolese money and its collections had been exported without the original owners' consent. When Belgian publications took up the question, the Government in Brussels admitted that Congo had a share in the collections of the museum. This acknowledgement was supported by '*many in the government*', for whom the ownership of the Tervuren objects counted less than the co-ownership of the mining company UMHK (*Union Minière de Haut Katanga*) and other Belgian economic interests.[649]

Like director Pott of the Museum Volkenkunde in the case of Indonesia, Cahen developed a strategy to minimise the loss of cultural objects in the colonial era. Apart from emphasising that they had been acquired properly, he summed up what museums in Congo themselves had and pointed to the many outstanding Congo collections elsewhere in Europe and North America. His museum was not '*a unique and rich centre of Congolese ethnography*' and could '*not be held accountable to fill a national museum*' in Congo. To accommodate restitution claims, the Belgian Foreign Office recognised '*the partial merit of the Congolese positions*' and proposed to send some of the non-exhibited reserves in Tervuren '*as a gift*' and to help set up a national museum. This early agreement is mentioned in correspondence but not in any official document.[650]

With Mobutu Sese Seko as the new strongman (1965 – 1997), the tension increased. Although in the end he gained little appreciation for his presidency, he became one of the champions of the restitution of colonial cultural objects throughout Africa.[651] He expressed his anger, when the Tervuren Museum made two hundred highly insured objects[652] available for a travelling exhibition in the USA (1967 – 1969). In his view, the exclusion of Congo illustrated the Western assumption of the inability of former colonies to present their cultural heritage abroad.[653]

In 1969, Cahen initiated talks that would lead to a breakthrough. As director with two hats and close contacts with Congolese officials, he came up with a phased proposal, which combined a transfer of objects by Belgium with collecting in Congo itself, cultural cooperation and strengthening Congo's museum infrastructure. The two governments accepted it in 1970.[654] Again, any official document remains untraceable.[655] In the first phase, which was financed by Belgian

---

648 Placide Mumbembele, email April 1, 2015.
649 Sarah Van Beurden, *Authentically African*, 89, 135, 136.
650 ibid., 137 – 142; 146; 148.
651 Tshiluila, ibid., 184. Nigeria was another one (Greenfield, *Return of Cultural Treasures*, 122).
652 Placide Mumbembele, email May 5, 2014.
653 Sarah Van Beurden, ibid., 143.
654 Van Geluwe, ibid., 33; Tshiluila, ibid., 184.
655 Sarah Van Beurden, ibid., 148.

overseas aid and implemented by the IMNZ (*Institut des Musées Nationaux de Zaïre*), 30,000 objects from all corners of the country were collected. In the second phase, specified objects were collected that were defined as Congolese national heritage. The third phase consisted of repatriations and gifts from Belgium. Congo continued to press Belgium to return the two hundred objects of the travelling exhibition in the USA.

The 1970 agreement of his country with Belgium and the 1970 UNESCO Convention, of which DR Congo would become state party in 1974,[656] inspired Mobutu to call, at a conference of the *International association of Art Criticism* in Kinshasa in September 1973, for the return of part of Africa's traditional art to their countries of origin. In Congo, the speech marked the beginning of what became known as *zairisation*, Mobutu's campaign for authenticity, a pre-colonial past, restitution of cultural treasures and nationalisation of foreign assets.[657] Mobutu announced Resolution 3187 (XXVIII) 1973 on the Restitution of Works of Art to Countries Victim of Expropriation (6.2.) for the 28th meeting of UN General Assembly in October 1973. After extensive discussions, a large majority of member states voted in favour, while most former colonial powers voted against it. The Resolution deplored the involuntary loss of many art objects, *'frequently as a result of colonial or foreign occupation'* and asked member states for their *'prompt restitution'*.[658]

After Mobutu's speech and as part of the third phase of the agreement between the two countries, the Belgian government expressed its intention to donate artefacts from Tervuren.[659] This was delayed, however, when Mobutu announced the nationalisation of Belgian interests. After a slight reversion of this policy in 1975 and 1976 and the reinstatement of some former European owners into their enterprises, the relationship eased and the third phase could be implemented. From the various enumerations of transfers[660] a list has been compiled (Box: *Repatriations and gifts to Congo*).

The first object was transferred on March 29, 1976, and concerned a valuable royal Kuba statue. It was the only one of the two hundred objects of the travelling exhibition that was ever returned.[661] That Belgium *'did not keep its promise'* and never handed over the other 199, was *'unfair play'* and led to a painful and so far unresolved dispute.[662] As with Diponegoro's kris, nobody knows where the objects are. Congo has never claimed them anew. The value of 114 other objects that Belgium came up with was said *'to be considerably lower'*.[663] The 114 were explicitly defined as gifts, not as restitution or returns. Just as the Netherlands,

656 http://www.unesco.org/eri/la/convention.asp?KO=13039&language=E&order=alpha (July 7, 2016).
657 Sarah Van Beurden, ibid., 149.
658 Prott, *Witnesses to History*, 27, 28.
659 Sarah Van Beurden, ibid., 150.
660 Tshiluila; Wastiau; Sarah Van Beurden; and Mumbembele.
661 Wastiau, *Congo – Tervuren: Aller – Retour*, 3. Sarah Van Beurden, ibid., 162.
662 Mumbembele, email May 7, 2014.
663 Mumbembele, email April 1, 2015.

Repatriations and gifts to Congo

Repatriations

- 31 Objects of the *Musée de la vie indigène* in Kinshasa (1977), shipped to Brussels in 1958 for the World's Fair and then exhibited in Germany and Austria until August 1960; they had remained in Belgium because of the instability in Congo.
- Over one hundred objects of the former *Institut de Recherche Scientifiques de l'Afrique Centrale* (IRSAC) (1978), which had been in Belgium from before independence.
- Six hundred other objects from IRSAC Rwanda.[1]

Gifts

- Wooden statue, representing a Kuba King (1976).
- 114 special objects from the storerooms of the Tervuren Museum meant to fill the gaps in the new museums set up. The last shipment (54 objects) arrived in Congo in 1982.

Notes

1 The year, in which these were returned, was not found.

Belgium wanted to prevent accusations of illicit appropriation. When the IMNZ in Kinshasa was plundered in 1990, most objects disappeared.[664]

Less than ten percent of all objects, which were transferred, came from the well-stocked Tervuren depots. The others came from Rwanda or from custodianships in Belgium, which were comparable with the custodianship of ethnographic objects from Papua in Museum Volkenkunde in Leiden that were repatriated in 1975. According to Belgian government sources, Brussels and Kinshasa never envisioned a formal exchange of archives or any archival cooperation, as was agreed in the Dutch – Indonesian case; there have only been incidental and informal exchanges of information.[665]

Nowadays, cultural cooperation between Belgium and DR Congo continues,[666] but is low on the list of priorities of the Kinshasa government. The instability and poor governance in the country are major obstacles in return discussions.

In conclusion, the case study reveals that DR Congo lost a great many cultural and historical treasures in the colonial era, where direct, structural and ideological violence characterised the forms of acquisition. Belgians were not the only ones involved, as nationals from other European countries have also played a role. The case study further emphasises the relevance of acknowledging underlying interests. As in the Dutch – Indonesian case, the return of colonial cultural objects was not about such objects or about undoing injustice, but was intended as an instrument in Belgium's foreign policy and cultural diplomacy to safeguard major economic

---

664 ICOM, *One Hundred Missing Objects: Looting in Africa* (Paris: ICOM, 1994/1997), 81, 82.

665 Email Filip Strubbe, Algemeen Rijksarchief – Archives générales du Royaume, Brussels, July 1, 2014. Email Gérard Alain, Foreign Ministry, Brussels, August 27, 2014.

666 http://www.africamuseum.be/research/projects/prj_list (May 7, 2014).

interests. Unlike the Netherlands, where the coming of a progressive government had accelerated the negotiations, the frequent change of governments in Belgium in the 1960s and 1970s, with either the Christian Democrats or the Social Democrats in the lead, did not noticeably influence the speed of the negotiations with Congo. Like the Netherlands, Belgium was not a generous returner. DR Congo was particularly after recognition of being equal to its former coloniser and of its ability to take responsibility itself for its cultural heritage. As in the Dutch – Indonesian case, media played a role in advancing the return discussion.

Chapter 10

Nordic model for Denmark, Iceland and Greenland?

As in the Dutch – Indonesian and the Belgian – Congolese cases, there has been an increase in research publications about Scandinavian colonialism. Many of them challenge the view that distant possessions were only something of non-Scandinavian European powers and break with the downplaying of Scandinavia's colonial past. Not only were Denmark and Sweden colonial powers, albeit smaller and shorter-lived than the Dutch, the British and the French, but Scandinavians also played an active role in the colonialism of other European powers. Scandinavian countries have always portrayed themselves as good colonisers and supporters of the UN's decolonisation efforts, but extensive collections of colonial cultural objects in their museums reveal another aspect, an aspect that is scarcely dealt with in the new publications. Some returns by Denmark offer an opportunity to explore it.

10.1. Scandinavian colonialism

Sweden had colonial possessions in the Baltic provinces and trade companies elsewhere: the East India Company, the West India Company and an African Company. Until today, it likes to present itself as *'a nation without a colonial past, but with a long history of international trade'*. The colonial context, however, was *'a necessary condition'* for its international trade.[667] Sweden tried to colonise Madagascar in vain, but succeeded in establishing a colony in North America, New Sweden, which was located close to Dutch New Amsterdam. Around 1660, it had to give up its interests in Africa and North America to the much stronger Dutch.[668] That Sweden did not have its own colonies *'was due to a failure to obtain them rather than a result of having higher moral standards than other European countries.'* Sweden and Swedes never *'actively choose not to participate in the colonial venture in far-away territories'*.[669]

---

667 Mikela Lundahl, "Nordic Complicity? Some aspects of Nordic identity as 'non-colonial'and non-participatory in the European colonial event" (2006), https://www.academia.edu/245966/Nordic_Complicity_Some_Aspects_of_Nordic_Identity_As_Non-Colonial_and_Non-Participatory_In_the_European_Colonial_Event (October 9, 2014), 5.
668 Naum and Nordin, *Scandinavian Colonialism*, 6.
669 Lundahl, "Nordic Complicity?", 6.

The Danish Crown established trading posts in Asia and Africa. In the 17th century, a Danish East India company operated in South Asia. It was 'reasonably successful' in the spices and textiles trade[670] and soon outpaced Portuguese shipping to the East, while Danish ship movements and trade volume remained incomparably smaller than those of the Dutch and British trade companies.[671] The Danish Crown's company more closely resembled the smaller private mercantile enterprises of the time.[672] Denmark held some of its trading posts in Asia for over two hundred years, and then sold them to other European powers.[673] In Africa, it set up trading posts and forts on the Western coast and participated in the slave trade between the Danish Gold Coast and the Danish West Indies. Around 1750, enslaved Africans constituted ninety percent of the population in the Danish West Indies, with 'hardly any restrictions' on their mistreatment.[674] Around 1700, Denmark acquired some islands in the Caribbean, which were known for sugar cultivation. In 1916 it sold them to the USA, which renamed them the Virgin Islands.[675]

Denmark's most extensive possessions, however, were in Nordic areas. Thanks to a 1380 royal marriage, Norway had become part of a personal union with Denmark, along with 'the so-called secondary countries of Iceland, the Faroe Islands, Orkney and Greenland'. When in the aftermath of Napoleon's defeat in 1815, this union fell apart and Norway was ceded to Sweden, the colonial possessions remained under Danish rule.[676] Denmark established trade stations 'to cope with the competition from Dutch whalers and tradesmen'.[677] That not land, but only water separated these possessions from the metropolis made the commercial, geographical and cultural

---

670 Wesseling, *European Colonial Empires*, 7, 94, 96.

671 Francisco Contente Domingues. "The India Route. Comparative Paths of a Maritime Venture", in ed. Amândio Barros, *Discoveries and the Origins of Global Convergence*, 116.

672 P.R. Rasmussen, "Tranquebar – The Danish East India Company 1616 – 1669"(Copenhagen: University of Copenhagen, http://scholiast.org/history/tra-narr.html, 2006) (July 02, 2014). Also https://www.academia.edu/2312688/Indian_textiles_in_17th_and_18th_century_Denmark._Colonialism_and_the_rise_of_a_global_consumer_culture (July 3, 2014).

673 E.g. in 1620, Denmark negotiated a trade-treaty with the King of Tanjore in Tamil Nadu about the city of Tranquebar. Denmark sold this post, together with the post Serampore in Bengal, to the British Empire in 1845, in: Esther Fihl and Stine Simonsen Puri, "Introduction : The study of cultural encounters in Tharangampadi/Tranquebar", in eds. Esther Fihl and A.R. Venkatachalapathy, "Cultural Encounters in Tranquebar: Past and Present", Special issue *Review of Development and Change*, (Madras: Madras Institute of Development Studies, 2009,), vol. XIV, No. 1-2. http://natmus.dk/fileadmin/user_upload/natmus/forskning/dokumenter/Tranquebar/RDC_XIV_Tranquebar.pdf: 8, 9 (February 10, 2016).

674 Anne Marie Lindgreen Pedersen and Lykke L. Pedersen, *Danish Modern History: Stories of Denmark 1660 – 2000* (Copenhagen: National Museum, 2005), 104. Honoured author Thorkild Hansen (1927 – 1989) wrote a documentary trilogy about the Danish slave-trade: *Coast of Slaves, Ships of Slaves*, and *Island of Slaves* (Accra: Sub-Saharan Publishers, 1972).

675 The Danish National Archives and other Danish institutions hold extensive archival material concerning the history of the islands, http://www.virgin-islands-history.dk/eng/a_other.asp (February 9, 2016).

676 Lucas and Parigoris, "Icelandic Archaeology and the Ambiguities of Colonialism", in Naum and Nordin, *Scandinavian Colonialism*.

677 Robert Petersen, "Colonialism as seen from a former colonized area", in *Arctic Anthropology* (Wisconsin: University of Wisconsin, 1995), 32/2: 118-126.

distance smaller than that between the British and continental colonial empires and their distant possessions.[678]

Sweden, Norway, Denmark and Finland had indigenous minorities that had been colonised. The biggest were the Sámi (English: Lapps), who lived spread over Norway, Sweden, Finland and the Kola Peninsula of Russia.

Greenland was undisputedly a Danish colony. That the colonisation proceeded with less direct violence than elsewhere, was due to the fact that Greenlanders were organised at the household level and rarely offered resistance against the Danish presence. The Danish structural and ideological violence, however, were comparable with that in distant possessions. Danish officials and arctic explorers marginalised the family-based production in favour of the export of whales, fish, seal blubber, baleen, skin and narwhal tooth to Europe and, later, of the mineral cryolite and they established trade posts and factories.[679] From 1721 onwards, the *'hordes of European – mostly Dutch, Spanish and Portuguese – whalers and sealers'* in the waters around Greenland[680] brought the Danish King to finance missionaries to convert the Greenlanders and to abolish their traditional faith, rituals and ritual objects.[681] The Danish were contemptuous of Greenlanders, whom they considered to be *'at the bottom'* of the *'hierarchy of civilisation'*.[682] Greenland's colonial status would last until 1953.

Defining Denmark's relationship with Iceland is more complicated. The economic, political and cultural facets do *'not necessarily paint the same picture'*.[683] In the late 9th century, Vikings from Norway and the British Isles arrived in Iceland. In 1262, it was united with Norway and lost its independence. After the merging of the Norwegian and Danish crowns in 1380, it became part of the Danish Kingdom. In the 16th century, the Danish King imposed Lutheranism. The Roman Catholic bishop was decapitated, and Roman Catholic silver crosses, chalices and other religious objects were shipped to Denmark, where they were melted down (3.1.). In 1602 – the same year that the VOC was established – Denmark imposed a trade monopoly, which was *'a clear example of Danish oppression'* and *'colonial arrangements'*.[684]

The *'entanglement of colonialism and nationalism'* sharpened contradictions between the Danish *'self'* and the Icelandic *'other'*.[685] Denmark considered Iceland *'backward and simple'*, this to *'the great distress of the more educated Icelanders'*,[686] and presented its culture at the World Fair in Paris of 1900 as *'primitive'* and itself as a country with a civilising mission. Danish academics rarely deal with this

---

678 Burbank and Cooper, *Empires in World History*, 149.
679 Petersen, ibid., 3. Peter A. Toft and Inge Høst Seiding, "Circumventing colonial policies: Consumption and family life as social practices in the early nineteenth-century Disko Bay" in: Naum and Nordin, *Scandinavian Colonialism*, 108.
680 Gabriel, *Object on the Move*, 78, 79.
681 Toft and Seiding, ibid. 107, 108.
682 Lucas and Parigoris, "Icelandic Archaeology", 98.
683 Ibid., 92.
684 Ibid., 93.
685 Ibid., 94.
686 Kristín Loftsdóttir and Gísli Pálsson, "Black on White: Danish colonialism, Iceland and the Caribbean" in: Naum and Nordin, ibid., 38.

ideological violence. At the same time, Iceland surprised scholars all over Europe as *'the cradle of... a democratic society of brave, free people and the creation and cultivation for centuries of a classic literary heritage of the Sagas'*.[687] It had always kept certain autonomy through its *Althing*, Europe's oldest running parliament (dating from 930 AD).[688] The language of the law courts and the church remained Icelandic. Since the Danish were impressed by the Icelandic sagas, they took serious responsibility for their preservation. High-ranking officials in the Danish administration could be of Icelandic origin, a well-known example being Árni Magnússon (1663 – 1730), secretary of the Royal Archives and first Danish Antiquities professor at Copenhagen University. Magnússon played a pivotal role in moving Icelandic manuscripts to Copenhagen, which would become the main issue in the return negotiations. Iceland *'resembled the core of the Danish monarchy through the Christian religion yet not those aspects of modernity so as to be equated with the other civilised nations'*.[689]

In 1918, Iceland became an independent sovereign state but it remained connected to Denmark in a personal union under the Danish King. In twenty-five years, a national referendum on the island's future would be held. Between 1924 and 1927, Denmark and Iceland exchanged a number of administrative documents and archives, including four ancient Icelandic manuscripts. Iceland rejected a Danish request *'that no further demands would be made'*.[690] In the Second World War, the two countries started as neutral, but soon Germany occupied Denmark, while Britain invaded Iceland. This encouraged the Althing to hold the promised plebiscite. Based on the outcome, it severed its ties with the Danish monarchy in 1944.

The discussion about the return of manuscripts shows the different views on the Danish – Icelandic relationship. Greenlander Peterson, Icelander Magnusson (who spent most of his life in Scotland) and outsider Greenfield allot the country a *'colonial status'*, in which the Danish *'colonial masters'* caused *'unbelievable penury and misery'*.[691] In the trilogy *Iceland's Bell* about the country's history, ancient manuscripts and the role of Árni Magnússon, Nobel Prize-winner Halldór Laxness views his country a Danish colony too.[692]

Danish Royal Library director, Erland Nielsen, rejects a *'colonial status'*. In his view, Iceland was a dependency and the transfer of ancient manuscripts, discussed below, *'was a normal practice'*, that had occurred after the partition of Sweden in 1658, in relation to Norway that proclaimed its independence in 1814, and so also in relation to Iceland from 1971 onwards. All three transfers had been a *'purely internal political matter resulting from the dissolution of the state and later political*

---

687 Ibid., 37.
688 http://europa.eu/youth/article/short-history-al%C3%BEingi-oldest-parliament-world_en (July 30, 2014).
689 Lucas and Parigoris, "Icelandic Archaeology", 98.
690 Greenfield, *Return of Cultural Treasures*, 20.
691 Magnus Magnusson, "Introduction", in Greenfield, *Return of Cultural Treasures*, 2, 4.
692 Halldór Laxness, *IJslands Klok* (trilogy) (Hasselt: Heideland, 1957).

union between Denmark and Iceland'.[693] The transfer to Iceland does not feature in the 1979 issue of UNESCO's *Museum* on good practices or in Prott's (2009) list of bilateral agreements between former colonisers and colonised.

All in all, the controversy over the Danish – Icelandic relationship makes clear that *'simplistic oppositions of colonisers and colonised do not always apply'*,[694] but conclude that Nordic colonialism was a reality. Denmark and Sweden had the explicit intention of establishing colonies and the naval power to control them, and Iceland was one of them. In varying degrees, it was politically dominated, economically exploited and culturally subjugated by Denmark. Denmark's colonial empire was modest in comparison with other European powers. The direct, structural and ideological violence applied by Denmark in tropical colonies was comparable with what other European powers did, but could differ in Denmark's Nordic, cold colonies.

10.2. Danish colonial collecting

Nordic countries acquired large collections of cultural objects from their own cold and tropical possessions and from those of other European powers. Between 1,500 and 2,000 Nordic missionaries, traders, collectors, explorers and scientists, for instance, *'played significant roles in colonization and exploitation of the Congo'*. They could move freely to collect, and at least *'38,000 objects'* are abundant evidence of Nordic museums being thankful recipients. Many others can be found in private collections (Box: *Cultural objects from non-Scandinavian colonies*).[695] It emphasises the European dimension of the colonial era.

Earlier (3.1.), mention was made of how, between 1550 and 1570, the Danish Lutheran King expelled Roman Catholicism from Iceland and how medieval Icelandic religious silver objects were massively melted down, one result being three silver lions in Slot Rosenborg in Denmark. Direct, structural and ideological violence came together in the forceful confiscation of treasured objects, damage to the Icelandic identity and Danish contempt of another religion. They contrasted with the more peaceful arrival of Christianity in Iceland around the year 1000 *'resulting from both direct missionary activities and the Vikings' indirect relationship with Christian people in Europe'*.[696]

The history behind the migration of ancient Icelandic manuscripts to Copenhagen is even more remarkable. Icelandic bishops had sent the *Flateyjarbók*, the *Codex Regius* and other manuscripts to the King of Denmark, who had them preserved in the Royal Library. Around 1700, Árni Magnússon came with Danish and Swedish emissaries to Iceland to collect more ancient parchments and paper manuscripts. He was *'begging, borrowing or buying wherever he went, at almost any*

---

693 Erland Kolding Nielsen, 2002. "Denmark to Iceland. A Case without Precedence: Delivering Back the Islandic Manuscripts 1971-1997" (Glascow: *68th IFLA Council and General Conference*, 2002), http://archive.ifla.org/IV/ifla68/papers/Kolding_Nielsen02.pdf (December 22, 2016), 5.

694 Loftsdóttir and Pálson, "Black on White", 38.

695 Waehle, *Entrepreneurs in the Congo?*

696 Steinunn Kristjánsdóttir, *The awakening of Christianity in Iceland – Discovery of a timber church and graveyard at Þórarinsstaðir in Seyðisfjörður,* (Gothenburg: University of Gothenburg, Ph.D., 2004), 24.

Cultural objects from non-Scandinavian colonies

Sweden

Most of the ten thousand masks, ancestral sculptures, items of jewellery and other objects from DR Congo in the ethnographic museums of Stockholm and Gothenburg were collected by members of the Swedish Missionary Society.[1] The Museum of Ethnography in Stockholm received its largest donation of Benin objects form German scholar and collector Hans Meyer.[2]

Finland

The Persian carpets, ritual objects from DR Congo, and tools and weapons from South America, Papua New Guinea and Alaska, which are on display in the Museum of Cultures in Helsinki, were *all fetched from afar by earlier generations of Finnish explorers and traders*.[3]

Norway

The Oslo University Ethnographic Museum received: ritual objects from DR Congo, the Pacific and the Americas through Norwegian sea captains, a sea pilot and a medical doctor; ethnographic objects from Santal areas in North India from an Ebenezer missionary; cult objects from southern India through the Norwegian wife of a British judge; and Thai and Burmese Buddhist statues through a Norwegian explorer.[4] Items from Congo comprise eleven percent of its total collection.[5]

Denmark

The Royal Library received ancient manuscripts from Dunhuang, China, seized by a Danish explorer, and an Inca chronicle about the vices of colonialism, which a Danish diplomat had taken from Spain around 1660.[6]

Notes

1 Tygesen and Waehle, *Congospor*, 75 ff. Gustafsson Reinius, *Touring Congo*, 81.

2 Stockholm Museum of Ethnography, *Whose Objects? Art Treasures from the Kingdom of Benin in the Collection of the Museum of Ethnography in Stockholm* (Stockholm: Museum of Ethnography, 2010), 28.

3 James Symonds, "Colonial Encounters of the Nordic Kind", in Naum and Nordin, 307.

4 Bouquet, *Sans og Samling… hos Universitetes Etnografiske Museum / Bringing it all back home… to the Oslo University Ethnographic Museum*, 77, 82, 86, 88.

5 Waehle, *Entrepreneurs in the Congo?*

6 Hvidt, Birgitte and Skovgaard – Petersen, Karen *Skatte/Treasures*, 12, 32.

---

price' to enlarge his private collection. In 1720, they shipped them in fifty-five crates to Copenhagen. When, on October 20, 1728, a fire in Copenhagen reached the university quarter, where Magnússon kept his collection, he and his helpers saved the most precious manuscripts, but others and the copies that he had made in Iceland disappeared in the flames. Magnússon never recovered from this tragedy. On his deathbed, fifteen months later, he bequeathed his private collection to the University of Copenhagen and his savings for the study and publication of the ancient manuscripts.[697]

---

697 Greenfield, ibid., 13. Magnússon even took pieces used as *'an insole for a shoe'* or as *'pattern for the back of a waistcoat'* (Magnusson, ibid., in: Greenfield, ibid., 3).

Collecting in Greenland occurred as it did in tropical colonies. Employees of the Royal Greenland Trading Company, clerics and explorers between the 17th and the early 20th century brought archaeological and ethnographic objects, water-colour paintings, archival material from pre-historic sites, oral materials, drum songs and remains of 1,641 persons to museums and institutions in Denmark.[698] In 1913, Greenlander poet and catechist, Josva Kleist, complained about *'the comprehensive grave lootings conducted by Danes and other foreigners especially in southern Greenland'*. The Greenlander had *'no other history than found in his graves'*, especially *'weapons and tools that were used'* and was *'totally stripped of old finds and similar items of national value'*.[699]

The Danish National Museum functioned in a way that was similar to that of the Tervuren Museum in Belgium. Objects of scientific value *'always had to be sent to and remain'* in Copenhagen.[700] The museum was responsible for study and public dissemination, and for the administration of cultural heritage sites and monuments in Greenland.[701] The Greenlandic museum was only a provincial museum. The National Museum in Copenhagen thus obtained the largest *'archaeological collections relating to palaeo- and neo-Eskimo cultures as well as the Norse people..., ethnographic objects from the late 19th- early 20th centuries, water colour paintings from the middle of the 19th century, archival information on prehistoric sites in Greenland and collections of oral material'*.[702]

Both Iceland and Greenland attached major importance to the return of cultural heritage that had disappeared. To show the public support for it, the following briefly describes the public welcome of Iceland's most precious manuscripts.

10.3. Ancient sagas back to Iceland

On April 21, 1971, shops and schools in Iceland remained closed. People listened to the radio or watched television. In Reykjavík 15,000 people were astir to watch the arrival of a ship with three carefully wrapped boxes that contained the country's most valuable manuscripts – the two-volume *Flateyjarbók* and the one-piece *Codex Regius*.[703] The country's largest manuscript contained two hundred and twenty-five written and illustrated vellum leaves with late 14th century sagas. The late 13th century Codex Regius counted 45 pages with poems.[704] Their importance for Iceland was comparable with that of the Nagarakertagama palm-leaf for Indonesia.

---

698 Bjarne Grønnow and Einar Lund Jensen, "Utimut: Repatriation and Collaboration Between Denmark and Greenland", in eds. Mille Gabriel and Jens Dahl, *Utimut: Past Heritage – Future Partnerships* (Copenhagen: International Working Group for Indigenous Affairs, 2008), 180. Aviâja Rosing Jakobsen, "The repatriation of Greenland's cultural heritage from Denmark to Greenland", in eds. Laura Van Broekhoven, Cunera Buijs and Pieter Hovens, *Sharing Knowledge & Cultural Heritage: First Nations of the Americas – Studies in collaboration with indigenous peoples from Greenland, North and South America* (Leiden: Sidestone Press, 2010), 80.

699 Gabriel, *Objects on the Move*, 106.

700 ibid., 108.

701 Grønnow and Lund Jensen, "Utimut", 181.

702 Daniel Thorleifsen, "Preface" in eds. Gabriel and Dahl, ibid. 9. Grønnow and Lund Jensen, "Utimut", 181.

703 For images: http://handrit.is/en (July 07, 2014).

704 Magnus Magnusson, in: Greenfield, *Return of Cultural Treasures*, 1- 4. Greenfield, *ibid.*, 13 ff.

Their arrival was the start of the repatriation of two thousand manuscripts about local history and peasant life, which had been created by Icelandic priests. Fifteen hundred manuscripts that did not cover exclusively Icelandic matters but the Scandinavian monarchies, religious affairs or translations from Latin, were kept in Copenhagen.[705] On Thursday June 19, 1997, the last of them were handed over.[706] Again, they came by boat, and again, upon arrival they were met '*by large numbers of Reykjavik citizens in circumstances similar to those*' of April 21, 1971.[707]

In the 1830s, the bishop of Iceland had formally asked for their repatriation. Between 1907 and 1938, the Althing had issued five return calls. Although there had been some modest returns between 1924 and 1927, Denmark's uncooperative attitude influenced the decision of the Althing of 1944 to break away from the Danish Monarchy. From then on, the sagas were '*a burning issue*' in Denmark. Danish society was divided. In 1947, the government installed a study commission with politicians and scholars. Folk High School principals submitted a petition *Give Iceland her treasures back*, while university teachers publicly opposed restitution. In its 1951 report, the study commission appeared divided too. Some members favoured a return on historical and moral grounds, following Icelandic politicians, who were aware that they '*had no absolute judicial right*' to the manuscripts but '*a moral obligation*' to return them. Others considered the manuscripts as Old Nordic, pan-Scandinavian heritage and Iceland as technically and scholarly unequipped to preserve them, and were against returning them.[708]

In 1959, a new round began. The electoral victory of the pro-return Danish Social-Democrats and Radicals over the anti-return Conservatives paved the way for negotiations. It was comparable with the impact of a progressive government taking office in the Netherlands in 1973. Most authors agree on the three steps that followed and which made a solution possible – legal interventions, the role of scholars on both sides and Iceland's position of not claiming any '*absolute judicial right*' to the manuscripts.[709]

In February 1961, the new Danish Government asked Iceland for a wish list. After it had been submitted, the two countries did some '*hard horse-trading behind the scenes*' and then agreed upon a final version. The next hurdle was legal: most manuscripts would have to come from the private collection of Árnu Magnussón's descendants, and according to the Danish parliamentarian opposition and university circles, their removal would be '*tantamount to an illegal expropriation of private property*'[710] and require compensation.[711] The Danish Government solved the inalienability hurdle by submitting a bill to change Magnussón's will. His collection was divided in two so that manuscripts and documents '*that were seen as being part of Iceland's cultural heritage*' could be handed over to the University

---

705 Nielsen, "Denmark to Iceland", 5.
706 Greenfield, ibid., 37, 38.
707 Nielsen, ibid., 2.
708 Greenfield, ibid., 19 – 21.
709 Ibid., 21.
710 Ibid., 21, 22.
711 Prott, *Witnesses to History*, 343.

of Iceland.[712] The bill was passed in May 1965. But the opposition asked the Danish High Court to declare the bill invalid. The Court rejected the appeal with the argument that the public interest and Denmark's relationship with Iceland outweighed the protection of private property principle.[713] This verdict paved the way for a return treaty.

On April 1, 1971, the two countries ratified it.[714] In Art. 1, the division of Magnússon's private collection into two was adopted from the 1965 law; one part was '*to be transferred to Iceland*'. Art. 2 stipulated that Iceland was to be a good guardian and to set up its own specialised Árni Magnússon Institute in Reykjavik. Art. 6 stipulated that the arrangement was '*to be recognised as a complete and final resolution of all Icelandic wishes concerning the transfer of national Icelandic heritage items of any kind, residing in Denmark*'. A committee of two Icelandic and two Danish scholars made the final selection of manuscripts that were to be transferred. Before their departure from Denmark, they were restored and copied on microfilm.

The transfer has been marked as unique and '*without any legal precedence in international law whatsoever*'.[715] For Lyndel Prott, the High Court decision and prioritising the public above someone's private interest were crucial. Jeanette Greenfield emphasises the reasonableness of the stakeholders. The parties negotiated firmly but were never at daggers drawn, and Iceland, although tough in 1944 when it unilaterally declared itself independent, never initiated legal action against the former colonial power. The outcome was one '*of astonishing goodwill.... The greater part of the manuscripts covered Icelandic matters and they were written by and for Icelandic people*', explained Greenfield to the British Select Committee on Culture, Media and Sport. '*These manuscripts mean to Icelanders what Shakespearean literature means to the English.*' She wonders why Iceland never asked other institutional possessors of ancient manuscripts to return these.[716]

This '*conflictual*' process with Iceland helped Denmark to act more smoothly in repatriations to the Faroe Islands (see Box: *Repatriation by Denmark to Faroe Islands*) and to Greenland (10.4.).[717]

---

712 Nielsen, "Denmark to Iceland", 4.
713 Prott, ibid., 344. Nielsen, ibid., 4.
714 The Articles (English version) are quoted from: Greenfield, *ibid.*, 35. The italics are mine.
715 Nielsen, "Denmark to Iceland", 5.
716 Greenfield mentioned the Royal Library in Stockholm (300 manuscripts), British Museum (250), Bodleian Library in Oxford (150), National Library of Scotland in Edinburgh (100), Uppsala University Library (50) and Harvard University Library (45). http://www.publications.parliament. uk/pa/cm199900/cmselect/cmcumeds/371/371ap20.htm (July 04, 2014).
717 Lily Eilertsen, "Breaking the Ice: Conflicts of Heritage in the West Nordic Regions" (Brussels: Conference National Museums and the Negotiations of Difficult Pasts, *EuNaMus Report no. 8*, January 26/27, 2012), 172.

Repatriation by Denmark to Faroe Islands

After repeated requests and an agreement in 1977, Denmark repatriated two pew ends and some chair gables to the Faroe Islands in 2002. The Faroe Islands, between Norway and Iceland, were Christianised around the year 1000. St. Olav's Church in Kirkjubøur is the oldest church still in use on the Faroe Islands. During restoration works in 1875, a well-carved medieval interior with remarkable pew ends was removed from this church and shipped to the National Museum in Copenhagen. Between 1901 and 1938, proponents of Faroese independence repeatedly claimed their return. The fact that only half of the Faroese population were pro-independence allowed Denmark to ignore the claim. Discussions from 1955 onwards showed no progress. In 1958, a new request was made during a visit of the Danish prime minister to the Faroe Islands. Finally, Denmark agreed to repatriate the pew ends, albeit on the condition that a proper museum was built. A positive side effect of the negotiations was that much information was found about the provenance of the objects.[1] The construction of the Faroese National Museum was finished in 1995. Seven years later the treasures went back.[2]

Notes

1   Lily Eilertsen, "Breaking the Ice", 158 - 161.
2   http://www.savn.fo/00647/ (August 6, 2014).

10.4. Peculiar agreement with Greenland

In 1913, the first Greenlandic return request was made, followed by several others.[718] Greenland also wanted museums. In 1953, it climbed on the political ladder and became a full part of the Danish Kingdom. It was in a period that many colonies became independent and former colonisers and colonised had to redefine their relations, as occurred between the Netherlands and Suriname and the Dutch Antilles.[719] However, all this time nothing was returned. In the capital Nuuk, the Grønlands Landsmuseum was set up and finds from excavations were to be curated there. It enabled the museum to build up its own collection, while continuing its cooperation with Denmark's National Museum.

In the late 1970s, the further acceptance of decolonisation and emancipation of indigenous peoples strongly influenced the new head of the ethnographic department and later director of Denmark's National Museum, Torben Lundbaek.[720] He 'played a central role in developing… new museum standards'. The museum should transfer collections to Greenland, when museum conditions there had improved.[721] He differed from Pieter Pott in the Netherlands and Lucien Cahen in Belgium, who had used the prioritisation of better museum facilities in former colonies to minimise returns. Greenland's director of the National Museum and Archives, Daniel Thorleifsen, avoided confrontations and had 'chosen to believe' that the Danish colonial empire had taken Inuit ethnographical objects, artefacts and human remains, 'among other reasons,

---

718 Gabriel, *Objects on the Move*, 105 ff.
719 The Hague: *Government of the Netherlands*, State-budget 1954, Chapter XIII, November 9, 1953, No. 9, http://resourcessgd.kb.nl/SGD/19531954/PDF/SGD_19531954_0000636.pdf (February 9, 2016).
720 Grønnow and Lund Jensen, "Utimut", 189.
721 Gabriel 2010: 67.

in the name of science', and that this '*was done in good faith, obviously with a wish to save a dying Inuit cultural heritage from oblivion*'.[722]

The attitude of the two main players and the pressure of young Greenlanders for self-government and recognition of them as a people with its own history and unique culture led to negotiations between Nuuk and Copenhagen.[723] One result was that, from January 1, 1981, Greenland became responsible for its own museums and monuments, and another that Denmark, claiming to be a supporter of decolonisation, could no longer evade the return issue.

In 1982, a thousand years after the arrival of the first Norse people in Greenland, the Danish Queen Margrethe II handed over two hundred and four watercolour paintings by Greenlandic hunters Aron of Kangeq (1822 – 1869) and Jens Kreutzmann (1828 -1899) to Greenland. They had once been acquired by a colonial official. His widow had more paintings, but she had separated those with conflict motifs from the paintings with Greenlandic life and folklore and sold the latter for a symbolic price to the National Museum of Denmark. While it is remarkable that none of Aron's returned pictures are exhibited in the museum in Nuuk, they are found on postcards, posters and stamps.[724] The paintings with conflict motifs ended up in the storerooms of the Ethnographic Museum of the University of Oslo.[725]

In 1983, the directors of the two national museums signed an agreement for the repatriation of thirty-five thousand archaeological and ethnographic items and the further strengthening of the Nuuk museum and staff.[726] The legal problem that the Danish National Museum was owner of Greenland's cultural heritage, which meant that Danish property had to be alienated, was solved by the Danish minister for Culture and the Parliament. He asked Greenland to pay a symbolic amount.

Danish and Greenlandic experts selected the objects. They were repatriated in nine phases; each phase encompassed the objects from a region or a type of material. One hundred thousand items remained in Copenhagen. This might look like '*an uneven share*', but Greenland's holding and curating of archaeological finds from 1966 onwards meant that '*the two national museums today hold collections of equal importance*'.[727] The clause with the provision that, if one of the two countries wishes the return of specific finds or objects, such a wish shall be respected, was also part of the 1975 Joint Recommendations between the Netherlands and Indonesia. All items were to be registered in a database. Those that were returned had to be cleaned and preserved before departure. Thanks to a Danish subsidy, the Arctic research centre SILA could be founded; it is based in the National Museum of Denmark.

While the agreement received ample attention in Denmark and Greenland and from UNESCO, it was as good as overlooked elsewhere. Greenfield mentions it only as a smooth return after the Danish experience with the return to Iceland. Prott does not include it in her list of bilateral agreements. There are voices that this return '*with appropriate modifications ..... might be applicable to certain*

---

722 Thorleifsen, ibid., 9.
723 Grønnow and Lund Jensen, "Utimut", 181.
724 Eilertsen, ibid., 162.
725 https://www.duo.uio.no/handle/10852/26508 (August 7, 2014).
726 Grønnow and Lund Jensen, "Utimut", 183.
727 Gabriel, *Objects on the Move*, 112.

minority groups and to other countries' that need cultural treasures from *'the custody of their former overlords'*.[728] The approach has a *'spirit of reconciliation and equitable exchange'*[729] and *'overlapping values'* with little or no 'colliding perspectives'.[730] With, as remarked, a key role for the National Museum of Denmark, which did not view *'Greenlandic wishes as a problem or a threat to its collections'* but *'took up the challenge and dialogue'*, established cooperation with the national and regional museums in Greenland and was even willing to contribute more to their collections.[731]

Greenland also made a remarkable agreement with Denmark on the remains of 1,641 persons. For the time being, they stay in Denmark, which is better equipped to preserve them, but they are under Greenland's authority.[732] Greenland's National Museum received objects from the Netherlands (*'one of the oldest kayaks in the world'*), Norway (archaeological collection) and the United States (human remains).[733] It faces a new challenge, one that is also felt in, for instance, Indonesia and touches the relation between a national museum and regional museums. Greenland's sixteen regional museums are asking the National Museum in Nuuk for more objects from their region, while the capacity of some of them to preserve and make objects accessible is disputed.[734]

In conclusion, in the colonial era both Iceland and Greenland faced massive migration of cultural and historical objects to Denmark. The nature and the extent of the violence that accompanied it differed in the two colonies. There was respect in Denmark (and elsewhere in Europe) for the Icelandic sagas. Greenland was confronted with more ideological violence. Both former colonies were eager to retrieve their heritage. This case study emphasises the relevance of geographical and cultural distance in return negotiations. Although Denmark had imposed its religion on Iceland, it helped that the two countries had shared the same religion for centuries. Thanks to the Danish upbringing of Greenlandic elite, Denmark and Greenland had overlapping values.

728 Helge Schultz-Lorentzen H. 1988, "Return of cultural property by Denmark to Greenland: From dream to reality", in *Museum* (Paris: UNESCO, 1988), 205.

729 Gabriel and Dahl, "Utimut", 13.

730 Gabriel, *Objects on the Move*, 116. Overlapping values are diminishing. Students have their own Greenlandic university and orient themselves at institutions in Canada and the USA, where they meet students from other indigenous communities and become part of an international community. Interview Mille Gabriel, National Museum, Copenhagen, August 24, 2015.

731 Grønnow and Jensen, "Utimut", 190.

732 Gabriel, *Objects on the Move*, 115.

733 Rosing Jakobson, "Repatriation of Greenland's cultural heritage", 80.

734 Interview Mille Gabriel, Copenhagen, August 25, 2015.

No indications have been found that Denmark (or Sweden) have been more generous towards *tropical* colonies with return requests than other European colonial powers. So, if a Danish or Nordic return model exists, it has worked for Denmark's dealing with nearby *cold* colonial possessions, thus in the Northern hemisphere. That such a model has limitations is proven by the many years that both Iceland and Greenland spent in the Danish waiting room and by the Danish application of the practice of 'giving-in-order-to-keep'. Denmark took good care of itself.

The case study further shows how one can deal with the inalienability of privately owned objects. Denmark took special measures to overcome the inalienability of Árni Magnússon's private collection and of the Greenlandic collection of the National Museum in Copenhagen. It is significant that Denmark's highest judge motivated his decision in the case of the Icelandic objects with the argument that Denmark's public interest and its relationship with Iceland outweighed the interests of private owners.

Chapter 11

Melanesian model for Australia and Papua New Guinea?

People have been living in New Guinea for over forty thousand years. Divided over more than one thousand groups, they have preserved much of their collective living, languages and customs. Their contact with Europeans dates from the 16th century, when a Spanish explorer arrived and, without consulting them, named the island after a similarly looking Spanish possession in West Africa – New Guinea. In the course of time, the European powers divided the island into two. From the early 17th century, the western part came under Dutch control. In 1824, the British agreed for it to become a formal part of the Dutch East Indies. In 1962, it joined Indonesia. It has over 3.5 million people, spread over more than three hundred language groups.

This chapter deals with the eastern part, which has over seven million inhabitants that represent eight hundred languages. It was colonised in the same years that King Leopold II started his Congo enterprise, in the 1880s. The British took the southwest area of the island. Initially, they left the administration of the new possession to the British Crown Colony of Queensland, but London annexed it in 1888. German companies, such as the *German New Guinea Company*, took the north-east plus nearby island groups. They explored the new possession, developed copra and rubber plantations and set up trading posts.[735] Later Germany installed a colonial administration.

In 1901, Great Britain united Queensland and five other colonial possessions into the Commonwealth of Australia and four years later, in 1905, it transferred its part of New Guinea to Australia. During the 1914 – 1918 Great War, Australia took over the German part and, in 1921, the League of Nations granted it to Australia as a mandatory area.[736] Australia's domination of the western part of the island would last until 1975, when it gained independence as Papua New Guinea. In the same period, the last Dutch colonies, the nearby East Timor and other Portuguese colonies became independent too; East Timor was soon invaded by Indonesia (7.2.). Australia and Papua New Guinea are separated only by water – Torres Strait has a minimum width of 150 kilometres and the distance between the capital Port Moresby and Cairns in North Queensland is less than one thousand kilometre.

---

735 Buschmann, "Exploring tensions in material culture".
736 http://www.naa.gov.au/collection/fact-sheets/fs148.aspx (August 15, 2014).

Until the arrival in 1606 of the Duyfken (little dove), Australia's Aboriginal peoples had lived undisturbed.[737] The VOC in Batavia had sent out the ship to explore the southern coast of New Guinea for spices, but the captain had ended up on Australia's coast. Other VOC ships followed and the Dutch called the area New Holland (just as they named the present New York New Amsterdam in 1625). In 1788, Captain James Cook arrived at the eastern side and occupied the *terra australis incognita* (unknown southern country) as *terra nullius* for Britain.[738] The British set up settlements and a penal colony. Initially, Aboriginals and newcomers were unaware of each other's existence. When the Europeans penetrated the interior, they pushed back the Aboriginals, showing little respect for their spiritual traditions and artistic skills. Capturing human remains and ritual objects was not a problem for them.[739] As a result, '*many living cultures and languages vanished*'.[740]

11.1. Colonial collecting in Papua New Guinea

More curators than historians have published about colonial collecting and about the returns by Australia to Papua New Guinea and to nearby islands. Two of them, Dirk Smidt, director of the museum in Port Moresby, and Jim Specht, curator of the Australian Museum in Sydney, were pivotal in these returns.

As in other colonies, the collectors of the late 19th and first half of the 20th century were driven by a mix of the salvage paradigm, curiosity and greed.[741] As will be shown, British officials and German enterprises sometimes played opposing roles in collecting. Collections have been spread over Australia, New Zealand, Europe, North and Central America. Australia's role in return matters is widely praised.[742] No evidence was found of German institutions returning objects to the country.

Collecting in the German colonial period
Residential traders, plantation owners, colonial officials, scientists and missionaries experienced a '*golden age of collecting*' during the brief period of German control.[743] For most of them, it was a profitable side activity that helped to show the colony's

---

737 http://www November 2010, Sydney: Netherlands gives important maritime collection to Australia. heritage-activities.nl/ancods/ (August 8, 2014).

738 Barkan, *Guilt of Nations*, 232.

739 Sydney Morning Herald, January 31, 1955, "One overseas collector made a request to the trooper that he shoot a native boy to furnish a complete exhibit of an Australian aboriginal skeleton, skin and skull", in *Creative Spirits*, http://www.creativespirits.info/aboriginalculture/people/aboriginal-remains-repatriation (August 12, 2014).

740 http://australianmuseum.net.au/Aboriginal-and-Torres-Strait-Islander-Collection-Overview#sthash.48aIjrXD.dpuf (August 11, 2014).

741 Gosden, "On his Todd: Material culture and colonialism", in eds. O'Hanlon and Welsch, *Hunting the Gatherers*, 237.

742 The Australian Museum in Sydney is considered '*a world leader in the return of cultural property to its country-of-origin*', in which Specht '*made the difference*'. Val Attenbrow and Richard Fullagar, "A Pacific Odyssey: Archaeology and Anthropology in the Western Pacific. Papers in Honour of Jim Specht", in *Records of the Australian Museum* (Sydney: Australian Museum, 2004, Supplement 29), 5, 6.

743 Charles Knowles and Chris Gosden, "A Century of Collecting: Colonial Collectors in Southwest New Britain", in Attenbrow and Fullagar, ibid., 66.

economic potential.[744] They showed little respect for indigenous cultures and scarcely documented their findings. German enterprises regularly quarrelled about prices and quality with museums and collectors in Europe and the USA. The German New Guinea Company, set up by Berlin entrepreneurs, was averse to research and used artefacts for 'company propaganda' to attract 'prospective German settlers'. Later on, it offered objects for sale e.g. to the newly established Museum of Ethnography in Berlin. When this failed, it considered the possibility of setting up its own colonial museum. Only one enterprise, the *Goddefroy Company*, is known to have hired a trained curator to describe items. It even published a cultural magazine.[745]

When, in 1914, Australian troops took over German New Guinea and many German expatriates returned to Europe, some of them left their collections behind. Of their ethnographic objects, 484 ended up in the Australian War Museum in Melbourne. Later, it loaned them to the National Museum of Victoria, where they remain until today.[746]

Collecting in the British and Australian colonial periods

Because of its proximity, missionaries, scientists and explorers easily crossed over from Queensland to British New Guinea. Preachers persuaded local villagers to destroy religious objects and to burn down the longhouses where they held their ceremonies. The intruders kept many objects for themselves or for their institutions and orders.[747] There is evidence of travellers, who cheated villagers and stole ritual objects from longhouses, and of explorers, who took human remains.[748] While they collected for the Australian Museum in the 1920s, photographer Frank Hurley and curator Allan McCulloch uttered threatening language to get seventeen ritual bullroarers exchanged for tobacco and rice. They pilfered eighteen others.[749] Coastal villagers profited from the exchange of artefacts for European metal tools and eagerly produced new artefacts.[750] Such objects for outsiders were also produced in the Dutch-controlled part of the island.[751]

744 Gosden, "On his Todd: Material culture and colonialism", 229.
745 Buschmann, "Exploring tensions in material culture", 57 – 65.
746 Barry Craig, "Edgar Waite's north-west Pacific expedition – the hidden collections", in eds. Susan Cochrane and Max Quanchi, *Hunting the collectors: Pacific collections in Australian museums, art galleries and archives* (Newcastle: Cambridge Scholars Publishing, 2007), 174. Busse, "Short history of the Papua New Guinea National Museum", 6.
747 Specht, *Pieces of Paradise*, 21, 24.
748 Redmond O'Hanlon discovered in a museum in Florence, Italy, the head of a headman in Papua New Guinea. Italian explorer Luigi D'Albertis (1841 – 1901) had the head sawn off around 1877, put it in a glass jar with alcohol and taken it home. The headman's descendants invoked O'Hanlon's help for the head's return. Until 2012 nothing was done (2012 TV documentary, broadcasted by Dutch TV station VPRO, http://historiek.net/redmond-ohanlon-ontdekt-lang-verdwenen-kannibalenhoofd/39723/ (January 19, 2014).
749 http://www.themonthly.com.au/issue/2008/june/1276830104/anna-cater/such-desirable-objects (August 8, 2014). The pilfered bullroarers were among eight hundred objects that ended up in Australia's National Museum, which is unable to identify them.
750 Specht, *ibid.* Quinnel, "'Before it is too late'".
751 Jacobs, *Collecting Kamoro-objects*, 42.

Papua New Guinean objects in foreign museums

Australia: 80,000
New Zealand; 16,000
UK and Ireland: 40,000
USA and Canada: 70,000.[1]
Ethnological Museum, Berlin: 65,000 objects from the South Seas (unclear how many from German New Guinea).[2]
Ethnological Museum in Hamburg: large collections from Bismarck Islands (which is a part of Papua New Guinea).[3]
National Museum of Ethnology in Leiden: large collection.[4]

mention the source, but it must be Dirk Smidt's *Report of the Symposium: The art of Oceania, held at Hamilton, Canada, (from 21 Aug. till 27 Aug. 1974) and of visits to museums in Australia, New Zealand, Mexico and the United States of America from 25 July till 6 Sept. 1974* (Port Moresby: Papua New Guinea Museum, 1974).

———— Notes ————

1   http://www.themonthly.com.au/issue/2008/june/1276830104/anna-cater/such-desirable-objects (August 8, 2014). The Monthly does not

2   http://www.smb.museum/en/museums-and-institutions/ethnologisches-museum/about-the-collection.html (August 20, 2014).

3   http://www.voelkerkundemuseum.com/70-0-Masken-der-Suedsee.html (August 20, 2014).

4   http://collectie.wereldculturen.nl/ (February 17, 2016).

Michael Somare, chairman of the Board of Trustees of the National Museum in Port Moresby and Papua New Guinea's first Prime Minister,[752] has praised two British officials for their share in the preservation of his country's heritage – William MacGregor, who worked from 1888 until 1897 in British New Guinea, and Hubert Murray, who was there between 1904 and 1940 (4.1. Box: *Relocating to preserve better: From Papua New Guinea to Australia*).[753]

When Lieutenant-governor MacGregor found out that ancient stone axes had become rare, he began to collect these and other materials. During inspection visits – often the first western contact with indigenous New Guineans; some lasted no longer than half an hour – he exchanged iron articles and coloured clothes for ethnographic objects. The primary aim of his visits was '*the spreading of government influence and exploration*'. Collecting new flora and fauna was secondary. Finding ethnographic objects came third. MacGregor set rules for collecting and had improperly acquired collections confiscated.[754]

In 1889, he agreed with the Queensland Museum in Brisbane that it should take in 10,800 objects from 178 different places, collected over ten years. There was no safe place in Port Moresby for them. The Brisbane museum labelled 2,550 as '*duplicates*' and passed these to other museums in Australia and to the British Museum. MacGregor agreed with the Queensland Museum that it would return the remaining objects back to the colony, once it had its own proper museum.

752 http://www.museumpng.gov.pg/index.php/news/view/living-spirits-with-fixed-abodes (August 12, 2014).
753 Michael Somare, in: "Foreword" to Craig, *Living Spirits with Fixed Abodes*.
754 Quinnell, "Before it is too late", 83 – 85.

Hubert Murray, Acting Administrator of the Territory of Papua, was an ardent collector too.[755] He began to construct a museum in Port Moresby and developed legislation for the protection of cultural heritage.[756] In 1915, he agreed with the Australian Museum in Sydney that it would house the collections, which he had gathered, temporarily. Part of the agreement was that the museum could keep a small representative portion for its own use. In archival documents of the decades thereafter, this temporary stay in Australia is confirmed.[757] Between 1915 and 1930, Murray shipped 3,200 objects to Sydney. When the Australian Museum had no more storage space, it selected four hundred objects for itself and sent the rest to the Australian Institute of Anatomy in Canberra. After the closure of the Canberra Institute in 1984, the collection went back to the Australian Museum in Sydney.

Upon the independence of Papua New Guinea in 1975, a quarter million objects were estimated to be in Western museums, while the National Museum and Art Gallery in Port Moresby itself had 30,000 pieces, ranging in size from small body-decoration items to ocean-going canoes (Box: *Papua New Guinean objects in foreign museums*).[758]

Jim Specht links the flow of colonial treasures to the post-independence one-way traffic of artefacts. Whereas in colonial times, colonial administrators, military, missionaries, explorers and traders had dominated it, '*in a neo-colonial relationship the world's art-market has assumed the right to treat the culturally significant artefacts of other people as commercial goods to be traded for profit.*'[759]

The way in which Australia dealt with archival records from the German, British and Australian periods, echoes the custodian principle of MacGregor and Murray. On two occasions, Australia evacuated records from Papua New Guinea – in 1937, following a volcanic eruption and in 1942, when Japan invaded Papua New Guinea -,[760] thus keeping fairly complete records of the British New Guinean administration over the period 1884 to 1942. It preserved around 1,500 files with records of the former German New Guinea, hand-written in the German language; most are about road and plantation development, exploration and health. From 1963 onwards, so twelve years before Papua New Guinea's independence, the two administrations began to make plans to microfilm archival records for the National Archives in Canberra and return the originals to Papua New Guinea. In 1968, the first phase of microfilming was completed and the originals were sent back to Port Moresby. By 1997, all had been microfilmed and returned. It coincided with Dutch and Indonesian dealings with archival matters (7.2.).

---

755 Quinnell, ibid., 91. Busse, ibid., 6.
756 Barry Craig, *Samting Bilong Tumbuna: The collection, documentation and preservation of the material cultural heritage of Papua New Guinea* (Adelaide: Flinders University, Thesis, 1996), 112.
757 Ibid., 206.
758 http://www.museumpng.gov.pg/index.php/collections (August 12, 2014).
759 Specht, *Pieces of Paradise*, 5.
760 http://www.naa.gov.au/collection/fact-sheets/fs148.aspx (August 16, 2014).

11.2. The return process

Prime Minister Somare was moderate about the impact of colonialism in his own country: *'Our late colonisation has protected us from many atrocities... committed against indigenous peoples all over the world. Many of our cultures and traditions are still alive because contact with the outside world was so recent.*[761] As his country faced the challenge of keeping hundreds of ethnic groups together, it began to search for representative heritage. In 1974, Somare asked Western museums *'to co-operate with us in returning our ancestral spirits and souls to their homes in Papua New Guinea... It is not right that they should be stored in New York, Paris, Bonn or elsewhere.... There is a burning desire among our people that our ancient values, wisdoms and unique forms of artistic expression should be preserved....'.* But the Western museums did not cooperate. At best, they were willing to exchange or loan objects.[762]

In spite of the examples of colonial officials who had helped to secure objects and archives for Papua New Guinea, Australia was divided on the issue of return. In 1972, the same year in which the national museums of Papua New Guinea and Australia began a constructive discussion about returns, the *Commonwealth Arts Advisory Board of Australia* sponsored an expedition, without informing the museum in Port Moresby.[763] It wanted to remove as much cultural property as possible before the country's independence, fearing that return requests would empty Australian museums. To underpin its position, it referred to a blanket demand of the National Museum of Solomon Islands for cultural heritage materials in Australian museums.[764]

At the same time, Australia was a country that had also retrieved colonial cultural objects. In 1972, it agreed with the Netherlands that all rights to four Dutch shipwrecks, which had been discovered off the West Australian coast, went to Australia. New finds – bricks, lead ingots, pipes, skulls, elephant tusks, cannonballs, navigational instruments and coins – were to be divided between both countries. From the 1980s on, all objects remained de facto in Australia.[765] In 2006, it was agreed that the Dutch part of the collection would be reunited with the collection in Australia. This was implemented in 2010. The United Kingdom gave a vellum copy of the Commonwealth of Australia Constitution Act of 1901, which had been kept in the British Parliament in London until then (1.2.).[766]

---

761 Somare, ibid., VII.
762 Smidt, ibid., Appendix b; 34.
763 Specht, "The Australian Museum and the return of artefacts to Pacific Island countries", 28.
764 New Zealander Raymond Firth, who had collected on the island of Tikopia in 1928 and 1929 and again in 1956, supported the blanket claim but suggested leaving some objects in Australia. Australia turned down the demand. The thus threatening deadlock was broken by offering the Solomon Islands' National Museum the opportunity to select two items to celebrate the opening of a new building in Honiara. In return the museum donated, as a typically Melanesian gesture, two items to Australia's National Museum, in: Elisabeth Bonshek, "Ownership and a Peripatetic Collection: Raymond Firth's Collection from Tikopia, Solomon Islands" in: eds. Attenbrow and Fullagar, ibid., 38.
765 Jos Van Beurden, *Return of Cultural and Historical Treasures*, 49, 50.
766 http://pmtranscripts.dpmc.gov.au/browse.php?did=8103 (April 30, 2015).

Several developments influenced the return debate in Australia. One was the growth of a civil rights movement among Aboriginal peoples from the early 1960s. It claimed land and self-determination, including the restitution of ancestral remains and ritual objects and fitted in '*the growth of the human rights movement in other democracies*', especially in the USA, and in the increased attention for '*the human rights of indigenous people in the international arena*'.[767] Aboriginal efforts to show their culture as a living one, as part of Australia's identity and as '*essential for the Australian national patrimony*' had effect. While they had never been asked to play a role and to be part of the Australian nation, Australian museums '*could no longer unilaterally determine how indigenous cultures represented in their collections were preserved and displayed*'.[768] It lasted until 2006, before the Australian Government admitted[769] that the Aborigines had lost thousands of human remains to museums and scientific institutions in Australia and Europe during the late 19th and early 20th century. Australian institutions possessed nearly twenty-five thousand secret and sacred objects from different Aboriginal and Torres Strait Islander cultures. Renegotiating their relations with Aboriginal communities, they repatriated over one thousand human remains and three hundred and sixty ethnographic objects and began to involve Aboriginals in the making of exhibitions.[770]

Another development occurred from the late 1970s. The Australian government shifted its focus '*away from (colonial) British ties to the Asia Pacific region*' and emphasised its connectedness with Aboriginals, Papua New Guinea and other nearby (new) states.[771] A practical result was the return by Australia's National Museum of two canoe-prow carvings to the Solomon Islands on the occasion of its independence in 1978 [772] and, in 1988, of some items which were underrepresented in the national museums of Papua New Guinea, the Solomon Islands and Vanuatu.[773]

The adoption of the 1970 UNESCO Convention was a development that encouraged new states in the Pacific to renew their relationship with Australia. It led to intense debates about past and present acquisition policies of Australian museums and increased Australia's generosity towards Papua New Guinea.[774] New states, such as Papua New Guinea, Vanuatu and Solomon Islands, felt encouraged to claim cultural objects. They did so in spite of the fact that they were (and still are) not states parties to the Convention – too small states for the big legal implications – while Australia acceded in 1989.[775]

---

767 Barkan, ibid., 239, 233.

768 Vrdoljak, *International Law, Museums and the Return of Cultural Objects*, 221, 223.

769 http://www.environment.gov.au/node/22561 (August 11, 2014); http://australianmuseum.net.au/ Aboriginal-and-Torres-Strait-Islander-Collection-Overview#sthash.48aIjrXD.dpuf (August 11, 2014).

770 http://www.nma.gov.au/history/aboriginal-torres-strait-islander-cultures-histories/repatriation (August 12, 2014).

771 Vrdoljak, ibid., 221, 220.

772 Specht, "The Australian Museum and the return of artefacts to Pacific Island countries", 28.

773 Prott, *Witnesses to History*, 418.

774 Quinnell, ibid., 95. Vrdoljak, ibid., 224.

775 http://www.unesco.org/eri/la/convention.asp?KO=13039&language=E&order=alpha (July 14, 2015).

In 1972, a Labour Government took office, which had an effect comparable with that of the coming of progressive Governments in Denmark in 1959 and in the Netherlands in 1973. It saw cultural heritage as having intrinsic value – for itself, for other countries and for Aboriginal peoples and did not oppose return negotiations.[776]

Papua New Guinea's museum infrastructure was a topic in the return negotiations. Objects were held in an old metal-roofed building without environmental control and with periodical flooding. Among the staff were few Papua New Guineans. Change began in 1972. The museum attracted new trustees – Michael Somare and four other local experts. Dirk Smidt, the museum's first director and a white Dutchman, asked the *Australian Council of Museum Directors* for the repatriation of Papua New Guinean collections, especially those of MacGregor and Murray. The Council replied that it was willing to send *'representative cultural material'*, but it would do so as a gift, thereby denying the nature of the custodianship that MacGregor and Murray had stipulated. It was the first time the Australian heritage sector made such a commitment. Smidt had the support of pro-return curators in Australia, organised in the Conference of Museum Anthropologists, CoMA, who took care that the Council kept its promise.[777] Papua New Guinea increased its credibility through a campaign with police and customs officials against the on-going smuggling of cultural objects and the seizing of seventeen cases with objects from known dealers in June 1972. They were ready to be flown out of the country to New York and Honolulu. Although no dealer was ever prosecuted,[778] the authorities showed over one hundred of the objects[779] and probably made the first post-1970 exhibition of stolen and smuggled objects. In 1973, the planning of a new national museum began, and in a few years the construction was well under way.[780] In 1974, a cultural heritage law was adopted, protecting objects manufactured prior to 31st December 1960.[781]

That the museum officials involved were scarcely bothered by formal, diplomatic hassles eased the negotiations. It is possible that hidden hierarchies played a minor role – with a western chief-negotiator and the inspired and inspiring Michael Somare at the Papua New Guinea side. Specht wrote that *'the close relationship with the museums… permitted honest discussions even though initially they were occasionally hard-hitting and heated'.*[782] The Australians were unaware of similar negotiations, except for those between Indonesia and the Netherlands, but, as an Australian insider wrote,[783] their sympathy for the Indonesian claims dwindled

---

776 Barkan, ibid., 233. Vrdoljak, ibid., 221.
777 CoMA was an informal, independent network for more collaboration between museums and indigenous minorities inside and outside Australia, email Jim Specht, May 13, 2015.
778 Craig, *Samting Bilong Tumbuna*, 163, 164.
779 Dirk Smidt, *The seized collections of the Papua New Guinea Museum* (Port Moresby: Port Moresby University, Creative Arts Centre, 1975). Busse, ibid., 11.
780 Busse, ibid., 12.
781 Craig, ibid., 199.
782 Specht, ibid., 30.
783 Email exchange May 13, 2015.

after the killing of five Australian journalists in Indonesia and the Indonesian invasion of East Timor in 1975.

At the opening of new buildings of the National Museum and Art Gallery in Port Moresby in 1977, seventeen artefacts were handed over. Australia's National Museum Trust had selected them from its collection, bearing in mind the gaps and weaknesses of existing collections in Papua New Guinea. It presented them as a gift.

In those years, a major part of the MacGregor collection was also transferred. It became '*a foundation icon for the Papua New Guinea National Museum*'.[784] In 1969, the Australian Administration had declared the MacGregor collection the property of the Queensland Government. If the colony wanted it back, it had to submit a formal request. In 1970, museum officials of both countries recommended that a representative selection was to be returned. There followed some legal wrangling, in which the Port Moresby museum claimed a moral and legal right to the whole collection, and the museum in Brisbane a right to the share that had been agreed upon in 1897. In 1973, the Queensland Museum offered a selection that would be transferred, when facilities in the museum in Port Moresby had become adequate.

In 1979, the two parties achieved a consensus with a Melanesian touch. First, the Queensland Museum repatriated an early Gogodala drum to Papua New Guinea. In return, the museum in Port Moresby announced that it no longer laid claim to the entire MacGregor collection. The two parties then agreed that the collection '*would have two homes*'. Unique items and best examples would be returned. The remainder would be divided, taking the holdings in the two museums into consideration. After a laborious selection process, 3,297 items of the MacGregor collection were returned, while 2,675 remained in Queensland. Another 2,277 items await selection.[785]

In 2015, the Hubert Murray collection was still in the National Museum of Australia and no steps have been taken to discuss repatriation.[786] No evidence was found of (requests for) repatriation made by Papua New Guinea to museums in Germany, the UK and other former European colonial powers.

In conclusion, although Papua New Guinea suffered less under colonial violence than many other colonies, the maldistribution of cultural and historical treasures inside and outside the country and the instances of inappropriate acquisitions show that the losses, which it suffered during the European colonial era, were considerable.

This case study highlights the relevance of distance and the role of committed heritage professionals. Even more than in the case study of Denmark, Iceland and Greenland, the small geographical and cultural distance made the negotiations go smoothly. It helped that Australia had been a colony itself, had internally colonised the Aboriginal peoples, who have since emancipated themselves, and had owned an external colony, albeit briefly.

---

784 Quinnell, ibid., 98.
785 Ibid., 97.
786 Barry Craig, email May 19, 2015. Busse, ibid., 14.

Returns to Papua New Guinea[1]

Australian Museum, Sydney:
- 17 objects (1977)
- 140 objects of F.K.G. Mulleried's stone-axe-adze collection (ca. 1998)

Queensland Museum, Brisbane:
- Gogodala drum (1979)
- 3.297 items of MacGregor collection (1979 – 1992)

Macleay Museum, Sydney:
- 37 objects (year unknown)

National Archives of Australia:
- Original materials returned (1968 – 1997)

——————— **Notes** ———————

1   Craig, *Living Spirits*, 261. Quinnell, ibid., 95 – 97; http://www.nma.gov.au/history/ aboriginal-torres-strait-islander-cultures-histories/ repatriation (August 12, 2014).

In 1977, committed heritage professionals played a role in Australia's gift of seventeen artefacts to the National Museum and Art Gallery of Papua New Guinea. It shows the weight of extensive research on the part of heritage officials in institutions of the former coloniser. Papua New Guinea showed commitment by tackling the illicit trade.

Australia's generosity, however, should be put in perspective. The country had a strong anti-return lobby and returns have remained limited. Stakeholders are still quarrelling about the Murray collection and part of the MacGregor collection. Nothing ever happened with the 484 objects left behind by Germans in 1914 and appropriated by museums in Australia. Australian museums were more willing to help curb the illicit trade than to negotiate returns. They preferred returns of skeletal remains to those of cultural objects.

As in the previous case studies, Australia and Papua New Guinea agreed on a package deal consisting of returns, strengthening museum infrastructure in the former colony financed by the former coloniser, and forms of collaboration. In my view, Australia used this package deal less than other former colonisers to create negotiation space to minimise or evade returns.

The case study raises the question of a Melanesian model for dealing with disputes about colonial cultural objects. The transfer of the MacGregor collection has been described as *'a typically Melanesian consensus'* and *'a very Melanesian act of reciprocity'*.[787] If a Melanesian country wants objects back, it offers something in return. This occurred more often, for instance between Australia and the Solomon Islands, and between New Zealand and Papua New Guinea. In 1975, the National Museum in Wellington handed over the valuable *Lockyer Collection* (prehistoric stone mortars and pestle, and a rare wickerwork figure), after which the National Museum in Port Moresby offered four objects in return.[788] Sometimes, there was a Melanesian touch, but not always.

---

787   Quinnell, ibid., 96, 98.
788   Craig, *Samting Bilong Tumbuna*, 199.

Chapter 12

The Benin Dialogue (2010 – ....)

In the late 19th century, European colonial powers tried to strengthen their hold on the coasts of Africa. When a conflict arose between the British and the Oba (traditional King) of Edo in Benin City about opening the borders for trade, early in January 1897, the Oba's soldiers happened to kill the British Consul-General and some of his men. A few weeks later over one thousand British soldiers arrived. After ransacking the palace of the King of Edo in 1897, they discovered peculiar objects. They did not understand that a brass head could represent a '*defeated or decapitated*' royal person, nobleman or warrior[789] and that a plaque told the Kingdom's long history, but rather considered the objects as expressions of '*decay, deterioration and degradation*'.[790] Nigerian, African and Western authors have described the journey of these objects in contradictory ways. What was a punitive expedition for the British was looting, pillaging and sacking for the Beninese.[791]

While the Oba and other royal family members could not elucidate the meaning of the technically well-made objects, since they had been killed or sent into exile, local people did not explain much either and '*the expedition was as usual unaccompanied by any scientific explorer*'.[792] Although European researchers wondered whether they had been produced with outside help – from Egypt or Portugal – initially,[793] within a year, many museums acquired their first Benin object. At the same time, they kept displaying their makers, the kings and people as the 'other', as inferior, thus defining an unmistakable hierarchy.[794] The objects continued to fascinate scholars and soon studies appeared about the objects, their clumsy acquisition, their makers, Benin's history, its ritual of human sacrifices and their dispersal. One conclusion was that Benin objects were entirely African

---

789 Staffan Lundén, *Displaying Loot: The Benin Objects and the British Museum* (Gothenburg: Gothenburg University, Ph.D., 2016), 2.

790 Annie E. Coombes, *Reinventing Africa – Museums, material culture and popular imagination* (New Haven and London: Yale University Press, 1994), 11.

791 Layiwola, "The Benin Massacre: Memories and Experiences", 83.

792 Augustus Pitt Rivers, *Antique Works of Art from Benin collected by Lieutenant- General Pitt Rivers* (London: printed privately, 1900), IV.

793 In 1485-6, Portugal was the first European power to reach the Benin Court. Beninese craftsmen included images of the Portuguese on plaques and other objects. Stefan Eisenhofer, "Olokun's Messengers – The Portuguese and the Kingdom of Benin", in ed. Plankensteiner, *Benin Kings and Rituals,* 55. Lundén, *ibid.*, 288.

794 Armand Duchâteau, *Vroege hofkunst uit Afrika* (Leiden: Museum Volkenkunde, 1990). Franziska Bedorf and Wilhelm Östberg, "African *objets d'arts* currency in a bid for the Polar Star – and for recognition on the European scene", in Stockholm Museum for Ethnography, *Whose Objects?*, 2010: 42.

creations.[795] Felix von Luschan of the Ethnological Museum in Berlin compared the Benin casting technique with the best in Europe and amassed a large collection.[796]

12.1. Dispersal over Europe and North America

Confiscated items – estimates vary from 2,400 to over 4,000 – entered Europe along two channels.[797] One was the Foreign Office in London, which had many objects auctioned to cover the costs of the expedition. Purchasers were British and European museums and collectors. German trading companies in West Africa were the second channel. They re-sold to museums and collectors in Europe. I would like to add private soldiers as a third. They took many objects, kept, re-sold, donated or loaned them to museums, traders and collectors. After a few decades, American collectors and museums joined the competition for Benin items.[798]

The quantity and quality of objects that have remained in Nigeria is disputed. Wilhelm Östberg of Stockholm's Ethnological Museum says *'more than a thousand'* and confirms the assertion of the director of the Glasgow Museums that Nigerian museums have *'one of the world's finest representations of this great culture and our collections would not add significantly to this'*.[799] Barbara Plankensteiner points to museum collections in Nigeria before the country's independence in 1960, while numerous objects disappeared especially in the aftermath of the Biafra War (1967 – 1971), mostly to Western museums and private collections.[800] Ekpo Eyo writes about only *'few unimportant objects'* and the need for his country to ask for returns and to purchase objects from the British Museum. As shown later, Nigeria actually did this.[801] In 2013, Dutch Africa curator, Annette Schmidt, was in Nigeria. She confirmed Eyo's argument: *'The quality and the quantity of the objects is less than that of the major European collections'*.[802] Some are fakes. The number of objects that Nigeria lent for the 2007/8 exhibition *Benin Kings and Rituals – Court Arts from Nigeria* in Vienna, Berlin, Paris and Chicago was 19 out of 275 exhibited items, or seven percent.

The literature for this chapter uncovers several efforts to list Benin collections in European and North American museums and private collections. Although the outcomes differ and although the British Museum tries to downplay the number of objects in its possession and claims that the Ethnological Museum in Berlin is

---

795 Lundén, *ibid.*, 288.

796 Paula Ivanov and Barbara Plankensteiner, *Benin – 600 Jahre höfische Kunst aus Nigeria* (Berlin: Ethnological Museum, 2008), 10, 12.

797 Duchâteau, *ibid.*, 137; Plankensteiner, *ibid.*, 34; Lundén, *ibid.*, 7, note 2.

798 P.J.C. Dark, *The Art of Benin, catalogue of an exhibition of the A.W.F. Fuller and Chicago Natural History Museum Collections of Antiquities from Benin, Nigeria,* (Chicago: Natural History Museum, 1962), 17. Kate Ezra, *Royal Art of Benin – The Perls Collection* (New York: Metropolitan Museum of Art, 1992), 25. Plankensteiner, ibid., 36.

799 Wilhelm Östberg. "The coveted treasures of the Kingdom of Benin", in Stockholm Museum of Ethnography, *Whose Objects?*, 2010: 67, 56.

800 Barbara Plankensteiner, "The Benin treasures -Difficult legacy and contested heritage", in eds. Brigitta Hauser-Schäublin and Lyndel V. Prott, *Cultural property and contested ownership – The trafficking of artefacts and the quest for restitution* (London and New York: Routledge, 2016), 138, 141.

801 Ekpo Eyo, "Nigeria", in: *Museum* (Paris: UNESCO Quarterly review, 1979), XXXI/1, 21.

802 Interview Annette Schmidt, National Museum of Ethnology, Leiden, September 29, 2014.

the biggest owner of Benin objects, Staffan Lundén has shown that the London institution comes first, with about 700 objects, and the Berlin museum second, with 535 items.[803] In the United Kingdom, the Pitt Rivers Museum in Oxford and the Glasgow Museums have considerable collections. In Germany they can also be found in museums in Cologne, Hamburg, Dresden, Leipzig, Stuttgart, Munich and Mannheim. The World Museum in Vienna is a major possessor. Not many are found in France, although the Musée du quai Branly in Paris has a few objects, or in Russia, where the Peter the Great Museum of Anthropology and Ethnography in Saint Petersburg keeps a few. In the USA, Benin collections can be found in museums in places such as New York, Washington, Boston and Chicago. Many objects have shifted from private hands to museums[804] or circulate in the art market.[805] That their chaotic dispersion has made them *a fragmented experience*[806] is evident from their scattered distribution in the Netherlands. While Museum Volkenkunde in Leiden has an extensive collection, other museums house only a few Benin objects. In private residences, auction houses and art fairs an unknown number of Benin objects circulate (Box: *Benin treasures in the Netherlands*).

12.2. Prelude to the Dialogue

At the opening of the exhibition *Benin Kings and Rituals – Court Arts from Nigeria* in Vienna, Oba Erediauwa of Benin prayed *'that the people and the government of Austria will show humaneness and magnanimity and return to us some of these objects which found their way to your country'*.[807] The answer of the World Museum in Vienna (167 Benin treasures) was a flat no, as *'state-property'* could not be alienated.[808] It had the support of the three other organising museums, all signatories of the 2002 *Declaration on the Importance and Value of the Universal Museum*. Their introduction in the catalogue echoed the declaration: it was their merit to have brought *'these works of art to far broader attention. They are now forever on the map of world art'* and they trusted *'that this exhibition contributes to an ongoing dialogue between the past and the present, and between Africa and*

---

803 Lundén, *Displaying Loot*, 8.

804 Pitt Rivers' collection went to the museum named after him in Oxford (Pitt Rivers 1900). A.W.F. Fuller donated his to the Chicago Natural History Museum (Dark, ibid.). The 160 items of the Perls collection and the Rockefeller collection, which includes an exceptional ivory pendant mask and two dozen of other sculptures, are in the Metropolitan Museum of Art in New York (Ezra, ibid., VI). In 2014, the R.O. Lehman collection went to the Museum of Fine Arts in Boston (https://www.mfa.org/give/gifts-art/Lehman-Collection [August 16, 2014]).

805 Sotheby, *Catalogue of Works of Art from Benin: The property of a European private collector – Monday, 16th June 1980*. In February 2011 Sotheby withdrew an ivory-made pendant mask of Queen Idia from auction, together with five other Benin items coming from descendants of Lieutenant Colonel Sir Henry Galway, who had participated in the 1897 raid. At the 2014 TEFAF Maastricht art fair, Entwistle offered a 15th – 17th century Benin ivory bracelet and a rare bronze plaque for sale, (http://www.entwistlegallery.com/pages/museums.html (August 13, 2014), (http://www.chapeaumagazine.com/media/61051/TEFAF-Gids_2014.pdf, 14). The Art Newspaper, Special Report, No. 255, March 2014, 13.

806 Layiwola, "The Benin Massacre", 87.

807 In Plankensteiner, *Benin – Kings and Rituals*, 13.

808 Interview Plankensteiner, Weltmuseum in Vienna, July 21, 2014.

Benin treasures in the Netherlands

Museum Volkenkunde, Leiden

Twenty objects, purchased shortly after 1897; seventy purchased between 1900 and 1902 (from dealers in Hamburg and London); later thirty were added, amongst them a 19th century bronze head from the Tropenmuseum in Amsterdam.[1]

A. Schwartz, collector in Amsterdam

Eighteen bronze and brass and six ivory objects, auctioned in 1980.[2]

World Museum, Rotterdam

Bronze bell, belt plate and staff.[3]

Museum Klok & Peel in Asten

Bronze bell, belonging to a dignitary.[4]

Tropenmuseum in Amsterdam

Brass plaque of a Benin titleholder with calabash-type musical instrument (from the collection of German Jewish banker, George Tillmann).[5]

Afrika Museum in Berg en Dal

Brass head from between 1380 and 1530, most probably a gift of the Oba to a subordinate ruler (provenance: collection Holy Spirit Fathers, who founded the museum in 1954).[6]

Museum Fundatie in Zwolle

Brass plaque with catfish (symbol of wealth, peace and fertility), 16th or 17th century (gift from museum-director Dirk Hannema, who purchased it in 1937 for an amount equivalent to between € 180 and €225 from Amsterdam art-dealer Carel van Lier, who had purchased it from Charles Ratton in Paris in 1935).[7]

TEFAF, Maastricht

In 2014, art-gallery Entwistle London offered a 15th – 17th century Benin ivory bracelet and a rare bronze plaque for sale.[8]

Private collections

No evidence was found of Benin objects in private collections in the Netherlands. This does not mean there are none.

Notes

1   Rogier Bedaux. "De geschiedenis van de Leidse Benin-verzameling". In: Duchâteau, *Benin: Vroege hofkunst*, 159. J. Macquart. *Die Benin-Sammlung des Reichsmuseum für Völkerkunde in Leiden* (Leiden: E.J. Brill, 1913).

2   Sotheby, *Catalogue of Works of Art from Benin*.

3   http://www.wereldmuseum.nl/nl/decollectie/zoeken.html (August 16, 2014). Inv. Nos. 15984, 29965, 46651.

4   Asten: *Museum Klok & Peel*, Inv. No. 937 F 362. Visit March 11, 2016.

5   Before fleeing to the USA in 1939, Tillmann loaned his collection of two thousand (mostly Indonesian) items to the museum. After his death (1941) the collection remained there. In 1994 his descendants donated it to the museum. See Coos van Brakel, David Van Duuren and Itie Van Hout. *A Passion for Indonesian Art – The George Tillmann Collection at the Tropenmuseum, Amsterdam* (Amsterdam: KIT Publishers, 1996): 7; 56, 57. Paul Faber, ea. *Africa at the Tropenmuseum* (Amsterdam: KIT Publishers, 2011), 132, 133. http://upload.wikimedia.org/wikipedia/commons/7/70/COLLECTIE_TROPENMUSEUM_Bronzen_plaat_paleisversiering_met_als_centrale_figuur_een_hofdignitaris_TMnr_1772-2018.jpg?uselang=nl (August 16, 2014).

6   http://www.afrikamuseum.nl/collectie/collectie.html (August 16, 2014). Inv. No. 254 – 1. Email exchange August 22, 2014.

7   Email information, provided by Museum Fundatie, August 21, 2014. Inv. No. 557.

8   http://www.entwistlegallery.com/pages/museums.html (August 13, 2014).

Return requests between 1972 and 2008[1]

1972: Nigeria sent a letter to the Austrian embassy in Lagos asking for help in securing the release of Nigerian antiquities from international museums. Austria rejected the request. Two visits of Ekpo Eyo, then director of the National Museum in Lagos, announced for 1973 and 1975, never took place.

1977: Upon a request of the National Museum of Nigeria to loan the popular Queen Idia ivory pectoral mask the British Museum asked for an insurance bond of two million pound sterling. Nigeria was unable/unwilling to pay. The museum later declared the mask to be too fragile to move and, later again, that it never had intended to loan it.

Early 1980s: Bilateral negotiations with various countries and the purchase of a number of objects with no result.

1991: The Oba of Benin petitioned for the return of Benin treasures with no result.

1996: British MP Bernie Grant, supported by the Oba of Benin, submitted a return request to the Director of the Glasgow Museums; this was rejected.

2000: Testimony was given by two members of the Benin Court to the House of Commons in London; no result.[2]

2001: Nigerian cultural heritage law specialist, Folarin Shyllon, claimed the objects at a UNESCO conference in London to no effect.

2002: Nigerian Parliament unanimously passed a motion, urging the President of the country to request the repatriation of the Benin treasures; no result.

2007: Request for the Queen Idia mask was repeated, but nothing happened.

2007: The Oba's request in the catalogue *Benin – Kings and Rituals – Court Art from Nigeria* was turned down.

2008: Letter with return request by the Oba to museum in Chicago had no result.

Notes

1   Sources: Lundén, *Displaying loot*, 436 – 439. Layiwola, "The Benin Massacre", 88. Peju Layiwola, "Walker and the restitution of two Benin bronzes", in: *Premium Times*, Nigeria, June 20, 2014. Folarin Shyllon, *Museums and universal heritage: Right of return and right of access*, http://www.blackherbals.com/museums_and_universal_heritage. htm (2007) (August 21, 2014). Greenfield, *Return of Cultural Treasures*, 122 – 129. The Art Newspaper (April 2002). Plankensteiner "The Benin treasures -Difficult legacy and contested heritage", 137 – 145.

2   https://www.publications.parliament.uk/pa/cm199900/cmselect/cmcumeds/371/371ap27. htm (February 16, 2017).

Returns between 1937 and 2014[1]

1937: Private return by G.M. Miller, son of a member of the Benin expedition, to Akenzua II, Oba at that time, of two coral bead crowns and a coral bead tunic of Oba Ovonramwen, who had been arrested in 1897.

1950s – 1970s: Nigeria purchased thirty Benin objects from the British Museum, which needed to raise money for the purchase of other objects.

1957: Josephine Walker, widow of Captain Herbert Sutherland Walker, who was involved in the capture of Benin, donated a six-foot-tall Benin ivory tusk to the museum in Jos, Nigeria.

1972: British Museum sold one plaque with a mudfish and one with a crocodile to Nigeria.

2014: Descendants of Captain H.S. and Mrs. J. Walker bring back a bronze bird and a bronze bell.

2014: Museum of Fine Arts, Boston transferred illicitly acquired antiquities back to Nigeria, including an early 20th century Benin bronze altar figure stolen from the Benin Palace in 1976.[2]

--- **Notes** ---

1   Sources: Lundén, *Displaying loot*, 436 – 439. Layiwola, "The Benin Massacre", 88. Peju Layiwola, "Walker and the restitution of two Benin bronzes", in: *Premium Times*, Nigeria, June 20, 2014. Folarin Shyllon, *Museums and universal heritage: Right of return and right of access*, http://www.blackherbals.com/museums_ and_universal_heritage.htm (2007) (August 21, 2014). Greenfield, *Return of Cultural Treasures*, 122 – 129. The Art Newspaper (April 2002). Plankensteiner "The Benin treasures -Difficult legacy and contested heritage", 137 – 145.

2   http://www.mfa.org/news/nigeria-transfer (September 11, 2014).

Europe and North America'.[809] The *ongoing dialogue* was about cooperation between the NCMM (Nigerian Commission for Museums and Monuments), the Benin Court and some European museums.

Such dealings between Nigeria and Europe were not new. There have been many return requests, coming from the Nigerian Government, the Benin Court, a Nigerian cultural specialist and a British MP (Box: *Return requests between 1977 and 2008*). In the wake of the 1997 Great Benin Centenary, the Oba of Benin himself became an active claimant of objects.[810] There have been few actual returns; some were the result of sales by the British Museum, others were handed over by private possessors (Box: *Returns between 1938 and 2014*).

809 In Plankensteiner, *Benin – Kings and Rituals*, 17.
810 Plankensteiner, "The Benin treasures -Difficult legacy and contested heritage", 142.

Folarin Shyllon and Kwame Opoku warn of exaggerations and untruths in enumerations of return requests and actual returns made public by return-lobby groups.[811] They criticise Nigerian Governments for not seeking the help of UNESCO's ICPRCP (6.1.), set up to deal with return and restitution, although Nigeria twice had a seat on this committee.

In 2014, Adrian Mark Walker, grandson of Captain Herbert Sutherland and Josephine Walker returned a bird, a bell and part of his grandfather's diary; and his motivation to do so deserves attention. According to Walker, his grandfather had been *'ahead of his time in the civil manner he referred to Benin natives... as gentlemen'*. His reason to return the objects was that he realised *'that if they meant a lot to me because of their connection with my grandfather, they must mean a lot more to the people of the place from where they had come'*.[812] It is reminiscent of the motivation of the descendants of Dutch Governor-general J.C. Baud, who returned Diponegoro's ancient pilgrim's staff to Indonesia (8.1.).

12.3. The dialogue[813]

Barbara Plankensteiner, initiator of the Dialogue from the European side when she was chief curator of the World Museum in Vienna,[814] defines the Benin Dialogue as *'a long-term project'* that began with *'joint conversations about the aims, needs and fears'* and building *'trust'*.[815] When the Vienna museum started preparations for the Benin Kings and Rituals exhibition in 2002, she met Omotoshu Eluyemi, Director-general of Nigeria's NCMM (National Commission for Museums and Monuments), who she says *'was open minded and supported collaboration. The NCMM was willing to loan us objects.'* Her subsequent visit to Nigeria was the first by a Viennese curator. In the following years, a longer-term contact between Western museums and the NCMM was discussed.

In 2006, a delegation of the Viennese museum and the ethnological museum in Berlin visited the Benin Court. The two museums and the NCMM agreed that the Vienna museum *'would invite four delegates from the Oba and give them a podium to express their opinion and pronounce a message from the Oba.'* In 2007, Oba Erediauwa wrote his modest return request in the Preface of the exhibition-catalogue. At the opening, his brother warned that their presence was *'a royal gesture'* that *'should not be mistaken for the King's approval or legitimisation of the forceful removal of the items from his palace.... The accent is to keep his demand for the*

---

811 Shyllon, *Museums and universal heritage*, 7. Kwame Opoku, "Benin Plan of Action (2): Will the miserable project be the last word on the looted Benin artefacts?" (Accra: *Modern Ghana*, 2013), http://www.modernghana.com/news/451636/1/benin-plan-of-action-2-will-this-miserable-project.html (September 12, 2014).

812 Layiwola, "Walker and the restitution of two Benin bronzes", 2014.

813 Sources for the Benin Dialogue are interviews with Barbara Plankensteiner (World Museum, Vienna) and Annette Schmidt (National Museum of Ethnology, Leiden), speeches by a representative of the Benin Court and reactions by Nigerian and African critics and exchanges with Folarin Shyllon.

814 Africa curator at the Yale University Art Gallery since late 2015, http://artgallery.yale.edu/sites/default/files/pr/pdf/pr_mitchell_plankensteiner_008.pdf (June 22, 2016).

815 Interview Barbara Plankensteiner, July 21, 2014.

repatriation of this Benin cultural property on World conscience'.[816] The removal had been a *'rape on the colonised people'*. Plankensteiner praises the *'crucial and positive'* role of Eluyemi's successor, Yusuf Abdallah Usman, and points to the difficult context of Nigeria's cultural sector: *'The museum system in Nigeria is hierarchically organized.... Security of the collections and fear for thefts are a major issue.'*

After the exhibition, the Vienna museum and NCMM initiated *'an open dialogue on the accessibility of the art treasures of the Benin Kingdom for the Nigerian public'*. This led to the signing of a Memorandum of Understanding about mutual support, transfer of knowledge and a commitment to advance the dialogue in 2010. Workshops and conferences were held in Vienna, Lagos and Benin City on issues such as conservation, restoration and exhibition design. A discussion platform was set up and the two parties organised a joint exhibition and research project on African lace in Vienna (2010) and Lagos (2011).[817]

In December 2010, the two-day workshop in Vienna, *New Cultures of Collaboration. Sharing of Collections and Quests for Restitution: the Benin Case* became a real result of the dialogue. Participants were the NCMM, the Benin Court, the ethnological museums of Vienna, Berlin and Stockholm and the British Museum (joint supporter of the 2002 *Declaration on the Importance and Value of Universal Museums* with the Berlin museum and other museums). Nigerian and Austrian legal experts also joined the workshop. Usman tried to convince his European counterparts of Nigeria's ability to preserve Benin objects, admitting that corruption had to be further attacked. The Lagos museum would get sufficient storage facilities; security personnel would be trained and better equipped.[818] The participants decided to exchange overviews of their Benin collections and to involve more European museums in the dialogue.

During the second workshop, *New Cultures of Collaboration. Sharing of Collections*, also held behind closed doors in Berlin in October 2011, German programmes for research and scholarships were presented and the Benin collections of the participating museums became virtually accessible. Thanks to an intervention of Nigerian legal expert Folarin Shyllon, Nigeria accepted that there was no juridical basis or hard law instrument to support a restitution claim. The Europeans suggested that the Nigerian stakeholders should organise the next meeting, as it would enable them to study the situation in Nigeria and be proof of Nigeria's interest in the dialogue.

During the third meeting, held in Benin City in February 2013, the NCMM's Director-General and representatives of the Vienna and Berlin museums presented a *Benin Plan of Action* (Appendix: *Benin Plan of Action*) with measures for better cooperation and for a stronger NCMM. It did not contain a single paragraph on returns. However, the NCMM Director-general is keeping the door open for

---

816 Edun Agharese Akenzua of the Benin Court in 2007 at the opening of the Benin exhibition in Vienna, in http://africanartswithtaj.blogspot.nl/2011/12/benin-monarch-govt-and-looted-artefacts. html (September 5, 2016).

817 http://www.weltmuseumwien.at/de/entdecken/das-museum/kooperationen/die-national-commission-for-museums-and-monuments-nigeria-ncmm/ (September 12, 2014).

818 http://tourism-news-nigeria.blogspot.nl/2011/01/looted-artifact-worries-director.html (October 7, 2014).

returns, stating that '*the return of the Benin treasures is actually an integral part of the dialogue but under a mutual collaborative engagement*'.[819] Curators from museums in Stockholm, Dresden, Berlin, Vienna and Leiden, present at the meeting, signed the Plan. The British Museum was not present, as its representative had not received a visa in time. It promised to host the next meeting.

According to Plankensteiner, there were never '*serious fights or contradictions*'. While it was agreed from the start to keep the dialogue '*on an internal basis*', the third meeting started with a public event with politicians and journalists.[820] The Dialogue turned out to be '*a very political issue in Nigeria*'. The representatives of European museums were said to have misappropriated the Benin objects. Annette Schmidt of the Leiden museum was '*not prepared for such a press conference and did not say anything at that moment*', but wondered later '*whether this would be the tone of their input, since in that case a conversation would be useless*'.

The Plan of Action evoked sharp reactions in Africa. Nigerian artist/blogger Tajudeen Sowole argued that '*for the first time*' a claimant country was using the means of dialogue and '*hosted representatives of possessor museums*' or the '*keepers of Nigeria's looted cultural objects*'. He considered the dialogue as a '*fresh strategy*' in the restitution game and compared it with the conference *International Cooperation for the Protection and Repatriation of Cultural Heritage* in Cairo in April 2010. This conference was organised by Zawi Hawass, who was then the vociferous head of Egypt's Supreme Council of Antiquities. Nigeria was one of twenty-two participating countries. These '*agitator countries*', Sowole wrote, had '*called for a collective approach for restitution*'.[821] NCMM Director-general Usman admits the difference with the Cairo conference, which '*was "demanding" for return,* whereas the Benin Dialogue '*is "requesting" return through collaboration and sharing*'.[822] After careful reading of the Cairo Communiqué,[823] one finds more focus on reducing the ongoing illicit trade and on new dispute settlement mechanisms than on restitution of colonial cultural objects.

Opoku criticises the Plan for avoiding the return issue. Its goal '*is to lead to the display of the objects in Nigeria*' but display is not equal to restitution. Nor are '*training, internship and scholarships*' a substitute '*for the precious artefacts that are part of Nigeria's national treasures*'. He notes that Westerners do not show '*regret or remorse for what their predecessors did in violently dispossessing Africans of their*'

819 Email from NCMM Director-general Yusuf Abdallah Usman, November 14, 2014.
820 Plankensteiner, "The Benin treasures – Difficult legacy and contested heritage", 147.
821 Sowole, T. 2013. *Benin Plan of Action… plotting repatriation of looted artefacts*, February 28, http://africanartswithtaj.blogspot.nl/ (September 12, 2014).
822 Email NCMM Director General Yusuf Abdallah Usman, November 14, 2014.
823 http://www.sca-egypt.org/eng/pdfs/RST_ICHC_SA%20Communique_2010-08-20.pdf (September 12, 2014).

cultural artefacts' and asks who need the Benin objects more, the people of Benin or the museums in Europe?[824]

According to Folarin Shyllon, who attended the meetings as a legal expert, the Dialogue has failed, stating that through the years '*return and restitution has been relegated to the background*'. He has come up with the remarkable suggestion of a '*midway house, … the establishment of branches of Universal museums in Africa*' in places like Abuja, Kinshasa and Benin City, more or less comparable with the British Institute and the German Archaeological Institute in Rome or the American School of Classical Studies at Athens.[825]

Before commenting on this midway house, the picture of commentators on the outcome of the Benin Dialogue has to be completed with Barbara Plankensteiner's rather defensive remarks against '*agitators for restitution*' who '*mostly reside in Europe*' and miss contact with the African '*circumstances, objectives or priorities*', while '*exhibiting a somewhat paternalistic form of behaviour*'. She substantiates these words with the observation that '*Nigerian and Africa institutions cannot comply*' with the '*usual conservational and facility standards asked from the European side in loan procedures*', not '*at present and probably also not in the near future*'.[826]

Scholars have listed numerous return methods, varying from simple return to virtual return and withdrawal of the claim for return in exchange for financial compensation.[827] The establishment of branches of Universal museums in Africa would be an addition to this list. Shyllon's argument is that with branch museums '*former colonised countries would have possession and former colonisers would retain ownership and control*'. It is a pragmatic approach of a complicated, multi-layered problem, which is also applied in Abu Dhabi, for instance, where a 2007 intergovernmental agreement led to the opening of the *Louvre Abu Dhabi* in 2017.[828] So, why not in Africa? It would enable Africans to get to know treasures, to which most people in Africa have no access. The management of such museums would be up to Western standards and be controlled from the old metropolis. Branch museums could be a great help to countries without sufficient facilities

---

824 Kwame Opoku, "'Benin Plan of Action for Restitution'- Will this ensure the return of looted Benin artifacts?" in http://www.modernghana.com/news/449521/1/benin-plan-of-action-for-restitution-will-this-ens.html. (February 27, 2013). Kwame Opoku, "Benin Plan of Action (2): Will the miserable project be the last word on the looted Benin artefacts?" in http://www.modernghana.com/news/451636/1/benin-plan-of-action-2-will-this-miserable-project.html (September 12, 2014).

825 Folarin Shyllon, "Imperial Rule of Law Trumping the Return of Benin Bronzes and Parthenon Sculptures and the Failure of the Dialogue for the Return of Benin Bronzes" (Amsterdam: Network Conference of the Historical Dialogues, Justice and Memory Network, December 1 – 3, 2016, unpubl.), 14, 17.

826 Barbara Plankensteiner, "Return and Dialogue – two sets of experiences from Vienna", in eds. Marcel Buehler and Anja Schaluske, *Positioning Ethnological Museums in the 21st Century* (Berlin: Deutschen Museumbund, Museumkunde, 2016, Band 81), 62.

827 See also 2.1. Prott, *Witnesses to History*, XXI – XVI. In "New Developments in the Restitution of Cultural Property: Alternative Means of Dispute Resolution" (in: *International Journal of Cultural Property* [Cambridge University Press, 2010/17], 18 – 22), Marie Cornu and Marc-André Renold mention: Simple restitution; conditional restitution; restitution accompanied by cultural cooperation measures; formal recognition of the importance of cultural identity; loans; donations; setting up special ownership regimes; production of replicas; withdrawal of the claim for restitution in exchange for financial compensation; other solutions.

828 http://louvreabudhabi.ae/en/about/Pages/intergovernmental-agreement.aspx (January 17, 2017).

and trained staff, allowing corruption, theft and mismanagement to be avoided. The establishment of such institutions would be recognition of the view that, at this stage, many African countries are insufficiently equipped to preserve and show colonial and other precious objects. It might work as a wake-up call for Africa to strengthen museum policies.

However, a considerable obstacle in the establishment of branch museums is the burden of colonialism and the nature of the European museums. These museums, signatories of the 2002 *Declaration on the Importance and Value of Universal Museums*, see themselves as superior to most others. They control the heritage discourse, belong to the largest owners of contestable colonial objects and have a poor record in openness about the provenance of these objects. Does an invitation to open a branch museum not border on adopting their discourse and legalising their ownership of these objects? While many Africans feel that these objects have been unjustly removed from their countries, Abu Dhabi does not have that burden, and because of its financial resources, there is more equality between Abu Dhabi and France, Britain and Belgium than between these European countries and Nigeria, DR Congo and other African countries. Is building branch museums in Africa not like admitting defeat and recolonising the material cultural heritage sector? From what I know, the idea of Western branch museums has not come up in Asia or Latin America.

12.4. Elements for the model

Up to the end of 2016, the British Museum has not announced a fourth meeting of the Benin Dialogue. Changes in staff and leadership on several sides are said to be the cause. Does this mean that the Benin Dialogue has come to a standstill? Plankensteiner admits that *'at the moment there is a little bit quietness'*.[829] It has *'failed'*, Shyllon observes.[830] Such a standstill is a relevant issue in relation to a model for negotiating the future of colonial cultural objects. How should one handle this? Even if the British Museum will not organise a fourth workshop, the Benin objects will keep their chair at the return table. The lengthiness of the Dutch – Indonesian negotiations in the 1970s shows that such a process has its ups and downs and that one should not give up quickly (8.2.). It is no different here.

Another issue is the absence of a return paragraph in the Plan. It is a step back compared with the post-independence bilateral negotiations of the 1970s and 1980s, in which returns were an explicit goal. There is agreement about the maldistribution of Benin objects and that the way the objects were acquired would be unacceptable today. It is clear that feelings have been hurt and also that Western curators feel uneasy about it. Dealing with the return issue requires more exchange and trust between stakeholders. In Plankensteiner's view, *'the greatest challenge is the lack of an adequate legal framework or a set of regulations and guidelines... that could help museums to deal with this complicated legacy'*.[831]

---

829 Personal communication with Barbara Plankensteiner, Hannover, June 22, 2015.
830 Shyllon, "Imperial Rule of Law", 2016.
831 Plankensteiner, "Return and Dialogue – two sets of experiences from Vienna", 62.

A third issue is that, unlike the negotiations in the 1970s and 1980s, more stakeholders are involved in the Dialogue. Among the Nigerian stakeholders there exists a hierarchy, with the NCMM at the top, and the Benin Court second. The European stakeholders face two problems. First of all, they are museum curators and they work under directors, whose commitment to dialogues, such as the one about Benin objects, is not as certain. Secondly, the internal organisation of the European delegation is unclear and the commitment of the various members differs. The slowest one in the chain determines the speed of the train. Would it be more effective if a *coalition of the willing* is built of likeminded European museums without museums that are notorious for their unwillingness to consider return-issues? A coalition of the willing that could be the basis for a Europe-wide commitment towards the issue of contestable colonial cultural objects.

A final issue has to do with arguments pro and con return and underlying interests. Some arguments are obvious, others less self-evident or opportunistic. They relate to legal issues and justice, connectedness with Benin objects and Nigeria's capacity to preserve cultural heritage. It is also relevant that Benin is business.

Possessors adduce legal arguments against a return: the Vienna museum cannot return inalienable state property; the Glasgow museums cannot return objects to a private institution like the Benin Kingdom.[832] Stockholm curator Östberg reasoned that only after the The Hague conferences of 1899 and 1907 – so after the British raid – spoils of war were no longer considered the legitimate property of the victor.[833] How strong are the arguments? What can be behind them? In the case studies of transfers by Denmark to Iceland and to Greenland, the inalienability issue was solved through extra legislation. At the 1815 Congress of Vienna the restitution of war booty was dealt with, but the Edo Kingdom was not recognised as a state in the Europe dominated international law discourse. Legal arguments of possessors can be a hurdle but also seem slightly opportunistic. They are not insoluble and can hide unwillingness to relinquish objects.

Most legal arguments in favour of returns are related to justice and equality. In 2007, Prince Edun Akuenza, speaking in Vienna, wondered why the royal items could not be returned on the same grounds as those on which Italy had returned the *Axum obelisk* to Ethiopia and *Nazi-looted art* had been returned to rightful owners.[834] The argument that the seizure of the objects had been a great injustice and sign of disrespect towards the Benin rulers and their culture is brought forward by many, including Östberg and other possessors. Legal arguments in favour can help prepare the ground for returns, but they lack a hard legal basis.

Both opponents and proponents of return bring in their close connection to Benin objects. European museums have a long history with them and have taken care of them. If the Glasgow Museums were to let their items go, they argue, they

---

832 Shyllon, "Museums and universal heritage: Right of return and right of access", 7.

833 Östberg, "Coveted treasures of the Kingdom of Benin", 58.

834 Kwame Opoku, "Blood antiquities in respectable heavens: Looted Benin artefacts donated to American museum", in Accra: *Modern Ghana*, http://www.modernghana.com/news/405992/1/blood-antiquities-in-respectable-havens-looted-ben.html (July 13, 2012), Annex II.

would limit three million visitors' understanding of the Beninese culture, British imperialism and the world. The Stockholm Museum of Ethnography cannot miss Benin objects, as these '*confer status, … attract visitors and are truly magical portals, opening peoples' eyes to African history*'.[835] Östberg is willing to meet the Oba's request for some Benin objects, but the museum '*should not return everything*', as museums '*are not willing to undertake such an "ethnic cleansing" of their collections*'.[836] That Benin objects are business, is hardly a hidden interest.

For the Beninese people, the objects are '*records of our soul*', produced and cared for by themselves in a society without written history, '*like pages torn of a book*', as Prince Akuenza said in Vienna. In a 2000 memorandum to the British Parliament, the Benin royal family stressed their religious and historical importance.[837] A few exceptional Benin treasures – such as the Queen-mother Idia mask, withdrawn from auction by Sotheby in 2010 – have become Pan-African symbols.

Are they really so important for the Beninese people, wonders Östberg of the Stockholm Museum. He argues that '*many of the people of Benin City are critical of the monarchy, which they consider passé, authoritarian, heathen*'. Evangelical Christian church members '*have done away with their family altars and have sold or even burned the loathsome objects on them*'. One can contest that the royal Benin treasures were and are part of all Beninese or Nigerian people's identity, but it cannot be argued that they do not belong to their history. Östberg compares the Benin loot with valuably ancient illuminated manuscripts, sculptures of Adriaen de Vries and works by Titian, Michelangelo and Dürer that the Swedish army took from Prague in 1648. He wonders why no one '*is urging the return of the works stolen from Prague*', and why it is self-evident '*that the objects from Benin are returned to Benin… Is colonialism a phenomenon that is decisively different from other forms of conquest?*'[838] It is a broader question, to which I will return (13.1.).

There are serious concerns about Nigeria's ability to preserve the Benin treasures, also among Nigerians themselves. Does the country have the mentality, the facilities and the personnel to preserve them and to keep them accessible to researchers and the general public? Ekpo Eyo recognises this bottleneck implicitly, when listing how his country lost '*more than half*' of its cultural property – through the systematic imposing of foreign religions, gifts either '*as a mark of hospitality or in exchange of knick-knacks or gewgaws*', sheer plunder and via research workers. With 'gifts' he also meant the bronze head that Nigeria's President, General Yakubu Gowon, unexpectedly took from the National Museum in Lagos on the eve of a state-visit in 1973 to Great Britain. Gowon wanted to thank Queen Elizabeth for the British support during the 1967 – 1971 Biafra War.[839] When Eyo, then director of the museum, heard about the President's plan, he quickly hid some of the most unique items in store. That is more than four decades ago, but twenty

---

835 Östberg, ibid., 55.

836 Östberg, ibid., 62, 68.

837 Kwame Opoku, "Reflections on the abortive Queen-mother Idia mask auction: Tactical withdrawal or decision of principle?" (2011) http://www.museum-security.org/ (January 01, 2011).

838 Östberg, ibid., 59, 58.

839 http://www.telegraph.co.uk/news/uknews/1407331/President-liberated-bronze-for-Queen-from-museum.html (May 14, 2015); http://news.bbc.co.uk/2/hi/entertainment/2260924.stm (May 14, 2015).

years later, Nigerian-American art historian Dele Jegede could not but write that Nigeria's National Museum in Lagos still has leaks, that its personnel is involved in the disappearance of objects and that the country is a cultural sieve, whereby they have Western and other collectors as greedy buyers. He asks African nations to tackle the disorder in their own houses.[840] Plankensteiner, of the Vienna museum, argues that '*the neglect of the cultural heritage… by the political elites*' often plays a role.[841] Nowadays, the NCMM is fighting abuses and openly accepts that Nigeria respects the international standards for loans of objects.[842] Discussing a country's capability to preserve cultural heritage is sensitive but is to be included in the model presented later (chapter 14). Doing this in a balanced way and not abusing this to hide unwillingness to consider returns requires professionalism, trust and commitment from all stakeholders.

In conclusion, this case study offers abundant evidence that the one-way traffic of colonial cultural objects, in this case of Benin objects, was massive and that their confiscation in 1897 was an act of direct violence (burning, looting, and acquisition by force), structural violence (identity damage, destruction of historical sources) and ideological violence (disbelief that Benin artisans were their creators, and that these could be the products of a degenerate culture and race). The early and on-going study of these objects, their visibility in public collections and Nigerian efforts to retrieve them have made some Benin objects iconic in the return debate in Africa. The fact that returns are not an explicit agenda point in the Benin Dialogue confirms the impasse in the discussion about the future of colonial cultural objects. Except for a few, Western museums and private owners have done little to undo this historical injustice. Naming the return of Benin objects a form of ethnic cleansing of one's own Western museum or waiting for the British Museum – well-known for its unwillingness to return – to act are not conducive to this. This case study of the Benin Dialogue confirms the need for a framework or model for negotiating the future of colonial cultural objects.

---

840 Dele Jegede, "Nigerian art as endangered species", in eds. Peter Schmidt and Roderick McIntosh, *Plundering Africa's Past* (Bloomington and Indianapolis: Indiana University Press, 1996), 135, 137, 139.
841 Interview Plankensteiner (July 21, 2014).
842 Email of DG Yusuf Abdallah Usman (NCMM), November 14, 2014.

Appendix: Benin Plan of Action[1]

Museum professionals in Europe with holdings of Benin art collections* and the National Commission for Museums and Monuments of Nigeria**, a scholar on copyright law*** and representatives of the court of Benin*, met in Benin, Nigeria on the 19th and 20th of February 2013, in continuation of previous meetings in Vienna, Austria and Berlin, Germany and proposed that a Memorandum of Understanding be made between the collaborating institutions on the following issues:

1. Developing a data bank by the collaborating institutions on Benin art collections in their holdings in the form of a digital archive of electronic and hard copies. This data will be submitted and made available to the general public.

2. That all collaborating institutions, upon request, shall have right of producing free of charge photographs of Benin art objects in the collection of collaborating institutions particularly for scholarly purposes.

3. That staff of the collaborating institutions shall have access to Benin Collections in their holdings in accordance with the existing procedures of the institutions.

4. That the National Commission for Museums and Monuments shall improve the university education of its staff working on the collections and on this basis collaborating institutions will assist in securing support for internship and scholarship for postgraduate studies on the Benin collections.

5. That collaborating institutions assist with expertise in the establishment of a conservation laboratory in Nigeria.

6. That collaborating institutions shall assist the National Commission for Museums and Monuments in developing its library and archive facilities.

7. That the National Commission for Museums and Monuments and collaborating museums shall create an enabling environment for an increased exchange of touring/travelling exhibitions for the Benin art objects and other art traditions where the European and Nigerian museum experts will work together in the planning and execution of such exhibitions.

8. That these individual steps are part of the dialogue which goal is to lead to the display of the objects in Nigeria.

The meeting resolved that there is a need at the next meeting to discuss:
The issue of fake Benin art objects on the international art markets and its consequences for museums,
The 1970 UNESCO Convention,
The publication of their inventories.

Yusuf Abdallah Usman
Director-General, National Commission for Museums and Monuments, Nigeria

* *to wit*: Dr. Michael Barrett and Dr. Lotten Gustafsson-Reinius representing the National Museum of Ethnography of the Museums of World Culture Stockholm, Sweden, Dipl. Ethn. Silvia Dolz representing Museum für Völkerkunde Dresden, Staatliche Ethnographische Sammlungen Sachsen of the Staatliche Kunstsammlungen Dresden, Germany, Dr. Peter Junge representing Ethnologisches Museum-Staatliche Museen zu Berlin, Germany, Dr. Barbara Plankensteiner representing Museum für Völkerkunde, Vienna, Austria, Dr. Annette Schmidt representing the National Museum of Ethnology of the Netherlands
** *to wit* Yusuf Abdallah Usman, Rosemary Bodam, Peter Odeh and Babatunde Adebiyi
*** Prof. Folarin Shyllon
**** Prince Edun Egharese Akenzua MFR – Enogie of Obazuwa, Chief Stanley Obamwonyi – Esere of Benin

Notes
1   Source: Barbara Plankensteiner, email October 9, 2014.

NEW INSIGHTS, A NEW APPROACH

Part VI - New insights, a new approach

Thanks to soft law instruments created during recent decades, more agreement has come on how to handle colonial human remains and artworks that disappeared in the Nazi-period. For these categories the option of repatriation or restitution has become accepted. The 1970 UNESCO Convention has changed how disputes about stolen or smuggled objects can be handled. There is much less agreement about what should be done with objects and collections acquired during the European colonial era. Political, economic and cultural changes in the world, research findings about the contestable nature of colonial acquisitions and the unremitting quest of former colonies for their vanished objects ask for an approach of this neglected aspect of European colonialism. This study therefore has raised three questions:

1. How can the loss of cultural and historical treasures during the European colonial era be charted?

2. What lessons can be drawn from the way other contested categories of such treasures have been handled?

3. How to devise a model for negotiating the future of cultural objects acquired in colonial times, including the option of their return?

This Part deduces and elaborates the answers to these questions from the earlier Parts about colonialism and colonial cultural objects, legal aspects, case studies of bilateral negotiations on post-independence returns and successful and failed return examples. First chapter 13 charts the loss of treasures and draws lessons from the way in which other contested categories are being handled. Then the final chapter 14 presents principles for dealing with colonial objects and a model with seven phases for negotiating their future.

Photograph previous page: Lost relics from East and Southeast Asia.

Chapter 13

The neglected effect of colonialism

Having started in the 15th century, European colonialism still has an impact on states and people. As is clear from earlier chapters, this is experienced differently in former colonial possessions than in former metropolis. Generally, the first suffered from the severe violence committed by the second. In depicting the impact of colonialism, Galtung's definition of violence as avoidable insults to basic human needs has been instrumental, as has been his division into direct, structural and cultural violence, where I have replaced the last term with ideological violence. Ideological violence serves to justify direct and structural violence (2.2.). The colonialism practised by the powers of the continent where I grew up, and later also by the United States of America and Japan was full of varying degrees of avoidable insults. In order to expand and strengthen their own position, they subjugated, exploited, enslaved, degraded and dehumanised other powers and peoples. Writers such as Anton de Kom, Gayatri Spivak, Edward Said, Amartya Sen and Achille Mbembe have helped to increase our understanding of how ideological, avoidable insults continue to work. Distance, which distinguishes European colonialism from other types of colonialism, has worsened ideological violence and 'othering', more so in Africa and South America than in Asia and the Northern Atlantic.

13.1. Towards an overview of colonial one-way traffic

To map the one-way traffic of objects, three steps have been taken: a definition of colonial cultural objects (Part I), a typology of such objects (Part I) and a division in periods of the European colonial era (Part II). The era has been split into three periods: colonial expansion, settler and exploitation colonialism, and decolonisation. A division in three is not unusual, but the periods often overlap each other. The start, length and end of each differ per coloniser and colony. While decolonisation usually covers the years of the independence struggle and negotiations up to the independence, it has been defined here as the period starting from the rise of anti-colonial groups and the signs of the disintegration of the European colonial empires often leading up to the present day. As it continues to have an impact, decolonisation is an unresolved conflict, and contestable colonial cultural objects and the need for both the ex-colonised and ex-colonisers to further decolonise their minds are part of this conflict. Moreover, there is continuity between the one-sided flow of objects before and after the independence of former colonies, only the actors have changed. Conflict researchers have neglected this conflict (5.4.).

The definition of a colonial cultural object as an object of cultural or historical importance acquired without just compensation or involuntarily lost during the European colonial era has been helpful (2.2.). It excludes objects that were exchanged for money or European goods or were specifically produced for European visitors. The definition has created several discussions. One has emerged in the case study about the Dutch – Indonesian negotiations (Part IV). The Indonesian team of experts had defined three categories of objects that it wanted to retrieve – cultural objects, historical objects and objects of aesthetic value. The definition does not cover the third category. Why? One reason is that aesthetically important objects have rarely figured separately in other negotiations or examples. Another reason is that a discussion about the inclusion of aesthetic objects can be overcome by defining a desired object of great aesthetic value as culturally or historically important.

A second discussion is whether the definition covers objects from countries that were never colonised but suffered under the European colonial yoke of unequal treaties and invasions (2.2.). China and Ethiopia were such countries. Both were confronted by European raids, China in 1860, Ethiopia in 1868, in which they lost cultural and historical relics. It happened again to China around 1900. These lost items are also considered colonial cultural objects.

A third discussion is how long a colonial cultural object can be claimed? Nazi-looted art is almost at our fingertips, while contested colonial cultural objects are more remote in time. By way of comparison, the artworks that the Netherland lost in its independence war against Spain (1568 – 1648), are even farther away. So, what does one do, when e.g. the Keeper of the records of Deventer asks Spain to return ancient drawings of this Dutch city that Spanish soldiers took,[843] when Belgium approaches France, as it did recently, about two hundred works of mostly Flemish painters, which French revolutionaries took in 1794,[844] or when the Czech government asks Sweden for the return of treasures lost in 1648? The definition of colonial cultural objects can help answer such questions. If an object still has cultural or historical importance, if it is still known, if the descendants of those who lost it miss it, a return claim might receive more understanding than in other cases. In the 1990s the Chinese authorities never came to take up precious porcelain objects, seized from smugglers by the Customs officers of the Port of Rotterdam. Apparently, their cultural and historical value did not appeal sufficiently to them.[845] The same authorities have outspoken policies for retrieving cultural relics lost between 1860 and 1945.

From the start of the research, examples of objects disappearing have been collected and mostly put in boxes. As they quickly increased in number, they have been divided into five categories – gifts to colonial administrators and institutions; objects acquired during private expeditions; objects acquired during military expeditions; missionary collecting; and archives (2.3.). In naming them, an eye has

---

843 Jos Van Beurden, *Return of Cultural and Historical Treasures*, 11.
844 Belgian national daily *De Standaard*, January 22, 2016; Dutch national daily *Trouw*, January 25, 2016.
845 Jos van Beurden, ibid., 47.

been kept on the 'how' of their acquisition, on whether colonial actors acquired objects by purchase or barter, in accordance with the laws of the time, but at an unequal level, or in violation of contemporary laws. A distinction has also been made between public institutions that acquired objects on behalf of the colonial authorities and private persons or institutions.

Gifts to colonial administrators and institutions

For many local rulers presenting gifts to foreign visitors was part of their culture. European traders like those of the VOC often carried gifts with them for local rulers. Some colonial administrators were also known for their culture of gift-giving. At the beginning of the first period – colonial expansion – the exchange of gifts could occur at fairly equal level. From the moment that colonial powers wanted to dominate and impose their will on local rulers, gifts from these rulers became an expression of subjugation, and those from colonial administrators were rewards for loyalty. It was cultural diplomacy back and forth. Gift-giving by local rulers reached a peak in the second period, that of settler and exploitation colonialism (4.1.). Evidence of gifts is rarer in the first part of the decolonisation period. After independence, gifts became a means of cultural diplomacy between two states.

Objects acquired during private expeditions

When the demand of private collectors and newly established museums increased, collecting became more profitable and special expeditions were organised. In places like Central America, Congo Free State and the Dutch East Indies, their organisers had to respect regulations of the colonial administrators. In places like Papua New Guinea, German enterprises collected objects autonomously in the phase of colonial expansion. In South America, the drain of colonial cultural objects through expeditions continued after the independence of colonies.

In many expeditions pillage and cheating, justified by ideological violence, were a dominant mode of acquisition; sometimes the local inhabitants were involved in or benefitted from exchanges. Expedition leaders are said to have been driven by the salvage paradigm, but greed and profit were important motives too. They brought tens of thousands of objects to Europe and the USA. Sometimes museums received so many that they did not know how to handle them (4.1.). Most objects are still in those museums, even though the history of their forceful acquisition is known. The freedom of movement for collectors and the many expeditions in, for instance, the Dun Huang area in China around 1900 by collectors from six powerful countries are evidence of a European dimension of colonial collecting.

The term 'private expeditions' raises dilemmas. An expedition is usually understood to be a journey by a group of people with a clear purpose. It is a joint, focussed effort. In the early colonial period, collecting by individual colonial officials, army men and merchants occurred mostly on a small and scattered scale; it was not planned. Yet, to keep the categorisation uncluttered, a special category of 'objects acquired by individuals' has not been included. The other dilemma is that expeditions took place in certain cooperation with state museums in the metropolis; they were examples of public-private cooperation – think of the expeditions on Cyprus and in Dun Huang (4.1.), German expeditions in German New Guinea (11.1.) or Dutch collector Groenevelt's acquisitions in Papua (8.1.). The cooperation could vary from rather direct, when an expedition collected exclusively for one museum, to rather loose, when expeditions members approached several museums with their finds afterwards.

Objects acquired during military expeditions

Violent conflicts to expand territory, to subjugate local rulers or keep them subjugated occurred massively in all three periods. Victory in a conflict often meant confiscation of the symbols of the defeated ruler – his flag, weapons, treasures – and pillaging his palace grounds (3.1.; 4.1.; 5.1.). Some raids with extensive booty are well known, such as those in the 1860s in China and Korea or those at the end of the 19th century on the island of Lombok and in the Edo Kingdom (Nigeria), but this study has collected new findings showing numerous lesser known raids with extensive booty. One can think of the flags and regalia appropriated by Dutch VOC soldiers in South and East Asia, the properties of Namibian resistance fighter Hendrik Witbooi, or regalia from West Africa captured by French soldiers. Many more objects arrived as war booty in public and private collections in the countries of the former colonisers than their possessors were aware of or wanted to admit. Examples can be found in collections of Dutch elite families (8.1.) or in the British Museum (4.1.). Some of these have become showpieces, while others linger in dusty depots.

Missionary collecting

Collecting by missionaries was extensive. They committed large-scale iconoclasm, and it was not unusual for local headmen to offer a helping hand in the destruction of objects; they had their own motives to become Christian. The missionaries' freedom of movement and the distribution of confiscated objects throughout Europe increased the European dimension of colonial collecting. In the first period of colonialism the destruction of indigenous religious objects must have outweighed their confiscation, examples being the large-scale destruction of Aztec and Maya temples, objects and codices in the 16th century (3.1.). In the instance of the confiscation of Roman Catholic objects by Danish Lutherans in Iceland between 1550 and 1570, Christian missionaries attacked other Christians (10.2.). Although such intra-Christian competition occurred also elsewhere, non-Christian religions were mostly the targets. In the second half of the 19th century, in the period of settler and exploitation colonialism, collecting by missionary orders reached its peak. European powers had their own Protestant missionary societies. They and their Roman-catholic colleagues needed the objects for educating new missionaries and raising funds at home for their work. The Swedish Missionary Society, for instance, gathered ten thousand objects from DR Congo that can be seen in museums in Stockholm and Gothenburg (9.1.). Collecting diminished during the decolonisation.

Archives

Although little evidence was found of explicit claims of former colonies of archival materials, enough other evidence was found to justify their inclusion in the typology. The economic and political weight of certain archives and the incriminating information they could contain were reason for the Belgian and British colonisers, for example, to order their destruction or to have them shipped away quickly. Archives were a haunting background presence during negotiations, a clear example being archival materials on precious minerals in DR Congo in the Tervuren Museum (9.2.). They were part of return agreements between Germany and Namibia (1.2.), between Australia and Papua New Guinea (11.1.) and between the Netherlands and Indonesia and Suriname (1.2.; 2.3.5.). The 1913 agreement between Suriname and the Netherlands that defined the archives as Surinamese property and led to their return to Suriname a century later (between 2010 and 2017) and Australia's care in pre-independence days and return of archives to Papua New Guinea later are good examples of how to deal with them.

The overview has yielded more findings. One is that ideological violence led to more rough and random confiscation of objects in South America and Africa than in Asia. Colonial actors were eager to acquire objects associated with Buddhism and Hinduism, but despised religious objects belonging to indigenous religions in Africa and South America. In the latter continent, they were more interested in the precious metals – gold and silver – of many objects than in their meaning for subjugated people.

Another finding is that several colonial officials, missionaries and scientists, as well as contemporary heritage officials from former colonial powers have been crucial in the protection and sometimes return of colonial cultural objects. Their role deserves to be rescued from oblivion, also to show that return issues ought to be part of their professional ethics.

The third finding has to do with Europe. While most studies focus on bilateral, one-country or one-object category issues, it was found that the acquisition of many colonial cultural objects and the position, taken by colonisers in return negotiations, have European traits. Europeans from different nations were allowed to collect items in the colonial possessions of other nations. Objects coming from a possession of one coloniser, such as Congo, were distributed all over Europe. In the post-independence era, European countries worked together to obstruct the working of the 1970 UNESCO Convention and the return of colonial cultural objects. These European traits deserve more research and make one wonder whether there should be a Europe-wide commitment or guideline on how to approach matters of colonial cultural objects.

13.2. Overview of returns so far

Over the course of time, colonial cultural objects have been going back to their place of origin, a movement that has been described by the umbrella term 'return'. Although it has been accepted as open and neutral internationally, the term worried former colonial powers for fear of being associated with guilt and inappropriate acquisitions. They pressed for the term 'transfer' to be used in agreements. I have stuck to return, as it also opens avenues for solutions in negotiations that serve deeper goals and can help promote restoration of relations, reconciliation and healing, or a source country's integrity (2.1.).

Most literature mentions three sets of negotiations for the redefinition of post-independence cultural relations and the return of objects – those between the Netherlands and Indonesia (7. and 8.), Belgium and DR Congo (9.) and Australia and Papua New Guinea (11.). In all of these cases, a demonstrable gap remained between the desire of former colonies to recover their cultural and historical treasures and the willingness of former colonisers to meet this desire. In the 1970s, both the Netherlands and Belgium claimed to have been generous returners, but in practice their returns were meagre (8.2.; 9.2.). This study has shown supporting evidence that the Netherlands did not keep its promise in the 1975 Joint Recommendations to contact private possessors of cultural and historical treasures and stimulate them to return these objects, or to search for objects such as those that had belonged to Prince Diponegoro. Museum Volkenkunde in Leiden minimised the number of items it had to hand over. The number of objects that Belgium selected in the Tervuren Museum differed greatly from what DR Congo had asked for. Australia showed its internal dissension on return issues by generously returning some objects and collections to Papua New Guinea, while keeping the big Murray collection and part of the MacGregor collection. Yet it is well known that these two colonial officials had stipulated that Australia would offer their collections some sort of a safe haven as long as this did not exist in Port Moresby and to return them if Papua New Guinea had sufficient facilities (11.1.).

Two more sets of bilateral negotiations have been added: one between Denmark and Iceland (10.3.), the other between Denmark and Greenland (10.4.). In these the gap between the desires of the two former colonies and Denmark's willingness to return objects was somewhat smaller. The hand-over to Iceland is instructive in a double sense. Since part of the ancient Icelandic manuscripts was private property, the Danish government had to prepare special legislation to expropriate them. Moreover, the Danish-Icelandic agreement shows the impact of distance: geographical and cultural distance played a smaller role than in many other cases. Distance in the 15th and following centuries differs, however, from what it is today in the global village. Denmark's agreements with its former colonies deserve to be more generally known.

Since the 1980s, no new negotiations between former colonisers and colonies about cultural relations and the return of objects have been initiated. Since 2010, the Benin Dialogue has taken place between Nigerian authorities, the Benin Court and Western museums (12.). So far, the exchange of information and strengthening of Nigeria's museum infrastructure have far outweighed return issues. Although the dialogue has been in an impasse since 2013 due to the absence of a framework and a lack of guidance, the European approach of dealing with colonial war booty is new and can provide direction for such negotiations.

Incidental returns of colonial cultural objects have always occurred. Throughout the book dozens of them have been mentioned (1.2.; 2.3.5.; 3.1.; 5.2.; case study chapters). Their returners were driven by a wide variety of motives. There are examples of descendants of colonial officials and military who had kept war booty from Ghana and Nigeria or regalia from Indonesia for themselves, who felt that the objects were better at home in the country of origin than in their own houses. In some cases, a colonial power, or one of its museums or nationals gave a present on the occasion of a colony's independence. Incidental returns were not infrequently motivated by economic interests. France excelled in this, with returns of Ottoman era documents to Algeria, ancient manuscripts to South Korea and a rat and a rabbit of the Summer Palace zodiac to China. The wish to undo injustice might have played a role, when Germany handed over its part of the Great Zimbabwe Bird. An instance was found of a missionary order handing over objects to regional museums on the Indonesian islands, whence they came, as it became too difficult to store them, and because '*after all, they are theirs*'. Great chances are being missed here, as more orders are wondering what to do with colonial collections, while there is an upsurge of regional museums in former colonies that have no older objects. In 1939, South-Asian Buddhist immigrants successfully pressured for the return of relics by museums in London. Sometimes a heritage institution wanted to get rid of a superfluous collection. Examples are the Brooklyn Museum in New York returning archaeological artefacts to Costa Rica, and the Nusantara Museum in Delft, the Netherlands, returning remnants of its collection to Indonesia. Below two examples are presented of the former Dutch colonies Suriname and Indonesia that objected to a Dutch return offer. They illustrate old and new sensitivities (Box: *Objections against return offers*).

All in all, the many incidental returns do not amount to more than a dripping tap and it is hard to discover patterns in them. They have helped to improve relations between the stakeholders involved, and they were often a means in the cultural diplomacy of former colonisers.

13.3. Returns and other categories of contested objects

Dealing with other categories of contested objects, notably Nazi-looted art and colonial human remains, contributes to discussing colonial objects (6.2.). There are differences between these categories that generally relate to their relationship with history: the time span, limited provenances and evidence that has been lost or was never available. Nazi-looted artworks are all items confiscated by the Nazi's during a certain number of years. They could be any art work, including colonial objects. Content does not always matter, provenance and the 'how' of the acquisition are more relevant. For objects of cultural and historical importance that were taken without just compensation or were involuntarily lost in the much lengthier European colonial era, contents matter more. Most are expressions of certain religions and cultures. Colonial human remains are a better comparison with colonial cultural objects, as they were removed in the same era. Doubts about and protests against collecting human remains began as early as the beginning of the 20th century, and quickly intensified after the Nazi racial policies had become known.

Objections against return offers

Marron in Suriname refuse ceremonial chair

Johannes King (1830 – 1898) and his half-brother Noah Adrai were Maroons of Suriname.[1] Noah was a headman who adhered to Maroon cults. Johannes was a Moravian missionary. When Noah died, Johannes was to be the new headman. When he renounced the position, a headman's chair and some other objects from his legacy ended up with a company in Paramaribo run by the Moravian Church. Some of these were passed to the museum of the church in Herrnhut near Dresden, Germany. Upon Maroon requests, the museum sent a copy of the chair to a descendant of the Maroon headman in Suriname in 2006. When this descendant died soon after receiving the chair, his relatives blamed the chair for being cursed and did not want to keep it. The Maroon diaspora in the city of Tilburg in the Netherlands is less bothered by the curse and has set up a Foundation that can preserve the chair.[2]

Indonesia objects to return

On November 23, 2016, Dutch Prime Minister Mark Rutte, who headed an economic mission to Indonesia, handed over a golden Buginese kris to President Joko Widodo. It was the first out of 1,465 objects that are to be returned in 2017. While it was claimed that 'never before heritage was repatriated at this scale',[3] it was not gold that glittered through the leading up to this repatriation. After the closure of the Museum Nusantara in Delft in 2013, a Dutch committee prepared the de-accession of its largely Indonesian collection. Ethnological museums in the Netherlands selected several thousand items. For the remaining fourteen thousand objects, the committee asked the National Museum in Jakarta to distribute them inside Indonesia. The committee did not approach regional museums in the archipelago, as it considered this paternalistic in regard to the National Museum. It put pressure on the de-accessioning, since the Delft municipality subsidised the storage of the collection for only one year.[4]

The Director-general of Indonesia's Ministry of Culture and Elementary and Secondary Education reacted positively and the return of the fourteen thousand objects was planned for April 2016. The Jakarta Post suggested preserving them in a new warehouse in the Indonesian capital. A reader wanted objects connected to the history of Yogyakarta to be transferred to the Sultan's museum there.[5] With the appointment of a new Director-general in Jakarta however, the situation changed. He did not wish to accept the objects.[6] It is possible that Indonesia found it difficult to accept that museums in the Netherlands were allowed to select the best items, whereas the National Museum in Jakarta had to settle for the remaining ones, and this also en bloc.[7] After new negotiations, the Dutch Committee and the National Museum in Jakarta agreed that only around ten percent of the remnants of the Nusantara collection would be returned.[8]

Notes

1   Surinamese Maroons are descendants of enslaved Central and West-Africans who escaped from Dutch slave owners, set up communities and concluded peace agreements with the Dutch in the 1760s.

2   Thomas Polimé, "Maroon collections in Western museums and their meaning" in: Jean Moomou,

Sociétés marronnes des Amériques – Mémoires, patrimoines, identités et histoire des XVIIe et XXe siècles (Matoury, IBIS Rouge Editions, 2015), 353 – 361. Personnel communication with Thomas Polimé, January 21 and March 22, 2016. http://www.skd.museum/en/museums-

institutions/herrnhut/ (February 4, 2016); http://
www.humboldt-forum.de/fileadmin/media/
dokumente/HLD_Begleitheft_Surinam.pdf
(February 4, 2016).

3 https://tropenmuseum.nl/nl/pers/Premier-
Rutte-overhandigt-gouden-kris-aan-president-
Indonesi%C3%AB (December 23, 2016.

4 Jos Van Beurden. "Aangepaste LAMO bij
ontmanteling Nusantara – Repatriëring: hoe
werkt dat?". In: *Museumvisie*. Amsterdam:

Nederlandse Museum Vereniging, 2015: 02.

5 Jakarta Post, October 19, 2015, http://
verreculturendelft.nl/archief%20
nusantara/2015-10-19%20jakarta%20post-
nusantara.pdf (April 11, 2016).

6 http://nusantara-delft.weebly.com/ (July 13, 2016)

7 Personal communication with two Dutch insiders
(July 06, 2016).

8 At the time of writing, no new developments
were known.

The translation of the 1998 Washington Conference Principles on Nazi-Confiscated Art (6.2.2.; 14.2) into principles for dealing with colonial cultural and historical objects can offer the sort of embedding that is lacking in the Benin Dialogue. They ask for commitment and understanding that evidence is a major problem, and help to avoid the legal path and to look for non-judicial solutions. So far, these alternative mechanisms have been rarely used in disputes about colonial cultural objects. The final chapter will elaborate on this.

All in all, the conclusion is that there has been a massive one-way flow and maldistribution of cultural and historical objects in the European colonial area from the colonial possessions to Europe. This book does not offer much more than the beginning of an overview. To make it complete, more provenance research is needed. Compared to what is now known about the total amount, only few colonial cultural objects have been returned. Four colonial powers agreed upon return matters after the independence of their colonies, but their generosity was of rather different levels. Even if the Netherlands had only stuck to what it agreed upon in the 1975 Joint Recommendations, many more objects would have been prepared for a return home (8.2.). In my view, the returns by Denmark to Iceland and to Greenland, those by descendants of former colonial officials and military and the one by a missionary order deserve to be followed by others. There have been many incidental returns of objects, but it is hard to discover general lines in them. What strikes one in most returns is that they are not about the objects and where they belong, but rather an instrument for cultural diplomacy for the returning country, and sometimes also for the recipient country. The ways of dealing with other categories of contested objects offer lessons for dealing with colonial cultural objects. These lessons are elaborated in the next and final chapter.

Chapter 14

A new commitment and a new approach

In this study decolonisation has been defined as a *conflict* that has remained unresolved, with the maldistribution of cultural and historical objects over former colonial possessions and former European colonisers being part of this conflict (5.4.). One or two words about conflicts per se: There always have been conflicts and ways to deal with them. At best they strengthen a relationship; in such cases the conflict helps stakeholders to mature and come closer to each other. At worst conflicts cause distance and destruction. Both outcomes have been found in the case studies and examples of successful and failed returns. Systematic approaches to solving such conflicts have been rare.

In this chapter an effort is made to contribute to the solution of unresolved conflicts and to reopen or strengthen the dialogue about the future of colonial objects. Two tools are provided. One is a set of principles akin to the 1998 Washington Principles for dealing with colonial objects, which can help all stakeholders to adjust their attitude. The other is a model with seven phases for negotiating the future of such objects. It is up to the stakeholders involved to decide which solution gives the best future.

14.1. Principles for dealing with colonial cultural and historical objects

When discussing soft law instruments for dealing with Nazi looted objects (6.2.2.), it was claimed that these instruments have lifted the issue of this Nazi loot to an international level, to prompt possessors of such objects to take their responsibility and offer them guidelines on how to solve claims in a just and fair manner. Building on this, it has been proposed that the 1998 Washington Conference Principles and the input from other such declarations be adapted to principles for dealing with colonial objects. Especially the case study about the Benin Dialogue and some examples of failed or as yet unmet return claims have given arguments to further implement this proposal. Such principles create awareness and offer the necessary substance to the commitment needed to solve the issue of lost colonial objects. The two sets of principles will be put next to each other at the end of this chapter (Appendix: *1998 Washington Principles adapted for Colonial Objects*). The adaptation and translation into principles for colonial objects that follows now should be considered as a work in progress and a start of a discussion.

Principles for Dealing with Colonial Cultural and Historical Objects
In developing a consensus on non-binding principles to assist in resolving issues relating to objects of cultural or historical importance that were taken in the European colonial era without just compensation or were involuntarily lost in the European colonial era, it is recognised that among participating nations, there are differing legal systems and that countries act within the context of their own laws.

1. Objects of cultural or historical importance taken in the European colonial era without just compensation or involuntarily lost in a territory controlled by European, American or Asian colonial powers and not subsequently returned should be identified.

2. Relevant records and archives should be open and accessible to researchers, in accordance with the guidelines of the International Council on Archives.

3. Resources and personnel should be made available to facilitate the identification of all objects of cultural or historical importance taken without just compensation or involuntarily lost in the European colonial era and not subsequently returned.

4. In establishing that an object of cultural or historical importance was taken without just compensation or was lost involuntarily in the European colonial era and not subsequently returned, consideration should be given to unavoidable gaps or ambiguities in the provenance in light of the passage of time and the circumstances of the European colonial era.

5. Every effort should be made to publicise objects of cultural or historical importance that are found to have been taken without just compensation or were lost involuntarily during the European colonial era and not subsequently returned in order to locate its rightful claimants.

6. Efforts should be made to establish public registries of such information on a bilateral basis.

7. Rightful parties should be encouraged to come forward and make known their claims to objects that were taken without just compensation or lost involuntarily in the European colonial era and not subsequently returned.

8. If the rightful claimants can be identified, steps should be taken expeditiously to achieve a just and fair solution, recognising this might vary according to the facts and circumstances surrounding a specific case.

9. If no rightful claimants can be identified, steps should be taken expeditiously to achieve a just and fair solution.

10. Committees established to identify objects of cultural or historical importance that are found to have been taken without just compensation or to have been lost involuntarily in the European colonial era and to assist in addressing return issues should have a balanced membership.

11. Nations, including the minorities and indigenous peoples in these nations, are encouraged to develop national and international processes to implement these principles, particularly as they relate to alternative dispute resolution mechanisms for resolving ownership issues.

The adaptation requires explanation. The terms 'artworks', 'confiscated' or 'looted' and 'pre-War owners' from the 1998 Washington Principles had to be adjusted. The definition of the objects concerned, mentioned in the first principle, builds on the definition of colonial cultural objects mentioned earlier (2.2.): objects of cultural or historical importance acquired without just compensation or involuntarily lost during the European colonial era. Objects of cultural or historical importance is a broader concept than '*artworks*' in the 1998 Washington Principles; other declarations of principles for dealing with Nazi looted objects also opt for a broader definition. The use of the terms confiscation or looting, as in principles for dealing with Nazi-Confiscated art creates problems. The colonies from which they were taken were part of a colonial power's empire and an empire is entitled to confiscate objects inside its own territory. Acquired is therefore a more suitable term, if the proviso is added that the objects were involuntarily lost or taken without just compensation. These objects were acquired in unequal and often violent circumstances (Part II). The addition distinguishes these objects from objects that were purchased, exchanged or taken in relatively equal circumstances. The term 'pre-War owners', used in the 1998 Washington Principles, is unsuitable, since both 'war' and 'owners' are unfit. Defining the whole European colonial era as 'war' creates many problems. The rightful owners of Nazi looted items are usually identifiable individuals or families, while those of colonial cultural objects are much harder to identify. The term 'rightful claimants' has been chosen as the colonial equivalent of 'pre-War owners'. 'Rightful' should not be taken in a strictly legal sense, but rather in terms of morality and justice. They can be states and state related institutions, communities, descendants of former local rulers, etc. It must also be taken into account that they live under different legal systems and that countries act within the context of their own laws.

It is also important that heritage institutions should open their records and archives, actively stimulate provenance research to fill gaps and ambiguities in questions of provenance, and make the outcomes accessible. This pro-active duty is in line with most sets of principles for dealing with Nazi-looted objects and colonial human remains. Rightful claimants should be encouraged to present their claims.

The 1998 Washington Principles ask for a central register with contested objects. Considering the volume of objects at stake and the over 500 years during which they have migrated to Europe, such a central register seems unpractical. Creative ways should be developed to set up registers on a bilateral basis that are accessible for everyone. The Benin Plan of Action for example, asks for the virtual exchange of information about Benin war booty between stakeholders (12.4.).

Since Committees negotiating about colonial objects should have a balanced membership, they should involve multiple stakeholders from both sides that are to be found in the biographies of the objects. There should be room for state and non-state stakeholders.

The last principle mentions alternative dispute resolution mechanisms, which this chapter also contributes to.

14.2. A model for negotiating the future of colonial cultural objects

The case studies have shown that, regardless of the outcome, negotiations about the future of colonial objects are not a quick-fix. A stiff relationship, irritations back and forth, prejudices about each other and neither party being accustomed to this sort of negotiations made the Dutch – Indonesian (1949 – 1975) and the Danish – Icelandic (1947 – 1971) negotiations last a long time. The negotiations between Belgium and Congo took a decade. Greenland and Iceland were kept in the Danish waiting room for a very long time as well. The talks between Papua New Guinea and Australia were an exception: because of their proximity and the attitude of Australian museum curators, a deal was made within five years. The warming up for the Benin Dialogue began in 2002, and the three meetings and the 2013 Benin Plan of Action do not necessarily mean the end. More time is needed and trust-building and communication remain key issues. To maintain clarity about such time-consuming negotiations and to structure them, it is useful to have a model that consists of distinguished phases, each with its own characteristics.

The model presented here is based on two pillars: the discipline of conflict studies, and the case studies and examples of successful and failed returns. With the maturing of conflict studies and the Internet revolution, the number of conflict resolution models has become vertiginous (5.4.). This book does not pretend to add a new one. The integration of the wishes of both parties into the final solution as the aim of conflict resolution has been adopted from Parker-Follett. Lewis' plea for the inclusion of the wisdom of the minority into the majority's decision has been incorporated, as well as Malan and Zeleke's emphasis on reconciliation and sustainability of the community in conflict resolution. Some guidelines of the Harvard Program on Negotiation, notably that of focussing on underlying interests, returns in the model. The cosmopolitan conflict resolution of Ramsbotham ea. with both state and non-state stakeholders has also been used.

Several elements have been taken from the case studies of bilateral negotiations in the 1970s and 1908s. Elements from the Dutch – Indonesian case study (8.2.), such as the time that it takes to come to a solution and the usefulness of socialising between stakeholders and of insight into the internal dynamics of each stakeholder, are part of the model. (In)equality and hidden interests had to be considered. From the case studies and other examples, it has also become evident that provenance issues, stakeholders, the contested or disputed objects, and the context differ per case, and that a specific, thought out approach is therefore

Phases in negotiations about colonial objects

0: Facilitating factors
1: Inviting the Other Party
2: Preparation by the Two Parties:
3: Approach of the Other Stakeholders
4: First Round of Decision-making
5: Deepening
6: Second and Subsequent Rounds of Decision-making

required for each new situation. The model presented can always be adapted to case-specific circumstances. It splits the process into seven phases (Box: *Phases in negotiations about colonial objects*).

Seven phases
None of the following phases that define a negotiation process is new, except perhaps *Phase 0*. It has been included to establish context and preconditions that are not part of negotiations but influence them. The other phases relate to the formal start, the definition of the conflict, the number of stakeholders, the need to include discussions about unspoken assumptions, including hurt feelings, and the option of more rounds.

Phase 0: Facilitating factors
In most case studies varying factors were identified that helped to create or obstruct an atmosphere, in which negotiations were to take place. Stakeholders have to be aware of them. Among these factors were the global anti-colonial wind in the 1970s, the public, media and civil society support in former colonies for returns and sympathising heritage officials in countries of the former colonisers. In several instances, governments, a member of a royal family or a museum of a country returned objects prior to the start of negotiations, examples being a palm-leaf manuscript and paintings returned to Indonesia, watercolour paintings to Greenland and a drum to Papua New Guinea. Other factors were the impact of claims of internally colonised peoples in several former colonisers and the taking office of progressive governments in Denmark, the Netherlands and Australia.

Obstructive factors were efforts of European countries such as the United Kingdom, Belgium and the Netherlands to minimise claims, the low priority that former colonies themselves gave to cultural policies and the poor management of their heritage sector.

Factors that help create an atmosphere conducive or obstructive to negotiations rarely figure in conflict resolution models. That is why they have been called Phase 0: Facilitating factors.

Phase 1: Inviting the Other Party

To lift negotiations to a formal level, one stakeholder has to take the initiative, to formally invite the other and to make a claim. This book offers evidence of former colonies and their heritage institutions that underestimate the need of a formal approach and a clearly formulated claim. The other party can ignore claims expressed e.g. via the media and other informal channels with more ease than when they are submitted officially. In some instances, a former coloniser used the absence of a formal claim to hide his unwillingness to discuss colonial objects.

Usually it was the claiming party – Indonesia, Congo, Iceland – that made the invitation. Papua New Guinea, Greenland and Nigeria were helped by the encouragement of heritage officials from the possessor's side. In Australia an informal network of critical museum officials helped. A Danish museum official surprised his Greenlandic colleagues with the suggestion to make a return claim. The proposal for the Benin Dialogue came from a curator of a Western museum and the Director-general of Nigeria's National Commission for Museums and Monuments (NCMM). The government of the state of Benin announced in 2016 to open negotiations with France and UNESCO about the return of war booty and other colonial objects but because the claim is not as distinct as it should be the Musée du quai Branly can pretend to be unaware of it.

Phase 2: Preparation by the Two Parties

Stakeholders have to define the contestation that lies at the basis of their dispute – colonial objects or collections – and must decide about procedures, places to meet, language, etc. In the case studies most inviting parties knew what they wanted and which objects they were after. Indonesia showed a list of ten thousand objects in Dutch public museums. Congo asked Belgium for the return of two hundred highly-valued objects that had been part of a travelling exhibition, amongst others. Iceland wanted ancient manuscripts that had once been taken to Copenhagen. For Greenland and Denmark the list of archaeological and other materials to be negotiated was no major bottleneck. Papua New Guinea asked for the repatriation of the MacGregor and Murray collections. A lack of clarity about the contestation has negatively impacted the Benin Dialogue.

Although the bilateral negotiations were a government-to-government affair, government delegations were usually composed of officials with divergent backgrounds and sometimes conflicting interests. This created a dynamic inside some delegations that influenced the outcome of the negotiations.

Thinking about this Phase of Preparation, the Benin Dialogue raises several questions: about the stakeholders, their commitment, the need of a mediator and a European approach. On the Nigerian side the stakeholders are the state, represented by the NCMM, and a private institution, the Benin Court. The European stakeholders are a semi-open group of museum curators from several countries. The power of the latter to act, as well as their commitment to the negotiations varied. They needed the approval of their directors for crucial decisions and in the case of a return, of the government of their country. It meant that the slowest of the participating museums determined the speed of the process. Should the Western museums not delegate their directors and should the Nigerian

authorities not press for their participation, in case the Dialogue is continued? That the British Museum has not organised a fourth meeting can be evidence of a divergent commitment of the museums involved and raises the question whether it is more efficient in a dialogue like this to form a *coalition of willing museums*.

It is certainly true that the impasse in the Benin Dialogue was due to a lack of a model to conduct this sort of negotiations. Another factor, in my view, was the absence of independent, external supervisors. They could have kept an eye on the technical process of the Dialogue itself, including agreements about the goals of the dialogue and about publicity, and on the progress in the negotiations. They have the competence to call stakeholders to order or to intervene when the discussions get bogged down.

Finally, the Benin Dialogue has given the negotiations about the future of colonial objects a European dimension. The distribution of Benin objects and many other contestable objects over countries in Europe raises the question whether a European level initiative is needed to deal with the issue of contestable colonial cultural acquisitions.

The explicit or implicit sharing of values can help negotiations. Denmark and its two colonies had certain values in common, although the commonality with Greenland had resulted from isolating the colony and educating Greenlandic experts in Denmark. Below the commonality there were a hidden hierarchy and inequality.

The hard-to-handle issue of equality is dealt with in the Box: *Address (in)equality.*

Phase 3: Approach of the Other Stakeholders

In the case studies of the 1970s and 1980s the only stakeholders were states. There was no room for non-state outsiders such as representatives of traditional courts. In Indonesia, local princes saw their loyalty to the Dutch colonial administration unrewarded. By being the only stakeholder, a central government demonstrated itself to be a state with a capable administration, equal to the former coloniser.

The biographies of most objects, however, also show other institutions and people with a strong relationship to them – their makers, the first and subsequent local and trans-ocean possessors, the people and institutions that have taken care of them, and their descendants and successors. This finding, plus the increasing space nowadays for regional and local initiatives in many former colonies, offers the possibility of including other stakeholders.

From the beginning, representatives of the Benin Court have been a stakeholder in the Benin Dialogue. Their attitude has been critical and constructive. A British private citizen did not return Benin objects inherited from his grandfather to the Nigerian state, but to the Benin Court. A Dutch missionary order returned ancient objects to two regional museums in Indonesia.

Involving more stakeholders can obstruct progress in negotiations, but if handled with care, it strengthens the dynamics and helps to bring a solution within reach.

Address (in)equality

The stakeholders in the case studies of the 1970s and 1980s were internationally recognised states and thus formally equal partners. Did this equality also exist *de facto*? Did they have equal chances and equal capabilities? One state was a possessor of objects, the other claiming them. One was an experienced international negotiator, the other a relative new-comer. Their unresolved conflict was asymmetric. Was there a hidden hierarchy between key players in negotiations? This study has abundant evidence of inequality.

In Congo, few people had been educated for manning the cultural heritage sector. High cultural positions were, even in the first years after independence, filled by Belgians, among them Tervuren Museum-director Lucien Cahen. The museum director in the Dutch Team of Experts had been the university professor of the museum director in the Indonesian Team. Did equality increase in cases where the geographical and cultural distance was smaller? One can doubt this in the case of colonial Greenland, which Denmark had

placed on the lowest rung of the civilisation ladder (10.1.). There was more equality between Denmark and Iceland because of their shared religion and the Danish respect for Iceland's ancient sagas. In the delegation that negotiated with Australia in the early 1970s, there were no Papua New Guinean nationals. The Australian National Trust selected the objects to be repatriated, although this was endorsed by its Papuan counterparts. In the Benin Dialogue stakeholders intend to hold frank and open discussions, but while the European curators are well-educated specialists, who keep developing their skills, their colleagues in Nigeria face more bureaucracy, as well as frequent staff changes.

Equality and inequality are a sensitive issue. Stakeholders have to face it, and in case of serious inequalities, one can invoke the capabilities approach of Amartya Sen and Martha Nussbaum to handle it (6.2.2.). Possessing stakeholders can also invoke this to strengthen their capability to un-dramatize their continuing possession of objects.

In the Benin Dialogue, legal experts are involved. A Nigerian legal expert made his countrymen accept that there is no legal base for restitution of the Benin treasures. The help of specialists, such as legal experts, art historians and heritage scholars, is more often invoked. They attend meetings and offer advice but do not have the position of a stakeholder. Experts should guard their independence and abstain from a role in the decision-making phase.

Phase 4: First Round of Decision-making

The case studies offer clues to the demarcation of clear rounds of negotiation. In the quarter century that the Netherlands and Indonesia needed, three rounds have been distinguished. For Belgium and Congo the years 1960 – 1969, from the independence until the eve of the negotiations, can be defined as the first round, with a second round following after. For Greenland and Denmark the first round started in 1981, when Greenland got Home Rule. It was concluded in 1983 when the two sides agreed. Papua New Guinea and Australia began their first and only round in 1972. It lasted until 1977 with the transfer of seventeen objects. It would not come as a surprise, if the first three Benin Dialogue meetings are later defined as round one, with the Benin Plan of Action as the outcome.

Phase 5: Deepening

One round is rarely sufficient to reach a solution. Negotiations often get stuck. What factors cause stagnation? A few can be mentioned. Among them are the different values assigned to the objects at stake, or the negative assumptions about the other stakeholder – such as unspoken mistrust of the capability of the one to take care of objects or of the supposed unwillingness of the other to consider a return. (Hidden) economic interests can also cause stagnation.

Such hidden or underlying interests can sometimes influence stakeholders more than open and obvious ones. To prevent or move on from stagnation, it is crucial to deepen such interests and to bring them into the open, which usually requires a mediator. He or she can bring the underlying interests into the open and point to the wisdom that they can add to the solution. Deepening can create understanding for the arguments of other stakeholders. It can help to integrate the wisdom in these arguments into the final solution.

The study offers several indications of underlying interests. One is the hidden longing of a former colony to be seen as equal to the former coloniser. This was behind Indonesia's dislike of the patronising attitude of the Dutch towards them strengthening their museum and archival infrastructure and behind Congo's effort to retrieve all two hundred objects that had travelled through the USA. A former colony's longing to point out injustice and to be confirmed as rightful owner can also be behind a claim for the return of war booty. Behind the willingness to transfer part of war booty there can be the hidden interest to clear booty that can be kept. Behind the unwillingness to return an object there can be the longing for recognition of the many years of care for the object. Many former colonisers minimised the transfers and gave some objects so that they could keep others: the giving occurred openly, the keeping was a hidden agenda.

Most returns function as part of a country's cultural diplomacy. Belgium used the return of colonial objects to diminish the chance of a loss of commercial interests in Katanga. The Netherlands agreed to return certain objects in order to nullify damage to its reputation and to renew and safeguard the cooperation with Indonesia's heritage sector. Western participants in the Benin Dialogue want to be seen as enlightened members of the world community and remove the embarrassment about the unequal distribution of Benin treasures. Underlying interests played a role in the language: the use of the term transfer enabled a country to avoid the terms return or restitution, which it associated with unpleasant discussions about its past wrongs.

In the case studies, deepening often occurred in an unorganised manner and was not restricted to one phase. In several instances it took place in Phase 0 (Facilitating factors) or in the first round. In the Dutch – Indonesian and Belgian – Congolese cases deepening occurred throughout the negotiations, though not systematically. In the Danish – Icelandic negotiations, deepening occurred especially in one stakeholder, Denmark, when it went through an internal process of adjusting to the idea of a transfer. There was less need for deepening during the negotiations between Australia and Papua New Guinea, and Denmark and Greenland. Deepening in the Benin Dialogue occurred in the statements of representatives of the Benin Court in Vienna in 2007, so before the start of the

Dialogue, as well as during the three meetings and in a way also during a press spontaneous conference, where some European stakeholders felt taken by surprise. The last was a way of unproductive deepening.

Phase 6: Second and Subsequent Rounds of Decision-making

One or more additional rounds of decision-making can be necessary, certainly if stakeholders have a complicated history and strongly opposed interests, as was the case in the Dutch – Indonesian and Belgian – Congolese negotiations, for instance. It was also the case for Denmark and Iceland, which needed ten years before the contours of an agreement emerged.

Part of the final round is agreeing about how the shared conclusions will be implemented. Who is responsible for what? When are steps to be taken, and when? And what is done if one side does not stick to the agreement? The 1975 Joint Recommendations between the Netherlands and Indonesia lacked such a provision, which enabled the Netherlands to not fulfil some of its promises.

In conclusion, the adaptation of the 1998 Washington Principles to Principles for Dealing with Colonial Cultural and Historical Objects helps to internationalise the discussion about the future of colonial objects. It creates awareness and indicates what commitment is needed to solve the issue of lost colonial objects. The other tool for this, the seven-phase model for negotiating the future of colonial cultural objects, has been developed within the limits of existing conflict resolution models. The special nature of the contestation – colonial cultural objects – gives it extra characteristics. In the application of the model, the help of a process supervisor, facilitator or mediator is recommended. UNESCO's Intergovernmental Committee, ICOM, and other institutions can be approached.

The model is meant for dealing with conflicts about objects that qualify for corrective justice (6.2.2.). One can think of war booty, objects confiscated by missionaries and objects taken by private persons and institutions in violation of the laws of the time. It can also be used to fix the maldistribution of colonial objects, as the collections in the West are significantly larger than the often meagre collections in countries of origin. It can also be of help to discuss objects that are needed more in a former colony than in a museum or in a private house in a Western country. It can even help to discuss objects that have been acquired by purchase or barter in a win-win situation but that might fit better in their country of origin nowadays. The model has a built-in guarantee that all stakeholders are respected and that painful questions can be raised and must be addressed.

Nigerian-American art historian Dele Jegede and cultural heritage law expert Folarin Shyllon criticised Nigeria for not using the opportunities that UNESCO and its Intergovernmental Committee for Return and Restitution offer to get back Benin treasures. They called upon Nigeria and other African countries to put their own house in order. I want to adapt their call for Europe. What I have learnt most is that it is time for Europe, for the former colonisers, to put their own house in order, to face this greatly neglected effect of colonialism, to do more pro-active provenance research into the acquisitions from the colonial era, both in public institutions and private collections, and to become genuinely generous in taking the consequences of it. New return policies should be developed, not to serve as a means of cultural diplomacy and to promote other foreign policy goals, but for the sake of justice and to create conditions in which colonial cultural and historical objects end up in trusted hands.

In the Preface I wrote about a dream of a round table with a colonial cultural object on top of it and its major stakeholders sitting around it. They are telling each other about their involvement with the object. Harsh words are uttered, but in the end a consensus is reached on where and how the object ends up best in trusted hands. Hopefully this book has helped to make the table steadier and less wobbly.

Appendix: 1998 Washington Principles adapted for Colonial Objects

Washington Conference Principles on Nazi-Confiscated Art	Principles on objects of cultural or historical importance, taken without just compensation or involuntarily lost in the European colonial era
In developing a consensus on non-binding principles to assist in resolving issues relating to Nazi-confiscated art, the Conference recognizes that among participating nations there are differing legal systems and that countries act within the context of their own laws.	In developing a consensus on non-binding principles to assist in resolving issues relating to objects of cultural or historical importance, that were taken without just compensation or were involuntarily lost in the European colonial era, it is recognized that among participating nations, there are differing legal systems and that countries act within the context of their own laws.
1. Art that had been confiscated by the Nazis and not subsequently restituted should be identified.	1. Objects of cultural or historical importance taken without just compensation or involuntarily lost in a territory controlled by European, American or Asian colonial powers and not subsequently returned should be identified.
2. Relevant records and archives should be open and accessible to researchers, in accordance with the guidelines of the International Council on Archives.	2. Relevant records and archives should be open and accessible to researchers, in accordance with the guidelines of the International Council on Archives.
3. Resources and personnel should be made available to facilitate the identification of all art that had been confiscated by the Nazis and not subsequently restituted.	3. Resources and personnel should be made available to facilitate the identification of all objects of cultural or historical importance taken without just compensation or involuntarily lost in the European colonial era and not subsequently returned.
4. In establishing that a work of art had been confiscated by the Nazis and not subsequently restituted, consideration should be given to unavoidable gaps or ambiguities in the provenance in light of the passage of time and the circumstances of the Holocaust era.	4. In establishing that an object of cultural or historical importance was taken without just compensation or had been lost involuntarily in the European colonial era and not subsequently returned, consideration should be given to unavoidable gaps or ambiguities in the provenance in light of the passage of time and the circumstances of the European colonial era.
5. Every effort should be made to publicize art that is found to have been confiscated by the Nazis and not subsequently restituted in order to locate its pre-War owners or their heirs.	5. Every effort should be made to publicise objects of cultural or historical importance that are found to have been taken without just compensation or were lost involuntarily during the European colonial era and not subsequently returned in order to locate its rightful claimants.
6. Efforts should be made to establish a central registry of such information.	6. Efforts should be made to establish a registry of such information on a bilateral basis.
7. Pre-War owners and their heirs should be encouraged to come forward and make known their claims to art that was confiscated by the Nazis and not subsequently restituted.	7. Rightful parties should be encouraged to come forward and make known their claims to objects that were taken without just compensation or lost involuntarily in the European colonial era and not subsequently returned.

8. If the pre-War owners of art that is found to have been confiscated by the Nazis and not subsequently restituted, or their heirs, can be identified, steps should be taken expeditiously to achieve a just and fair solution, recognizing this may vary according to the facts and circumstances surrounding a specific case.	8. If the rightful claimants can be identified, steps should be taken expeditiously to achieve a just and fair solution, recognizing this may vary according to the facts and circumstances surrounding a specific case.
9. If the pre-War owners of art that is found to have been confiscated by the Nazis, or their heirs, cannot be identified, steps should be taken expeditiously to achieve a just and fair solution.	9. If no rightful claimants can be identified, steps should be taken expeditiously to achieve a just and fair solution.
10. Commissions or other bodies established to identify art that was confiscated by the Nazis and to assist in addressing ownership issues should have a balanced membership.	10. Commissions or other bodies established to identify objects of cultural or historical importance that are found to have been taken without just compensation or to have been lost involuntarily in the European colonial era and to assist in addressing ownership issues should have a balanced membership.
11 Nations are encouraged to develop national processes to implement these principles, particularly as they relate to alternative dispute resolution mechanisms for resolving ownership issues.	11. Nations, including the minorities and indigenous peoples in these nations, are encouraged to develop national and international processes to implement these principles, particularly as they relate to alternative dispute resolution mechanisms for resolving ownership issues.

Sources

Abraham, Kinfe. *Adowa – Decolonisation, Pan-Africanism and the Struggle of the Black Diaspora.* Addis Ababa: Ethiopian International Institute for Peace and Development, 2012.

Abungu, George O. "'Universal Museums': New contestations, new controversies". In: Gabriel and Dahl, *Utimut*, 32 – 43.

Achterhuis, Hans. *Met alle geweld.* Rotterdam: Lemniscaat, 2008.

Akinade, Olalekan Ajao. "Illicit traffic in cultural property in Nigeria: Aftermaths and antidotes". In: *African Study Monographs*, 20 (2), June 1999: 99 – 107. Kyoto: Kyoto University, Center for African Area Studies (CAAS), 1999.

Alonso, Hilario Casado. "The Geographical Discoveries: New economic Opportunities in a Globalising World". In: Barros, *Discoveries and the Origins of Global Convergence*, 170 – 202.

Anheier, Helmut K. and Isar, Yudhishthir Raj, eds. *Conflicts and tensions.* Los Angeles: Sage Publications, 2007.

Appadurai, Arjun.
- *The Social Life of Things.* Cambridge: Cambridge University Press, 1986.
- *Modernity at large – Cultural Dimensions of Globalization.* Minneapolis, London: University of Minnesota Press, 1996.
- *The future as a cultural fact – Essays on the global condition.* London/New York: Verso Books, 2013.

Appiah, Kwame A. *Cosmopolitanism: Ethics in a World of Strangers.* Hammondsworth: Penguin, 2007.

Arendt, Hannah. *The Origins of Totalitarianism.* Orlando: Harcourt Inc., [1950] 1968.

Aristoteles, *Ethica Nicomachea.* Vertaald en ingeleid door C. Pannier and J. Verhaeghe. Groningen: Historische uitgeverij, 1999.

Attenbrow, Val and Fullagar, Richard, eds. "A Pacific Odyssey: Archaeology and Anthropology in the Western Pacific. Papers in Honour of Jim Specht". Sydney: Australian Museum, *Records of the Australian Museum*, Supplement 29, 2004.

Baay, Reggie. *Daar werd wat gruwelijks verricht – Slavernij in Nederlands-Indië.* Amsterdam: Athenaeum – Polak & Van Gennep, 2015.

Balk, Louisa, Dijk, Frans Van, Kortlang, Diederick, Gaastra, Femme, Niemijer, Hendrik, Koenders, Pieter, *The archives of the Dutch East India Company (VOC) and the local institutions in Batavia (Jakarta).* Jakarta: Arsip Nasional Republik Indonesia, and Leiden: Brill, 2007.

Bandle, Anne Laure. "Auschwitz Suitcase – Pierre Lévi Heirs and Auschwitz-Birkenau State Museum Oswiecim and Shoah Memorial Museum Paris". In: *Arthemis database.* Geneva: University of Geneva, Art-Law Centre, 2012. https://plone.unige.ch/art-adr.

Barbalet, Jack. *A characterisation of trust and its consequences.* Canterbury: University of Kent, 2006. https://www.kent.ac.uk/scarr/publications/Barbalet%20Wk%20Paper(2)%2013.pdf.

Barkan, Elazar. *The Guilt of Nations: Restitution and Negotiating Historical Injustices.* New York/London: W.W. Norton & Company, 2000.

Barros, Amândio, ed. *Os Descombrimentos e as Origens da Convergência Global/The Discoveries and the Origins of Global Convergence*. Porto: Câmara Municipal do Porto, 2015.

Bedaux, Rogier M.A.
- "De geschiedenis van de Leidse Benin-verzameling". In: Duchâteau, *Benin: Vroege hofkunst uit Afrika*, 159 – 167.
- *Rendez-nous notre bélier – Het behoud van cultureel erfgoed in Mali*. Leiden: CNWS, 1998.

Bellisari, Andrew H. "The art of decolonization: The battle for Algeria's French art, 1962 – 1970". Cambridge: Cambridge University, conference *Looted Art and Restitution in the Twentieth Century*, 2014 (unpubl.).

Bercovitch, Jacob, Kremenyuk, Victor and Zartman, I.William, eds. *The SAGE handbook of conflict resolution*. Los Angeles, CA: SAGE, 2009.

Bercovitch, Jacob. "Mediation and conflict resolution". In: Bercovitch ea., *SAGE handbook of conflict resolution*, 2009: 340 – 357.

Bedorf, Franziska and Östberg, Wilhelm. „African *objets d'arts* currency in a bid for the Polar Star – and for recognition on the European scene". In: Stockholm Museum for Ethnography, *Whose Objects?*, 2010: 30 – 43.

Bergvelt, Ellinoor and Kistemaker, Renée, eds. *De Wereld binnen Handbereik*. Amsterdam: Amsterdams Historisch Museum, 1992.

Beurden, Jos Van
- "Mali – Losing the race to preserve its cultural heritage". In: *The Courier*. Brussels: European Commission, 2000: 181, June-July, 74 – 77.
- *Goden, Graven en Grenzen: Over Kunstroof uit Afrika, Azië en Latijns Amerika*. Amsterdam: KIT Publishers, 2001. Amsterdam: Querido Fosfor, 2013, e-book.

- "A holy cross and the necessity for international conventions". In: *Culture Without Context*. Cambridge: Cambridge University, 2001: 9/ Autumn, 30 – 31.
- *Partnerships in Cultural Heritage – The International Projects of the KIT Tropenmuseum in Amsterdam*. Amsterdam: KIT Publishers, 2005, Bulletin 364.
- "An Etruscan Cuirass". In: *Culture Without Context*. Cambridge: Cambridge University, 2006: 18/ Spring, 8 – 10.
- "The Dutch Treatment of Tainted Objects". In: Scholten ed., *Sense and Sensitivities*, 2010: 16 – 23.
- *The Return of Cultural and Historical Treasures: The Case of the Netherlands*. Amsterdam: KIT Publishers, 2012, https://issuu.com/kitpublishers/docs/the_return_of__cultural_lr.
- "Dutch Heritage Institutions, Return-Practice and Return-Potential". In: *Transnational Dispute Management (TDM)*, OGEMID, 2013: 10/5, http://www.transnational-dispute-management.com/about-author-a-z-profile.asp?key=2292
- "How to Break the Deadlock in the Debate about Colonial Acquisitions?". In: Vadi and Schneider, *Art, Cultural Heritage and the Market*, 2014: 165 – 181.
- "Aangepaste LAMO bij ontmanteling Nusantara – Repatriëring: hoe werkt dat?". In: *Museumvisie*. Amsterdam: Nederlandse Museum Vereniging, 2015/02.

Beurden, Sarah Van
- *Authentically African: African arts and postcolonial cultural politics in transnational perspective (Congo [DRC], Belgium and the USA, 1955 – 1980)*. Philadelphia: University of Pennsylvania, Ph.D., 2009.

- "The art of (re)possession: Heritage and the cultural politics of Congo's decolonization". In: *The Journal of African History*. Cambridge: Cambridge University Press, 2015: 56/1: 143 – 164.

Bilsen, Jef Van. *Kongo – Het Einde van een Kolonie*. Leuven: Davidsfonds, 1993.

Bleeker, Mô
- 2010. "Preface". In: *Politorbis*: 7 – 9.
- 2010. "The right to know: a key factor in combating impunity". In: *Politorbis*: 31 – 40.

Bonshek, Elizabeth. "Ownership and a Peripatetic Collection: Raymond Firth's Collection from Tikopia, Solomon Islands". In: Attenbrow and Fullagar, *Pacific Odyssey*, 37 – 46.

Bouquet, Mary. *Sans og Samling... hos Universitetes Etnografiske Museum / Bringing it all back home... to the Oslo University Ethnographic Museum*. Oslo: Scandinavian University Press, 1996.

Bouquet, Mary and Freitas Branco, Jorge. *Artefactos Melanésios – Reflexões pós-modernistas/Melanesian Artefacts – Postmodernist reflections*. Lisbon: Museo de Etnologia, 1988.

Bowman Proulx, Blythe. "Archaeological Site Looting in 'Glocal' Perspective: Nature, Scope and Frequency", in: *American Journal of Archaeology* (Forum article, 2013): 111 – 125. http://www.ajaonline.org/sites/default/files/1171_Proulx.pdf

Boz, Zeyneb B. "Bogazkoy Sphinx and Turkey's policy on return and restitution cases". Seoul: Conference of Experts on the Return of Cultural Property, 2012. https://www.academia.edu/6644263/Bogazkoy_Sphinx_and_Turkeys_Policy_on_Return_and_Restitution_Cases.

Brakel, Coos Van. "Hunters, gatherers and collectors: Origins and early history of the Indonesian collections in the Tropenmuseum in Amsterdam". In: Schefold and Vermeulen, *Treasure Hunting?*, 169 – 182.

Brakel, Coos Van, Duuren, David Van, Hout, Itie Van. *A Passion for Indonesian Art – The George Tillmann Collection at the Tropenmuseum, Amsterdam*. Amsterdam: KIT Publishers, 1996.

Brekke, Torkel. "Bones of Contention: Buddhist Relics, Nationalism and the Politics of Archaeology", in: *Numen*. Leiden: Brill, 2007: 54/ 3: 270 – 303.

Brigg, Morten. *The New Politics of Conflict Resolution,* Palgrave: Macmillan, 2008.

Brinkgreve, Francine. "Balinese Chiefs and Dutch Dominion: Building a Collection and Politics". In: Hardiati and Ter Keurs, *Discovery of Indonesia,* 2005: 122 – 145.

Brinkgreve, Francine and Van Hout, Itie. "Java: Gifts, Scholarship and Colonial Rule". In: Hardiati and Ter Keurs, *Discovery of Indonesia,* 2005: 100 – 121.

Brodie, Neil, Kersel, Morag, and Tubb, Kathy W., eds. *Cultural heritage, and the antiquities trade*. Gainesville: University Press of Florida, 2006.

Broekhoven, Laura Van, ed. *Kuifje naar de Inca's – Strijdbaar heden, roemrijk verleden*. Leiden: Museum Volkenkunde, 2003.

Broekhoven, Laura Van, Buijs, Cunera and Hovens, Pieter, eds. *Sharing Knowledge & Cultural Heritage: First Nations of the Americas – Studies in collaboration with indigenous peoples from Greenland, North and South America*. Leiden: Sidestone Press, 2010.

Budiarti, Hari.
- "The Sulawesi collections – Missionaries, Chiefs and Military Expeditions". In: Hardiati and Ter Keurs, *Discovery of Indonesia*, 2005: 160 – 271.

- "Heirlooms of an archipelago". In: Sitowati and Miksic, *Icons of Art*, 2006: 126 – 165.
- "Taking and Returning Objects in a Colonial Context – Tracing the Collections acquired during the Bone-Gowa military expeditions". In: Schefold and Vermeulen, *Treasure Hunting?*, 2007: 123 – 144.

Bullough, Nigel and Carey, Peter, "The Kolkata (Calcutta) Stone and the bicentennial of the British Interregnum in Java, 1811 – 1816". In *The Newsletter*. Leiden: IIAS, 2016, No. 74: 4 – 5.

Burbank, Jane and Cooper, Ferdinand. *Empires in world history – Power and the politics of difference*. Princeton and Oxford: Princeton University Press, 2010.

Buschmann, Rainer. "Exploring tensions in material culture: Commercialising ethnography in German New Guinea, 1870 – 1904". In: O'Hanlon and Welch, *Hunting the Gatherers*, 2000: 55 – 80.

Busse, Mark. "Short history of the Papua New Guinea National Museum". In: Craig, *Living Spirits*, 2010: 6 – 15.

Campen, Jan Van and Hartkamp-Jonxis, Ebeltje. *Aziatische Weelde – VOC-kunst in het Rijksmuseum*. Zutphen: Walburg Pers, 2011.

Campfens, Evelien.
- "Alternative Dispute Resolution in Restitution Claims and the Binding Expert Opinion Procedure of the Dutch Restitutions Committee". In: Vadi and Schneider. *Art, Cultural Heritage and the Market*, 2014: 61 – 91.
- *Fair and just solutions? Alternatives to litigation in Nazi-looted art disputes: status quo and new developments*. The Hague: Eleven International Publishing, 2015.

Carey, Henri Charles. *The Slave Trade, Domestic and Foreign: Why It Exists, and How It May Be Extinguished*. Philadelphia: A. Hart, late Carey and Hart, 1853, http://cecaust.com.au/foodcrisis/H%20Carey%20British%20free%20trade.pdf (November 16, 2015)

Carey, Peter B.R.
- *The British in Java, 1811 – 1816. A Javanese Account*. London: Oxford University Press for the British Academy, 1992.
- *The power of prophecy – Prince Dipanagara and the end of an old order in Java, 1785 – 1855*. Leiden: KITLV Press, 2008.

Carrington, Michael. "Officers, gentlemen and thieves: The looting of monasteries during the 1903/4 Younghusband Mission to Tibet". In: *Modern Asian Studies*. Cambridge: Cambridge University Press, 2003: 37/1, 81 – 109.

Casalis, Eugène. *My life in Basutoland – A story of missionary enterprise in South Africa*. Piccadilly: The Religious Tract Society, 1889.

Casas, Barthelomé de las. *Brevisima relacion de la destruccion de las Indias*. Sevilla: 1522 http://www.verbodengeschriften.nl/html/zeerbeknoptrelaasvandeverwoesting.html.

Célestin, Kanimba Misago and Pee, Lode Van. *Rwanda – Its cultural heritage, past and present*. Nyanza: Institute of National Museums of Rwanda, 2008.

Césaire, Aimé. *Discourse on Colonialism*. New York and London: Monthly Review Press, Editions Presence Africaine, [1955] 1972. http://www.rlwclarke.net/theory/SourcesPrimary/CesaireDiscourseonColonialism.pdf.

Chakrabarty, Dipesh. *Provincializing Europe*. Princeton: Princeton University Press, 2000.

Chamberlain, Kevin and Vrdoljak, Ana F. "Controls on the Export of Cultural Objects and Human Rights". In: Nafziger, J.A.R. & Paterson R.K., *Handbook on the Law of Cultural Heritage and International Trade*. Cheltenham: Edward Elgar, 2014: 532 – 570.

Chang, Jung. *De keizerin – Het verhaal van de vrouw die bijna vijftig jaar over China heerste*. Amsterdam: Boekerij, 2014.

Chechi, Alessandro. "Some reflections on International Adjudication of Cultural Heritage-related Cases". In: Vadi and Schneider, *Art and Heritage Disputes*, 2013.

Chechi, Alessandro, Bandle, Anne-Laure, and Renold, Marc-André. "Case Venus of Cyrene – Italy and Libya". In: *Platform ArThemis*. Geneva: University of Geneva, Art-Law Centre, 2012. http://unige.ch/art-adr.

Chutiwongs, Nandana. "Pieces of the Borobudur puzzle re-examined". In: Hardiati and Ter Keurs, *Discovery of Indonesia*, 2005: 40 – 48.

Cochrane, Susan and Quanchi, Max, eds. *Hunting the collectors: Pacific collections in Australian museums, art galleries and archives*. Newcastle: Cambridge Scholars Publishing, 2007.

Cohan, John Alan. "An examination of archaeological ethics and the repatriation movement – Respecting cultural property". In: *Environs*. Davis: University of California, Fall 2004: 28, 1 – 116.

Cohn, Bernard S. *Colonialism and its forms of knowledge – The British in India*. Princeton: Princeton University Press, 1996.

Colombijn, Freek and Lindblad, J. Thomas. *Roots of Violence in Indonesia: Contemporary violence in historical perspective*. Leiden: KITLV Press, Verhandelingen KITLV 194, 2002.

Contel, Raphael, Chechi, Alessandro, and Renold, Marc-André. "Affaire Obélisque d'Axoum – Italie et Ethiopie". In: *Plateforme ArThemis* (http://unige.ch/art-adr). Genève : Université de Genève, Centre du Droit de l'Art, 2012.

Coombes, Annie. E. *Reinventing Africa – Museums, material culture and popular imagination*. New Haven and London: Yale University Press, 1994.

Coombs, Philip H. *The fourth dimension of foreign policy: Educational and cultural affairs*. New York/Evanston: Harper and Row, 1964.

Corbey, Raymond. *Tribal Art Traffic: A Chronicle of Taste, Trade and Desire in Colonial and Post-Colonial Times*. Amsterdam: KIT Publishers, 2000.

Corbey, Raymond and Weener, Frans-Karel. "Collecting while converting: missionaries and ethnographies". In: *Journal of Art Historiography*. Birmingham: University of Birmingham, 2015, No. 12: 1 – 14. https://arthistoriography.files.wordpress.com/2015/06/corbey-weener.pdf.

Cornu, Marie. "The concepts of original heritage and adoptive heritage in French law". In: Prott, *Witnesses to History*, 2009: 326 – 342.

Cornu, Marie and Renold, Marc-André. "New Developments in the Restitution of Cultural Property: Alternative Means of Dispute Resolution". In: *International Journal of Cultural Property*. Cambridge: Cambridge University Press, 2010: 17, 1 – 31.

Couttenier, Maarten. "Between Regionalization and Centralization: The Creation of the Musée Léopold II in Elisabethville (Musée national de Lubumbashi), Belgian Congo

(1931 – 1961)". In: *History and Anthropology*. London: Routledge, 2014: 25/1, 72 – 101.

Craig, Barry.
- *Samting Bilong Tumbuna: The collection, documentation and preservation of the material cultural heritage of Papua New Guinea*. Adelaide: Flinders University, Ph.D., 1996.
- "Edgar Waite's north-west Pacific expedition – the hidden collections". In: Cochrane and Quanchi, *Hunting the Collectors*, 2007: 174 – 195.
- ed. *Living Spirits with Fixed Abodes*. Adelaide: Crawford House Publications, 2010.

Cultural Heritage Inspectorate (Erfgoedinpectie, ICB),
- *Analyse van 105 dossiers van de Inspectie Cultuurbezit m.b.t. de Invoer van Cultuurgoederen*. The Hague: ICB, 2004.
- *Grenzen overschreden? Onderzoek naar onrechtmatig handelen op de gebieden van archeologie en archieven*. The Hague: ICB, 2012.
- *Verslagen van het Toezicht* (annual reports of the inspection). The Hague: ICB.

Cuno, James.
- "View from the universal Museum". In: Merryman, *Imperialism, art and restitution*, 2006: 15 – 36.
- *Who Owns Antiquity? Museums and the Battle over Our Ancient Heritage*. Princeton: Princeton University Press, 2008. http://press.princeton.edu/chapters/i8602.pdf

Dark, P.J.C. *The Art of Benin, a catalogue of an exhibition of the A.W.F. Fuller and Chicago Natural History Museum Collections of Antiquities from Benin, Nigeria*. Chicago: Natural History Museum, 1962.

Davidson, Douglas. "Just and fair solutions: A view from the United States" in: Campfens, *Fair and Just solutions?*, 2015: 91 – 101.

Dembélé, M, Schmidt, Annette and Waals, Diederik Van der. "Prospections de sites archéologiques dans le delta intérieur du Niger". In: *Vallées de Niger*. Paris: Editions de la Réunion des Musées Nationaux, 1993: 218 – 232.

Derix, Jan. *Brengers van de Boodschap – Geschiedenis van de katholieke missionering vanuit Nederland van VOC tot Vaticanum II*. Nijmegen: Valkhof Pers, 2009.

Derrida, Jacques. "To forgive: The unforgiveable and the imprescriptible". In: Caputo, John D., Dooley, Mark, and Scanlon, Michael J., eds., *Questioning God*. Bloomington and Indianapolis: Indiana University Press, 2001.

Deutsches Historisches Museum, *German Colonialism – Fragments Past and Present*. Berlin: Deutscher Historisches Museum, 2016.

Dewey, William J. and Palmenaer, Els De, eds. *Zimbabwe – Legacies of Stone: Past and Present*. Tervuren: Royal Museum for Central Africa (2 Vol.), 1997.

Dijk, Cees Van. "Gathering and describing: Western interest in Eastern nature and culture". In: Schefold and Vermeulen, *Treasure Hunting?*, 2002: 23 – 46.

Dinnie, Keith. *Country of origin 1965 – 2004: A literature review*. Tokyo: Temple University Japan, 2003. http://www.brandhorizons.com/papers/Dinnie_COO_litreview.pdf

Djojonegoro, Wardiman. "The evolution of the National Museum". In: Sitowati and Miksic, *Icons of Art*, 2006: 34 – 71.

Domingues, Francisco Contente. "The India Route. Comparative Paths of a Maritime Venture". In: Amândio Barros, *Discoveries and the Origins of Global Convergence*, 110 – 125.

Doorn, J.A.A. Van and Hendrix, W.J. *Het Nederlandsch/Indonesisch Conflict – Ontsporing en Geweld.* Dieren: De Bataafsche Leeuw, [1970] 1983.

Drees, Willem. *Zestig jaar levenservaring.* Amsterdam: Arbeiderspers, 1962.

Drieënhuizen, Caroline. *Koloniale collecties, Nederlands aanzien: De Europese elite van Nederlands Indië belicht door haar verzamelingen, 1811 – 1957.* Amsterdam: University of Amsterdam, Ph.D., 2012.

Duarte, Luís Miguel. ""Grey hairs to the fore!" The Portuguese Conquest of Ceuta in 1415". In: Amândio Barros, *Os Descombrimentos e as Origens da Convergência Global/The Discoveries and the Origins of Global Convergence*, 87 – 109.

Duchâteau, Armand. *Benin: Vroege hofkunst uit Afrika.* Leiden: Museum Volkenkunde, 1990.

Dutch Restitutions Committee (in full: Advisory Committee on the Assessment of Restitution Applications for Items of Cultural Value and the Second World War). *Annual reports.* Den Haag: Restitutions Committee, 2006 – 2015. http://www.restitutiecommissie.nl/

Dutton, Dennis. "Authenticity in Art". In: Levinson, Jerrold. *The Oxford Handbook of Aesthetics.* New York: Oxford University Press, 2003. http://denisdutton.com/authenticity.htm.

Duuren, David Van.
- ed. *Physical Anthropology Reconsidered: Human Remains at the Tropenmuseum.* Amsterdam: KIT Publishers, 2007.
- ed. *Oceania and the Tropenmuseum.* Amsterdam: KIT Publishers, 2011.
- "Expeditions, collections, science – The Dutch fascination for the Papuans of New Guinea" In: Legêne and Dijk, *The Netherlands East Indies*, 2011: 97 – 109.

Effert, Rudolf. "The Royal Cabinet of Curiosities and the National Museum of Ethnography in the nineteenth century: From the belief in the superiority of western civilization to comparative ethnography". In: Bergvelt, E., Meijers, D.J., Tibbe, L. and Van Wezel, E., eds. *Museale Spezialisierung und Nationalisierung ab 1830. Das Neue Museum in Berlin im internationalen Kontext.* Berlin: G + H Verlag, Berliner Schriften zur Museumsforschung, 2011: Band 29, 153 – 164.

Effiboley, Patrick. "Les musées béninois: du musée ethnographique au musée d'histoire sociale". In: *French Studies in Southern Africa.* Gauteng: Sabinet, 2015: 30 – 61.

Eickhoff, Martijn and Bloembergen, Marieke. "Decolonizing Borobudur: Moral Engagements and the Fear of Loss. The Netherlands, Japan and (Post) Colonial Heritage Politics in Indonesia". In: Legêne, Susan, Purwanto, Bambang, and Schulte Nordholt, Henk, eds. *Sites, Bodies and Stories: Imagining Indonesian History.* Singapore: NUS Press, 2015: 33 – 66.

Eilertsen, Lily. "Breaking the Ice: Conflicts of Heritage in the West Nordic Regions". Brussels: Conference National Museums and the Negotiations of Difficult Pasts, *EuNaMus Report no. 8*, 2012: January 26/27, 153 – 172.

Ekkart Committee. *Origins Unknown – Final report.* Zwolle: Waanders, 2006.

Eoe, S.M. "The role of the National Museum in contemporary Papua New Guinea". In: Craig, *Living Spirits*, 2010: 19 – 24.

Ernawati, Wahyu. "The Lombok treasure". In: Hardiati and Ter Keurs, *Discovery of Indonesia*, 2005: 146 – 159.

Estienne, René, ed. *Les Compagnies des Indes.* Paris: Coédition Gallimard/Ministère de la Défense – DMPA, 2013.

Eyo, Ekpo.
- "Nigeria". In: *Museum*. Paris: UNESCO Quarterly review, 1979: XXXI/1, 18 – 21.
- *Two thousand years of Nigerian Art*. Lagos: Ethnographica London with National Commission for Museums and Monuments, 1990 [1977].
- "Repatriation of Cultural Heritage: The African Experience". In: Kaplan, Flora S., *Museums and the Making of 'Ourselves': The Role of Objects in National Identity*. London: Leicester Press, 1996: 330 – 350.

Ezra, Kate. *Royal Art of Benin – The Perls Collection*. New York: Metropolitan Museum of Art, 1992.

Faber, Paul, ea. *Africa at the Tropenmuseum*. Amsterdam: KIT Publishers, 2011.

Fagan, Brian M. *The Rape of the Nile; Tomb Robbers, Tourists, and Archaeologists in Egypt*. London: Book Club Associates/Macdonald and Jane's Publishers, 1977.

Fasseur, Cees. *Juliana & Bernard – Het verhaal van een huwelijk. De Jaren 1936 – 1956*. Amsterdam: Balans, 2008.

Ferguson, Niall. *Kissinger (1923 – 1968) – The idealist*. London: Allen Lane, 2015.

Fihl, Esther and Simonsen Puri, Stine. "Introduction: The study of cultural encounters in Tharangampadi/Tranquebar". In: Fihl, Esther and A.R. Venkatachalapathy, eds., "Cultural Encounters in Tranquebar: Past and Present", Special issue *Review of Development and Change*. Madras: Madras Institute of Development Studies, 2009: Vol. XIV, No. 1-2.

Finaldi, Giuseppe. "'The peasants did not think of Africa': empire and the Italian state's pursuit of legitimacy, 1871 – 1945". In: MacKenzie, *European Empires and the People*, 2011: 195 – 228.

Fisher, Roger and Ury, William. *Getting to yes – Negotiating agreement without giving in*. London: Penguin Books, [1981] 2011.

Fitz Gibbon, Kate, ed. *Who owns the past? Cultural policy, cultural property and the law*. New Brunswick: Rutgers University Press, 2005.

Flyvbjerg, Bent. "Case Study". In: Denzin, N.K. and Lincoln, Y. S., eds., *The SAGE Handbook of Qualitative Research*. Thousand Oaks, CA: Sage, 2011.

Fontein, Jan. "Piecing together the fragments of the past". In: *Aziatische Kunst*. Amsterdam: Vereniging van Vrienden der Aziatische Kunst, December 1996: 2 – 24.

Förster, Larissa. "Problematic Provenances – Museum and University Collections from a Post-colonial Perspective". In: Deutsches Historisches Museum, *German Colonialism*, 154 – 171.

Frederick, William H. "The killing of Dutch and Eurasians in Indonesia's national revolution (1945 – 1949): a 'brief genocide' reconsidered". In: *Journal of Genocide Research*. Taylor and Francis, 2012: 14/3 – 4 (September-November), 359 – 380.

Freyer, Bryna. *Royal Benin Art in the collection of the National Museum of African Art*. Washington DC: Smithsonian Institution Press, 1987.

Fur, Gunlög. "Colonialism and Swedish history: Unthinkable connections?". In: Naum and Nordin, *Scandinavian Colonialism*, 2013: 17 – 36.

Gabriel, Mille. *Objects on the Move – The Role of Repatriation in Postcolonial Imaginaries*. Copenhagen: University of Copenhagen, Ph.D., 2010.

Gabriel, Mille and Dahl, Jens, eds. *Utimut: Past Heritage – Future Partnerships*. Copenhagen: International Working Group for Indigenous Affairs, 2008.

Galeano, Eduardo. *De aderlating van een continent – Vier eeuwen economische exploitatie van Latijns-Amerika*. Amsterdam: Van Gennep, 1976.

Gallagher, John and Robinson, Ronald. "The Imperialism of Free Trade". In: *The Economic History Review*. London: London School of Economics, Economic History Society, 1953: 6/1, August: 2 – 15.

Galtung, Johan.
- "A Structural Theory of Imperialism". In: *Journal of Peace Research*. Los Angeles: Sage Publications, 1971: 8/2, 81- 117
- "Cultural Violence", in: *Journal of Peace Research*. Los Angeles: Sage Publications, 1990: 27/3.

Gamboni, Dario. *The destruction of art – Iconoclasm and vandalism since the French Revolution*. London: Reaktion Books, 1997.

Gänger, Stefanie. *Relics of the past: The collecting and study of pre-Columbian antiquities in Peru and Chile, 1837 – 1911*. Oxford: Oxford University Press, 2014.

Gaugue, Anne. "Musées et colonisation en Afrique tropicale". In: *Cahiers d'études africaines*. Paris: École des hautes études en sciences sociales, 1999 : 39/155 – 156: 727 – 745.

Gelder, Roelof Van.
- "De wereld binnen handbereik: Nederlandse kunst- en rariteitenverzamelingen, 1858 – 1735". In: Bergvelt and Kistemaker, *Wereld binnen Handbereik*, 1992: 15 – 38.
- "Liefhebbers en geleerde luiden: Nederlandse kabinetten en hun bezoekers". In: Bergvelt and Kistemaker, *Wereld binnen Handbereik*, 1992: 259 – 292.

Geluwe, Huguette Van. 1979. "Belgium's contribution to the Zairian cultural heritage". In: *Museum*. Paris: UNESCO, 1979: XXXI/1: 32 – 37.

George, Alexander L. and Bennet, Andrew. *Case Studies and Theory Development in the Social Sciences*. Cambridge, MA: MIT Press, 2005.

German Museum Association, *Recommendations for the Care of Human Remains in Museums and Collections*. Berlin: German Museum Association, 2013, http://www.museumsbund.de/fileadmin/geschaefts/dokumente/Leitfaeden_und_anderes/2013__Recommendations_for_the_Care_of_Human_Remains.pdf.

Geschiere, Peter. *The perils of belonging – Autochthony, citizenship and exclusion in Africa & Europe*. Chicago: University of Chicago Press, 2009.

Ghani, Ashraf and Lockhart, Claire. *Fixing Failed States: A Framework for Rebuilding a Fractured World*. Oxford: Oxford University Press, 2008.

Ghemawat, Pankaj. *World 3.0: Global prosperity and how to achieve it*. Boston, MA: Harvard Business Review Press, 2011.

Gienow – Hecht, Jessica C.E. and Donfried, Mark, eds. *Searching for Cultural Diplomacy*. New York/Oxford: Berghahn Books, 2010.

Gissibl, Bernard. "Imagination and beyond: cultures and geographies of imperialism in Germany, 1848 – 1918". In: MacKenzie, *European Empires and the People,* 2011: 158 – 194.

Glendinning, Victoria. *Raffles and the golden opportunity*. London: Profile Books, 2012.

Goddeeris, Idesbald and Kiangu, Sindani E. "Congomania in Academia. Recent Historical Research on the Belgian

Colonial Past". In: *BMGN – Low Countries Historical Review*. The Hague: KNHG, 2007/4: 54 – 74.

González-Casanovas, Roberto. "Religious-Secular Politics of Jesuit Frontier Missions as Colonies in Ibero-America". In: Christopher Hartney, ed. *Secularisation: New Historical Perspectives*. Cambridge: Cambridge Scholars Publishing, 2014: 34 – 57.

Gordon, Daniel A. "World Reactions to the 1961 Paris Pogrom". In: *University of Sussex Journal of Contemporary History*. Sussex, University of Sussex, 2000: 1.

Gorkom, Lodewijk Van. *Door Europa en de wereld: Een trektocht in Buitenlandse Dienst*. Amsterdam: Boom, 2009.

Gosden, Chris. "On his Todd: Material culture and colonialism". In: O'Hanlon and Welsch, *Hunting the Gatherers*, 2000: 227 – 250.

Gosepath, Stefan. "Equality" in: E.N. Zalta, *Stanford Encyclopaedia of Philosophy*. Stanford: Stanford University, 2011, §2, http://plato.stanford.edu/archives/spr2011/entries/equality/.

Greenfield, Jeanette. *The Return of Cultural Treasures*. Cambridge: Cambridge University Press, 2007.

Greiff, Pablo De. 2010. "A normative conception of Transitional Justice". In: Politorbis, *Dealing with the Past*, 210: 17 – 29.

Grønnow, Bjarne and Lund Jensen, Einar. "Utimut: Repatriation and collaboration between Denmark and Greenland". In: Gabriel and Dahl, *Utimut: Past Heritage*, 2008: 180 – 191.

Groot, Hans. *Van Batavia naar Weltevreden: Het Bataviaasch Genootschap van Kunsten en Wetenschappen, 1778 – 1867*. Leiden: KITLV, 2009.

Gulik, Willem Van. "Holding or losing: The return of cultural property". In: Zoest, Rob Van, ed. *Generators of Culture: The museum as a stage*. Amsterdam: AHA Books, 1989: 49 – 53.

Gustafsson Reinius, Lotten.
- *Touring Congo – Mobility and materiality in missionary media*. Stockholm: Museum of Ethnography, 2011.
- "Sacred matter and (post)secular frames in a Swedish Museum", in: Minucciani, V., *Religion and museums – Immaterial and material heritage*. Torino: Allemandi & C., 2013: 37 – 44.

Hansen, Thorkild. *Coast of Slaves, Ships of Slaves*, and *Island of Slaves* (trilogy). Accra: Sub-Saharan Publishers, 1972.

Hardiati, Endang Sri and Ter Keurs, Pieter, eds. *Indonesia: The discovery of the past*. Amsterdam: KIT Publishers, 2005.

Hardiati, Endang Sri.
- "From Batavian Society to Indonesian National Museum". In: Hardiati and Ter Keurs, *Discovery of Indonesia*, 2005: 11 – 19.
- "The Borobudur temple as a place of pilgrimage". In: Hardiati and Ter Keurs, *Discovery of Indonesia*, 2005: 49 – 51.

Hardjasoemantri, Koesnadi. "Penyerahan Benda Budaya kepada Indonesia" (Transfer of art objects to Indonesia – A cooperation between Indonesia and the Netherlands). In: *SSNB* (Indonesian Bulletin). The Hague: Embassy of Indonesia, [after] 1980: 8/13: 45.

Harvey, Miles. *The island of lost maps – A true story of cartographic crime*. Portland: Broadway books, 2001.

Herskovitch, Corinne and Rykner, Didier. *La Restitution des Œuvres d'Art*. Paris: Hazan, 2011.

History News Network. Reykjavik: Reykjavik Academy, 2006. http://historynewsnetwork.org/article/23720

Hochschild, Adam. *De geest van Koning Leopold II en de plundering van de Congo*. Amsterdam: Meulenhoff, 2000.

Hoffman, Carl. *Savage harvest – A tale of cannibals, colonialism, and Michael Rockefeller's tragic quest*. New York: Harper Collins, 2014.

Hol, Roelof.
- "A shared Legacy", congress-paper for '*Archives without Borders*'. The Hague: National Archive, 2010.
- "Gedeelde historie & archieven". In: *Vitruvius*. Rotterdam: Educom, January 2012: Vol. 18, 26 – 29.

Hollander, Hanneke. *Een man met een speurneus – Carel Groeneveldt (1899 – 1973), beroepsverzamelaar voor Tropenmuseum en Wereldmuseum in Nieuw Guinea*. Amsterdam: KIT Publishers, Bulletin 379, 2007.

Honoré, Tony. *About Law: An Introduction*. Oxford: Clarendon Press, 1995.

Hopkirk, Peter. *Barbaren langs de Zijderoute – Op zoek naar de verloren steden en schatten van Chinees Centraal Azië*. Baarn: Hollandia, 1991.

Hvidt, Birgitte and Skovgaard – Petersen, Karen. *Skatte – Treasures*: Copenhagen: Royal Library, 2003.

ICOM
- *One Hundred Missing Objects: Looting in Angkor*. Paris: ICOM, 1993/1997.
- *One Hundred Missing Objects: Looting in Africa*. Paris: ICOM, 1994/1997.
- *Illicit traffic of cultural property in Africa*. Paris: ICOM, 1995.
- *Illicit traffic of cultural property in Latin America*. Paris: ICOM, 1996.
- *One Hundred Missing Objects: Looting in Latin America*. Paris: ICOM, 1997.
- *One Hundred Missing Objects: Looting in Europe*. Paris: ICOM, 2000.
- *Protection of Cultural Heritage in Southeast Asia – Workshop proceedings, Hanoi, Vietnam 9 – 13 April 2001*: Paris: ICOM, 2000.
- *ICOM Code of Ethics for Museums*. Paris: ICOM, 2013, http://icom. museum/fileadmin/user_upload/pdf/ Codes/code_ethics2013_eng.pdf.
- ICOM ad hoc Committee for the Return of Cultural Property. *Return of Cultural Property to their Countries of Origin: Bangladesh*. Paris: ICOM, 1980.

ICOM-WIPO Art and Cultural Heritage Mediation,
http://icom.museum/programmes/ art-and-cultural-heritage-mediation/ icom-wipo-art-and-cultural-heritage- mediation/.

Ivanov, Paula and Plankensteiner, Barbara. *Benin – 600 Jahre höfische Kunst aus Nigeria*. Berlin: Ethnological Museum, 2008.

Jacobs, Karen. *Collecting Kamoro-objects, encounters and representation on the southwest coast of Papua*. Leiden: Sidestone Press, Mededelingen van Museum Volkenkunde 40, 2011.

Jacobs, Karen, Chantal Knowles and Chris Wingfield, eds. *Trophies, relics and curios? Missionary heritage from Africa and the Pacific*. Leiden: Sidestone Press, 2015.

Jacques, Claude. *Angkor*. Cologne: Könemann Verlagsgesellschaft, 1999.

Jansen, Maarten and Pérez, Gabina A. "Renaming the Mexican Codices". In: *Ancient Mesoamerica*. Cambridge: Cambridge University Press, 2004: 15/02, July 2004.

Jansen, Michael. *War and cultural heritage: Cyprus after the 1974 Turkish invasion*. Minneapolis: University of Minnesota, 2005.

Jansen van Galen, John.
- "De Weggemoffelde held". In: national daily *Trouw*, May 5. 2012.
- *Afscheid van de Koloniën – Het Nederlandse Dekolonisatiebeleid 1942 – 2012*. Amsterdam/Antwerpen: Atlas/ Contact, 2013.

Jegede, Dele. "Nigerian art as endangered species". In: Schmidt, Peter and McIntosh, Roderick, eds. *Plundering Africa's Past.* Bloomington and Indianapolis: Indiana University Press, 1996: 125 – 142.

Jong, Joop De. *De Waaier van het Fortuin – De Nederlanders in Azië en de Indonesische Archipel 1595 – 1950.* Den Haag: Sdu, 2000.

Junne, Gert and Verkoren, Willemijn, eds. *Postconflict development: Meeting new challenges.* London: Boulder, 2005.

Kalmeijer, Ans M.
- "Verslag van de reis naar Indonesië van de Nederlandse delegatie van het 'Team of Experts' betreffende de culturele samenwerking tussen Indonesië en Nederland op het gebied van archieven en musea – 10 t/m 22 november 1975". In: *National Archive,* Archive Foreign Ministry 1975 – 1984, Inv. No. 10266.
- *Verslag reis Indonesië 8 april – 6 mei 1978,* private archive (through Susan Legêne).

Karabinos, Michael Joseph. "Displaced archives, displaced history: Recovering the seized archives of Indonesia". In: *Bijdragen tot de Taal-, Land- en Volkenkunde.* Leiden: Brill, 2013/169: 279 – 294.

Kartiwa, Suwati. "Pusaka and the Palaces of Java". In: Soebadio, *Pusaka – Art of Indonesia,* 1992: 158 – 164.

Kluijver, Robert. *Contemporary Art in the Gulf – Context and Perspectives.* 2013 (self-published), http://www.sciencespo.fr/psia/sites/sciencespo.fr.psia/files/Contemporary%20Art%20in%20the%20Gulf%20for%20print.pdf.

Knaap, Gerrit, Den Heijer, Henk and Jong, Michiel De. *Oorlogen overzee – Militair optreden door Compagnie en Staat buiten Europa 1595 – 1814.* Amsterdam: Boom, 2015.

Knowles, Charles and Gosden, Chris. "A Century of Collecting: Colonial Collectors in Southwest New Britain". In: Attenbrow and Fullagar, *Pacific Odyssey,* 2000: 65 – 74.

Kom, Anton De. *Wij slaven van Suriname.* Amsterdam/Antwerpen: Contact [1934] 2009.

Kopytoff, Igor. "The cultural biography of things: commoditization as process". In: Appadurai, *Social Life of Things,* 1986: 64 – 91.

Kowalski, Wojciech. "Types of Claims for Recovery of Lost Cultural Property". In: *Museum International.* Paris: UNESCO, 2005: 57/4, 85 – 101.

Kriesberg, Louis. "The Evolution of Conflict Resolution". In: Bercovitch ea., *SAGE Handbook of conflict resolution,* 2009: 15 – 32.

Kristjánsdóttir, Steinunn. *The awakening of Christianity in Iceland – Discovery of a timber church and graveyard at Þórarinsstaðir in Seyðisfjörður.* Gothenburg: University of Gothenburg, Ph.D., 2004.

Kyong-hee, Lee. "Joseon Royal Books return home after 145 years". In: *Koreana, A Quaterly on Korean Culture and Arts.* Korea Foundation, No. 1851, http://www.koreana.or.kr/months/news_view.asp?b_idx=1576&lang=en.

Layiwola, (Ade)peju.
- "The Benin Massacre: Memories and Experiences". In: Plankensteiner, *Benin – Kings and Rituals,* 2007: 82 – 89.
- "Walker and the restitution of two Benin bronzes". In: *Premium Times.* Nigeria, June 20, 2014, https://www.premiumtimesng.com/arts-entertainment/165632-walker-and-the-restitution-of-two-benin-bronzes-by-peju-layiwola.html#sthash.zHmDyYEu.dpbs.

Laxness, Halldór. *IJslands Klok* (trilogy). Hasselt: Heideland, 1957.

Legêne, Susan.
- *De Bagage van Blomhoff en Van Breugel – Japan, Java, Tripoli en Suriname in de negentiende eeuwse Nederlandse cultuur van het imperialisme.* Amsterdam: KIT Publishers, 1998.
- Speeches and interviews (archive Legêne), 1998 – 2006.
- *Ratification/Implementation/ Commitment – What is the problem for our Governments?.* Copenhagen: Danish UNESCO Committee, Lecture, 2007.
- *Spiegelreflex – Culturele sporen van de koloniale ervaring.* Amsterdam: Bert Bakker, 2010.

Legêne, Susan and Postel-Coster, Els. "Isn't it all culture? Culture and Dutch development policy in the post-colonial period". In: Nekkers and Malcontent, *Fifty Years of Dutch Development Cooperation*, 2000: 271 – 288.

Legêne, Susan and Dijk, Janneke Van, eds. *The Netherlands East Indies and the Tropenmuseum.* Amsterdam: KIT Publishers, 2011.

Leiris, Michel. *L'Afrique fantôme.* Paris: Gallimard, [1934] 1981.

Lequin, Frank. *Het personeel van de Verenigde Oost-Indische Compagnie in Azië in de 18de eeuw, meer in het bijzonder in de vestiging Bengalen.* Alphen aan den Rijn: Canaletto, [1982] 2005.

Leturcq, Jean-Gabriel. "La question des restitutions d'oeuvres d'art : différentiels maghrébins ». In : *L'Année du Maghreb, 2008,* IV: 79 – 97, http:// anneemaghreb.revues.org/431.

Leyten, Harry. *From idol to art – African 'objects-with-power': A challenge for missionaries, anthropologists and museum curators.* Leiden: African Studies Centre, 2015.

Lewis, Myrna. *Inside the No – Five steps to decisions that last.* Johannesburg: 2008.

Lidwina, Intan. *Het Landsarchief – The history of the Landsarchief in Indonesia (1892 – 1942).* Leiden: Leiden University, 2012, Master thesis.

Lindgreen Pedersen, Anne Marie and Pedersen, Lykke L. *Danish Modern History: Stories of Denmark 1660 – 2000.* Copenhagen: National Museum, 2005.

Liu, Zuozhen. *The Case for Repatriating China's Cultural Objects.* Singapore: Springer, 2016.

Loftsdóttir, Kristín and Pálsson, Gísli. "Black on White: Danish colonialism, Iceland and the Caribbean". In: Naum and Nordin, *Scandinavian Colonialism,* 2013: 37 – 52.

Longhena, Maria. *Het oude Mexico: De geschiedenis en de cultuur van de Maya's, Azteken en andere pre-Columbiaanse volkeren.* Lisse: Zuid Boekproducties, 1998.

Longhena, Maria and Alva, Walter. *De Inca's: Geschiedenis en cultuur van de beschavingen in de Andes.* Lisse: Zuid Boekproducties, 1999.

Lubina, Katja. *Contested Cultural Property: The return of Nazi-spoliated art and human remains from public collections.* Maastricht: Maastricht University, Ph.D., 2009.

Lucas, Gavion and Parigoris, Angelos. "Icelandic Archaeology and the Ambiguities of Colonialism". In: Naum and Nordin, *Scandinavian Colonialism,* 2013: 89 – 105.

Lundahl, Mikela. *Nordic Complicity? Some aspects of Nordic identity as 'non-colonial' and non-participatory in the European colonial event.* 2006. https://www.academia.edu/245966/ Nordic_Complicity_Some_Aspects_ of_Nordic_Identity_As_Non-Colonial_and_Non-Participatory_In_ the_European_Colonial_Event.

Lundén, Staffan. *Displaying Loot: The Benin Objects and the British Museum.* Gothenburg: Gothenburg University, Ph.D., 2016.

Lunsing Scheurleer, Pauline. "Collecting Javanese Antiquities: The appropriation of a newly discovered Hindu-Buddhist civilization". In: Ter Keurs, *Colonial Collections Revisited,* 2007: 71 – 114.

MacGregor, Neil. *A history of the world in 100 objects.* London: Penguin, [1996] 2012.

MacKenzie, John M.
- *Museums and empire, natural history, human cultures and colonial identities,* Manchester: Manchester University Press, 2010.
- ed. *European empires and the people – Popular responses to imperialism in France, Britain, The Netherlands, Belgium, Germany and Italy.* Manchester: Manchester University Press, 2011.

Macquart, J. *Die Benin-Sammlung des Reichsmuseum für Völkerkunde in Leiden.* Leiden: E.J. Brill, 1913.

Maddison, Angus. *Contours of the world economy, 1 – 2030.* Oxford: Oxford University Press, 2007.

Malan, Jannie. "Indigenous dispute resolution and reconciliation: Past, present and future". Paper *International Conference on Indigenous Peace building and Dispute Resolution.* Gabarone: University of Botswana, Centre for Culture and Peace Studies, 2010, September 23 – 24.

Mann, Charles. *1493 – How Europe's Discovery of the Americas Revolutionized Trade, Ecology and Life on Earth.* London: Granta Books, 2011.

Marangou, Ana. *Life & Deeds – The Consul Luigi Palma di Cesnola 1832 – 1904,* Nicosia: Popular Bank Group, Cultural Centre, 2000.

Marck, Annemarie and Muller, Eelke. "National panels advising on Nazi-looted art in Austria, France, the United Kingdom, the Netherlands and Germany". In: Campfens, *Fair and Just Solutions?,* 2015: 41 – 89.

Mark, Simon. *A greater role for cultural diplomacy.* The Hague: Institute Clingendael, 2009, https://www.clingendael.nl/sites/default/files/20090616_cdsp_discussion_paper_114_mark.pdf.

Mauss, Marcel. *The gift: the form and reason for exchange in archaic societies.* London: Routledge, 1990.

Mayer, Carol E. "A green dress, Vanuaatu". In: Jacobs ea., *Trophies, Relics and Curios?,* 2015: 131 – 138.

Mbembe, Achille. *Kritiek van de zwarte rede.* Amsterdam: Boom, 2015.

M'bow, Amadou-Mahtar. "A plea for the return of irreplaceable culture heritage to those who created it". In: *UNESCO Courier.* Paris: UNESCO, 1978: July, 4 – 5.

Merryman, John Henry, ed. *Imperialism, art and restitution.* Cambridge: Cambridge University Press, 2006.

Metcalf, H. and Urwick, L. *Dynamic Administration – The Collected Papers of Mary Parker Follett.* London: Sir Isaac Pitman & Sons, [1941] 1963.

Mills, Andrew. "Female statuette, Tonga". In: Jacobs ea., *Trophies, Relics and Curios?,* 2015: 37 – 44.

Mishra, Pankaj. *From the Ruins of Empire – The Revolt against the West and the Remaking of Asia.* London: Allan Lane, 2012.

Moor, Jaap A. De and Velde, Paul Van der. *Uit menschlievendheid zoude ik barbaar kunnen worden – Reizen in Azië 1770 – 1830.* Amsterdam: Veen, 1992.

Moor, Jaap A. De, and Wesseling, Henk L., eds. *Imperialism and War: Essays on Colonial Wars in Overseas History*. Leiden: E.J. Brill, 1989.

Moyn, Samuel. *The last Utopia – Human Rights in History*. Princeton: Belknap Press of Harvard University Press, 2010.

Murdock, Graham. "Thin descriptions: Questions of method in cultural analysis". In: McGuigan, J., *Cultural Methodologies*. London: SAGE, 1997.

Musée National des Arts d'Afrique et d'Océanie. *Vallées du Niger*. Paris: Editions de la Réunion des Musées Nationaux, 1993.

Musonda, F.B.
- "How accurate are interpretations of African objects in western museums". In: Schmidt and McIntosh, *Plundering Africa's Past,* 1996: 164 – 169.
- "Decolonising the Broken Hill Skull: Cultural loss and a pathway to Zambian archaeological sovereignty". In: *African Archaeological Review*. New York: Springer, 2013: 30/195 – 220.

Naum, Magdalena and Nordin, Jonas, eds. *Scandinavian Colonialism and the Rise of Modernity – Small Time Agents in a Global Arena*. New York: Springer, 2013.

Ndoro, Webber. "Great Zimbabwe". In: http://www.scientificamerican.com/article/great-zimbabwe-2005-01/.

Nekkers, J.A.M. and Malcontent, P., eds. *Fifty Years of Dutch Development Cooperation 1949 – 1999*. The Hague: Sdu Publishers, 2000.

Neuman, W. Lawrence. *Understanding Research*. Boston: Pearson – Prentice Hall, 2012.

Nicholas, Lynn H. *The Rape of Europe: The Fate of Europe's Treasures in the Third Reich*. New York: Vintage Books, 1995.

Nielsen, Erland Kolding. "Denmark to Iceland. A Case without Precedence: Delivering Back the Islandic Manuscripts 1971-1997", paper *68th IFLA Council and General Conference*. Glascow: August 18 – 24, 2002. http://archive.ifla.org/IV/ifla68/papers/Kolding_Nielsen02.pdf.

Nooy-Palm, Hetty. "Treasure hunters in the field: Collecting ethnographic artefacts in the Netherlands East Indies (1750 – 1940)". In: Schefold and Vermeulen, *Treasure Hunting?*, 2002: 47 – 80.

Noyes, James. *The politics of Iconoclasm – Religion, violence and the culture of image-breaking in Christianity and Islam*. London/New York: Tauris, 2016.

Nussbaum, Martha. *Creating capabilities: The human development approach*. Cambridge/Massachusetts/London: Belknap Press of Harvard University Press, 2011.

Ogbechie, Sylvester Okwunodo. *Making History: African Collectors and the Canon of African Art*, http://olaleredot.blogspot.nl/2012/02/making-history-femi-akinsanya-art.html.

O'Hanlon, Michael and Welch, Robert L., eds. *Hunting the gatherers – Ethnographic collectors, agents and agency in Melanesia, 1870s -1930s*. New York/Oxford: Berghahn Books, 2000.

O'Keefe, Patrick J.
- *Commentary on the 1970 UNESCO Convention – Second Edition*. Pentre Moel, Crickadarn, Builth Wells: Institute of Art and Law, 2007.
– "A comparison of the Washington and Vilnius Principles and Resolution 1205". In: Prott, *Witnesses to History*, 2009: 158 – 162.

O'Keefe, Patrick J. and Prott, Lyndel V.
- "'Cultural Heritage' or 'Cultural Property'?". In: *International Journal of Cultural Property*. Cambridge: Cambridge University Press, 1992/1: 307 – 320.

- *Cultural Heritage Conventions and Other Instruments: A compendium with commentaries.* Pentre Moel, Crickadarn, Builth Wells: Institute of Art and Law, 2011.

Okoro, Mazi Azubike. *Perspectives on Aro history and civilization: The splendour of a great past, Vol. 2.* Lulu Public Services (self-publishing), 2015, www.aronewsonline.com/files/Articles.doc.

Opoku, Kwame.
- "Can we condemn contemporary looting of artefacts without condemning colonial loot and plunder? Comment on Lord Renfrew's Statement on Looted Artefacts". In: *Modern Ghana.* Accra: 2008. http://www.modernghana.com/news/193144/50/can-we-condemn-contemporary-looting-of-artefacts-w.html.
- "Reflections on the abortive Queen-mother Idia mask auction: Tactical withdrawal or decision of principle?". In: *Museum Security Network*, 2011, http://www.museum-security.org/.
- "When will Britain return looted golden Ghanaian artefacts? A history of British looting of more than 100 objects". In: *Modern Ghana.* Accra: 2011.
- "Virtual visits to museums holding looted Benin objects". In: *Museum Security Network*, 2012, http://www.museum-security.org/opoku_benin_virtual_museum.htm.
- "Nigeria Reacts to Donation of Looted Benin Artefacts to Museum of Fine Arts, Boston". In: *Museum Security Network*, 2012.
- "Blood antiquities in respectable heavens: Looted Benin artefacts donated to American museum". In: *Modern Ghana.* Accra: 2012, http://www.modernghana.com/news/405992/1/blood-antiquities-in-respectable-havens-looted-ben.html.
- "Declaration on the Importance and Value of Universal Museums: Singular failure of an arrogant imperialist project". In: *Modern Ghana.* Accra: 2013. http://www.modernghana.com/news/441891/1/declaration-on-the-importance-and-value-of-univers.html.
- "'Benin Plan of Action for Restitution'- Will this ensure the return of looted Benin artifacts?". In: *Modern Ghana.* Accra: 2013, http://www.modernghana.com/news/449521/1/benin-plan-of-action-for-restitution-will-this-ens.html.
- "Benin Plan of Action (2): Will the miserable project be the last word on the looted Benin artefacts?". In: *Modern Ghana.* Accra: 2013, http://www.modernghana.com/news/451636/1/benin-plan-of-action-2-will-this-miserable-project.html.
- "Will Nigeria finally raise restitution of Benin Bronzes at UNESCO Governmental Committee". In: *Museum Security Network*, 2013, http://www.museum-security.org/will%20nigeria%20finally%20raise%20restitution%20of%20benin%20bronzes%20at%20unesco%20intergovernmental%20committee.htm.
- "Rat and rabbit sculptures returned to China by owner of Christie's". In: *Modern Ghana.* Accra: 2013, http://www.modernghana.com/news/462152/1/rat-and-rabbit-sculptures-returned-t.html.
- "What are they really celebrating at the Musée du quai Branly, Paris?". In: *Pambazuka News.* Wantage Oxon: May 5, 2016, http://www.pambazuka.org/arts/what-are-they-really-celebrating-mus%C3%A9e-du-quai-branly-paris.

Östberg, Wilhelm. "The coveted treasures of the Kingdom of Benin". In: Stockholm Museum of Ethnography, *Whose Objects?*, 2010: 52 -71.

Pakenham, Thomas. *The scramble for Africa – The white man's conquest of the dark continent from 1876 to 1912*. New York: Random House, 1991.

Panella, Cristiana. *Les terres cuites de la discorde: Deterrement et écoulement des terres cuites anthropomorphes de Mali*. Leiden: Research School of Asian, African and Amerindian Studies, Leiden University, Ph.D., 2002.

Pasztory, Esther. *Pre-Columbian art*. London: Weidenfeld and Nicholson, 1998.

Pentz, Peter, ed. *Utimut – Return: The Return of more than 35.000 Cultural Objects to Greenland*. Nuuk/Copenhagen: Greenland National Museum & Archives/National Museum of Denmark, 2004.

Pesch, A.M.C. Van and Campbell, H.W. *Missionaire collecties in beeld: Een onderzoek naar de omvang en herkomst van verspreide volkenkundige collecties van missionaire oorsprong*. Maarssen: self published, 1992.

Petersen, Robert. "Colonialism as seen from a former colonized area". In: *Arctic Anthropology*. Madison: University of Wisconsin, 1995: 32/2: 118-126.

Pigeaud, Theo G. *Literature of Java – Catalogue raisonné of Javanese manuscripts in the Library of the University of Leiden and other public collections in the Netherlands*. Leiden: Bibliotheca Universitatis Leidensis – Codices Manuscipti:
- *Volume I Synopsis of Javanese Literature 900 – 1900 AD* (1967)
- *Volume II Descriptive list of Javanese manuscripts* (1968)
- *Volume II Illustrations and facsimiles of manuscripts, maps, addenda and a general index* (1970)

Pitt Rivers, Augustus H.L. *Antique Works of Art from Benin collected by Lieutenant- General Pitt Rivers*, printed privately, 1900 (via library Museum Volkenkunde, Leiden).

Plankensteiner, Barbara.
- ed. *Benin Kings and Rituals – Court Arts from Nigeria*. Wien: Museum für Völkerkunde, 2007.
- "The Benin treasures -Difficult legacy and contested heritage", in: eds. Hauser-Schäublin, Brigitta and Prott, Lyndel V. *Cultural property and contested ownership – The trafficking of artefacts and the quest for restitution*. London and New York: Routledge, 2016: 133 – 155.
- "Return and Dialogue – two sets of experiences from Vienna". In: eds. Buehler, Marcel and Schaluske, Anja. *Positioning Ethnological Museums in the 21st Century*. Berlijn: Deutschen Museumbund, 2016: Museumkunde, Band 81.

Polimé, Thomas. "Maroon collections in Western museums and their meaning". In: ed. Moomou, Jean. *Sociétés marronnes des Amériques – Mémoires, patrimoines, identités et histoire du XVIIe et XXe siècles*. Matoury: IBIS Rouge Editions, 2015: 353 – 361.

Politorbis, magazine. "Dealing with the Past". Bern: Swiss Foreign Ministry, 2010/3.

Pool, Mariska. *Vergeten vlaggen: De trofeeën van het eskader – Van Braam in de Indische archipel, 1784*, http://collectie.legermuseum.nl/sites/strategion/contents/i004530/arma36%20vergeten%20vlaggen.pdf.

Pott, Pieter.
- "Rapport inzake de gouden sieraden in het bezit van het Rijksmuseum voor Volkenkunde te Leiden". Leiden: *Museum Volkenkunde*, Archive P. Pott – 'divers – divers', 1949.

- "Kort verslag van de missie van deskundigen naar Indonesië ter bespreking van problemen en mogelijke oplossingen terzake van de overdracht van voorwerpen en archieven in het kader van de culturele samenwerking tussen Nederland en Indonesië, 10 – 22 november 1975". Leiden, *Museum Volkenkunde*, Seriearchief NL-LdnRMV 360-1.

Pott, Pieter and Sutaarga, M. Amin. "Arrangements concluded or in progress for the Return of Objects: the Netherlands – Indonesia". In: *Museum*. Paris: UNESCO, 1979: XXXI: 38 – 42.

Powers, John. *History as Propaganda: Tibetan exiles versus the People's Republic of China*. Oxford: Oxford University Press, 2004.

Prashad, Vikaj. *The Darker Nations – A People's History of the Third World*. New York/London: The New Press, 2007.

Prott, Lyndel. V.
- "UNESCO and UNIDROIT: a Partnership against Trafficking in Cultural Objects". Paris: 1996, http://www.unidroit.org/english/conventions/1995culturalproperty/articles/s70-prott-1996-e.pdf
- ed. *Witnesses to History: Documents and Writings on the Return of Cultural Objects*. Paris: UNESCO Publishing, 2009.
- "Strengths and Weaknesses of the 1970 Convention: An Evaluation 40 years after its adoption – Background paper (2nd edition) for Second Meeting of States Parties in the 1970 Convention". Paris: UNESCO, 20 – 21 June, 2012.

Quinnell, Michael. "'Before it is too late' – The making and repatriation of Sir William MacGregor's official collection from British New Guinea". In: eds. O'Hanlon and Welch, *Hunting the Gatherers*, 2000: 81 – 102.

Rainero, R. H. "The Battle of Adowa on 1st March 1896: A Reappraisal". In: Moor and Wesseling, *Imperialism and War*, 1989: 189 – 200.

Raffles, Thomas S. *The History of Java* (2 Vol.). Oxford: Oxford University Press, [1817] 1978.

Ramsbotham, Oliver, Woodhouse, Tom, and Miall, Hugh. *Contemporary Conflict Resolution: The prevention, management and transformation of deadly conflicts*. Cambridge, UK/ Malden, USA: Polity Press, 2011.

Rasmussen, Peter Ravn. *Tranquebar – The Danish East India Company 1616 – 1669, University of Copenhagen*. 1996, http://scholiast.org/history/tra-narr.html.

Rassool, Ciraj. "Human remains, the disciplines of the dead and the South African memorial complex". In: Peterson, Derek, Gavua, Kodzo and Rassool, Ciraj. *The politics of heritage in Africa*. Cambridge: Cambridge University Press, 2015: 133 – 156.

Raven – Hart, R. *The Dutch Wars in Kandy*. Colombo: Government Publications Bureau, 1964, via http://www.defonseka.com/ref_dutch_wars02.htm.

Ray, Himanshu Prabha. *The Return of the Buddha: Ancient Symbols for a New Nation*. Abingdon: Taylor and Amp, 2013.

Reid, Andrew and Ashley, Ceri Z. "A context for the Luzira Head". In: *Antiquity*. Cambridge: Cambridge University Press, 2000: 82 (315) 99 – 112.

Renfrew, Colin.
- *Loot, Legitimacy and Ownership*. London: Duckworth, 2001.
- "Museum Acquisitions: Responsibilities for the Illicit Traffic in Antiquities". In: Brodie ea., *Cultural heritage, and the antiquities trade*, 2006: 245 – 257.

Renold, Marc-André., Bandle, Anne-Laure, and Chechi, Alessandro. "Case Great Zimbabwe Bird – Zimbabwe and Prussia Cultural Heritage Foundation, Germany". In: *Platform ArThemis.* Geneva: University of Geneva, Art-Law Centre, 2013, http://unige.ch/art-adr.

Reybrouck, David Van. *Congo – Een geschiedenis.* Amsterdam: De Bezige Bij, 2010.

Roque, Ricardo. *Headhunting and colonialism – Anthropology and the circulation of human skulls in the Portuguese empire, 1870 – 1930.* Basingstoke: Palgrave – Macmillan, 2010.

Rosing Jakobsen, Aviâja. "The repatriation of Greenland's cultural heritage from Denmark to Greenland". In: Laura Van Broekhoven ea., *Sharing Knowledge & Cultural Heritage*, 2010: 75 – 82.

Rossum, Matthias Van. *Kleurrijke tragiek – De geschiedenis van de slavernij in Azië onder de VOC.* Hilversum: Verloren, 2015.

Said, Edward. W.
- *Orientalism.* New York: Vintage Books, [1978] 2003.
- *Culture and Imperialism*, London: Vintage, 1994.

Salem, Paul. "Critique of Western Conflict Resolution from a Non-Western Perspective". In: *Negotiation Journal.* Cambridge, MA: Harvard Law School, 1993: 9/4: 361 – 369.

Santa Barbara, Joanna, Galtung, Johan and Perlman, Diane. *Reconciliation: Clearing the Past, Building a Future.* Basel: Transcend University Press, 2012.

Saunders, Harold H. "Dialogue as a Process for Transforming Partnerships". In: Bercovitch ea., *SAGE handbook of conflict resolution*, 2009: 376 – 391.

Schefold, Reimar and Vermeulen, Han F., eds. *Treasure Hunting? Collectors and collections of Indonesian artefacts.* Leiden: Mededelingen van het Rijksmuseum voor Volkenkunde 30, 2002.

Schildkrout, Enid and Keim, Curtis A., eds. *The scramble for art in Central Africa*, Cambridge: Cambridge University Press. 1998

Schmidt, Peter R. and McIntosh, Roderick. *Plundering Africa's Past.* Bloomington: Indiana University Press, 1996.

Scholten, Steph, ed. *Sense and Sensitivities: The Dutch and Delicate Heritage Issues.* Rotterdam: ICOM Netherlands, 2010.

Schulte Nordholt, Henk. "A genealogy of violence". In: Colombijn and Lindblad, *Roots of Violence in Indonesia*, 2002: 33 – 62.

Schulze, Dorothee. *Die Restitution von Kunstwerken: Zur Völkerrechtlichen Dimension der Restitutionsresolutionen der Generalversammlung der Vereinigten Nationen.* Bremen: Ganslmayr, 1983.

Schuylenbergh, Patricia Van. *La Mémoire des Belges en Afrique Centrale – Inventaire des Archives Historiques Privées du Musée Royal de l'Afrique Centrale de 1858 á Nos Jours.* Tervuren: Royal Museum of Central Africa, 1997: Inventory of Historical Archives, Vol. 8.F

Scott, Cynthia.
- "Sharing the divisions of the colonial past: an assessment of the Netherlands-Indonesia shared cultural heritage project, 2003 – 2006". In: *International Journal of Heritage Studies.* London: Taylor & Francis Online, 2012.
- *Negotiating the colonial past in the age of European decolonization: Cultural property return between the Netherlands and Indonesia.* Claremont: Claremont Graduate University, Ph.D., 2014.

Scott, Geoffrey .R. "Spoliation, cultural property, and Japan". In: *Journal of International Law*. Philadelphia: University of Pennsylvania Law School, 2008: 29/4: 803 – 902.

Sedyawati, Edi. "The Sculpture of the Singasari Period". In: Hardiati and Ter Keurs, *Discovery of Indonesia*, 2005: 34 – 39.

Sen, Amartya.
- *Development as Freedom*, Oxford: Oxford University Press, 1999.
- *Identity and Violence: The illusion of Destiny*. New York – London: Norton, 2006.
- *The Idea of Justice*, London: Penguin Books, 2010.

Shatanawi, Miriam. *Islam at the Tropenmuseum*. Arnhem: LM Publishers, 2014.

Shipway, Martin. *Decolonisation and its impact: A Comparative approach to the end of colonial empires*. Malden: Blackwell, 2008.

Shyllon, Folarin.
- 2000. "The recovery of cultural objects by African States through the UNESCO and UNIDROIT Conventions and the role of arbitration". In: *Revue de droit uniforme*. Paris: UNIDROIT, 2000: 2, 219 – 241.
- *Museums and universal heritage: Right of return and right of access*. 2007, http:// www.blackherbals.com/museums_and_ universal_heritage.htm.
- 2016. "Imperial Rule of Law Trumping the Return of Benin Bronzes and Parthenon Sculptures and the Failure of the Dialogue for the Return of Benin Bronzes". Amsterdam: paper *Network Conference of the Historical Dialogues, Justice and Memory Network*, December 1 – 3, 2016 (unplubl.).

Shyllon, Folarin, Négri, Vincent and Schneider, Marina. "The role of national and international legal instruments in the protection of African cultural goods". Addis Ababa: paper *2nd Pan African Cultural Congress*, 5 – 7 October, 2009 (unpubl.).

Schultz-Lorentzen, Helge. "Return of cultural property by Denmark to Greenland: From dream to reality". In: *Museum*. Paris: UNESCO, 1988.

Sidibé, Samuel.
- 1996. "The fight against the plundering of Malian cultural heritage and illicit exportation: National efforts and international cooperation". In: Schmidt and McIntosh, *Plundering Africa's Past*, 1996: 79 – 86.
- "Priver des communautés de leur patrimoine n'est pas justifiable ». In: *La Recherche – L'actualité des sciences*. Paris: Mensuel 445/Octobre 1, 2010: 82.

Silva, P.H.D.H. De.
- *A catalogue of antiquities and other cultural objects from Sri Lanka (Ceylon) abroad*. Colombo, National Museums of Sri Lanka, 1975.
- "Sri Lanka". In: *Museum*. Paris: UNESCO, Quarterly review, 1979: XXXI/1, 22 – 25.

Sitowati, Retno S. and Miksic, John N. *Icons of Art – National Museum of Jakarta*. Jakarta: National Museum, 2006.

Smidt, Dirk.
- "Report of the Symposium: The art of Oceania held at Hamilton, Canada: (from 21 Aug. till 27 Aug. 1974) and of visits to museums in Australia, New Zealand, Mexico and the United States of America from 25 July till 6 Sept. 1974". Port Moresby: *Papua New Guinea Museum*, 1975.
- *The seized collections of the Papua New Guinea Museum*. Port Moresby: Creative Arts Centre, University, 1975.

Smith, Laurajane. *Uses of heritage*. London: Routledge, 2006.

Soebadio, Haryati, ed. *Pusaka – Art of Indonesia*. Jakarta: Archipelago Press with National Museum, 1992.

Soerjaningrat, R.M. Soewardi. *Als ik eens Nederlander was....*, Bandoeng: Inlandsch Comité tot Herdenking van Neêrlands Honderdjarige Vrijheid, 1913.

Sotheby. *Catalogue of Works of Art from Benin: The property of a European private collector – Monday*. Amsterdam: Sotheby, 16th June 1980.

Southworth, William A. "The Disembodied Human Head in Southeast Asian Art". In: *Aziatische Kunst*. Amsterdam: Rijksmuseum, 2013: 43/2/June: 27 – 30.

Soyinka, Wole. *The burden of memory, the music of forgiveness*. Oxford: Oxford University Press, 1999.

Specht, Jim.
- "The Australian Museum and the return of artefacts to Pacific Island countries". In: *Museum*. Paris: UNESCO, 1979: XXXI/1: 28-31
- *Pieces of Paradise*. Sydney: Australian Museum Trust, Australian Natural History, Supplement 1, 1988.

Spivak, Gayatri. "Can the Sub-altern speak?". The article was revised in: Rosalind C. Morris ed., *Can the Subaltern Speak – Reflections on the history of an idea*, New York: Columbia University Press, 2010.

Stevens, Harm.
- "Collecting and 'The rough work of subjugation' – Van Daalen, Snouck Hurgronje and the ethnographic exploitation of North Sumatra". In: Hardiati and Ter Keurs, *Discovery of Indonesia*, 2005: 76 – 84.
- "The resonance of violence in collections". In: Legêne and Dijk, *The Netherlands East Indies*, 2011: 28 – 37.

- *Bitter spice – Indonesia and the Netherlands from 1600*. Nijmegen: Vantilt, 2015.

Stevens, Harm, Stoopman, Jos and Verhoeven, Pauljac. *De laatste Batakkoning – Koloniale kroniek in documenten 1883 – 1911*. Arnhem: Museum Bronbeek, 2010.

Stockholm Museum of Ethnography. *Whose Objects? Art Treasures from the Kingdom of Benin in the Collection of the Museum of Ethnography in Stockholm*. Stockholm: Museum of Ethnography, 2010.

Straaten, Harald Van der. "Terug of houden zo? Restitutie van cultuurschatten". In: *Verre Naasten Naderbij*. Leiden: Museum Volkenkunde, 1985: 19/1, april, 19 – 36.

Stuurman, Siep. *De Uitvinding van de Mensheid: Korte Wereldgeschiedenis van het Denken over Gelijkheid en Cultuurverschil*. Amsterdam: Bert Bakker, 2010.

Sudarmadi, Tular. *Between colonial legacies and grassroots movements: Exploring cultural heritage practice in the Ngadha and Manggarai Region of Flores*. Amsterdam: Free University, Ph.D., 2014.

Sumadio, Bambang. "Indonesia's Cultural Evolution". In: Soebadio, *Pusaka – Art of Indonesia*, 1992: 19 – 24.

Sutaarga, M. Amin. "The role of museums in Indonesia: Collecting documents from the past and the present for a better future". In: Schefold and Vermeulen, *Treasure Hunting?*, 2002: 281 – 282.

Sweet, Jonathan. "Colonial museology and the Buddhist chronicles of Sri Lanka: agency and negotiation in the development of the palm-leaf manuscript collection at the Colombo Museum". In: *Museum & Society*. Leicester: Leicester University, 2014, November, 12/3: 225 – 246.

Symonds, James. "Colonial Encounters of the Nordic Kind". In: Naum and Nordin, *Scandinavian Colonialism*, 2013: 307 -320.

Sysling, Fenneke.
- "Dead Bodies, Lively Debates: Human Remains in Dutch Museums". In: Scholten, *Sense and Sensitivities*, 2010: 52 – 61.
- *The archipelago of difference – Physical anthropology in the Netherlands East Indies, ca. 1890-1960.* Amsterdam: Free University, Ph.D., 2013.
- *De onmeetbare mens – Schedels, ras en wetenschap in Nederlands-Indië.* Nijmegen: Van Tilt, 2015.

Tarekat, Hasti. 2012. "Monumentenzorg in Indonesië". In: *Vitruvius/Indonesië-special.* Rotterdam: Educom, 2012: 1, 9 – 13.

Ter Keurs, Pieter.
- "Collecting in Central- and South Sumatra". In: Hardiati and Ter Keurs, *Discovery of Indonesia*, 2005: 85 – 89.
- ed. *Colonial Collections Revisited*, Leiden: CNWS Publications, 2007.

Thorleifsen, Daniel.
- "Preface", In: Gabriel and Dahl, *Utimut*, 2008: 8 – 11.
- "The repatriation of Greenland's cultural heritage". In: *Museum International.* Paris: UNESCO, 2009: Vol. 241/242, 25-29.

Tómas, Jordi. "The traditional authorities cross the border: Opposing views on the role of the religious leaders of the Jola Huluf and Ajamaat of the Lower Casamance", in *Africana Studia*, 9. Porto: University of Porto, 2006, 73 – 97. http://www.theguardian.com/world/2014/nov/03/france-museums-restitution-colonial-objects .

Tshiluila, Shaje'a. "Measures for the Protection of Cultural Heritage in Developing Countries". In: *Illicit Traffic of Cultural Property in Africa.* Paris: ICOM, 1995: 183 – 187.

Toft, Peter A. and Seiding, Inge Høst. "Circumventing colonial policies: Consumption and family life as social practices in the early nineteenth-century Disko Bay". In: Naum and Nordin, *Scandinavian Colonialism*, 2013: 105 – 129.

Trigangga, Sukati, Peni Mudji and Ismail, Djunaldi. "Three centuries of collections". In: Sitowati and Miksic, *Icons of Art*, 2006: 72 – 89.

Tygesen, Peter and Waehle, Epsen. *Congospor: Norden I Congo – Congo I Norden.* Copenhagen: National Museum, 2006.

Tythacott, Louise. "Trophies of War: Representing 'Summer Palace' Loot in Military Museums in the UK". In: *Museum & Society.* Leicester: Leicester University, November 2015, 13/4: 469 – 488.

UK Department for Culture, Media and Sport. *Working group on human remains report*, November 14, 2003 (Updated February 9, 2007). London: Department for Culture, Media and Sport, 2003, http://webarchive.nationalarchives.gov.uk/20100113212249/http://www.culture.gov.uk/reference_library/publications/4553.aspx.

UNESCO. "Return and restitution of cultural property". In: *Museum Quarterly review.* Paris: UNESCO, 1979: XXXI/1.

Urbinati, Sabrina. "Alternative Dispute Resolution Mechanisms in Cultural Property Related Disputes: UNESCO Mediation and Conciliation Procedures". In: Vadia and Schneider, *Art, Cultural Heritage and the Market*, 2014: 93 – 116.

Urice, Stephen K. "The beautiful one has come – To stay". In: Merryman, *Imperialism, Art and Restitution*, 2006: 135 – 165.

Vadi, Valentina and Schneider, Hildegard, eds.
- "Art and Heritage Disputes in International and Comparative Law". Issue in: *Transnational Dispute Management (TDM)*. OGEMID: 2013: 10/5, http://www.transnational-dispute-management.com/journal-browse-issues-toc.asp?key=50.
- *Art, Cultural Heritage and the Market*. Heidelberg: Springer, 2014.

Vanvugt, Ewald.
- *De Schatten van Lombok: Honderd Jaar Nederlandse Oorlogsbuit uit Indonesië*. Amsterdam: Jan Mets, 1994.
- *Nestbevuilers. 400 jaar Nederlandse critici van het koloniale bewind in de Oost en de West*. Breda: De Geus, 1996.
- *Roofgoed: Het Europese museum van overzeese gestolen schatten – met de monumenten voor de dieven*. Soesterberg: Aspekt, 2010.

Veraart, Wouter.
- *Ontrechting en rechtsherstel in Nederland en Frankrijk in de jaren van bezetting en wederopbouw*. Deventer: Kluwer, Ph.D., 2005.
- "Between justice and legal closure. Looted art claims and the passage of time". In: Campfens, *Fair and Just Solutions?*, 2015: 211 – 221.

Ver Loren van Themaat, Tessa. *Royaal geschenk of koninklijke buit? Een onderzoek naar de krissen die door het koninklijk Kabinet van Zeldzaamheden verzameld zijn tussen 1817 en 1835*. Amsterdam: Vrije Universiteit, Bachelor thesis, 2010 (unpubl.).

Vicien-Milburn, Maria, García Márquez, Asoid and Papaefstratiou, Fouchard: "UNESCO's role in the resolution of disputes on the recovery of cultural property". In: *Art and Heritage Disputes in International and Comparative Law, Transnational Dispute Management (TDM)*. OGEMID: 5/2013.

Vlasblom, Dirk. *Papoea – Een geschiedenis*. Amsterdam: Mets & Schilt, 2004.

Vrdoljak, Ana F.
- *International Law, Museums and the Return of Cultural Objects*, Cambridge: Cambridge University Press, 2008.
- "Restitution of Cultural Property Trafficked During Colonization: A Human Rights Perspective". In: Ministry of Foreign Affairs and Trade of Korea, *Strategies to Build the International Network for the Return of Cultural Property*. Seoul: Korean National Commission for UNESCO, 2011: 197 – 208.
- *Human Rights and Illicit Trade in Cultural Objects*, Berkeley: Berkeley Electronic Press, 2012, https://works.bepress.com/ana_filipa_vrdoljak/20/.

Waehle, Espen. *Entrepreneurs in the Congo? Two case studies on possibilities for making money among Norwegians in the Congo Free-state*. Bergen: University of Bergen, 2014, http://www.uib.no/en/rg/colonialtimes/78215/entrepreneurs-congo.

Wassing – Visser, Rita. *Koninklijke Geschenken uit Indonesië: Historische banden met het Huis Oranje-Nassau (1600 – 1938)*. Zwolle: Waanders, 1995.

Wastiau, Boris.
- *Congo – Tervuren: Aller – Retour: Le transfert de pièces ethnographiques du Musée royal de l'Afrique central à l'Institut des Musées nationaux du Zaïre 1976 – 1982*. Tervuren: Royal Museum for Central Africa, 2000.
- *Exit Congo Museum*. Tervuren: Royal Museum for Central Africa, 2000.

- "The Legacy of Collecting: Colonial Collecting in the Belgian Congo and the Duty of Unveiling Provenance". American Historical Association, 2009 Annual Meeting (unedited paper), https://aha.confex.com/aha/2009/webprogram/Paper3035.html.

Waxman, Sharon. *Loot: The battle over the stolen treasures of the ancient world*. New York: Times Books, 2008.

Weener, Frans-Karel. *Missionary exhibitions in the Netherlands*. 2010 (unpubl.).

Weiner, Annette. *Inalienable possessions – The paradox of keeping while giving*, Berkeley: University of California Press, 1992.

Wekker, Gloria. *White innocence: Paradoxes of colonialism and race*. Durham and London: Duke University Press, 2016.

Wengen, Ger Van.
- *'Wat is er te doen in Volkenkunde?' De bewogen geschiedenis van het Rijksmuseum voor Volkenkunde in Leiden*. Leiden: Museum Volkenkunde, 2002.
- "Indonesian collections in the National Museum of Ethnology in Leiden". In: Schefold and Vermeulen, *Treasure Hunting?*, 2002: 81 – 108.

Wesseling, Henk J.
- "Colonial wars: an introduction". In: De Moor and Wesseling, *Imperialism and War*, 1989: 2 – 11.
- *The European Colonial Empires 1815 – 1919*: Harlow, UK: Pearson, 2004.
- *De Man die nooit nee zei – Charles de Gaulle 1890 – 1970*. Amsterdam: Bert Bakker, 2013.

Westerman, Frank. *El Negro en ik*. Amsterdam: Atlas, 2004.

Westfries Museum. *Coen! Geroemd en verguisd*. Hoorn: Westfries Museum, 2012.

Wickramasinghe, Nikra. "The return of Keppetipola's cranium: The construction of authenticity in Sri Lankan nationalism". In: Pandey, Gyanendra and Geschiere, Peter. *The forging of nationhood*. New Dehli: Manohar, 2003: 129 – 155.

Williams, John. *A Narrative of missionary enterprises in the South Sea Islands*. London: Snow, 1838.

Williams, Susan. *Who killed Hammarskjöld? The UN, the Cold War and white supremacy in Africa*. London: Hurst, 2013.

Willink, Robert Joost.
- *De bewogen verzamelgeschiedenis van de West-Centraal-Afrikaanse collecties in Nederland (1856-1889)*. Leiden: Leiden University, Ph.D., 2006.
- *The Fateful Journey: The Expedition of Alexine Tinne and Theodor von Heuglin in Sudan (1863-1864)*. Amsterdam: Amsterdam University Press, 2011.

Wilson, John. *Failed Hope: The Story of the Lost Peace*. Toronto: Dundurn Books, 2012.

Zanten, Jeroen Van. *Koning Willem II 1792 – 1849*. Amsterdam: Boom, 2013.

Zantwijk, Rudolf Van, transl./ed. *De oorlog tegen de Goden – Azteekse kronieken over de Spaanse Verovering, uit het Nahuatl vertaald*. Amsterdam: Meulenhoff, 1992.

Zeleke, Meron. "*Ye Shakoch Chilot* (the court of the sheiks): A traditional institution of conflict resolution in Oromiya zone of Amhara regional state, Ethiopia". In: *African Journal on Conflict Resolution*. Mount Edgecombe, South Africa: 2010: 63 – 84.

Zweers, Louis. "Sukarno's art collection". In: *The Newsletter*. Leiden: International Institute of Asian Studies, 2014/Spring: 6 – 7.

Index

Algeria
- archives, 87;
- general, 81, 82, nt. 82, 86;
- returns, 25, 88, 237;
- war booty, 72.

Archives
deliberate destruction, 47, 86;
general, 24, 47, 48, 57, 60, 72, 77, 86,
    112, 124, 232, 235, 242 – 243;
returns to
- Algeria, 237;
- Australia, 24;
- Iceland, 190;
- Indonesia, chapter 7 and 8;
- Namibia, 25;
- Papua New Guinea, 205, 210;
- Suriname, 47, 48, 235.

Argentina
New Zealand (return Maori head), 109.

Aruba
the Netherlands, 19.

Australia
Aboriginal peoples, 105, 166, 202;
Australian Museum, Sydney, 202, 203,
    205, 210;
itself a colony, 201;
Papua New Guinea
- general, 68, 201, 203, 235, 244, 248;
- return of archives, 205, 210;
- return of human remains, 107;
Queensland Museum, Brisbane, 68, 204,
    209, 210;
return debate, 206 – 208, 236, 246;
returns from
- Austria, 107;
- Great Britain, 24, 206;
- the Netherlands, 206;
returns to
- New Zealand (Maori head), 109;
- Solomon Islands, 207, 210;
- Vanuaatu, 207;
Specht, Jim, 90, 202, 205, 208.

Austria
Benin Dialogue, 111, 213 – 226;
China, 69, 84;
kris of Diponegoro, 17;
Montezuma II, Aztec Emperor, 58;
New Zealand (return Maori head), 109;
South Africa (return San remains), 107.

Belgium
Berlin Conference, see *Berlin Conference*;
DR Congo, chapter 9;
DR Congo archives, 181, 184;
Cahen, Lucien, 179 – 182, 196, 248;
King Leopold II, 43, 45, 55, 71, 78, 86,
    177 – 179;
Mobutu Sese Seko, see *DR Congo*;
mineral wealth DR Congo, 83, 86, 89,
    177 – 179, 181, 235;
returns to DR Congo, chapter 9, 184;
return to Iran: Khurvin treasure, 104;
Tervuren Museum (Royal Museum for
    Central Africa), 25, 43, 78, 117,
    177 – 184.

Benin (State of)
claiming objects, 91, 117, 246;
lost objects, 71, 74, 116.

Berlin Conference 1884 – 1885
European interests, 42 nt. 92, 63, 77;
King Leopold II, 177, 178;
mobility missionaries, scientists and
    collectors, 42, 71.

Missionary collecting

Asia, 76;
concept/history, 22, 42, 45, 46 – 48, 57,
61, 71, 77, 79, 85, 95, 234, 235, 250;
China, 46, 76, 84, 85, 86;
DR Congo, 45, 71, 76, 180, 191, 192,
234;
Ethiopia, 24, 73;
European dimension, 45, 47, 71;
Greenland, 189;
Iceland, 191, 234;
India, 192;
Indonesia, 86, 123, 237, 239, 247;
Korea, 73;
Mexico, 57;
Namibia, 71;
Nigeria, 90;
Pacific, 45;
Papua New Guinea, 202, 203, 205;
South Africa, 46;
South America, 85;
West Africa, 46, 57, 83.

Model for negotiating the future of colonial objects

28, 92 – 93, 164, 187 ff., 199, 201 ff.,
210, 221 – 224, 244 – 251.

Myanmar

Norway, 192;
United Kingdom, 24.

Namibia

Germany, 22, 46, 71;
Germany (return), 107, 235;
Witbooi, Herman, 24 – 25, 234.

Nazi-looted art

1998 Washington Conference Principles
for Dealing with Nazi-looted Art, 98,
111 – 114, 118, 239, 241, 243, 250,
252;
1999 Resolution No. 1205 concerning
Looted Jewish Cultural Property of the
Parliamentary Assembly of the Council
of Europe, 111 – 112;

2000 Vilnius Principles, 111 – 112;
2007 UN Declaration on the Rights of
Indigenous Peoples, 110;
2009 Terezin Declaration on Holocaust
Era Assets and Related Issues,
111 – 112;
alternative dispute resolution, 111 – 113,
118, 239, 244;
restitution committees, 28, 33, 111, 113.

the Netherlands

1949 UN Security Council Resolution 67
with respect to Indonesia, 125;
1962 Agreement between Indonesia and
Netherlands concerning West New
Guinea, 129;
1965 Coup d'état, 130, 172 ;
1975 Joint Recommandations, 122 ff.;
archives, 124 – 125, 127, 131, 132,
137 – 144, 147 – 148, 151 – 152,
167, 170;
Aceh War, 72, 131;
Australia (return), 206;
Batavian Society for Arts and Sciences,
65, 66, 73, 74, 78, 88, 123, 124, 130,
142, 144, 145, 146, 158, 159;
Baud, J.C. (return pilgrim's staff
Diponegoro), 26, 160, 161, 168, 217;
Bernhard, Prince-Consort Bernhard,
Prince-Consort, Netherlands, 169;
Borobudur temple complex, 64, 136, 143,
143 nt. 501, 156, 168, 172;
Brandes, J.L.A. (art-protection officer),
126, 145;
Coen, J.P., 54, 55 nt. 150;
Cultural Agreement with Indonesia, 127,
130, 131, 138, 148, 165;
Ghana, (return Badu Bonsu head), 106,
110;
Indonesia, see *Indonesia*;
Juliana, Queen, 138, 169;
Lovink, T., High Representative in
Indonesia, 126;
New Zealand (return Maori head), 109
Kandy, Sri Lanka, looted by VOC, 44, 58;
Luwu insignia, 88, 136, 141, 142, 143;